KOVELS'
DEPRESSION GLASS
& AMERICAN
DINNERWARE
PRICE LIST

BOOKS BY
RALPH AND TERRY KOVEL

American Country Furniture 1780–1875

A Directory of American Silver, Pewter, and Silver Plate

Kovels' Advertising Collectibles Price List

Kovels' American Silver Marks

Kovels' American Art Pottery: The Collector's Guide to Makers,
Marks, and Factory Histories

Kovels' Antiques & Collectibles Fix-It Source Book

Kovels' Antiques & Collectibles Price List

Kovels' Book of Antique Labels

Kovels' Bottles Price List

Kovels' Collector's Guide to American Art Pottery

Kovels' Collector's Source Book

Kovels' Depression Glass & American Dinnerware Price List

Kovels' Dictionary of Marks—Pottery and Porcelain

Kovels' Guide to Selling, Buying, and Fixing Your Antiques and Collectibles

Kovels' Guide to Selling Your Antiques & Collectibles

Kovels' Illustrated Price Guide to Royal Doulton

Kovels' Know Your Antiques

Kovels' Know Your Collectibles

Kovels' New Dictionary of Marks—Pottery & Porcelain

Kovels' Organizer for Collectors

Kovels' Price Guide for Collector Plates, Figurines,
Paperweights, and Other Limited Editions

Kovels' Quick Tips: 799 Helpful Hints on How to Care for Your Collectibles

KOVELS'
DEPRESSION GLASS
& AMERICAN
DINNERWARE
PRICE LIST

Ralph and Terry Kovel

CROWN TRADE PAPERBACKS
NEW YORK

Published by Crown Publishers, Inc., 201 East 50th Street, New York, New York 10022. Member of the Crown Publishing Group.

Random House, Inc., New York, Toronto, London, Sydney, Auckland

CROWN TRADE PAPERBACKS and colophon are trademarks of Crown Publishers, Inc.

Originally published by Crown Publishers Inc., in 1980. Updated editions published in 1983, 1988, and 1991.

Manufactured in the United States of America

Design by Deborah Kerner

Library of Congress Cataloging-in-Publication Data is available upon request.

ISBN 0-517-88382-1

10 9 8 7 6 5 4 3 2 1

Fifth Edition

CONTENTS

ACKNOWLEDGMENTS   vi

DEPRESSION GLASS

INTRODUCTION   3
BIBLIOGRAPHY   6
CLUBS AND PUBLICATIONS   8
COLOR NAMES   10
MAIN LISTING   **11**
REPRODUCTIONS   82
FACTORIES   85
PATTERN LIST   88

AMERICAN DINNERWARE

INTRODUCTION   121
BIBLIOGRAPHY   124
CLUBS AND PUBLICATIONS   128
MAIN LISTING   **129**
FACTORIES   166
PATTERN LIST   169

ACKNOWLEDGMENTS

We want to thank the following companies and collectors who knowingly or unknowingly helped us to find pictures and prices for this book:

Al-Lin's Antiques, David Becker, Gary Beegle, Dennis Bialek, Helen Binder, Paul A. Bizub, Diane Brouhle, Linda Brown, Eileen Burns, C & K Collectibles, Chinamates, T. J. Cousins, Velma Dahl, Gloria DePasquale, The Dish Patch, Djanet, Dogdayz Glassware, Donna Marie's Antiques & Interiors, H. L. Douthitt, Fenner's Antiques, Fiesta Plus, Bob & Charmaine French, Front Porch Collectibles, Melissa Gallian, David C. Gaydos, Andy Gibbs, The Glass Connection, Sandra Handler, William Hatchett, Dianne Hermes, Arlene Higdon, Hogues Antiques & Curios, Paul & Carol Hrics, Larry & Ruby Jacques, Frank Jay, Jenkins Antiques, Troy Jenkins, Kevin & Barbara Kiley, Matt Koester, Laguna, Juan F. Lebron, Sandy Levine, Cadia Los, My Glass Duchess, Ellie Lowenstein, Mad Hatter's Tea Party, Debbie Maggard, L. A. Maness, Dottie Milanoski, Moore's Antiques, C. M. Murray, Dawn Nardi, Betty Newbound, Barbara Owens, Jim Pappas, Bob & Nancy Perzel, Diand & Bob Petripas, Robert Pierce, Dick & Sherryl Ponti, Popkorn, Lottie Porter, Richard G. Racheter, Chris Rainka, Roger Redwine, Ted & Lana Renner, William Rhoades, Nita & Curtis Ridgway, Bob Rothermel, Dan Russo, Arlene Sage, Roselle Scheleifman, Second Hand Rose, M. A. Setzer, Roni Sionakides, E. S. Snow, Jr., Florence Solito, Sparkle Plenty Glassware, Splendor in the Glass, Chris Stansell, Sugar Hill Antiques, T & J's Yesteryear Collectibles, Robert Taylor, M. E. Theobald, Bob F. Thistle, Bryant Turner, Nancy Wasserman, Margaret & Kenn Whitmyer, Leigh Williams, Arline V. Wise, Delmer H. Youngen, Z Mod Gallery, and Helga Zeches.

Special thanks to Vicky Kaffeman of Second Hand Rose, who helped find the pieces to picture, and to members of the Western Reserve Depression Glass Club, who gave us fill-in information and other advice. Another thank you to Benjamin Margalit, who took the color photos.

Putting a book like this together takes extra attention to details. Thanks to our staff, including Edie and Cherri Smrekar, who recorded prices, and Grace DeFrancisco, Harriet Goldner, Evelyn Hayes, Vijay Shah, and Hillary Stone. More thank yous to Crown Publishers and Sharon Squibb, our tireless editor, Ken Sansone, art director, Pam Stinson, production editor, Bill Peabody, production coordinator, and Merri Ann Morrell, compositor.

But special cheers for Gay Hunter, who became an expert on a new computer program to check manuscripts, pictures, charts, and dozens of other details to make the book accurate.

DEPRESSION GLASS

Introduction

Clear and pastel-colored glassware in matching sets became popular about 1925. The Fostoria Glass Company of Fostoria, Ohio, made the first of these glass sets, which included dinner plates, coffee cups, and other pieces to be used at a dinner table. The glassware was expensive and its popularity led to similar pieces being made by other companies that were able to produce a less expensive glass.

Inexpensive glass was made by a method called tank molding: Silica sand, soda ash, and limestone were heated, and the molten glass mixture was passed through pipes to the automated pressing mold. Patterns were acid-etched or tooled into the mold so the finished glassware had a design. Because the pressing process made a glass that often had flaws or bubbles, patterns used as decoration were often lacy in appearance to help hide the flaws.

During the late 1960s, interest in the inexpensive pastel glass led to several books, and the term "Depression glass" came into general use, even though the glassware was made before, during, and after the Depression. The name has gradually come to include other glassware made from 1925 through the 1970s. This price list includes lacy types, pseudo-Sandwich glass patterns, hobnail variations, solid-colored wares of ruby, cobalt, or green, and many opaque glass patterns. In the past few years another term, "elegant glassware of the Depression," has come into use. This refers to the better-quality glass made at the same time. There is much overlap between these types of glass, and even the exact name to use for a pattern may be in doubt. We have included those patterns most often offered for sale at glass shows, both Depression and some "elegant" patterns of glass. The pattern names used are from original catalogs if known, Depression glass books, lists, or shows.

Depression glass designs can be divided into groups. The etched designs, like Adam or Cherry Blossom, were made first, from about 1925 to 1935 in pastel colors.

Raised designs, often with fruit and flower patterns, such as Open Rose and Sharon, were made in the mid-1930s. Strong colors like cobalt blue or Royal Ruby, opaque glass, pastels, and clear glass were popular.

Geometric wares, such as Hobnail and Ribbon, were made during the late 1920s, and again in the late 1930s and early 1940s. Simple outlines and bold colors predominated. Art Deco–influenced geometric designs include Imperial Octagon and U.S. Octagon.

Enameled or silk-screened patterns were developed during the 1940s. White enameled designs were added to cobalt blue, Royal Ruby, Forest Green, and clear glass, the most popular colors decorated this way. Shirley Temple glasswares and White Sails are two examples.

A few patterns, Floral & Diamond Band for example, were made to resemble the cut glass of the nineteenth century, or the Lacy Sandwich patterns made by the Sandwich, Massachusetts, glassworks. About ten such pseudo-Sandwich patterns were made, most of which were referred to as Sandwich in the manufacturers' catalogs.

Depression glass utility wares were also made. The dishes were meant to be used in the kitchen and not on the table, and included ice-box dishes, lemon reamers, or canister sets.

Opaque glass was popular in the 1930s. Each of the colors was given a special name by the company that produced it. Monax or Ivrene are opaque white glasswares.

Opaque green glass was known by a variety of names. Jade green is a generic name used by many companies. Jade-ite was the green used by Anchor Hocking; Jadite was a color of glass and a pattern of green kitchenware made by Jeannette Glass Company. To avoid unnecessary confusion, we have chosen to always spell the word *Jadite* when referring to color in this book. Delphite, an opaque blue glass, is sometimes spelled "delfite" in the ads, but we have chosen to always use the Delphite spelling.

This book is not an in-depth study of Depression glass. The beginner who needs more information about patterns, manufacturers, color groups, or how and where to buy should see the Bibliography and club lists we have included.

Hundreds of patterns, many not listed in other price books, are included here. But if you wish to specialize in one pattern of Depression glass, there may be a book available that includes colored photographs of your pattern. There may also be a book available with special information about the factory making your pattern. The best way to learn about Depression glass is to attend the regional and national shows devoted to glass. Your local newspaper or the collectors' publications listed in this book will print the dates and locations.

There are lists of reproductions and known glass patterns and manufacturers following the last glass price entries.

This book is a price report. Prices are actual offerings in the marketplace. They are not an average. The high and low prices represent different sales. Prices reported are not those from garage or house sales or flea markets. They are only from dealers who understand the Depression glass market and who sell at shops, at shows, or through national advertising.

Information about American ceramic dinnerwares and the prices for these pieces can be found in the second half of this book.

Particular patterns can be found by using either the Depression Glass or American Dinnerware main listings, both of which are arranged alphabetically. Depression Glass begins on page 11 and American Dinnerware on page 129. There is no index of pattern names in this book because it would only duplicate the main listings. However, we have compiled lists of known Depression glass and American dinnerware patterns along with information on manufacturers, dates, alternate names, and descriptions. These can be found at the end of each section. When a dealer says a piece is "Book One," it is a pattern of glassware found in the book _A Guidebook to Colored Glassware of the 1920's and 1930's_ by Hazel Marie Weatherman. "Book Two" refers to patterns in the book _Price Trends for the Colored Glassware of the Depression Era 2_ by Weatherman. These books are out of print.

Patterns listed in the main sections of the book are those most popular with collectors. This book is a report of prices for pieces offered for sale during the past year. Most of the patterns included in earlier books are still to be found here because the collectors still buy these patterns. Many newly popular patterns are also included. We have made no effort to give an exact definition of the term "Depression glass." If a pattern of American glassware was made between 1925 and 1970 and if it is known to some collectors or dealers as Depression glass, we have included it here.

Ralph and Terry Kovel,
Accredited Senior Appraisers,
American Society of Appraisers
March 1995

Bibliography

Archer, Margaret and Douglas. *Imperial Glass.* Paducah, Kentucky: Collector Books, 1978.

Birkenheuser, Fred. *Tiffin Glassmasters.* Privately printed, 1979 (P.O. Box 524, Grove City, OH 43123).

Cambridge Glass Co. (catalog reprint). Privately printed, 1976 (P.O. Box 416, Cambridge, OH 43725).

Fine Handmade Table Glassware (catalog reprint). Privately printed, 1978 (P.O. Box 416, Cambridge, OH 43725).

Florence, Gene. *Collector's Encyclopedia of Depression Glass.* 11th edition. Paducah, Kentucky: Collector Books, 1994.

Florence, Gene. *Elegant Glassware of the Depression Era.* 5th edition. Paducah, Kentucky: Collector Books, 1993.

Florence, Gene. *Kitchen Glassware of the Depression Years.* 5th edition. Paducah, Kentucky: Collector Books, 1995.

Florence, Gene. *Very Rare Glassware of the Depression Years.* Paducah, Kentucky: Collector Books, 1988.

Fountain, Mel. *Swankyswigs, with Price Guide.* Privately printed, 1979 (201 Alvena, Wichita, KS 67203).

Heacock, William. *Fenton Glass—The First Twenty-five Years.* Privately printed, 1978 (P.O. Box 663, Marietta, OH 45750).

Kilgo, Garry and Dale; Jerry and Gail Watkins. *A Collectors Guide to Anchor Hockings Fire-King Glassware.* Privately printed, 1991 (K & W Collectibles, P.O. Box 473, Addison, AL 35540).

Klamkin, Marian. *Collector's Guide to Depression Glass.* New York, Hawthorn Books, Inc., 1973.

Kovel, Ralph and Terry. *Kovels' Antiques & Collectibles Price List.* 27th edition. New York: Crown Publishers, 1995.

Kovel, Ralph and Terry. *Kovels' Depression Glass & American Dinnerware Price List,* 4th edition. New York: Crown Publishers, 1991.

Kovel, Ralph and Terry. *Kovels' Guide to Selling, Buying, and Fixing Your Antiques and Collectibles.* New York: Crown Publishers, 1995.

Kovel, Ralph and Terry. *Kovels' Know Your Collectibles.* New York: Crown Publishers, 1981.

Luckey, Carl F., with Mary Burris, special consultant. *Identification & Value Guide to Depression Era Glassware.* 3rd edition. Florence, Alabama: Books Americana, 1994.

McGrain, Patrick, ed. *Fostoria—The Popular Years.* Privately printed, 1982 (Box 219, Frederick, MD 21701).

Meehan, Kathy and Bill. *Collector's Guide to Lu-Ray Pastels.* Paducah, Kentucky: Collector Books, 1995.

Schliesmann, Mark. *Price Survey.* 3rd edition. Privately printed, 1986 (Box 838-PS, Racine, WI 53403).

Stout, Sandra McPhee. *Depression Glass in Color.* Radnor, Pennsylvania: Wallace-Homestead Book Co., 1970.

Stout, Sandra McPhee. *Depression Glass Number Two.* Radnor, Pennsylvania: Wallace-Homestead Book Co., 1971.

Stout, Sandra McPhee. *Depression Glass III.* Radnor, Pennsylvania: Wallace-Homestead Book Co., 1976.

Stout, Sandra McPhee. *Depression Glass Price Guide.* Radnor, Pennsylvania: Wallace-Homestead Book Co., 1975.

Warner, Ian. *Swankyswigs, A Pattern Guide and Check List.* Privately printed, 1982 (Box 57, Otisville, MI 48463).

Washburn, Kent G. *Price Survey.* 4th edition. Privately printed, 1994 (8048 Midcrown, Suite 26, San Antonio, TX 78218-2334).

Weatherman, Hazel Marie. *Colored Glassware of the Depression Era.* Privately printed, 1970 (P.O. Box 4444, Springfield, MO 65804).

Weatherman, Hazel Marie. *Colored Glassware of the Depression Era 2.* Privately printed, 1974 (P.O. Box 4444, Springfield, MO 65804).

Weatherman, Hazel Marie. *Decorated Tumbler.* Privately printed, 1978 (P.O. Box 4444, Springfield, MO 65804).

Weatherman, Hazel Marie. *Fostoria—Its First Fifty Years.* Privately printed, 1972 (P.O. Box 4444, Springfield, MO 65804).

Weatherman, Hazel Marie. *Price Guide to the Decorated Tumbler.* Privately printed, 1979 (P.O. Box 4444, Springfield, MO 65804).

Whitmyer, Margaret and Kenn. *Bedroom & Bathroom Glassware of the Depression Years.* Paducah, Kentucky: Collector Books, 1990.

Clubs and Publications

CLUBS

Fenton Art Glass Collectors of America, Inc., *Butterfly Net* (newsletter), P.O. Box 384, Williamstown, WV 26187.

Fostoria Glass Collectors, *Fostoria Reflections* (newsletter), 21901 Lassen Street, #112, Chatsworth, CA 91311.

Fostoria Glass Society of America, Inc., *Facets of Fostoria* (newsletter), P.O. Box 826, Moundsville, WV 26041.

Heisey Collectors of America, *Heisey News* (newsletter), 169 West Church Street, Newark, OH 43055.

Michiana Association of Candlewick Collectors, *MACC Spyglass* (newsletter), 17370 Battles Road, South Bend, IN 46614.

Morgantown Collectors of America, *Morgantown Newscaster* (newsletter), 420 First Avenue NW, Plainview, MN 55964.

National Cambridge Collectors, Inc., *Cambridge Crystal Ball* (newsletter), P.O. Box 416, Cambridge, OH 43725-0416.

National Candlewick Collectors Club, *Candlewick Collector* (newsletter), 275 Milledge Terrace, Athens, GA 30606.

National Depression Glass Association, *News & Views* (newsletter), P.O. Box 69843, Odessa, TX 79769.

National Duncan Glass Society, *National Duncan Glass Journal* (newsletter), P.O. Box 965, Washington, PA 15301-0965.

National Imperial Glass Collectors Society, *Glasszette* (newsletter), P.O. Box 534, Bellaire, OH 43906.

National Milk Glass Collectors Society, *Opaque News* (newsletter), 1113 Birchwood Drive, Garland, TX 75043.

National Reamer Collectors Association, *NRCA Quarterly Review* (newsletter), Rt. 3, Box 67, 405 Benson Road, Frederic, WI 54837.

Old Morgantown Glass Collector Guild, *Old Morgantown Topics* (newsletter), 420 First Avenue NW, Plainview, MN 55964.

Tiffin Glass Collectors' Club, *Tiffin Glassmasters* (newsletter), P.O. Box 554, Tiffin, OH 44883.

Local clubs and their meeting dates are often listed in *The Daze Inc.*

PUBLICATIONS

Antique Trader Weekly (newspaper), P.O. Box 1050, Dubuque, IA 52004-1050.

Daze (newspaper), Box 57, Otisville, MI 48463.

Glass Collector's Digest (magazine), P.O. Box 553, Marietta, OH 45750-9979.

Kovels on Antiques and Collectibles (newsletter), P.O. Box 22200, Beachwood, OH 44122.

Matching Services: China, Silver, Crystal (leaflet), Ralph and Terry Kovel (P.O. Box 22900, Beachwood, OH 44122).

Color Names

This is a list of some of the most confusing color names:

AMBER	Topaz, Golden Glow
BLUE-GREEN	Ultramarine
CLEAR	Crystal
DEEP BLUE	Ritz Blue, cobalt, dark blue, deep blue
GREEN	Springtime Green, emerald, Imperial Green, Forest Green, Nu-green
MEDIUM BLUE	Madonna
OPAQUE BLACK	Black
OPAQUE BLUE	Delphite
OPAQUE GREEN	Jadite
OPAQUE OFF-WHITE	Azur-ite, Chinex, Clambroth, Cremax, Ivrene
OPAQUE WHITE	Milk white, Monax
PINK	Rose Marie, Rose, Rose Pink, Rose Tint, Rose Glow, Nu-rose, Wild Rose, Flamingo, Cheri-Glo
PURPLE	Burgundy, amethyst
RED	Royal Ruby, Ruby Red, Carmen

A

**ACCORDIAN PLEATS, see
Round Robin**

Adam

Adam, sometimes called Chain Daisy or Fan & Feather, is a glass pattern made from 1932 to 1934 by the Jeannette Glass Company, Jeannette, Pennsylvania. Sets can be found most often in pink, but crystal, Delphite, and green pieces were also made. A few pieces are known in yellow, but this does not seem to have been a standard production color. Reproductions have been made in green and pink.

CRYSTAL
Water Set, Box, 7 Piece 200.00
GREEN
Ashtray, 4 1/2 In. 15.00 to 22.00
Bowl, 4 3/4 In. 14.00
Butter, Cover 295.00
Cake Plate, Footed,
  10 In. .... 21.00 to 23.00
Creamer................... 19.00
Cup & Saucer 25.00
Grill Plate, 9 In..... 15.00 to 16.00
Pitcher, 8 In. 48.00
Plate, 6 In. 7.50
Plate, Square, 7 3/4 In. ...11.00 to
  15.00
Plate, Square, 9 In. 20.00
Saucer 7.00
Sherbet, Footed, 3 In. 45.00
Sugar, Cover 50.00

Tumbler,
  4 1/2 In. .... 20.00 to 22.00
Tumbler, Iced Tea,
  5 1/2 In. .... 40.00 to 45.00
PINK
Ashtray, 4 1/2 In. 23.00
Bowl, Cover, 9 In. 25.00
Bowl, Oval, 10 In........... 45.00
Butter, Cover..... 70.00 to 75.00
Cake Plate, Footed,
  10 In. .... 20.00 to 25.00
Candlestick, 4 In., Pair..... 80.00
Candy Jar, Cover........... 65.00
Cup...................... 20.00
Cup & Saucer ..... 26.00 to 35.00
Pitcher, 8 In. 35.00
Plate, 6 In. 7.50
Plate, Square, 7 3/4 In....... 13.50
Plate, Square,
  9 In............ 25.00 to 27.50
Platter,
  11 3/4 In. .... 21.00 to 35.00
Salt & Pepper,
  Footed, 4 In. 65.00
Saucer.................... 6.50
Sherbet, 3 In...... 27.50 to 30.00
Sugar & Creamer, Cover 50.00
Tumbler,
  4 1/2 In. .... 25.00 to 28.00

Akro Agate

Picture a marble cake with the irregular mixture of colors running through the batter. This is what Akro Agate is usually like—a marbleized mixture of clear and opaque colored glass. The Akro Agate Company, Clarksburg, West Virginia, originally made children's marbles. The marbleized dinnerware and other glass children's sets were made in many colors from 1932 to 1951.

AMBER
Creamer, Stippled Band.... 30.00
Cup & Saucer,
  Stippled Band.......... 32.50
Plate, Stippled Band,
  3 1/4 In. 15.00

BLUE
Bowl, Child's, Concentric
  Ring, 3 1/8 In. 22.50
Cornucopia, 3 1/8 In........ 4.50
Creamer, Child's,
  Octagonal.............. 10.00
Cup & Saucer, Interior
  Panel, Opaque.......... 29.00
Flowerpot, 2 1/4 In......... 3.50
Flowerpot, Stacked Disc,
  White, Footed, 2 3/4 In..... 4.50
Pitcher, Child's, 2 7/8 In.... 30.00
Planter, Oval, 6 In. 9.00
Plate, Child's, Concentric
  Ring, 3 1/4 In. 4.00
Plate, Child's, Concentric
  Rib, Opaque, 3 1/4 In. 6.00
Plate, Child's, Interior Panel,
  Opaque, 3 1/4 In. 7.50
Plate, Child's, Opaque,
  3 1/4 In. 6.00
Powder Jar, Scotty Dog 95.00
Sugar, Interior Panel,
  Opaque................. 22.50
Sugar & Creamer, Child's,
  Stacked Disc & Panel 60.00
Teapot, Child's, Playtime, White
  Cover, Octagonal 16.00
Teapot, Stacked Disc &
  Panel, 3 3/4 In. 25.00
Teapot, White Cover,
  Octagonal.............. 20.00
Tumbler, Child's, Stacked
  Disc & Panel, 2 Oz. 10.00
Window Box, Green, Footed,
  5 1/2 x 3 x 2 1/4 In. 9.00
CHARTREUSE
Flowerpot, Vertical Rib & Panel,
  Blue, Flared, 3 1/2........ 5.00
Flowerpot, Vertical Rib,
  2 1/2 In. 3.50
Wall Pocket, Brown,
  3 1/2 In. 9.00
GOLD
Plate, Concentric Ring,
  1/8 In. 4.50

GRAY

Flowerpot, Chevrons, Brown
& Blue, Flared, 3 3/4 In. ... 8.50

GREEN

Ashtray, Scalloped Shell, White,
4 x 3 3/4 In. 5.00

Cup, Child's, Chiquita,
1 1/2 In. 7.00

Cup, Child's, Concentric
Ring, 2 In. 4.50

Cup, Child's, Interior
Panel. 15.00

Cup & Saucer, Opaque 7.50

Cup & Saucer, White,
After Dinner 13.00

Cup & Saucer, White,
Octagonal 10.00

Flowerpot, 2 1/4 In. 3.00

Flowerpot, Chevrons,
Flared, 3 In. 6.00

Flowerpot, Vertical Rib
Top, 3 In. 7.00

Pitcher, Child's, Stacking ... 12.50

Pitcher, Stippled Band. 17.00

Planter, Vertical Rib,
6 x 3 1/2 x 2 1/2 In. 7.50

Plate, Child's, Concentric
Ring, 3 1/4 In. ..... 4.50 to 10.00

Plate, Child's, Interior
Panel, 3 1/4 In. 5.00

Plate, Child's, Octagonal,
3 3/8 In. 7.00

Powder Jar, Colonial Lady .. 95.00

Saucer, Child's, Stippled
Band. 4.00

Sugar, Child's, Chiquita...... 4.50

Sugar, Child's, Stacked
Disc & Panel 12.00

Tumbler, Child's, Interior
Panel, 2 Oz. 10.00

Tumbler, Child's, Stippled
Band, 2 Oz. 11.00

IVORY

Cup, Child's, 2 In. 8.00

LEMONADE

Cup, Oxblood, 1 In. 25.00

ORANGE

Cup & Saucer, White....... 13.00

Flowerpot, 3 1/2 In. 7.00

Flowerpot, Vertical Rib
Top, 1 7/8 In. 3.00

Vase, Oval, Flared, Handles,
4 3/8 x 4 3/4 In. 9.00

Window Box, Vertical Rib, 6 x
3 3/4 x 2 3/4 In. . . 10.00 to 12.00

OXBLOOD

Ashtray, Hexagonal,
3 3/4 x 2 In. 4.00

Planter, Footed,
5 1/2 x 3 x 2 1/4 In. 10.00

PINK

Powder Jar, Colonial Lady. . . 18.00

PUMPKIN

Ashtray, Leaf, Orange,
4 x 3 In. 4.00

Cup, Child's, Concentric
Ring 20.00

PURPLE

Cup, Child's, Concentric
Ring, 1 In. 25.00

Plate, Child's, Stippled
Band, 4 1/4 In. 6.50

TAN

Lamp, Stacked Disc,
6 1/2 x 6 In. 45.00

WHITE

Powder Jar, Colonial Lady. . . 75.00

YELLOW

Bowl, Child's, Interior
Panel. 25.00

Creamer, Child's, Interior
Panel, 3 1/8 In. 30.00

Flowerpot, Orange,
2 3/4 In. 5.00

Powder Jar, Ribbed 25.00

Saucer, Concentric Ring,
2 3/4 In. .... 3.00 to 7.00

Saucer, Interior Panel,
2 3/4 In. 4.00

Sugar, Green Cover,
Interior Panel 40.00

Tumbler, Octagonal, 2 Oz. . . . 8.00

Alice

An 8 1/2-inch plate, cup, and
saucer were apparently the
only pieces made in the Alice
pattern. This 1940s pattern
was made by the Anchor
Hocking Glass Corporation,
Lancaster, Ohio, in opaque
white with a pink or blue border and in Jadite. Other related

sections in this book are
Charm, Fire-King, Jadite, Jane-
Ray, Peach Lustre, Philbe,
Swirl Fire-King, Turquoise
Blue, and Wheat.

JADITE

Cup & Saucer ...... 3.50 to 9.00

Saucer. 1.00

WHITE

Cup & Saucer, Blue Trim. . . . 12.00

Plate, Blue Trim, 8 1/2 In. . . . 15.00

Alpine Caprice

Caprice and Alpine Caprice
were made from the same
molds. Alpine Caprice has a
satin finish, Caprice is transparent. Alpine Caprice, made
by the Cambridge Glass Company, Cambridge, Ohio, about
1936, was made in blue, crystal, and pink satin-finished
glass.

BLUE

Bonbon, Footed, Square 75.00

Bowl, Crimped, 4-Footed,
12 1/2 In. 75.00

Bowl, Footed, 13 In. 75.00

Candlestick, With Prism,
7 In., Pair .....110.00 to 150.00

Candy Dish, Cover, 6 In. 250.00

Compote, 2 Handles,
Low Footed, 7 In. 60.00

Cup & Saucer 45.00

Oyster Cocktail, 4 1/2 Oz....67.50

Plate, 16 In. 90.00

Relish, 3 Sections 38.00

Sugar. 22.00

Sugar & Creamer 45.00

Tumbler, Footed, 5 Oz. 40.00

Tumbler, Footed,
12 Oz. .... 40.00 to 45.00

CRYSTAL

Bowl, 3-Footed, 6 In. 45.00
Bowl, Cupped, 13 1/2 In. . . 100.00
Celery Dish, 12 In. 125.00
Compote, 5 In. 45.00
Cruet, Oil, 3 Oz. 37.50
Dish, Mayonnaise. 18.00

ALPINE CAPRICE, see also Caprice

American

American is a pattern made to resemble the pressed glass of an earlier time. It was introduced by Fostoria Glass, Moundsville, West Virginia, in 1915 and remained in production until the factory closed in 1986. Most pieces were made of clear, colorless glass known as crystal. A few pieces are known in amber, blue, green, yellow, and milk glass. It is similar to Cube pattern, but after looking carefully, you will soon learn to tell the two patterns apart. Many pieces of American pattern were reproduced after 1987.

AMBER

Lamp, Hurricane Shade,
Pair 500.00

CRYSTAL

Bowl, 5 In. 8.00
Bowl, Child's. 18.50
Bowl, Shrimp 300.00
Bowl, Wedding, Cover 75.00

Cake Plate, Pedestal,
12 In. . . . . 49.00 to 60.00
Candlestick, 3 In., Pair. 20.00
Candy Dish, Cover, 3 Sections,
Triangular. . . . . . 59.00 to 65.00
Celery Vase 62.00
Decanter, Stopper 65.00
Goblet, Water, 4 3/4 In. 12.00
Ice Bucket, Metal Handle,
6 In. . . . . 45.00 to 50.00
Mayonnaise, Ladle,
2 Piece 15.00
Punch Cup, Tom & Jerry,
Pair 26.50
Relish, 3 Sections, 11 In. . . . 30.00
Relish, 4 Sections,
Rectangular, 9 In. 32.00
Sugar & Creamer, Cover 35.00
Toothpick 18.00
Tray, 10 1/2 In. . . . . 30.00 to 35.00
Tumbler, Flared, 8 Oz.,
4 1/4 In. 11.00
Tumbler, Footed, 12 Oz.,
6 In. 11.00
Vase, Flared, 8 In. 40.00
Vase, Straight, 10 In. 110.00

AMERICAN BEAUTY, see English Hobnail

American Pioneer

Panels of hobnail-like protrusions and plain panels were used in the design of American Pioneer. It was made by Liberty Works, Egg Harbor, New Jersey, from 1931 to 1934. Crystal, green, and pink dishes are easily found. Amber is rare.

CRYSTAL

Cup. 9.00
Cup & Saucer . . . . . 12.00 to 14.00
Plate, 8 In. 9.00

GREEN

Cup & Saucer 22.00
Lamp, 8 1/2 In. 75.00
Plate, 8 In. 16.00

American Sweetheart

In 1930 Macbeth-Evans Glass Company introduced American Sweetheart. At first it was made of pink glass, but soon other colors were added. The pattern continued in production until 1936. Blue, Cremax, Monax, pink, and red pieces were made. Sometimes a gold, green, pink, platinum, red, or smoky black trim was used on Monax pieces. There is a center design on most plates, but some Monax plates are found with plain centers. One of the rarest items in this pattern is the Monax sugar bowl lid. The bowls are easy to find but the lids seem to have broken.

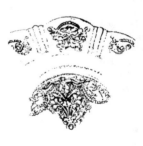

MONAX

Bowl, 6 In. . . . . 12.00 to 14.50
Bowl, 9 In. . . . . 53.00 to 60.00
Bowl, Vegetable, Oval,
11 In. 75.00
Chop Plate, 11 In. . . 13.00 to 15.00
Creamer . . . . 7.00 to 12.00
Cup & Saucer . . . . . . 9.50 to 13.00
Plate, 8 In. . . . . 6.00 to 8.00
Plate, 9 In. . . . . 10.00 to 11.00
Plate, 10 In. . . . . 20.00 to 22.00
Platter, Oval,
13 In. . . . . 58.00 to 65.00

Salver, 12 In. . . . . . . 19.00 to 22.00

Service For 8, 64 Piece 495.00

Sherbet, 4 In. . . . . . 15.75 to 18.50

Soup, Cream,
4 1/2 In. . . . . 85.00 to 110.00

Soup, Dish, 10 In. . 72.00 to 77.00

Sugar, Footed . . . . . . 6.00 to 10.00

Sugar & Creamer 16.00

Sugar Cover 325.00

PINK

Bowl, 6 In. . . . . . . 10.00 to 14.50

Bowl, 9 In. . . . . . . 28.00 to 40.00

Bowl, Vegetable,
Oval, 11 In. 60.00

Creamer . . . . 6.50 to 13.00

Cup 14.00

Cup & Saucer 18.00

Plate, 6 In. . . . . 2.50 to 5.00

Plate, 8 In. 14.50

Plate, 10 In. . . . . . . 30.00 to 32.00

Platter, 13 In. 45.00

Salt & Pepper, Footed 375.00

Salver, 12 In. . . . . . . 8.00 to 17.50

Saucer 2.50

Sherbet, Footed,
4 1/4 In. . . . . 13.00 to 15.00

Soup, Cream. 90.00

Soup, Dish,
10 In. . . . . 55.00 to 65.00

Sugar 3.00

Tumbler, 9 Oz., 4 1/4 In. . . . 65.00

RED

Salver, 12 In. 140.00

Tidbit, 2 Tiers 220.00

Anniversary

Although pink Anniversary pattern was made from 1947 to 1949, it is still considered Depression glass by collectors. Crystal pieces are shown in a 1949 catalog. In the 1970s crystal and an iridescent carnival-glass-like amber color were used. The pattern was the product of the Jeannette Glass Company, Jeannette, Pennsylvania.

CRYSTAL

Bowl, Gold Rim, 4 7/8 In. 2.50

Butter, Cover 25.00

Cake Plate, Gold Rim,
12 1/2 In. 5.00

Compote, 3-Footed 3.50

Creamer, Gold Rim 3.00

Cup, Gold Rim 2.00

Plate, Gold Rim, 9 In. 4.00

Soup, Dish, Gold Rim,
7 3/8 In. 6.00

Sugar & Creamer, Gold Rim . . 6.00

Vase, 6 1/2 In. 13.00

IRIDESCENT

Compote, 3-Footed 4.00

Cup & Saucer 5.00

Plate, 6 1/4 In. 1.50

Sugar, Cover 7.00

PINK

Butter, Cover 45.00

Cake Plate, 12 1/2 In. 14.00

Cup. 5.50

Plate, 6 1/4 In. 2.50

Plate, 9 In. 8.00

Sandwich Server,
12 1/2 In. 10.00

APPLE BLOSSOM, see Dogwood

Arcadia Lace

Arcadia Lace pattern was made by Jenkins Glass Company of Kokomo, Indiana, and Arcadia, Indiana. The company worked from 1901 to 1932. Arcadia was made of crystal green or iridescent amber

glass. Green was not used until 1929.

CRYSTAL

Bowl, Handles, 8 In. 19.00

Bowl, Sterling Footed,
8 In. 22.50

Candy Dish, Cover,
Footed 45.00

Compote, Handles,
6 1/2 In. 19.00

Dish, Mayonnaise,
2 Piece 35.00

Relish, 3 Sections, 8 In. 35.00

Sherbet, Footed 10.00

Aunt Polly

U.S. Glass Company, a firm with factories in Indiana, Ohio, Pennsylvania, and West Virginia, made Aunt Polly glass. Luncheon sets can be found in blue, green, and iridescent. Pink pieces have been reported. The pattern was made in the late 1920s until c.1935.

BLUE

Bowl, Oval, 8 3/8 In. 90.00

Butter, Cover. . . . 180.00 to 195.00

Compote, Handles,
5 1/4 In. 28.00

Pitcher, 48 Oz., 8 In. 165.00

Plate, 6 In. 9.00

Plate, 8 In. 18.00

Salt & Pepper 200.00

Tumbler, 8 Oz.,
3 5/8 In. . . . . 20.00 to 23.00

Vase, Footed,
6 1/2 In. . . . . 32.50 to 40.00

GREEN

Bowl, 4 3/4 In. 7.00

Bowl, Oval, 8 3/8 In. 35.00

Nappy, 7 7/8 In. . . . 16.00 to 25.00

Sherbet 6.00

Sugar, Cover 45.00

IRIDESCENT

Sherbet. 7.50

Aurora

The Hazel Atlas Glass Company made Aurora pattern glass in the late 1930s. Fewer than ten different pieces were made in Cobalt Blue and pink; an even smaller quantity in crystal and green.

BLUE

Bowl, 5 3/8 In. 18.00

Bowl, Deep,
4 1/2 In. . . . . 18.00 to 26.00

Cup. . . . . 7.50 to 9.00

Plate, 6 1/2 In. 9.00

Saucer 3.00

Tumbler, 4 3/4 In. 32.50

CRYSTAL

Creamer, 4 1/2 In. 17.00

Cup & Saucer 16.00

Tumbler, 10 Oz., 4 3/4 In. . . 19.00

PINK

Cup. 12.00

Avocado

Although the center fruit looks more like a pear, the pattern has been named Avocado. It was made originally from 1923 to 1933 by the Indiana Glass Company, Dunkirk, Indiana, primarily in green and pink. Some crystal pieces were also produced. In 1973, a reproduction line of pitchers and tumblers appeared in amethyst, blue, frosted pink, green, and pink. In 1982, amber-colored creamers and sugars, cups and saucers, plates and serving dishes were made. Pieces have also been made in red and amber. The pattern is sometimes called Sweet Pear or No. 601.

CRYSTAL

Water Set, 5 Piece. 95.00

GREEN

Bowl, 7 1/2 In. . . . . 50.00 to 55.00

Bowl, Handles, 5 1/4 In. 30.00

Bowl, Handles,
Oval, 8 In. . . . . . . 22.00 to 26.00

Bowl, Preserve,
Handle, 7 In. 25.00

Cake Plate,
Handles, 10 1/4 In. 50.00

Creamer. 38.00

Cup. .30.00

Cup & Saucer 54.00

Pitcher, 64 Oz., 6 3/8 In. 15.00

Plate, 6 3/8 In. 10.00

Plate, 8 1/4 In. . . . . . 15.00 to 19.00

Relish, Footed,
6 In. . . . . 25.00 to 27.00

Saucer. 30.00

Sherbet. . . . . 55.00 to 56.00

Sugar, Footed . . . . . 25.00 to 38.00

Sugar & Creamer . . 65.00 to 69.00

Tumbler. 215.00

PINK

Cake Plate,
Handles, 10 1/4 In. 35.00

Plate, 6 3/8 In. 9.00

Relish, Footed, 6 In. 25.00

Sherbet. 47.50

Sugar, Footed. . . . . .30.00 to 32.00

Tumbler 195.00

B

B PATTERN, see Dogwood

BALLERINA, see Cameo

Bamboo Optic

Bamboo Optic pattern was made by Liberty Works of Egg Harbor, New Jersey, about 1929. Pink and green luncheon sets and other pieces were made. The pattern resembles Octagon.

GREEN

Bowl, 5 1/2 In. 12.00

Candlestick, 5 1/2 In. 12.00

Cup. . . . . 5.00 to 6.50

Cup & Saucer 5.50

Plate, 7 1/4 In. 6.00

Plate, 8 In. 3.50

Salt & Pepper, Squatty 85.00

Saucer, Ring, 6 1/8 In. 9.00

PINK

Cup. .6.50

Plate, 8 In. 4.00

**BANDED CHERRY,
see Cherry Blossom**

**BANDED FINE RIB,
see Coronation**

**BANDED PETALWARE,
see Petalware**

**BANDED RAINBOW,
see Ring**

**BANDED RIBBON,
see New Century**

**BANDED RINGS,
see Ring**

Baroque

Fostoria Glass Company of Moundsville, West Virginia, made Baroque, or No. 2496, from 1936 to 1966. The pattern was made in crystal, blue (azure), Gold Tint, yellow (topaz), and green. The same molds were used to make other glass patterns decorated with etched designs.

BLUE

Bonbon, 3-Footed	95.00
Bowl, 6 1/2 In.	45.00 to 65.00
Bowl, Handles, Cupped, 8 1/2 In.	150.00
Compote, 5 1/2 In.	35.00 to 40.00
Cup & Saucer, Footed	30.00
Dish, Mayonnaise, Oval, 8 In., 2 Piece	135.00
Goblet, 9 Oz., 6 3/4 In.	30.00 to 47.50
Jam Jar, Cover, 7 1/2 In.	85.00 to 98.00
Punch Cup	25.00
Relish, 2 Sections, Square, 6 In.	35.00

Tray, Oval, 6 1/2 In.	65.00
Tumbler, Footed, 14 Oz., 5 7/8 In.	75.00
Tumbler, Old Fashioned, 3 1/4 In.	85.00

CRYSTAL

Bowl, Handle, 4 In.	11.00
Bowl, Handle, Footed, 10 1/2 In.	30.00
Cheese & Crackers, 11 In.	45.00
Creamer	12.00
Cup & Saucer	12.00
Goblet, 9 Oz., 6 3/4 In.	12.00 to 14.50
Mustard, Cover	22.00
Platter, 11 In.	35.00
Salt & Pepper	45.00
Sherbet	9.50
Sweetmeat, Cover, Large	175.00
Vase, 8 In.	35.00

GREEN

Tumbler, Footed, 14 Oz., 5 7/8 In.	75.00

YELLOW

Bonbon, Ruffled	30.00
Compote, 5 1/2 In.	22.50
Ice Bucket, 4 3/8 In.	85.00
Jam Jar, Cover, 7 1/2 In.	55.00
Nappy, Handle, Footed, 5 In.	18.00 to 22.50
Plate, 7 In.	9.50
Plate, 9 In.	42.50
Relish, 3 Sections, Handles, 10 In.	27.50 to 35.00
Rose Bowl	85.00
Salt & Pepper, Large	95.00
Sugar & Creamer, Tray, Individual	55.00
Sweetmeat, Cover	125.00
Tidbit, 3-Footed	24.00

BASKET, see No. 615

. . . .

If you discover a cache of very dirty antiques and you are not dressed in work clothes, make a temporary cover up from a plastic garbage bag.

. . . .

Beaded Block

Imperial Glass Company, Bellaire, Ohio, made Beaded Block from 1927 to c.1936. It was made in amber, crystal, green, Ice Blue, pink, red, Vaseline, and white. Frosted or iridescent pieces were also made, leading some collectors to name the pattern Frosted Block. Some iridescent pink pieces made recently have been found marked with the IG trademark used from 1951 to 1977.

AMBER

Plate, Square, 7 3/4 In.	8.00
Vase, 6 In.	18.00

CRYSTAL

Pitcher, 5 1/4 In.	80.00
Sugar, Footed	14.00

GREEN

Celery Dish, 8 1/4 In.	10.00
Creamer	25.00
Sugar & Creamer	45.00

PINK

Bowl, 2 Handles, 4 1/2 In.	4.50
Bowl, Square, 5 1/2 In.	4.50
Plate, Round, 8 3/4 In.	10.00
Sugar & Creamer	45.00

BERWICK, see Boopie

BEVERAGE WITH SAIL-BOATS, see White Ship

BIG RIB, see Manhattan

BLOCK, see Block Optic

Block Optic

Block Optic, sometimes called Block, was made from 1929 to 1933 by the Hocking Glass Company, Lancaster, Ohio. Slight variations in the design of some pieces, like creamers and sugars, show that the pattern was redesigned at times. Green is the most common color, followed by crystal, pink, and yellow. Amber and blue examples are harder to find. Some pieces were made with a black stem or a black flat foot.

CRYSTAL

Butter, Cover	30.00
Cup, Curly Handle	4.00
Goblet, 4 1/2 In.	10.00 to 16.00
Goblet, 5 3/4 In.	14.00 to 15.00
Goblet, 7 1/4 In.	14.00 to 16.00
Ice Bucket, Metal Handle	30.00
Plate, 8 In.	5.00
Sandwich Server, Center Handle, 10 1/4 In.	12.00
Sherbet, 4 3/4 In.	8.00
Sugar, Curly Handle	8.00
Tumbler, 9 Oz., 5 In.	10.00
Whiskey, 2 1/4 In.	10.00

GREEN

Bowl, 4 1/4 In.	6.00
Bowl, 5 1/4 In.	7.50 to 15.00
Bowl, 8 1/2 In.	16.00 to 26.00
Butter, Cover	200.00
Candlestick, 1 3/4 In., Pair	110.00
Creamer, Footed	12.00
Cup	5.00 to 6.00
Cup & Saucer	14.00 to 15.00
Goblet, 4 1/2 In.	30.00
Goblet, 5 3/4 In.	23.00
Ice Tub	35.00
Pitcher, 80 Oz., 8 In.	85.00
Plate, 6 In.	1.50 to 3.00
Plate, 8 In.	2.50
Plate, 9 In.	17.50 to 20.00
Salt & Pepper, Footed	34.00 to 38.00
Saucer	8.00
Saucer, Ring, 5 3/4 In.	6.00
Saucer, Ring, 6 1/8 In.	6.00
Sherbet, 3 1/4 In.	3.00 to 8.00
Sherbet, 4 3/4 In.	7.00 to 14.00
Sugar	10.00 to 12.00
Sugar, Cone	8.50 to 12.50
Tumble-Up	62.00
Tumbler, For Tumble-Up, 3 In.	40.00
Vase, 5 3/4 In.	350.00

PINK

Candleholder, 1 3/4 In., Pair	65.00 to 75.00
Cup	6.00
Cup & Saucer	13.50
Goblet, 4 In.	28.00
Goblet, 5 3/4 In.	16.00
Plate, 6 In.	2.50
Plate, 8 In.	4.00
Saltshaker	35.00
Sandwich Server, Center Handle	50.00
Sherbet, 3 1/4 In.	7.00
Tumbler, 10 Oz., 5 In.	16.00

YELLOW

Candleholder, 1 3/4 In.	95.00
Candy Jar, Cover	55.00
Creamer	12.00
Cup	8.00
Goblet, 5 3/4 In.	30.00
Goblet, 7 1/4 In.	32.00
Plate, 6 In.	2.50 to 5.00
Plate, 8 In.	5.00 to 6.00
Sugar	12.00

Boopie

With a name like Boopie, it must have some other attraction. This Anchor Hocking pattern was made in the late 1940s and 1950s. Only glasses of various sizes are known, including the 3 1/2-ounce, 4-ounce, 6-ounce, and 9-ounce. The pattern came in crystal, Forest Green, and Royal Ruby.

CRYSTAL

Sherbet	2.50 to 6.00
Tumbler, 3 3/4 In.	4.00 to 9.00
Tumbler, 5 1/2 In.	5.00 to 10.00

GREEN

Sherbet	10.50

ROYAL RUBY

Tumbler, 3 7/8 In.	7.00
Tumbler, 5 1/2 In.	12.00

BOUQUET & LATTICE, see Normandie

BRIDAL BOUQUET, see No. 615

Bubble

Names of Depression glass patterns can be depressingly confusing. Bubble is also known as Bullseye, the original name given by Anchor Hocking Glass Corporation, or as Provincial, the 1960s name. Bubble was made in many colors, originally in crystal, pale blue, and pink. Dark green was issued in 1954. Milk white and Ruby Red were made in the 1960s. Recently, yellow pieces have been seen, possibly made in the 1950s. Reproductions have appeared in the

1980s in green, Jadite, pink, and Royal Ruby. They usually have an anchor mark on the bottom.

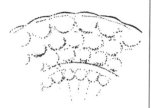

BLUE

Bowl, 4 In.	13.75 to 24.00
Bowl, 4 1/2 In.	9.00 to 10.00
Bowl, 5 1/4 In.	10.00 to 12.00
Bowl, 7 3/4 In.	8.50
Bowl, 8 3/4 In.	12.50
Creamer	30.00 to 32.00
Cup	3.50
Cup & Saucer	6.50
Grill Plate, 9 3/8 In.	16.00 to 19.00
Plate, 6 3/4 In.	2.25 to 4.00
Platter, Oval, 12 In.	10.75 to 15.00
Saucer	1.50
Soup, Dish, 7 3/4 In.	10.00 to 15.00
Sugar	17.50 to 20.00
Sugar & Creamer	50.00 to 53.00
Tumbler, Footed, 16 Oz., 5 7/8 In.	17.00

CRYSTAL

Bowl, 4 In.	3.00 to 5.00
Bowl, 4 1/2 In.	3.50 to 5.00
Bowl, 8 3/8 In.	6.00 to 9.50
Candlestick, 3 In., Pair	50.00
Champagne, Saucer	10.00
Creamer	6.00
Cup	3.25 to 5.00
Cup & Saucer	4.00 to 5.00
Grill Plate, 9 3/8 In.	5.00 to 10.00
Plate, 6 3/4 In.	2.50 to 8.00
Platter, Oval, 12 In.	16.00
Saucer	3.00

Soup, Dish, 7 3/4 In.	7.00 to 10.00
Sugar	5.00 to 6.00
Sugar & Creamer	10.00
Tumbler, 6 Oz.	6.50 to 8.50

GREEN

Bowl, 4 1/2 In.	6.00
Bowl, 5 1/4 In.	13.00 to 15.00
Creamer	11.00 to 12.00
Cup	8.00 to 9.00
Cup & Saucer	12.00
Grill Plate, 9 3/8 In.	14.00 to 20.00
Plate, 6 3/4 In.	6.00
Saucer	4.00 to 5.00
Sherbet	7.50
Sugar	11.00 to 12.00
Sugar & Creamer	18.00 to 28.00
Tumbler, 16 Oz., 5 7/8 In.	8.00 to 15.00

RED

Bowl, 4 1/2 In.	7.00 to 9.50
Bowl, 8 3/8 In.	15.00 to 25.00
Cup	5.00 to 7.00
Cup & Saucer	12.00 to 14.00
Grill Plate, 9 3/8 In.	15.00 to 16.00
Pitcher, Ice Lip, 64 Oz.	50.00 to 55.00
Sherbet	12.00
Tumbler, 12 Oz., 4 1/2 In.	9.00 to 12.00
Tumbler, 16 Oz., 5 7/8 In.	12.00 to 18.00

WHITE

Bowl, 4 In.	5.00
Bowl, 4 1/2 In.	6.00
Bowl, 7 3/4 In.	10.00
Bowl, 8 3/8 In.	4.00 to 8.00
Creamer	6.00
Cup	5.00
Plate, 9 3/4 In.	10.00
Saucer	3.00
Sugar	6.00

BULLSEYE, see Bubble

Burple

Burple is not a mistype but a real name used by the factory. Anchor Hocking Glass Corporation, Lancaster, Ohio, made crystal, Forest Green, and Ruby Red dessert sets in this pattern in the 1940s. There are also two sizes of bowls.

CRYSTAL

Bowl, 4 5/8 In.	3.00
Bowl, 8 1/2 In.	20.00
Sherbet, Footed, 4 In.	5.00 to 11.00
Tumbler, 14 Oz.	12.00 to 20.00

GREEN

Bowl, 4 5/8 In.	4.00
Sherbet, Footed, 4 In.	7.00
Tumbler, 14 Oz.	10.00

BUTTERFLIES & ROSES, see Flower Garden with Butterflies

BUTTONS & BOWS, see Holiday

By Cracky

A strange cracked-ice look to the glass must have inspired the name By Cracky for this pattern. It was made in the late 1920s by L. E. Smith Glass Corporation, Mt. Pleasant, Pennsylvania. Candleholders, flower frogs, 8-inch octagonal plates, and luncheon sets with sherbets were made. The luncheon set dish had several compartments. Amber, Canary Yellow, crystal, and green pieces were made. The pieces have an overall crackled pattern.

AMBER

Sherbet, Liner 3.50

CRYSTAL

Pitcher 14.00

Plate, Round, 8 In. 1.50

Sherbet, Round, Flared 1.50

GREEN

Plate, Octagonal, 6 In. 1.25

Plate, Round, 6 In. 1.25

Sherbet, Octagonal,
 Crimped. 3.00

Tumbler, Juice 1.75

YELLOW

Sherbet. 7.00

C

**CABBAGE ROSE,
 see Sharon**

**CABBAGE ROSE WITH
 SINGLE ARCH, see
 Rosemary**

Cameo

Cameo is understandably called Ballerina or Dancing Girl because the most identifiable feature of the etched pattern is the silhouette of the dancer. This pattern must have sold well when made by Hocking Glass Company from 1930 to 1934 because many different pieces were made, from dinner sets and servers, to cookie jars and lamps. The pattern was made in crystal, sometimes with a platinum trim, and in green, pink, and yellow. In 1981 reproductions were made of both pink and green Cameo salt and pepper shakers. Children's dishes have recently been made in green, pink, and yellow; but there were never any old Cameo children's dishes.

CRYSTAL

Console Set, 3 Piece 125.00

Grill Plate, 10 1/2 In. 5.50

Tumbler, 11 Oz., 5 In. 15.00

Tumbler, Platinum Trim,
 9 Oz., 4 In. 12.50

GREEN

Bottle, Whitehouse
 Vinegar. 20.00

Bowl, 5 1/2 In. . . . . 18.00 to 28.00

Bowl, 7 1/4 In. . . . . 50.00 to 57.00

Bowl, 8 1/4 In. . . . . 32.00 to 35.00

Bowl, Vegetable, Oval,
 10 In. . . . . 18.00 to 24.00

Butter, Cover. . . 185.00 to 200.00

Cake Plate,
 Footed, 10 In. . . . 18.00 to 27.00

Candlestick, 4 In. 46.50

Candlestick, 4 In.,
 Pair . . . . 95.00 to 110.00

Candy Jar, Cover,
 6 1/2 In. 175.00

Console, Footed,
 11 In. . . . . 57.00 to 85.00

Cookie Jar,
 Cover . . . . 46.00 to 50.00

Creamer, 3 1/4 In. 19.00

Cup 9.00

Cup & Saucer . . . . . 15.00 to 18.00

Decanter, Stopper,
 10 In. . . . . 125.00 to 140.00

Dish,
 Mayonnaise . . . . . 22.00 to 28.00

Dish, Mayonnaise,
 Ladle, 2 Piece. 42.00

Goblet, 4 In. . . . . . . 47.50 to 65.00

Goblet, 6 In. 55.00

Grill Plate,
 10 1/2 In. . . . . 7.50 to 10.00

Grill Plate, Closed Handles,
 10 1/2 In. . . . . 60.00 to 75.00

Pitcher, 36 Oz.,
 6 In. . . . . 35.00 to 45.00

Pitcher, 56 Oz.,
 8 1/2 In. . . . . 45.00 to 60.00

Plate, 6 In. 6.00

Plate, 8 In. . . . . 7.00 to 12.00

Plate, 9 1/2 In. 12.00

Plate, Handles, 10 In. 8.00

Plate, Square,
 8 1/2 In. . . . . 38.00 to 42.00

Platter, Closed
 Handles, 12 In. . . 19.00 to 20.00

Relish, 3 Sections, Footed,
 7 1/2 In. . . . . 25.00 to 28.00

Salt & Pepper. . . . . 59.50 to 69.00

Saltshaker. 40.00

Saucer. 4.00

Sherbet, 3 1/8 In. . . 12.00 to 15.00

Sherbet, 4 7/8 In.......... 35.00
Soup, Cream, 4 3/4 In. 125.00
Soup, Dish, 9 In.... 43.00 to 47.00
Sugar, 3 1/4 In..... 11.00 to 20.00
Sugar, 4 1/4 In............. 24.00
Tray, Domino, 7 In........175.00
Tumbler,
  3 3/4 In........ 27.00 to 32.00
Tumbler, 4 In. .... 22.00 to 27.00
Tumbler, 5 In. .... 26.00 to 32.00
Tumbler, Footed,
  5 In........... 23.00 to 27.00
Tumbler, Footed,
  5 3/4 In................ 55.00
Vase, 5 3/4 In. .. 145.00 to 150.00
Vase, 8 In......... 25.00 to 32.00

PINK

Console, Footed, 11 In...... 50.00
Plate, 9 1/2 In. 8.00
Tumbler, 3 3/4 In........ 185.00
Tumbler, 4 In. 150.00
Tumbler, Footed,
  5 3/4 In................ 160.00

YELLOW

Bowl, 5 1/2 In. .... 29.00 to 35.00
Bowl, Vegetable,
  Oval, 10 In. 40.00
Creamer 19.00
Cup & Saucer.............. 9.00
Grill Plate,
  10 1/2 In........ 5.00 to 22.00
Grill Plate, Closed
  Handles, 10 1/2 In........ 7.00
Plate, 6 In.......... 1.75 to 3.00
Plate, 9 1/2 In. ...... 8.00 to 9.00
Sherbet, 3 1/8 In.......... 32.00
Sherbet, 4 7/8 In.......... 38.00
Sugar & Creamer 30.00
Tumbler, Footed,
  5 In........... 12.00 to 14.00

Candlewick

Candlewick has been made
by Imperial Glass Company,
Bellaire, Ohio, from 1937 to
the present. Many similar patterns have been made by
other companies. The beaded
edge is the only design. Although the glass was first

made in crystal, it has also
been produced in black, Nut
Brown, Sunshine Yellow, Ultra Blue, and Verde (green).
Some pieces of crystal are
decorated with gold. Pieces
have been found in red, pink,
lavender, and amber, and
with fired-on gold, red, blue,
or green beading. Some sets
were made with etchings and
hand-painted designs.

CRYSTAL

Bowl, Footed, 6 In. 20.00
Butter, Cover, 1/4 Lb. 33.00
Butter, Square...........100.00
Candlestick, 5 In. 60.00
Candy Dish, Cover.........50.00
Celery Dish, Oval,
  13 1/2 In................35.00
Cocktail, 4 Oz. 9.50
Condiment Set, 4 Piece.....65.00
Cruet, Stopper, Handle,
  6 Oz....................65.00
Cup & Saucer 27.50
Muddler..................20.00
Pitcher, Footed, 80 Oz.....200.00
Plate, 7 In. 6.50
Plate, Heart Shape,
  9 In. 65.00
Platter, Toast..............75.00
Punch Bowl, Underplate,
  Ladle, 3 Piece 125.00
Punch Set,
  15 Piece ..... 275.00 to 400.00
Relish, 2 Sections,
  Gold Trim 40.00
Relish, 4 Sections,
  Gold Trim, 8 1/2 In.......65.00
Tidbit, Heart Shape,
  3 Piece 50.00
Tray, Deviled Egg.........110.00

Tumbler, Footed, 5 Oz......10.00

GREEN

Relish, 2 Sections 65.00
Relish, 3 Sections,
  7 1/2 In................48.00
Tidbit, 2 Tiers 550.00

ULTRA BLUE

Bowl, Chrome Stand 75.00
Dish, Mayonnaise,
  2 Piece 117.00
Plate, Frosted, 6 In. 24.00

Cape Cod

Cape Cod was a pattern made
by the Imperial Glass Company, Bellaire, Ohio, from 1932.
It is usually found in crystal,
but was also made in amber,
Azalea, light blue, cobalt blue,
green, milk glass, and ruby. In
1978 the dinner set was reproduced. The cruet was reproduced in 1986 without the
rayed bottom.

AMBER

Cruet, 4 Oz...............30.00
Goblet, Water 18.00
Salt & Pepper 40.00
Sherbet...................12.00
Tumbler, Footed,
  5 Oz........... 10.00 to 12.00
Wine....................17.50

AZALEA

Goblet, Water 24.00

BLUE

Goblet, Water 27.50

CRYSTAL

Bowl, Baked Apple, 6 In......5.00
Bowl, Footed, 10 In. 75.00

Bowl, Heart Shape 15.00
Cake Stand, Footed,
  11 In. . . . . 60.00 to 80.00
Champagne. 6.00
Cocktail, 3 1/2 In. 5.00
Compote, Footed. 15.00
Cup & Saucer 8.50
Dish, Sundae, 6 Oz. 3.00
Goblet, 11 Oz. 7.00
Parfait. . . . . 8.00 to 10.00
Pitcher, 32 Oz., 10 In. 95.00
Pitcher, Water, Blown,
  80 Oz. 125.00
Plate, 10 In. 35.00
Punch Set, 15 Piece 250.00
Relish, 5 Sections, 11 In. 30.00
Salt & Pepper 12.00
Sherbet, 6 Oz. . . . . 6.00 to 8.00
Sugar & Creamer, Tray,
  Square, 3 Piece 200.00
Tom & Jerry Set 450.00
Tumbler, Footed, 6 Oz. 6.00
Vase, 11 In. 60.00
Wine. . . . . 4.00 to 8.00

GREEN
Cruet, Stopper 30.00
Goblet, 11 Oz. 20.00

RED
Cocktail 15.90
Cologne, Stopper. 85.00
Goblet, 11 Oz. 25.00

Caprice

Caprice was advertised in 1936 as the most popular crystal pattern in America. It was made until 1953. Over 200 pieces were made in the line. Frosted pieces were called Alpine Caprice, the name given by the maker, Cambridge Glass Company, Cambridge, Ohio. The sets were made in amber, amethyst, blue, cobalt blue, Moonlight Blue, crystal, Emerald Green, light green, pink, and milk glass. Reproductions are being made in cobalt blue and Moonlight Blue.

AMBER
Ashtray, 3 In. 12.50
Jam Jar, 7 In. 65.00

BLUE
Ashtray, Triangular,
  2 1/2 In. 15.00
Bonbon, 2 Handles,
  Square, 6 In. . . . . . 48.00 to 65.00
Bonbon, Handle,
  Square, 4 In. 32.50
Bowl, Footed, 6 In. 40.00
Bowl, Salad, 10 In. 165.00
Candleholder, 3-Light,
  Pair 80.00
Claret, 4 1/2 Oz. . . . 35.00 to 37.50
Cocktail, 3 Oz. . . . . 55.00 to 65.00
Compote, Footed, 7 In. 50.00
Cup & Saucer 45.00
Dish, Mayonnaise, Footed,
  Handle . . . . 45.00 to 75.00
Goblet, Water . . . . . 45.00 to 48.00
Ivy Bowl, 5 In. 275.00
Oyster Cocktail,
  4 1/2 Oz. 67.50
Plate, 6 1/2 In. 25.00
Plate, 8 In. 22.00
Plate, Lemon, Handle,
  6 In. . . . . 25.00 to 35.00
Relish, 3 Sections,
  8 In. . . . . 38.00 to 45.00
Salt & Pepper 75.00
Sherbet, 6 Oz. . . . . 32.50 to 225.00

Sugar. 30.00
Sugar & Creamer. 45.00
Tray, Center Handle 75.00
Tumbler, Footed,
  5 Oz. . . . . 35.00 to 60.00
Tumbler, Footed, 12 Oz. 45.00
Vase, 4 In. 150.00

CRYSTAL
Candleholder, 2 1/2 In.,
  Pair 27.50
Compote, 6 In. . . . . 22.00 to 37.50
Cruet, Oil, 3 Oz. 37.50
Cup 8.50
Mayonnaise Set, 3 Piece. . . . 35.00
Plate, 7 1/2 In. 7.00
Salt & Pepper, Tray,
  Individual, 3 Piece 75.00
Sherbet, 6 Oz. 13.00
Tray, Center Handle 37.50
Tumbler, Footed, 5 Oz. 18.00
Tumbler, Footed,
  12 Oz. 37.50

MILK GLASS
Ashtray, 3 In. 45.00
Candy Dish, Cover,
  Footed. 295.00
Plate, 8 1/2 In. 75.00
Plate, Lemon, 6 In. 50.00
Sherbet, 6 Oz. 225.00
Vase, 4 1/4 In. 85.00

PINK
Ashtray, 3 In. 45.00
Candy Dish, Cover,
  Footed. 295.00
Plate, 8 1/2 In. 75.00
Plate, Lemon, 6 In. 50.00
Sherbet, 6 Oz. 225.00

CAPRICE, see also
  Alpine Caprice

. . . .

Shallow nicks and rough edges on glass can sometimes be smoothed off with fine emery paper.

. . . .

Caribbean

The rippled design of Caribbean is slick and modern in appearance and has attracted many collectors. It was made by Duncan & Miller Glass Company, Pittsburgh, Pennsylvania, from 1936 to 1955. Sets were made of crystal, crystal with ruby trim, amber, blue, and red glass. The Duncan & Miller catalogs identify the line as No. 112.

BLUE

Bowl, Flared, 9 1/2 In.	95.00
Bowl, Flower, Handle, Oval, 10 3/4 In.	65.00
Console, Flared, 12 In.	65.00
Plate, 7 1/2 In.	20.00
Plate, Torte, 16 In.	55.00
Relish, 5 Sections, 12 1/2 In.	95.00
Sherbet	45.00
Sherbet, 4 5/8 In.	25.00
Sugar & Creamer	50.00
Vase, Oval, 10 1/2 x 5 1/2 In.	75.00

CRYSTAL

Punch Bowl, Flared, 10 In.	70.00

Century

Century pattern was made by Fostoria Glass Company from 1926 until 1986. It is a plain pattern with a slightly rippled rim. Full dinner sets were made of clear crystal.

• • • • • • • • • • • • • •

Don't use ammonia on glasses with gold or silver decorations.

• • • • • • • • • • • • • •

Bonbon	22.50
Bowl, 5 In.	18.00
Bowl, Rolled Edge, Footed	30.00
Bowl, Utility, Handles, Oval	30.00
Butter, Cover, 1/4 Lb.	33.00
Candy Dish, Cover.	35.00
Cocktail	17.50
Compote, Round	17.50
Compote, Square	17.50
Cruet, Stopper, 5 Oz.	32.50
Cup	10.00
Cup & Saucer	12.50
Dish, Mayonnaise, Round, 3 Piece	37.50
Plate, 8 1/2 In.	25.00
Relish, 2 Sections, 7 3/8 In.	17.50
Relish, 3 Sections, 11 1/8 In.	27.50
Sugar & Creamer	14.00 to 29.00
Tidbit, Footed	17.50
Tumbler, Iced Tea	24.00
Vase, Bud, Footed, 6 In.	12.50

CHAIN DAISY, see Adam

Chantilly

As late as the 1960s the Jeannette Glass Company, Jeannette, Pennsylvania, made a pattern called Chantilly that is collected by Depression glass buffs. It was made in crystal and pink.

Compote, 6 In.	35.00
Cup	20.00
Goblet, 5 3/4 In.	30.00
Jam Jar, Cover	145.00
Jug, Martini, 9 In.	175.00
Plate, 10 In.	87.50
Sugar & Creamer	40.00

Charm

Charm is a pattern of Fire-King dinnerware made from 1950 to 1954. The square shaped dishes were made by Anchor Hocking Glass Corporation of Lancaster, Ohio. The dinnerware was made of Forest Green, Royal Ruby, Jadite (opaque green), and Azurite (opaque blue). Collectors often refer to the color name rather than the pattern name when describing these pieces. It is sometimes called Square. Other related sections in this book are Alice; Fire-King; Peach Lustre; Philbe; Swirl Fire-King; Turquoise Blue; and Wheat.

AZURITE

Cup & Saucer	3.00 to 8.00
Plate, 8 3/8 In.	4.00 to 6.50
Plate, 9 1/4 In.	22.00
Platter, 11 In.	22.00
Saucer	1.00
Soup, Dish, 6 In.	22.00

JADITE

Bowl, 6 In.	12.00
Bowl, 4 1/2 In.	6.00
Cup & Saucer	18.00
Plate, 7 In.	5.00 to 6.00
Plate, 9 1/2 In.	20.00
Saucer	1.00

Cherokee Rose

The Tiffin glass factory can be traced back to the 1840s, when Joseph Beatty made glass in Steubenville, Ohio. The factory failed and was purchased by Alexander Beatty in 1851. He was joined by his sons and moved to Tiffin, Ohio, in 1888. The company became part of U.S. Glass Company in 1892 and was still operating in 1963 when U.S. Glass went bankrupt. Employees bought the plant and it went through several changes of ownership until it closed in 1980. Cherokee Rose was one of the popular glass patterns made by Tiffin in the 1940s and 1950s. The glass was made only in crystal.

CRYSTAL

Candlestick, 2-Light	40.00
Champagne, 5 1/2 Oz.	16.00 to 18.00
Cocktail, 3 1/2 Oz.	24.00
Parfait, 4 1/2 Oz.	50.00
Plate, 8 In.	15.00 to 18.50
Relish, 3 Sections, 6 1/2 In.	35.00
Relish, 3 Sections, 12 1/2 In.	60.00
Sherbet	20.00
Sugar	22.50
Sugar & Creamer	45.00
Vase, Bud, 8 In.	45.00
Vase, Bud, 11 In.	45.00
Wine, 3 1/2 Oz.	25.00

CHERRY, see Cherry Blossom

Cherry-Berry

Two similar patterns, Cherry-Berry and Strawberry, can be confusing. If the fruit pictured is a cherry, then the pattern is called Cherry-Berry. If the strawberry is used, then the pattern has that name. The dishes were made by the U.S. Glass Company in the early 1930s in crystal, green, iridescent amber, and pink.

AMBER

Bowl, 7 1/2 In.	15.00
Sugar, Cover	45.00 to 60.00

GREEN

Bowl, 6 1/2 In.	55.00
Tumbler, 9 Oz., 3 1/2 In.	26.00

CHERRY-BERRY, see also Strawberry

Cherry Blossom

Cherry Blossom is one of the most popular Depression glass patterns. It has been called Banded Cherry, Cherry, or Paneled Cherry Blossom by some collectors. The pattern was made by the Jeannette Glass Company, Jeannette, Pennsylvania, from 1930 to 1939. Full dinner sets, serving pieces, and a child's set were made in a wide range of colors. Pieces were made in crystal, Delphite (opaque blue), green, Jadite (opaque green), pink, and red. During the course of production, molds were changed, resulting in several shapes and styles for some pieces. Many reproductions of Cherry Blossom pieces have been made and sold in recent years.

CRYSTAL

Bowl, Round, 8 1/2 In.	40.00

DELPHITE

Bowl, Oval, 9 In.	23.00
Child's Set, 14 Piece	240.00
Creamer, Child's	30.00 to 40.00
Cup, Child's	15.00 to 30.00
Plate, Child's, 6 In.	8.00 to 12.00
Saucer, Child's	6.00 to 9.00
Sugar, Child's	40.00
Tumbler, Footed, 4 1/2 In.	20.00

GREEN

Bowl, 2 Handles, 9 In.	30.00
Bowl, 4 3/4 In.	16.00
Bowl, 5 3/4 In.	30.00 to 32.00
Bowl, 8 1/2 In.	30.00 to 42.00
Bowl, Footed, 10 1/2 In.	68.00 to 75.00
Bowl, Oval, 9 In.	35.00 to 36.00
Bowl, Round, 8 1/2 In.	30.00
Butter, Cover	75.00 to 125.00
Cake Plate, 10 1/4 In.	23.00
Coaster	10.00 to 16.00
Creamer	15.00
Cup	12.00 to 15.00
Cup & Saucer	19.00 to 24.00
Grill Plate, 9 In.	22.00
Mug	220.00
Pitcher, Footed, 8 In.	40.00 to 55.00

Plate, 6 In. 6.00
Plate, 7 In. . . . . 18.00 to 20.00
Plate, 9 In. 22.00
Platter, 2 Sections,
13 In. 50.00
Saucer . . . . 4.75 to 6.00
Sherbet . . . . 14.00 to 17.00
Soup, Dish. 50.00
Sugar 13.00
Sugar, Cover . . . . . . 27.00 to 34.00
Sugar & Creamer,
Cover . . . . 28.00 to 43.00
Tumbler,
3 1/2 In. . . . . 24.00 to 26.00
Tumbler, Round Footed,
4 1/4 In. . . . . 22.00 to 26.00
Tumbler, Flat Footed,
4 1/2 In. 19.00

PINK

Bowl, 4 3/4 In. . . . . 12.00 to 15.00
Bowl, 5 3/4 In. 32.00
Bowl, 8 1/2 In. . . . . 34.00 to 45.00
Bowl, Footed,
10 1/2 In. . . . . 71.00 to 80.00
Bowl, Handles,
9 In. . . . . 25.00 to 26.00
Bowl, Oval, 9 In. . . 25.00 to 40.00
Butter, Cover . . . . . 75.00 to 80.00
Cake Plate, Footed,
10 1/2 In. . . . . 22.50 to 24.00
Creamer . . . . 10.00 to 19.50
Cup 13.00
Cup & Saucer . . . . . 20.00 to 26.50
Grill Plate, 9 In. . . . 20.00 to 24.00
Pitcher, 36 Oz., 6 3/4 In. . . . 50.00
Pitcher, Footed,
42 Oz., 8 In. 60.00
Plate, 6 In. 6.00
Plate, 7 In. . . . . 16.50 to 18.00
Plate, 9 In. . . . . 15.00 to 20.00
Platter, 13 In. . . . . . 50.00 to 60.00
Platter, 2 Sections,
13 In. . . . . 55.00 to 60.00
Platter, Oval, 11 In. 31.00
Salt & Pepper 1150.00
Saucer 5.00
Sherbet 15.00
Soup, Dish. . . . . 45.00 to 68.00
Sugar 15.00

Sugar, Cover 18.00
Sugar & Creamer 25.00
Tray, Sandwich,
10 1/2 In. 19.50
Tumbler,
4 1/4 In. . . . . 15.00 to 28.00
Tumbler, Footed,
4 1/2 In. 32.00

Chinex Classic

Chinex Classic and Cremax are very similar patterns made by Macbeth-Evans Division of Corning Glass Works from about 1938 to 1942. Chinex and Cremax are both words with two meanings. Each is the name of a pattern and the name of a color used for other patterns. Chinex is ivory colored, Cremax is a bit whiter. Chinex Classic, the dinnerware pattern, has a piecrust edge, and just inside the edge is an elongated feathered scroll. It may or may not have a decal-decorated center and colored edging. The Cremax pattern has just the piecrust edge. The decals used on Chinex Classic are either floral designs or brown-toned scenics.

IVORY

Bowl, 5 3/4 In. 6.50
Bowl, 7 In. 17.00
Creamer. 5.00
Plate, 6 1/4 In. 16.00
Plate, 9 3/4 In. . . . . . . 3.75 to 5.00
Plate, Sandwich,
11 1/2 In. . . . . 6.50 to 8.00
Saucer 1.75
Sugar 5.25

IVORY WITH DECAL

Bowl, 6 In. 17.00

Bowl, 9 In. 35.00
Bowl, Blue Rim, 7 In. 32.00
Butter, Cover. 70.00
Cup & Saucer 20.00
Plate, 6 1/4 In. 7.50
Plate, 9 3/4 In. 16.00
Plate, Sandwich,
11 1/2 In. 25.00
Plate, Yellow Border,
9 3/4 In. 16.00
Sherbet. 22.00
Soup, Dish . . . . 30.00 to 33.00

CHINEX CLASSIC,
see also Cremax

Chintz

Several companies made a glass named Chintz. To identify the pieces of Chintz pattern, remember the design is named for the etched pattern, not the shape, of the glass. Fostoria Glass Company made Baroque, a glass shape that included molded fleur-de-lis-shaped handles and ridges. This glass blank was then etched with design No. 338 and then sold as Chintz pattern. The etched design pictures branches of leaves and flowers. It was also used on some vases and other pieces that were not Baroque blanks. Only crystal pieces were made. Pieces were made from 1940 to 1972. To confuse this even more, the company made other etched designs (Navarre) on the Baroque blanks. Another Chintz pattern was made by A. H. Heisey Company from 1931 to 1938. It was an etched design of butterflies and encircled flowers. This Chintz pattern was made in crystal, green (Moongleam), orchid (Alexandrite, a glass that turned from blue to purple depending on the lighting source), pink (Flamingo), and yellow (Sahara). Pieces listed in this book are for Fostoria Chintz.

CRYSTAL

Bowl, Handle, 8 1/2 In.	42.00
Bowl, Handle, Footed, 10 1/2 In.	55.00
Cake Plate, Handle, 10 In.	45.00
Candleholder, 2-Light, Pair	75.00
Candleholder, 3-Light, Pair	70.00
Candleholder, Pair	45.00 to 55.00
Champagne, 6 Oz., 5 1/2 In.	16.00 to 20.00
Cheese & Cracker Set	95.00
Cocktail, 4 Oz., 5 In.	18.00 to 24.00
Cordial, 1 Oz., 3 7/8 In.	50.00
Creamer	20.00
Cup & Saucer	24.00
Goblet, 9 Oz., 7 5/8 In.	27.00
Jam Jar, Cover, 7 1/2 In.	95.00
Nappy, 3 Handles, 4 5/8 In.	20.00
Pickle, 8 In.	35.00
Plate, 7 In.	12.50 to 16.00
Plate, Torte, 14 In.	40.00 to 50.00
Relish, 3 Sections	32.00 to 39.50
Salt & Pepper	75.00
Server, Center Handle	45.00
Sherbet, 4 3/8 In.	16.00 to 25.00
Sugar	15.00 to 22.00
Sugar & Creamer	27.00 to 35.00
Sugar & Creamer, Tray, Individual, 3 Piece	67.00
Tumbler, 5 Oz., 4 3/4 In.	18.00
Tumbler, 13 Oz., 6 In.	24.00 to 26.00
Wine, 4 1/2 Oz., 5 3/8 In.	37.00 to 40.00

Christmas Candy

Christmas Candy, sometimes called Christmas Candy Ribbon or No. 624, was made by the Indiana Glass Company, Dunkirk, Indiana, in 1937. The pattern, apparently only made in luncheon sets, was made in crystal, a light green called Seafoam Green, a bright blue called Teal Blue, and dark Emerald Green.

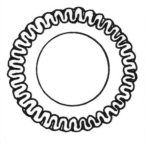

CRYSTAL

Creamer	8.00
Cup & Saucer	6.50 to 7.00
Plate, 8 In.	7.00
Plate, 9 In.	22.00
Platter, 11 In.	15.00
Sugar	8.00

TEAL BLUE

Bowl, 7 3/8 In.	26.00
Creamer	20.00
Cup	20.00
Cup & Saucer	25.00
Plate, 9 In.	29.00
Saucer	8.00
Soup, Dish	29.00
Sugar	16.00 to 20.00

CHRISTMAS CANDY RIBBON, see Christmas Candy

Circle

Circles ring the Circle pattern made by Hocking Glass Company, Lancaster, Ohio, in the 1930s. It is often found in green, but only luncheon sets were made in crystal and pink. It can be distinguished from the similar Hocking pattern called Ring by the number of groupings of rings—Circle has only one set, Ring has several sets with four rings in each group.

CRYSTAL

Sherbet, 3 1/8 In.	2.00
Sherbet, 4 3/4 In.	3.50
Tumbler, 4 Oz., 3 1/2 In.	1.75

GREEN

Bowl, 4 1/2 In.	8.00 to 11.00
Bowl, 8 In.	24.00
Bowl, Flared, 5 1/2 In.	14.00
Creamer	8.50
Cup, Flared	4.50
Cup, Round	5.25
Goblet, 4 1/2 In.	10.00 to 13.00
Goblet, 5 3/4 In.	5.00 to 13.00
Plate, 6 In.	2.00 to 7.50
Plate, 8 1/4 In.	5.00
Plate, 9 1/2 In.	9.00
Sherbet, 3 1/8 In.	3.00 to 5.00
Sherbet, 4 3/4 In.	4.00 to 7.25
Tumbler, 4 In.	9.75
Tumbler, 5 In.	16.00 to 17.00

PINK

Creamer	22.00
Cup	7.00
Plate, 6 In.	2.00 to 9.00
Sherbet, 3 1/8 In.	6.00
Sugar	22.00
Tumbler, 5 In.	10.00

CIRCULAR RIBS,
   see Circle

CLASSIC, see Chinex
   Classic

Cleo

In 1930 the Cambridge Glass Company, Cambridge, Ohio, introduced an etched pattern called Cleo. Many pieces are marked with the Cambridge C in a triangle. Sets were made in amber, blue, crystal, green, pink, and yellow.

AMBER
Candy Dish,
   Cover . . . . 165.00 to 175.00
Casserole, Cover, Small 210.00
Console, 12 In. 35.00

BLUE
Champagne 32.50
Compote, Tall, 7 In. 110.00
Cup 20.00
Goblet, 9 Oz. 47.50
Pitcher, Crystal Handle 145.00
Plate, 7 In. 12.50
Plate, Sandwich,
   Center Handle, 12 In. . . . 115.00
Vase, 9 1/2 In. 75.00

CRYSTAL
Champagne 32.50

GREEN
Champagne 32.50
Ice Pail, 4 In. 65.00
Oyster Cocktail, Liner 95.00
Plate, 9 1/2 In. . . . . 50.00 to 60.00
Vase, Footed, 11 In. 195.00

PINK
Bowl, Vegetable,
   Oval, 9 1/2 In. 65.00
Bowl, Vegetable,
   Oval, 11 In. 125.00
Champagne 35.00
Ice Pail, 4 In. 65.00
Platter, 11 In. 110.00

Cloverleaf

Three-leaf clovers form part of the border of Cloverleaf pattern made by Hazel Atlas Glass Company from 1930 to 1936. It was made in black, crystal, green, pink, and topaz.

BLACK
Ashtray, 4 In. 54.00
Creamer. 14.00
Cup. 11.00
Cup & Saucer . . . . . 15.00 to 22.00
Plate, 6 In. 30.00
Plate, 8 In. . . . . 13.00 to 22.00
Salt & Pepper . . . . . 69.00 to 75.00
Saucer 5.00
Sherbet. . . . . 15.00 to 18.00
Sugar 15.00
Sugar & Creamer 27.00

CRYSTAL
Cup. . . . . 3.50 to 5.00

GREEN
Bowl, 5 In. 24.00
Bowl, 7 In. 35.00
Candy Dish,
   Cover . . . . 40.00 to 43.00
Creamer. . . . . 6.00 to 9.50
Cup. 7.50

Cup & Saucer . . . . . . 9.00 to 11.00
Plate, 8 In. . . . . 6.00 to 7.00
Salt & Pepper . . . . . 25.00 to 38.00
Saucer. . . . . 2.00 to 3.50
Sherbet. 5.00
Sugar & Creamer 16.00
Tumbler, 4 In. 30.00
Tumbler, 5 3/4 In. 30.00

PINK
Bowl, 5 In. 10.00
Cup & Saucer 9.00
Plate, 8 In. . . . . 6.00 to 7.00
Sherbet. 6.50
Tumbler, 4 In. 16.00

YELLOW
Cup. 9.00
Plate, 6 In. 6.00
Plate, 8 In. 10.00
Sugar. 14.00

Colonial

Sometimes this pattern is called Knife & Fork, although Colonial is the more common name. It was made by Hocking Glass Company, Lancaster, Ohio, from 1934 to 1938. Crystal, green, and pink pieces are more common than opaque white.

CRYSTAL
Butter, Cover. . . . . . 35.00 to 38.00
Champagne,
   5 1/4 In. . . . . 8.00 to 9.00
Cocktail, 4 In. . . . . . 10.00 to 12.00
Cordial, 3 3/4 In. 15.00
Creamer, 5 In. 12.00
Cup. 7.00
Cup & Saucer 10.00

Goblet, 4 1/2 In.... 12.50 to 13.50
Goblet, 5 1/4 In.... 12.00 to 15.00
Goblet, 5 3/4 In.... 18.00 to 25.00
Plate, 8 1/2 In. 4.00
Spoon Holder 65.00
Sugar, Cover ...... 10.00 to 22.00
Tumbler, 9 Oz., 4 In........ 17.00
Whiskey, 2 1/2 In. 7.50

GREEN

Bowl, 9 In................. 30.00
Bowl, Vegetable,
Oval, 10 In. 35.00
Butter, Cover ..... 48.00 to 50.00
Cup...................... 11.00
Goblet, 4 1/2 In........... 25.00
Goblet, 5 3/4 In........... 27.00
Grill Plate, 10 In........... 27.50
Pitcher, 54 Oz., 7 In....... 45.00
Plate, 6 In................. 6.00
Plate, 8 1/2 In. 9.00
Plate, 10 In................ 50.00
Saucer 6.00
Sherbet.......... 14.00 to 15.00
Soup, Cream, 4 1/2 In. 60.00
Spoon Holder 120.00
Sugar 10.00
Tumbler, Footed, 3 1/4 In. ...24.50
Tumbler, Footed, 4 In. 40.00
Whiskey, 2 1/2 In. 12.50

OPAQUE WHITE

Cup & Saucer 10.00

PINK

Cake Plate 80.00
Cup...................... 10.00
Grill Plate, 10 In........... 25.00
Plate, 10 In....... 46.00 to 47.00
Sherbet........... 4.00 to 8.00
Tumbler, Footed, 3 1/4 In. ...16.50
Tumbler, Footed, 4 In. 20.00
Whiskey, 2 1/2 In. ... 7.00 to 12.00

Colonial Block

A small set of dishes, mostly serving pieces, was made in Colonial Block pattern by Hazel Atlas Glass Company, a firm with factories in Ohio, Pennsylvania, and West Virgin-

ia. The dishes were made in the 1930s in black, crystal, green, and pink and in the 1950s in white.

GREEN

Bowl, 4 In................. 6.00
Bowl, 7 In................ 10.00
Creamer.................. 10.00
Goblet, 5 1/2 In.... 10.00 to 12.00
Pitcher, 20 Oz., 5 3/4 In.... 15.00
Sherbet................... 7.00
Sugar..................... 9.00
Sugar, Cover 20.00

PINK

Sugar, Cover 18.00

Colonial Fluted

Federal Glass Company made Colonial Fluted or Rope pattern from 1928 to 1933. Luncheon sets were made primarily in green, although crystal pieces were also produced.

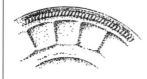

GREEN

Bowl, 4 In.......... 3.00 to 8.00
Creamer.................. 8.00

Cup & Saucer 11.50
Sherbet...........5.00 to 10.00
Sugar, Cover 28.00

Colony

Colony is a pattern that has also been called Elongated Honeycomb or Hexagon Triple Band because of the features in the molding. It was made by Hazel Atlas Glass Company in the 1930s in crystal, green, and pink. Another pattern, also named Colony, was made by Fostoria Glass Company.

CRYSTAL

Bowl, 14 In.............. 35.00
Bowl, Flared, 11 In. 32.50
Bowl, Handles, 5 In........8.00
Bowl, Vegetable, 2 Sections,
Oval, 10 1/2 In. 35.00
Cake Plate, 12 In......... 70.00
Candleholder, 3 1/2 In. 15.00
Console, 9 In. 35.00
Cup & Saucer 7.00
Goblet, 3 1/4 Oz., 4 1/4 In. . 18.50
Goblet, 9 Oz., 5 1/4 In. 12.00
Ice Bucket 95.00
Pickle, 9 1/2 In. 10.00
Pitcher, Ice Lip, 2 Qt...... 125.00
Plate, 6 In. 4.50
Plate, 7 In. 7.00
Plate, 8 In. 9.00
Plate, Sandwich, Center
Handle............... 24.50
Salver, Footed, 7 1/2 In..... 45.00
Sherbet, Footed............8.00
Sugar & Creamer,
Individual 10.00

Tumbler, Footed, 12 Oz.,
5 3/4 In. 12.00
Vase, Cupped, 7 In. 35.00

Columbia

Columbia pattern can be found in crystal but is rare in pink. It was made by Federal Glass Company, Columbus, Ohio, from 1938 to 1942.

CRYSTAL

Bowl, 5 In. . . . . . . 12.00 to 14.00
Bowl, 8 1/2 In. . . . . 9.00 to 18.00
Bowl, Ruffled,
10 1/2 In. . . . . . . 16.00 to 18.00
Butter, Cover . . . . . 18.00 to 20.00
Cup . . . . 4.00 to 7.00
Plate, 6 In. . . . . 2.50 to 3.50
Plate, 9 1/2 In. . . . . 5.00 to 10.00
Plate, 11 3/4 In. . . . 10.00 to 14.00
Saucer 1.00
Soup, Dish, 8 In. . . . 13.00 to 16.00
Tumbler, 9 Oz. 22.50

PINK

Cup & Saucer Set,
6 Plate Set 65.00
Plate, 6 In. 9.00

Coronation

Coronation was made, primarily in berry sets, by Anchor Hocking Glass Corporation, Lancaster, Ohio, from 1936 to 1940. Most pieces are crystal or pink, but there are also dark green and Ruby Red sets. The pattern is sometimes called Banded Fine Rib or Saxon. Some of the pieces are confused with those in Lace Edge pattern.

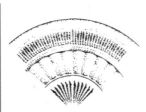

CRYSTAL

Cup. 4.00
Cup & Saucer 7.00
Plate, 6 In. 2.50
Plate, 8 1/2 In. 5.00
Sherbet. 5.00
Tumbler, Footed,
10 Oz., 5 In. . . . . . . 7.00 to 21.00

RUBY RED

Berry Bowl, 7 Piece 45.00
Bowl, 4 1/4 In. . . . . 6.00 to 15.00
Bowl, 8 In. . . . . 14.00 to 18.00
Bowl, Handles, 6 1/2 In. 15.00

Cracked Ice

Cracked Ice is an Art Deco-looking geometric pattern made by Indiana Glass Company in the 1930s. It was made in green and pink.

GREEN

Sherbet, 3 In. 20.00

PINK

Plate, 6 1/2 In. 20.00
Sherbet, 3 In. . . . . 14.00 to 15.00
Sugar 45.00

Craquel

Craquel was made by the U.S. Glass Company in 1924. It has an overall stippled finish. Pieces were made in crystal with green trim and in blue and yellow.

CRYSTAL

Plate, Green Trim, 6 In. 4.00
Saucer, Green Trim 3.00

YELLOW

Sherbet. 6.00

Cremax

Cremax and Chinex Classic are confusing patterns. There is an added piece of molded design next to the fluted rim trim on Chinex Classic. Also the names Cremax and Chinex refer to colors as well as patterns. Cremax, made by Macbeth-Evans Division of Corning Glass Works, was made from 1938 to 1942. It is a cream-colored opaque glass, sometimes decorated with floral or brown-tinted decals or with a colored rim.

. . . .
A glass vase or bowl can be cleaned with a damp cloth. Try not to put the glass in a sink filled with water. Hitting the glass on a faucet or the sink is a common cause of breakage.
. . . .

CREAM COLORED

Cup, Pink Border 3.50
Cup, Yellow Border 3.50
Cup & Saucer, After Dinner . . 7.00
Plate, 12 In. 6.00
Plate, Green Border,
   9 1/4 In. 5.00

CREMAX, see also Chinex Classic

CRISS CROSS, see X Design

CUBE, see Cubist

Cubist

Cubist, or Cube, molded with the expected rectangular and diamond pattern, was made by Jeannette Glass Company from 1929 to 1933. It was made first in pink and crystal. Later, green replaced crystal, and amber, blue, Canary Yellow, pink, Ultramarine, and white were added. Various shades of some of the colors were made. It has been made recently in amber, opaque white, and Avocado.

CRYSTAL

Bowl, 4 1/4 In. 2.25
Bowl, 6 1/2 In. 3.50
Sherbet 3.00
Sugar, 3 In. 1.00

GREEN

Butter, Cover 55.00
Candy Jar, Cover. . . 24.00 to 28.00
Coaster . . . . 5.00 to 6.50
Creamer, 3 9/16 In. 8.00
Cup 3.50
Pitcher, 45 Oz.,
   8 3/4 In. . . . . . . 195.00 to 225.00
Plate, 6 In. 2.50
Plate, 8 In. . . . . 5.00 to 6.50
Powder Jar, Cover 25.00
Salt & Pepper 30.00
Saltshaker 15.00
Sherbet . . . . 6.00 to 7.00
Sugar, Cover, 3 In. 18.00

PINK

Bowl, 4 1/2 In. . . . . . . 3.50 to 7.00
Candy Jar, Cover. . . 25.00 to 27.00
Coaster . . . . 6.00 to 7.00
Creamer, 3 In. . . . . . . 2.00 to 3.00
Cup & Saucer 9.00
Plate, 6 In. 3.50
Plate, 8 In. . . . . 3.00 to 5.50
Powder Jar, Cover 22.00
Salt & Pepper 28.00
Saucer 2.50
Sugar, 3 In. . . . . 2.00 to 6.50

D

DAISY, see No. 620

**DAISY PETALS,
   see Petalware**

DANCING GIRL, see Cameo

Decagon

Decagon, named for its 10-sided outline, was made by the Cambridge Glass Company of Cambridge, Ohio. The pattern, dating from the 1930s, was made in amber, dark blue

(cobalt), light blue (Moonlight), green, pink, and red.

AMBER

Cup & Saucer 7.00
Plate, 7 1/2 In. 7.00
Sandwich Server,
   Center Handle 15.00

LIGHT BLUE

Basket, Handles, 7 In. 45.00
Bonbon, Handles,
   5 1/2 In. 27.50
Cocktail, 3 1/2 Oz. 22.50
Compote, 5 3/4 In. 60.00
Creamer 17.50
Cup & Saucer 16.50
Ice Bucket . . . . 75.00 to 110.00
Plate, 8 1/2 In. . . . . . 12.50 to 15.00
Sherbet 19.50
Sugar & Creamer 45.00
Tumbler, Footed, 12 Oz. . . . 37.50

DARK BLUE

Ice Bucket 110.00
Sugar & Creamer 45.00

GREEN

Basket, Handles, 7 In. 35.00
Bouillon, Liner 20.00
Bowl, 3 3/4 In. 14.00
Bowl, 5 3/4 In. 22.00
Bowl, Belled, 5 1/2 In. 7.50
Cup & Saucer 12.50
Dish, Mayonnaise, Footed . . 18.00
Plate, 6 1/4 In. 5.00
Plate, 7 1/2 In. 6.00

• • • • • • • • • • • • • • • • •

Put a rubber collar on the faucet spout over the sink. This may save you from breaking a piece of glass or china you are washing.

• • • • • • • • • • • • • • • • •

Plate, 8 1/2 In. ..... 8.50 to 12.50
Platter, Handles, 10 1/2 In. .. 35.00
Sherbet 12.50
Soup, Cream............. 17.50
Soup, Cream, Liner 25.00
Sugar, Cover............. 17.50
Sugar & Creamer 25.00
Sugar & Creamer,
  Tray, 3 Piece 65.00
Tumbler, Footed, 5 Oz. 12.50
Tumbler, Footed, 10 Oz. ... 18.50

PINK
Basket, Handles, 7 In. 40.00
Bowl, 5 3/4 In. 15.00
Cup & Saucer............. 12.50
Plate, 7 1/2 In. 7.50
Plate, 8 1/2 In. 8.00
Plate, 10 In............... 45.00
Sandwich Server,
  Center Handle 30.00
Soup, Cream............. 20.00

Della Robbia

Della Robbia is a heavy glass with raised pears and apples as part of the design. It was made by the Westmoreland Glass Company, Grapeville, Pennsylvania, from 1926 to the 1960s. The pattern was made in crystal, Roselin, green, and amber. Crystal pieces often have fruit stained in natural colors.

CRYSTAL
Bowl, Heart Shape,
  Handle, 8 In. 50.00
Candy Jar, Cover, 7 In. 95.00
Compote, Bell, 8 In. 50.00
Goblet, 3 Oz., 4 1/4 In. 29.50
Goblet, 5 Oz., 4 3/4 In. 24.50
Goblet, 8 Oz.,
  6 In. .... 26.00 to 30.00
Plate, 7 1/4 In. 19.50

Plate, 10 1/2 In. 60.00
Plate, Torte, 14 In. 115.00
Punch Set, 8 Piece 240.00
Salt & Pepper 75.00
Sherbet.................. 24.50
Sugar & Creamer .. 25.00 to 30.00
Sugar & Creamer,
  Individual.............. 20.00
Tumbler, 5 Oz............. 29.50

Dewdrop

Although Dewdrop was made in 1954 and 1955, it is collected by some Depression glass buyers. It was made by Jeannette Glass Company, Jeannette, Pennsylvania, in crystal.

Bowl, 4 3/4 In. 3.50
Butter, Cover 25.00
Creamer.................. 12.00
Cup................. 3.00 to 5.00
Jug, 64 Oz................ 25.00
Punch Bowl 28.00
Punch Cup 4.00
Relish, Leaf Shape,
  8 In. .... 7.50 to 12.00
Snack Plate, Cup..... 7.50 to 9.00
Tray, Lazy Susan,
  11 1/2 In............. 15.00
Tumbler, Footed, 9 Oz...... 9.00

DIAMOND, see Windsor

DIAMOND PATTERN, see Miss America

Diamond Quilted

Imperial Glass Company, Bellaire, Ohio, made Diamond Quilted, sometimes called Flat Diamond, in the 1920s and early 1930s. It was made in amber, black, blue, crystal, green, pink, and red. Dinner sets, luncheon sets, and serving pieces, including a large punch bowl, were made, but not all items were made in all colors.

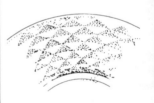

AMBER
Sherbet, 6 In............... 3.00
BLACK
Bowl, Crimp, 7 In. 22.50
Bowl, Flared, 7 In. 22.50
BLUE
Bowl, 5 In................. 16.00
Bowl, Flared, 7 In. 35.00
Cup & Saucer 45.00
Plate, 8 In................ 17.00
Soup, Cream 35.00
Sugar.................... 19.00
Sugar & Creamer 30.00
GREEN
Candleholder,
  Pair .... 20.00 to 22.00

Plate, 6 In.	3.50
Saucer	3.50
Sherbet.	4.00 to 6.00
Soup, Cream	9.00
Sugar	7.50

PINK

Bowl, Flared, 7 In.	24.00
Cup & Saucer	25.00
Plate, 6 In.	3.00

Diana

Diana is one of the many Depression glass patterns with swirls in the glass, which often cause confusion. Federal Glass Company, Columbus, Ohio, made this pattern, sometimes called Swirled Sharp Rib, from 1937 to 1941. It was made in amber, crystal, green, and pink and can be distinguished from other swirled patterns by the two sets of swirls used—one in the center of the piece, another on the rim. A pink bowl was reproduced in 1987.

AMBER

Bowl, 5 In.	10.00
Console, 11 In.	11.00
Creamer.	8.00
Cup.	4.00
Cup & Saucer	7.50
Plate, 6 In.	3.00
Plate, 9 1/2 In.	8.00
Platter, Oval, 12 In.	11.00
Salt & Pepper	95.00
Saucer	2.50
Sherbet	9.00 to 18.00

CRYSTAL

Bowl, 5 In.	3.50 to 4.50

Bowl, 9 In.	5.00
Bowl, Scalloped, 12 In.	6.00 to 7.00
Candy Jar, Cover.	13.00
Cocktail, 2 Piece	65.00
Cup & Saucer	4.00
Cup & Saucer, After Dinner.	8.00 to 13.00
Cup & Saucer, Child's	12.00
Dish, Mayonnaise, Liner	47.50
Plate, 9 1/2 In.	4.50
Plate, 11 3/4 In.	5.00
Platter, Oval, 12 In.	4.00
Salt & Pepper, Footed	60.00
Saucer.	1.00 to 1.50
Soup, Cream	4.00
Sugar & Creamer	5.50
Tumbler, 13 Oz., 4 1/8 In.	37.50

PINK

Bowl, 5 In.	4.50 to 8.50
Bowl, 9 In.	12.00 to 20.00
Coaster.	7.00 to 10.00
Creamer.	6.00 to 10.00
Cup.	9.00
Cup & Saucer	15.00
Cup & Saucer, After Dinner.	20.00 to 30.00
Plate, 6 In.	2.00 to 3.00
Plate, 9 1/2 In.	10.00
Platter, Oval, 12 In.	20.00
Saucer.	3.00 to 4.00
Sugar.	10.00

Dogwood

Dogwood is decorated with a strange flower that has been given many names. Collectors have called this pattern Apple Blossom, B pattern, Magnolia, or Wildrose. It was made from 1930 to 1934 by Macbeth-Evans Glass Company. It is found in Cremax, crystal, green, Monax, pink, and yellow. Sometimes the pink pieces were trimmed with gold. Some pieces were made with such thin walls the factory redesigned the molds to make the pieces thicker.

CRYSTAL

Pitcher, 80 Oz., 8 In.	185.00
Plate, 6 In.	2.50
Punch Set, 14 Piece	450.00
Saucer.	2.50
Tumbler, 10 Oz., 4 In.	24.00
Tumbler, 11 Oz., 4 3/4 In.	45.00
Tumbler, 12 Oz., 5 In.	60.00

GREEN

Bowl, 5 1/2 In.	22.00
Bowl, 10 1/4 In.	135.00
Cup & Saucer	30.00
Plate, 6 In.	4.50
Plate, 8 In.	7.00
Sugar, Thin, 2 1/2 In.	45.00
Tumbler, 10 Oz., 4 In.	85.00

PINK

Bowl, 5 1/2 In.	40.00
Bowl, 8 1/2 In.	46.00 to 55.00
Creamer, Thin	15.00 to 17.00
Cup	9.00
Cup & Saucer, Thick	17.00 to 23.00
Cup & Saucer, Thin	15.00 to 30.00
Grill Plate, 10 1/2 In.	20.00
Plate, 6 In.	8.00
Plate, 8 In.	4.75 to 10.00
Plate, 9 1/4 In.	20.00 to 31.00
Salver, 12 In.	18.00
Sherbet	24.00
Sugar, Thick	15.00 to 16.00
Sugar, Thin	13.50
Sugar & Creamer, Thin	27.00 to 35.00
Tumbler, 11 Oz., 4 3/4 In.	37.50 to 40.00
Tumbler, 12 Oz., 5 In.	45.00
Water Set, 6 Piece	365.00

YELLOW

Ashtray 60.00
Ashtray, Filigree Holder 85.00
Bowl, 10 1/4 In. 85.00
Grill Plate, 10 1/2 In. 55.00
Plate, 8 In. 13.50
Relish, 2 Handles, 8 In. 45.00
Salt & Pepper 150.00
Sugar & Creamer 47.50

Doric

Doric was made by Jeannette Glass Company, Jeannette, Pennsylvania, from 1935 to 1938. The molded pattern has also inspired another name for the pattern Snowflake. It was made in Delphite, green, pink, and yellow. A few white pieces may have been made.

DELPHITE

Sherbet .... 6.00 to 10.00

GREEN

Bowl, 4 1/2 In. 7.00
Bridge Set, Box,
   14 Piece 160.00
Candy Dish, Cover. 35.00
Creamer. .... 12.00 to 14.00
Cup 9.00
Plate, 6 In. 4.00
Relish, 4 Sections,
   4 x 8 In. 48.00
Relish, 4 x 4 In. ... 12.50 to 16.00
Salt & Pepper ..... 28.00 to 37.50
Saucer 4.00
Sugar & Creamer 55.00

PINK

Bowl, 4 1/2 In. 8.00
Bowl, 8 1/4 In. 16.00

Bowl, Handles, 9 In. 12.00
Butter, Cover 60.00
Candy Dish, Cover. 18.00
Coaster, 3 In. 22.00
Creamer. 15.00
Cup. .... 7.50 to 10.00
Pitcher, 36 Oz., 6 In. 20.00
Plate, 6 In. 5.00
Plate, 9 In. .... 12.00 to 16.50
Relish, 4 x 4 In. ..... 13.50 to 15.00
Salt & Pepper ..... 28.00 to 35.00
Tumbler, 9 Oz.,
   4 1/2 In. .... 42.00 to 62.00

Doric & Pansy

The snowflake design of Doric alternates with squares holding pansies, so, of course, the pattern is named Doric & Pansy. It, too, was made by Jeannette Glass Company, but only in 1937 and 1938. It was made in crystal, pink, and Ultramarine. The Ultramarine varied in color from green to blue. A set of child's dishes called Pretty Polly Party Dishes was made in this pattern.

CRYSTAL

Bowl, 4 1/2 In. 9.00
Cup & Saucer 17.00

PINK

Bowl, 4 1/2 In. 7.50
Creamer. 30.00
Creamer, Child's 30.00
Cup & Saucer, Child's 20.00
Plate, Child's, 6 In. 5.00
Sherbet, 6 In. 7.00
Sugar 30.00
Sugar, Child's 33.00

ULTRAMARINE

Bowl, 4 1/2 In. 12.00
Creamer. .... 145.00 to 180.00
Cup & Saucer 25.00
Plate, 6 In. .... 9.00 to 10.00
Plate, Child's 14.00
Salt & Pepper 340.00
Tumbler, 9 Oz.,
   4 1/2 In. .... 70.00 to 88.00

DORIC WITH PANSY,
   see Doric & Pansy

DOUBLE SHIELD,
   see Mt. Pleasant

DOUBLE SWIRL, see Swirl

DRAPE & TASSEL,
   see Princess

DUTCH, see Windmill

DUTCH ROSE,
   see Rosemary

E

EARLY AMERICAN HOB-
   NAIL, see Hobnail

EARLY AMERICAN ROCK
   CRYSTAL, see Rock
   Crystal

ELONGATED HONEY-
   COMB, see Colony

English Hobnail

Westmoreland Glass Company, Grapeville, Pennsylvania, made English Hobnail pattern from the 1920s through the 1970s. It is similar to Miss America except for more rounded hobs and the absence of the typical Hocking sunburst ray on the base. English Hobnail was made in amber, blue, cobalt blue, crystal, green, pink, red, and turquoise. There is much variation in the shading, and a darker amber was made in the 1960s. Red and pink reproduction pieces were made in the 1980s.

CRYSTAL

Bowl, Footed, 6 In.	9.00 to 12.00
Candy Dish, Cover	20.00
Champagne	7.00
Cocktail	6.00
Cordial, Ball	16.00
Cruet, Stopper	20.00
Cup	4.00
Goblet, 6 1/4 In.	7.00
Jam Jar, Cover	35.00 to 48.00
Lamp, Electric, 9 1/4 In.	90.00
Plate, 5 1/2 In.	7.00
Plate, Hole For Tidbit, 8 In.	5.00
Plate, Hole For Tidbit, 10 1/2 In.	8.00
Plate, Square, 9 In.	5.00
Punch Set, 15 Piece	550.00
Salt & Pepper	55.00
Sherbet	7.00
Tumbler, 5 Oz., 3 3/4 In.	5.00
Tumbler, Footed, 4 5/8 In.	7.00

GREEN

Bowl, 6 In.	10.00
Candy Dish, Cover	80.00
Lamp, Electric, 9 1/4 In.	95.00
Salt & Pepper	70.00
Vase, Flared, 7 1/2 In.	65.00

PINK

Candy Dish, Footed	45.00
Cup	18.00
Plate, 10 In.	22.00

ENGLISH HOBNAIL, see also Miss America

Everglades

Cambridge Glass Company of Cambridge, Ohio, made Everglades about 1934. The glassware was made in crystal, Eleanor Blue, Forest Green, and amber. The pattern had a wide border of leaves and a plain center design on the plate. Other pieces were made to look like they were made of layers of leaves.

AMBER

Salt & Pepper	150.00
Vase, 10 In.	295.00

BLUE

Bowl, Swan, Ruffled, 13 In.	150.00
Bowl, Tulip, 13 In.	125.00
Console Set, 3 Piece	175.00
Plate, 16 In.	150.00
Plate, Tulip, 16 In.	125.00

CRYSTAL

Compote, 6 In.	30.00
Plate, 8 1/2 In.	12.50
Relish, 3 Sections	12.00
Vase, Frosted, 5 In.	60.00

GREEN

Vase, Footed, 11 1/2 In.	195.00

F

Fairfax

Fairfax was made by Fostoria Glass Company, Fostoria, Ohio, from 1927 to 1960. The name Fairfax refers to a glass blank and to an etching pattern. The same glass blanks were used for other etched designs including June, Trojan, and Versailles. The undecorated blank, also known as No. 2375, is popular with collectors. The same shapes were used to make other patterns with etched designs. The glass was made in amber, black, blue, green, orchid, pink, ruby, and topaz.

BLACK

Salt & Pepper	150.00

BLUE

Bowl, 6 In.	30.00
Bowl, Cornucopia, 11 In.	125.00
Bowl, Whipped Cream, Handle	24.00
Butter, Cover	125.00
Candleholder, 3 In., Pair	25.00 to 47.50
Cordial	55.00
Cup & Saucer	10.00
Dish, Grapefruit, Insert	110.00
Dish, Sweetmeat, Handles	22.50
Jam Jar, Footed	37.50
Nut Cup, Footed	17.50 to 20.00
Plate, 6 In.	2.50
Plate, 9 In.	8.00 to 13.50
Plate, 10 1/4 In.	40.00
Plate, Lemon, Handles	17.50 to 20.00
Salt & Pepper, Footed	90.00
Sherbet, 6 In.	16.00
Soup, Cream, Liner	22.50
Sugar & Creamer	18.00
Tray, Center Handle, 11 In.	35.00
Tumbler, 10 Oz.	25.00

GREEN

Bouillon, Liner	175.00
Candy Dish, Cover, 3 Sections	67.50
Cup, After Dinner	10.00
Cup & Saucer	11.50
Dish, Grapefruit, Insert	65.00
Gravy Boat, Liner	75.00
Ice Bucket	45.00
Plate, 6 In.	11.00
Relish, 2 Sections, 8 1/2 In.	8.00 to 12.50
Relish, 3 Sections, Round, 11 1/2 In.	15.00

Salt, Footed, Square	12.50
Sugar	10.00
Sugar & Creamer	25.00
Vase, Optic, Footed, 7 In.	95.00
Whiskey, Footed	15.00

ORCHID

Cup & Saucer	15.00
Finger Bowl	20.00
Soup, Cream	24.00

PINK

Bowl, 6 In.	15.00
Bowl, Oval, 13 In.	55.00
Celery Dish, Oval, 11 1/2 In.	20.00
Cocktail	27.50
Compote, 6 In.	24.00
Cup	8.00
Cup, Footed	8.00
Cup & Saucer	12.50
Dish, Pickle, Oval, 8 1/2 In.	18.00
Goblet, Water	30.00
Plate, 6 In.	3.00
Plate, 7 In.	5.00
Plate, 8 3/4 In.	10.00
Plate, 9 1/2 In.	15.00
Platter, Oval, 12 In.	50.00
Relish, 3 Sections, Oval, 11 1/2 In.	15.00
Relish, 3 Sections, Round	16.00 to 18.00
Relish, Oval, 8 3/4 In.	20.00
Saucer	4.00
Sugar, Footed	10.00 to 15.00
Tumbler, Footed, 5 Oz., 4 1/2 In.	12.50
Tumbler, Footed, 6 In.	25.00

RUBY

Sugar & Creamer, Individual	45.00

TOPAZ

Compote, 6 In.	24.00
Cordial	32.00
Cup & Saucer, After Dinner	17.50
Dish, Sweetmeat, Handles	11.00 to 18.50
Plate, 7 In.	5.50

FAN & FEATHER, see Adam

FINE RIB, see Homespun

Fire-King

Fire-King or Fire-King Oven Glass, Fire-King Oven Ware, and Fire-King Dinnerware were all made by Anchor Hocking Corporation, Lancaster, Ohio, from 1941 through 1976. Fire-King Oven Glass is a transparent, pale blue glassware with a lacy decoration. A matching dinnerware set is called Philbe. It was made in crystal and pale blue. Philbe is listed under its own name in this book. Fire-King Oven Ware is an opaque glass made by Anchor Hocking in the 1950s. It was made in blue, Jadite, pink, and white, or ivory with gold or colored trim. Some mixing bowls and kitchen sets were made with tulips or red kitchen objects pictured on the sides. Fire-King Dinnerware sets were made in patterns named Alice, Charm, Jadite, Jane-Ray, Peach Lustre, Square, Swirl Fire-King, Turquoise Blue, and Wheat. These are listed in this book in their own sections.

BLUE

Bowl, 5 3/8 In.	12.50
Casserole, Knob Cover, 1 Pt.	12.50
Casserole, Knob Cover, 1 Qt.	10.00
Casserole, Knob Cover, 1 1/2 Qt.	13.00 to 15.00
Casserole, Knob Cover, 2 Qt.	16.00 to 25.00
Casserole, Knob Cover, Tab Handle, 10 Oz.	13.00
Custard Cup, 5 Oz.	4.00
Custard Cup, 6 Oz.	3.00 to 3.50
Grease Jar, Tulip	16.00
Measuring Cup, 1 Spout	15.00 to 18.00
Measuring Cup, 2 Spouts, 8 Oz.	24.00
Measuring Cup, 3 Spouts	28.00
Mixing Bowl, 6 7/8 In.	12.00
Mixing Bowl, 8 3/8 In.	12.00 to 16.00
Mixing Bowl, 10 1/8 In.	14.00 to 20.00
Mixing Bowl Set, 6 7/8, 8 3/8 & 10 7/8 In., 3 Piece	45.00
Mug, Coffee	30.00
Nurser, 4 Oz.	14.00 to 18.00
Nurser, 8 Oz.	24.00
Pan, Utility, 6 x 9 In.	10.00
Pan, Utility, 10 1/2 x 2 In.	20.00
Pan, Utility, 8 1/8 x 12 1/2 In.	16.00
Percolator Top, 2 1/8 In.	3.00 to 4.50
Pie Plate, 8 3/8 In.	8.00 to 9.00
Pie Plate, 9 In.	8.00 to 24.00
Pie Plate, Cover, 7 In.	9.00
Pie Plate, Juice Saver, 10 3/8 In.	90.00
Refrigerator Jar, Cover, 4 x 4 In.	7.00
Refrigerator Jar, Cover, 4 x 8 In.	24.00
Roaster, Cover, 8 3/4 In.	40.00
Roaster, Cover, 10 3/8 In.	60.00 to 70.00
Server, Tab Handles	15.00 to 18.00

CRYSTAL

Cake Pan, Square	7.00
Hot Plate, Handle	12.00
Nurser, 4 Oz.	11.00
Nurser, 8 Oz.	9.00
Pan, Utility, 10 1/2 x 2 In.	9.00
Refrigerator Jar, Cover, 4 x 4 In.	7.00

Refrigerator Jar, Cover,
4 x 8 In. 12.00

IVORY

Bowl, Fruit, 6 In. 5.00

Cake Pan, Fruit, Square,
8 In. 8.00

Casserole, Knob
Cover, 1 1/2 Qt. 20.00

Custard Cup, Pink Flower. . . . 2.50

Custard Cup, Thin 3.00

Grease Jar, Cover, Tulip 15.00

Mixing Bowl, Tulip,
Deep, 8 1/2 In. 20.00

Pan, Utility, Fruit, 6 x 9 In. . . . 8.00

Refrigerator Jar, Cover,
Fruit, 4 x 4 In. 4.00

Refrigerator Jar, Cover,
Pink Flower, 4 x 4 In. 4.00

Refrigerator Jar, Crystal
Cover, 4 x 4 In. 3.00

Relish, 3 Sections,
Gold Trim 10.00

JADITE

Casserole, Crystal
Cover, 10 Oz. 6.00

Reamer, 7 1/2 In. 20.00

Flanders

Flanders dinnerware was made by the U.S. Glass Company, at the Tiffin, Ohio, plant from 1914 to 1935. It was made in crystal and in pink or yellow (Mandarin) with crystal trim.

CRYSTAL

Cup & Saucer, Footed 35.00

Sandwich Server, Center
Handle 125.00

Vase, Dahlia, 8 In. 95.00

PINK

Goblet, Water 40.00

Plate, 6 In. 13.00

Plate, 8 In. 18.50

Sherbet. 27.50

**FLAT DIAMOND, see
Diamond Quilted**

Floragold

The iridescent marigold color of carnival glass was copied in this 1950s pattern made by Jeannette Glass Company, Jeannette, Pennsylvania. The pattern is called Floragold or Louisa, the name of the original carnival glass pattern that was copied. Pieces were made in crystal, iridescent, Ice Blue, Shell Pink, and reddish yellow.

CRYSTAL

Ashtray, 4 In. 4.50

Bowl, Ruffled, 5 1/2 In. 29.00

Bowl, Ruffled,
9 1/2 In. . . . . 25.00 to 35.00

Bowl, Ruffled, 12 In. 7.00

Bowl, Square, 4 1/2 In. 3.00

Bowl, Straight Sides,
9 1/2 In. 8.00

Butter, Cover, Oblong,
1/4 Lb. 7.00

Candy Dish, 4-Footed,
5 1/4 In. . . . . 3.50 to 6.00

Candy Dish, Cover,
6 3/4 In. 50.00

Candy Dish,
Handle . . . . 6.00 to 10.00

Creamer. . . . . 4.50 to 6.50

Cup. . . . . 2.50 to 4.00

Cup & Saucer 15.00

Pitcher, 64 Oz. 22.50

Plate, 5 3/4 In. 10.00

Plate, 8 1/2 In. 24.50

Platter, 11 1/4 In. 13.00

Sugar, Cover 17.00

Tray, Indentation,
14 In. . . . . 18.00 to 35.00

Tumbler, Footed, 10 Oz. . . . 15.00

Tumbler, Footed, 15 Oz. . . . 10.00

IRIDESCENT

Bowl, Ruffled,
5 1/2 In. . . . . 8.00 to 31.00

Bowl, Ruffled, 9 1/2 In. 36.00

Bowl, Ruffled,
12 In. . . . . 6.50 to 10.00

Bowl, Square,
4 1/2 In. . . . . 3.75 to 5.00

Butter, Cover,
Oval, 1/4 Lb. 22.50

Butter, Cover,
Round . . . . 38.00 to 45.00

Candleholder, Pair 45.00

Candy Dish, Footed,
5 1/4 In. . . . . 6.50 to 7.00

Creamer . . . . 8.00 to 9.00

Cup . . . . 5.25 to 6.50

Cup & Saucer 15.00

Eggnog Set, Tray, 64 Oz.,
10 Piece 95.00

Pitcher, 64 Oz. . . . 25.00 to 32.50

Plate, 8 1/2 In. 30.00

Saucer. 9.50

Sherbet. 12.00

Sugar & Creamer,
Cover . . . . 14.50 to 27.50

Tumbler, Footed, 10 Oz. . . . 17.50

Tumbler, Footed, 11 Oz. . . . 15.00

Tumbler, Footed,
15 Oz. . . . . 87.50 to 90.00

Vase, 7 In. 21.50

PINK

Cake Plate, 3 Tiers 18.00

Floral

Poinsettia blossoms are the decorations on Floral patterns made by Jeannette Glass Company from 1931 to 1935. Green is the most common color, although the pattern was also made in amber, crystal, Delphite, green, Jadite, pink, red, and yellow.

GREEN

Bowl, 4 In.	15.00 to 17.00
Bowl, Vegetable, Oval, 9 In.	16.00
Candleholder, 4 In., Pair	75.00
Candy Dish, Cover	35.00
Coaster	8.00 to 9.00
Creamer	10.00 to 15.00
Cup	12.50 to 13.50
Cup & Saucer	22.00 to 25.00
Lamp, Bulb	275.00
Pitcher, Footed, 32 Oz., 8 In.	34.00 to 37.00
Plate, 6 In.	6.00 to 7.00
Plate, 9 In.	14.00 to 20.00
Relish, 2 Sections, Oval	11.00
Salt & Pepper, Footed, 4 In.	50.00 to 60.00
Saucer	10.00 to 12.00
Sherbet	16.00 to 18.00
Sugar, Cover	29.00 to 32.00
Tumbler, Footed, 5 Oz., 4 In.	17.00
Tumbler, Footed, 7 Oz., 4 3/4 In.	19.00 to 22.00
Tumbler, Footed, 9 Oz., 5 1/4 In.	42.00 to 45.00

PINK

Bowl, 4 In.	15.00
Bowl, Cover, Vegetable, 8 In.	25.00
Bowl, Vegetable, Oval, 9 In.	12.00 to 15.00
Coaster, 3 1/4 In.	12.00 to 20.00

Creamer	9.50 to 12.00
Cup	10.00 to 12.00
Cup & Saucer	18.00
Pitcher, Cone Footed, 32 Oz., 8 In.	30.00 to 34.00
Plate, 6 In.	5.00 to 6.00
Plate, 8 In.	8.00 to 11.00
Plate, 9 In.	15.00 to 30.00
Platter, Oval, 10 3/4 In.	12.00 to 22.00
Relish, 2 Sections, Oval	12.00
Salt & Pepper, 6 In.	45.00
Salt & Pepper, Footed, 4 1/4 In.	42.00 to 55.00
Saucer	10.00
Sherbet	12.00 to 15.00
Sugar, Cover	23.50 to 27.00
Tumbler, Footed, 7 Oz., 4 3/4 In.	13.00 to 18.50
Tumbler, Footed, 9 Oz., 5 1/4 In.	44.00

Floral & Diamond Band

Floral & Diamond Band was made by the U.S. Glass Company from the late 1920s until c.1937. It features a large center flower and pressed diamond bands of edging. Luncheon sets were made mostly in varying shades of pink and green, but black, crystal, and yellow colors were also used. Some pieces are iridescent marigold and are considered carnival glass, called Mayflower by the collectors.

GREEN

Bowl, 4 1/2 In.	7.50
Bowl, 8 In.	12.00
Creamer, 4 3/4 In.	20.00
Plate, 8 In.	15.00
Sherbet	5.00 to 8.00
Sugar, Cover	70.00 to 71.50
Tumbler, 4 In.	12.00

FLORAL RIM, see Vitrock

Florentine No. 1

Florentine No. 1, also called Poppy No. 1, is neither Florentine in appearance nor decorated with recognizable poppies. The plates are hexagonal and have scalloped edges, differentiating them from Florentine No. 2 which has round pieces. The pattern was made by the Hazel Atlas Glass Company from 1932 to 1935 in cobalt blue, crystal, green, pink, and yellow.

COBALT BLUE

Bowl, 5 In.	10.00 to 15.00
Creamer, Ruffled	65.00

CRYSTAL

Creamer	9.00
Cup	8.00 to 11.00

• • • • • • • • • • • • • • •

Watch burning candles in glass candlesticks. If the candle burns too low, the hot wax and flame may break the glass.

• • • • • • • • • • • • • • •

Plate, 6 In. 5.00

Plate, 8 1/2 In. . . . . . . 6.00 to 7.00

Plate, 10 In. 14.00

Sherbet. . . . . 7.00 to 9.00

Sugar, Cover 8.00

Sugar & Creamer 16.00

GREEN

Ashtray, 5 1/2 In. 20.00

Bowl, 5 In. 10.00

Bowl, 8 1/2 In. 20.00

Bowl, Cover, Vegetable,
Oval, 9 1/2 In. 45.00

Butter, Cover 105.00

Creamer. 7.00

Creamer, Ruffled 23.00

Cup. . . . . 6.00 to 9.00

Cup & Saucer 15.00

Grill Plate, 10 In. . . . . 9.00 to 14.00

Pitcher, 54 Oz.,
7 1/2 In. . . . . 40.00 to 80.00

Pitcher, Footed, 36 Oz.,
6 1/2 In. . . . . 37.00 to 39.00

Plate, 6 In. . . . . 4.00 to 6.00

Plate, 8 1/2 In. 7.00

Plate, 10 In. 13.00

Platter, Oval,
11 1/2 In. . . . . . . 12.00 to 16.00

Salt & Pepper 33.00

Sherbet. 8.00

Sugar, Cover 9.00

Tumbler, Footed,
5 Oz., 3 3/4 In. 13.00

Tumbler, Footed,
10 Oz., 4 3/4 In. 19.00

PINK

Ashtray, 5 1/2 In. 26.00

Bowl, 5 In. 10.00

Bowl, 6 In. 20.00

Bowl, 8 1/2 In. 25.00

Butter, Cover 145.00

Compote, Ruffled. 18.00

Cup & Saucer . . . . . 10.00 to 15.00

Grill Plate, 10 In. 14.00

Pitcher, 54 Oz.,
7 1/2 In. . . . . . . 105.00 to 195.00

Pitcher, Footed,
36 Oz., 6 1/2 In. 40.00

Plate, 6 In. 5.00

Plate, 8 1/2 In. 9.00

Plate, 10 In. . . . . . . 22.00 to 25.00

Platter, Oval,
11 1/2 In. . . . . . . 16.00 to 18.00

Salt & Pepper 49.00

Sherbet. . . . . 8.00 to 14.00

Soup, Cream,
Ruffled . . . . 14.00 to 22.00

Sugar. 12.00

Sugar, Ruffled 18.00

Tumbler, Footed,
5 Oz., 3 1/4 In. . . 25.00 to 40.00

Tumbler, Footed, 10 Oz.,
4 3/4 In. . . . . 20.00 to 29.00

YELLOW

Bowl, 8 1/2 In. . . . . 22.50 to 25.00

Cup. 9.00

Sherbet. . . . . 6.00 to 10.00

Tumbler, Footed,
9 Oz., 4 3/4 In. 19.00

Florentine No. 2

Florentine No. 2, sometimes
called Poppy No. 2 or Oriental
Poppy, was also made by Hazel Atlas Glass Company from
1934 to 1937. It has round
plates instead of the hexagonal pieces of Florentine No. 1,
and larger and more promi-
nent flowers. It was made in
amber, cobalt blue, crystal,
green, Ice Blue, and pink.

. . . .

**If two tumblers get stuck
when stacked, try putting
cold water into the inside
glass, then put both into
hot water up to the lower
rim.**

. . . .

AMBER

Cup. 9.00

Grill Plate,
10 1/4 In. . . . . . . 10.00 to 12.00

Pitcher, Footed, 54 Oz.,
7 1/2 In. 27.00

Salt & Pepper. 45.00

Sherbet. 10.00

Sugar & Creamer. 20.00

CRYSTAL

Bowl, 8 In. 25.00

Coaster, 3 1/4 In. 12.00

Creamer. 6.00

Cup & Saucer 9.00

Pitcher, Cone Footed,
28 Oz., 7 1/2 In. 40.00

Plate, 6 In. 3.00

Plate, 10 In. 12.00

Platter, Oval, 11 In. 18.00

Saucer. . . . . 2.00 to 3.00

Soup, Cream 11.00

Sugar & Creamer,
Fired-On Yellow 75.00

Tumbler, 5 Oz., 3 1/2 In. 9.00

Vase, 6 In. . . . . 28.00 to 55.00

GREEN

Bowl, 4 1/2 In. . . . . . 8.00 to 10.00

Bowl, Cover, Vegetable,
Oval, 9 In. 42.00

Candy Dish, Cover 100.00

Creamer 8.00

Cup. .7.50

Pitcher, 76 Oz., 8 1/4 In. . . . 175.00

Pitcher, Cone Footed,
28 Oz., 7 1/2 In. . . 25.00 to 29.00

Plate, 6 In. 4.90

Plate, 8 1/2 In. 8.00

Plate, 10 In. . . . . 12.00 to 14.00

Relish, 3 Sections,
10 In. . . . . .17.00 to 18.00

Salt & Pepper . . . . . 35.00 to 42.00
Saucer 3.00
Sherbet 9.00
Soup, Cream . . . . . . 10.00 to 12.00
Sugar 7.50
Tumbler, 5 Oz.,
3 1/4 In. . . . . 10.00 to 13.50
Tumbler, 9 Oz., 4 In. 10.00
Tumbler, 12 Oz., 5 In. 30.00
Tumbler, Footed, 9 Oz.,
4 1/2 In. . . . . 17.00 to 25.00
Vase, 6 In. 28.00

PINK
Candy Dish, Cover. 110.00
Relish, 3 Sections,
10 In. . . . . 22.00 to 24.00
Soup, Cream . . . . . . 11.00 to 14.00
Tumbler, 5 Oz.,
3 1/4 In. . . . . 10.00 to 11.00
Tumbler, 9 Oz., 4 In. 13.00
Tumbler, 12 Oz., 5 In. 29.00

YELLOW
Ashtray, 3 3/4 In. 25.00
Bowl, 4 1/2 In. . . . . 14.50 to 17.00
Bowl, 6 In. 35.00
Bowl, 8 In. . . . . 25.00 to 26.00
Bowl, Cover, Vegetable,
Oval, 9 In. . . . . . . 60.00 to 70.00
Butter, Cover . . . 125.00 to 135.00
Candleholder, 2 3/4 In.,
Pair . . . . 45.00 to 57.00
Coaster, 3 1/4 In. 20.00
Creamer . . . . 9.00 to 10.00
Cup . . . . 8.00 to 8.50
Cup & Saucer . . . . . 12.00 to 14.00
Custard Cup 10.00
Gravy Boat . . . . 45.00 to 47.50
Pitcher, 54 Oz.,
7 1/2 In. 155.00
Pitcher, Cone Footed, 24 Oz.,
7 1/2 In. . . . . . 135.00 to 165.00
Plate, 6 In. . . . . 5.00 to 8.00
Plate, 8 1/2 In. . . . . . . 7.00 to 9.00
Plate, 10 In. . . . . 11.00 to 14.00
Platter, Gravy Boat,
11 1/2 In. 35.00
Platter, Oval,
11 In. . . . . 16.00 to 18.00
Relish, 3 Sections, 10 In. 26.00

Salt & Pepper . . . . . 45.00 to 48.00
Saucer . . . . 3.00 to 5.00
Sherbet. . . . . 9.00 to 10.00
Soup, Cream . . . . . . 18.00 to 20.00
Sugar 9.00
Sugar, Cover 30.00
Sugar & Creamer 18.00
Tray, Condiment, Round . . . 60.00
Tumbler, 5 Oz.,
3 1/2 In. . . . . 14.00 to 22.00
Tumbler, 9 Oz., 4 In. 20.00
Tumbler, Footed, 5 Oz.,
3 1/4 In. . . . . 9.75 to 12.00
Tumbler, Footed, 5 Oz.,
4 In. . . . . 10.00 to 16.00
Tumbler, Footed, 9 Oz.,
4 1/2 In. 30.00
Vase, 6 In. 55.00

FLOWER, see Princess Feather

FLOWER & LEAF BAND, see Indiana Custard

FLOWER BASKET, see No. 615

Flower Garden with Butterflies

There really is a butterfly hiding in the flower on this U.S. Glass Company pattern called Flower Garden with Butterflies, Butterflies and Roses, Flower Garden, or Wildrose with Apple Blossom. It was made in the late 1920s in a variety of colors, including amber, black, blue, Canary Yellow, crystal, green, and pink.

BLUE
Compote, Footed,
2 7/8 In. 37.50
CRYSTAL
Plate, 10 In. 22.00
GREEN
Plate, 8 In. 18.00
Powder Jar, Cover,
7 1/2 In. 120.00
PINK
Cheese & Cracker Set 65.00
Powder Jar, Cover,
3 1/2 In. 42.00

**FLOWER RIM,
see Vitrock**

Forest Green

There is no need to picture Forest Green in a black-and-white drawing because it is the color that identifies the pattern. Anchor Hocking Glass Corporation, Lancaster, Ohio, made this very plain pattern from 1950 to 1957. Other patterns were also made in this same deep green color, but these are known by the pattern name.

Ashtray, 3 1/2 In. 3.00
Ashtray, 4 5/8 In. 4.50
Basket, 5 In. 20.00
Batter Bowl, Spout 18.00
Bowl, 4 3/4 In. . . . . . 4.00 to 5.50
Bowl, 6 In. . . . . 6.50 to 12.00
Bowl, 7 3/8 In. . . . . 10.00 to 20.00
Bowl, Chrome
Pedestal, 10 In. 20.00
Creamer . . . . 5.00 to 6.50
Cup . . . . 4.00 to 5.00
Mixing Bowl, 4 1/2 In. 7.00
Mixing Bowl,
6 In. . . . . 6.00 to 8.50
Pitcher, Ball, Upright 25.00
Pitcher, Round,
3 Qt. . . . . 25.00 to 28.00
Plate, 6 5/8 In. 2.50
Plate, 8 3/8 In. . . . . . . 4.50 to 6.00
Plate, 9 1/4 In. . . . . . 20.00 to 32.50

Platter, Rectangular 25.00
Punch Bowl 45.00
Rose Bowl, Crystal Insert . . . 30.00
Saucer . . . . 1.00 to 1.50
Sherbet. . . . . 4.00 to 6.00
Soup, Dish . . . . 12.00 to 15.00
Sugar . . . . 5.00 to 6.50
Sugar & Creamer 12.00
Tumbler, 5 Oz.,
    3 1/2 In. . . . . 3.50 to 4.00
Tumbler, 9 Oz.,
    4 3/4 In. . . . . 4.00 to 5.00
Tumbler, Footed,
    10 Oz., 4 In. 6.00
Tumbler, Roly Poly,
    9 1/2 Oz., 6 In. . . . . 5.00 to 6.00
Vase, 6 1/2 In. . . . . . . 4.50 to 15.00
Vase, 9 In. 10.00
Vase, Hoover, 9 In. 20.00
Vase, Ivy, 4 In. . . . . . 7.00 to 10.00

Fortune

Anchor Hocking made Fortune pattern in 1937 and 1938. The simple design was made in crystal or pink.

PINK

Bowl, 4 In. . . . . 3.50 to 5.00
Bowl, Handle,
    4 1/2 In. . . . . 2.00 to 5.00
Candy Dish, Cover. 25.00
Cup. 6.00
Plate, 6 In. 6.00
Tumbler, 5 Oz.,
    3 1/2 In. . . . . 6.00 to 11.00
Tumbler, 9 Oz.,
    4 In. . . . . 8.00 to 9.00

FOSTORIA, see American

FROSTED BLOCK, see Beaded Block

Fruits

Pears, grapes, apples, and other fruits are displayed in small bunches on the pieces of Fruits pattern. Hazel Atlas and several other companies made this pattern about 1931 to 1933. Pieces are known in crystal, green, pink, and iridized finish.

CRYSTAL

Bowl, 8 In. 28.00

GREEN

Bowl, 5 In. 23.00
Bowl, 8 In. 53.00
Cup. . . . . 6.00 to 8.00
Cup & Saucer 12.00
Plate, 8 In. . . . . 6.00 to 7.50
Saucer. . . . . 4.00 to 4.50
Tumbler, Pears, 4 In. 17.00

G

Georgian

Georgian, also known as Lovebirds, was made by the Federal Glass Company, Columbus, Ohio, from 1931 to 1936. The pattern shows alternating sections with birds in one, a basket of flowers in the next. Dinner sets were made mostly in crystal, although green piec-

---

es were also manufactured. Notice that it is mold-etched and in no way resembles the Fenton glass pattern called Georgian, listed in this book as Georgian Fenton.

CRYSTAL

Tumbler, 12 Oz., 5 1/4 In. . . 95.00

GREEN

Bowl, 4 1/2 In. . . . . . . 6.50 to 8.00
Bowl, 5 3/4 In. . . . 20.00 to 22.00
Butter, Cover . . . . . . 55.00 to 75.00
Creamer, Footed, 3 In. 10.00
Creamer, Footed,
    4 In. . . . . 13.00 to 14.00
Cup & Saucer . . . . . 10.00 to 12.50
Plate, 6 In. 3.00
Plate, 8 In. . . . . 7.50 to 8.75
Plate, 9 1/4 In. 23.00
Saucer. 3.00
Sherbet . . . . 10.00 to 11.50
Sugar, 4 In. . . . . 9.00 to 9.50
Sugar, Cover,
    3 In. . . . . 28.00 to 44.50
Sugar & Creamer,
    Footed, 3 In. 30.00
Tumbler, 9 Oz.,
    4 In. . . . . 47.50 to 55.00

Georgian Fenton

Fenton Glass Company made this Georgian pattern tableware from about 1930. It came in many colors, some pale but many in the popular dark shades. Look for amber, black, cobalt blue, crystal, green, pink, ruby, and topaz. It is very different from the Georgian or

Lovebirds pattern made by the Federal Glass Company.

AMBER
Grill Plate, 10 1/2 In. 15.00
Tumbler, 5 Oz. 10.00
CRYSTAL
Tumbler, 2 1/2 Oz. 18.00
Tumbler, 7 1/2 Oz. 16.00
GREEN
Bowl, 4 1/2 In. 7.50
Butter, Cover . . . . . 35.00 to 72.00
Creamer, 3 In. 11.00
Cup & Saucer 13.00
Plate, 6 In. 5.50
Plate, 8 In. 8.50
Sherbet . . . . 3.00 to 12.00
Sugar, Cover, 3 In. 45.00
Tumbler, 9 Oz. 50.00
RUBY
Creamer 10.00
Cup & Saucer, Footed. 12.00
Goblet, 10 Oz. 12.50
Sugar 15.00
Tumbler, 5 Oz. 4.00
Tumbler, 12 Oz. 4.00
Tumbler, Footed, 9 Oz. 18.00

GLADIOLA, see Royal Lace

Gloria
Gloria is an etched glass pattern made by Cambridge Glass Company about 1930. It is similar to the Tiffin pattern called Flanders. Gloria was made in amber, crystal, Emerald Green, green, Heatherbloom (pink-purple), pink, and yellow. Full dinner sets were made as well as serving pieces, vases, and candlesticks.

CRYSTAL
Candlestick, 6 In., Pair. 47.50
Saltshaker, Footed 62.50
Vase, 9 1/2 In. 165.00
GREEN
Bonbon, 5 1/2 In. 35.00
Relish, 5 Sections, 12 In. 65.00
Vase, Footed, 11 1/2 In. . . . 195.00
YELLOW
Bowl, Pickle, Figure 8,
   9 In. 40.00
Candy Box, Cover 145.00
Compote 37.50
Plate, 9 1/2 In. 70.00
Salt & Pepper 150.00
Vase, 10 In. . . . . . 225.00 to 295.00

GRAPE, see Woolworth

GRAY LAUREL, see Peach Lustre

. . . .

To clean wax from glass candlesticks, scrape with a wooden stick, then wash off the remaining wax with rubbing alcohol.

. . . .

H

HAIRPIN, see Newport

**HANGING BASKET,
   see No. 615**

Harp
The pattern name Harp describes the small lyre-shaped instruments that are included on the borders of these pieces of glass. This Jeannette Glass Company pattern was made from 1954 to 1957. Pieces are found in crystal, crystal with gold trim, light blue, and pink.

BLUE
Cake Stand. 28.00
Cake Stand, 9 In. 22.00
CRYSTAL
Ashtray, 4 3/4 In. 5.00
Cake Stand,
   Gold Trim, 9 In. . 20.00 to 24.00
Tray, Handles, Gold Trim,
   Rectangular 32.00
Vase, Gold Trim, 7 1/2 In. . . . 19.00

Heritage
Federal Glass Company, Columbus, Ohio, made Heritage in the 1930s through the 1960s. Evidently the serving pieces were made in blue, light green, and pink, but the plates and dinnerware pieces were made only in crystal. Amber and crystal reproduction bowls were made in 1987.

Bowl, 5 In. . . . . 6.00 to 7.50
Bowl, 8 1/2 In. 45.00
Bowl, 10 1/2 In. . . . . 8.50 to 12.00
Cup. . . . . 7.00 to 10.00
Cup & Saucer . . . . . . 7.50 to 15.00
Plate, 8 In. . . . . 5.00 to 7.00
Plate, 9 1/4 In. . . . . . 6.00 to 10.00
Plate, 12 In. . . . . 10.00 to 12.00

HEX OPTIC, see Hexagon Optic

Hexagon Optic

Hexagon Optic, also called Honeycomb or Hex Optic, really does have an accurate, descriptive name. Pink or green sets of kitchenware were made in this pattern by Jeannette Glass Company, Jeannette, Pennsylvania, from 1928 to 1932. In the years near 1960 some iridized sets and some blue-green pieces were made.

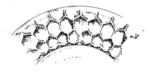

GREEN
Pitcher, 5 In. 35.00
Pitcher, Footed, 48 Oz.,
    9 In. 77.00
Plate, 8 In. 5.00
Salt & Pepper 37.00

Sherbet. 5.00
Tumbler, Footed, 7 In. 6.00
Whiskey, 2 In. 7.50
PINK
Bowl, Ruffled, 4 1/2 In. 6.00
Mixing Bowl, 8 In. 25.00
Plate, 6 In. 3.00
Sherbet 5.00

HEXAGON TRIPLE BAND, see Colony

HINGE, see Patrician

Hobnail

Hobnail is the name of this pattern, although many similar patterns have been made with the hobbed decorations. Hocking Glass Company, Lancaster, Ohio, made this pattern from 1934 to 1936, and it can be distinguished from other hobbed patterns by a honeycomb design with long sides and pointed ends. Mostly crystal or pink beverage sets were made. Some pieces were made with red rims or black feet.

CRYSTAL
Bowl, 5 1/2 In. 3.00
Cup. 4.00
Decanter, Stopper 24.00
Pitcher, 18 Oz. 18.00
Pitcher, 67 Oz. 23.00
Sugar, Footed 5.00
Tumbler, 5 Oz. 4.50
Tumbler, 10 Oz. 4.00
Tumbler, Footed, 3 Oz. 5.00
Tumbler, Footed, 5 Oz. 5.00

Whiskey, 1 1/2 Oz. 5.00
PINK
Cup 4.00
Plate, 6 In. 3.50

HOBNAIL, see also Moonstone

Holiday

Holiday is one of the later Depression glass patterns. It was made from 1947 through 1949 by Jeannette Glass Company. The pattern is found in dinnerware sets of crystal, iridescent, and pink. A few pieces of opaque Shell Pink were made. The pattern is sometimes also called Buttons & Bows or Russian.

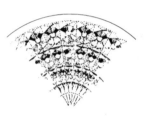

IRIDESCENT
Pitcher, 18 Oz., 4 3/4 In. . . . 19.00
Tumbler, Footed, 5 Oz.,
    4 In. 9.50
PINK
Bowl, 5 1/8 In. . . . . 11.00 to 17.00
Bowl, 8 1/2 In. 22.00
Bowl, Vegetable, Oval,
    9 1/2 In. 24.00
Butter, Cover 33.00

Candleholder, 3 In., Pair 82.00
Console,
   10 3/4 In. . . . . . . 99.00 to 125.00
Creamer . . . . 6.00 to 11.00
Cup . . . . 6.00 to 8.00
Cup & Saucer . . . . . . 9.75 to 13.00
Pitcher, 52 Oz.,
   6 3/4 In. . . . . 28.00 to 40.00
Plate, 6 In. 5.00
Plate, 9 In. . . . . 8.50 to 16.50
Sandwich Server,
   10 1/2 In. 17.00
Saucer 5.00
Saucer, Rayed 4.00
Sherbet . . . . 6.00 to 7.50
Soup, Dish . . . . 38.00 to 42.50
Sugar 6.00
Sugar, Cover 25.00
Sugar & Creamer, Cover 36.00
Tumbler, Footed,
   4 In. . . . . 35.00 to 47.00
Tumbler, Footed, 6 In. 140.00

Homespun

Homespun, often called Fine Rib, is a cause of confusion. Several writers have presented different views about whether this is really one pattern or two. We prefer to call all of these pieces Homespun because that is the way most collectors use the name. Jeannette Glass Company made crystal, light blue, and pink pieces in this pattern in 1939 and 1940. Hazel Atlas made other pieces in crystal and cobalt blue.

BLUE
Tumbler, 9 Oz.,
   4 1/4 In. . . . . 16.50 to 18.50

Tumbler, 13 Oz., 5 1/4 In. . . 24.00
Tumbler, Footed,
   5 Oz., 4 In. 14.50

CRYSTAL
Butter, Cover 35.00
Plate, Child's, 4 In. 6.50

PINK
Bowl, 8 1/4 In. 22.00
Bowl, Closed Handles,
   4 1/2 In. . . . . 9.00 to 17.00
Butter, Cover 60.00
Coaster-Ashtray . . . . 6.50 to 20.00
Cup 10.00
Cup & Saucer . . . . . 13.00 to 15.00
Plate, 6 In. . . . . 4.00 to 6.00
Plate, 9 1/2 In. . . . . 14.00 to 20.00
Plate, Child's, 4 In. 18.00
Platter, Closed Handles,
   13 In. . . . . 15.00 to 22.00
Saucer 3.00
Sherbet . . . . 15.00 to 16.00
Sugar & Creamer 30.00
Tumbler, 9 Oz.,
   4 1/4 In. . . . . 18.00 to 20.00
Tumbler, 13 Oz., 5 1/4 In. . . 55.00
Tumbler, Cone Footed,
   9 Oz., 6 1/4 In. 50.00
Tumbler, Cone-Footed,
   5 Oz., 4 In. 9.00

HONEYCOMB, see Hexagon Optic

HORIZONTAL FINE RIB, see Manhattan

HORIZONTAL RIBBED, see Manhattan

HORIZONTAL ROUNDED BIG RIB, see Manhattan

HORIZONTAL SHARP BIG RIB, see Manhattan

HORSESHOE, see No. 612

• • • • • • • • • • • • • • •
The best time to buy an antique is when you see it.
• • • • • • • • • • • • • • •

Indiana Custard

The design makes the old name Flower & Leaf Band clear, but collectors prefer to call this pattern Indiana Custard. It is an opaque glassware of custard color and ivory made by the Indiana Glass Company. Primarily luncheon sets were made from the 1930s to the 1950s. Some pieces have bands that are decorated with pastel colors or decal designs. The same pattern was made of milk glass in 1957. It was called Orange Blossom.

IVORY
Bowl, 5 1/2 In. 7.50
Bowl, 8 3/4 In. 33.00
Bowl, Vegetable, Oval,
   9 1/2 In. . . . . 26.00 to 35.00
Butter, Cover 60.00
Creamer . . . . 16.00 to 17.50
Cup 30.00
Cup & Saucer 42.00
Plate, 6 In. 6.00
Plate, 7 1/2 In. 10.00
Plate, 9 In. 12.00
Platter, Oval, 12 In. 32.50
Sherbet 85.00
Sugar . . . . 7.00 to 10.00
Sugar, Cover . . . . . . 20.00 to 30.00
Sugar & Creamer 25.00

Iris

The design of Iris is unusually bold for Depression glass. Molded representations of stalks of iris fill the center of a ribbed plate. Other pieces in the pattern show fewer irises, but the flower is predominant. Edges of pieces may be ruffled or beaded. It was made by Jeannette Glass Company, Jeannette, Pennsylvania, from 1928 to 1932 and then again in the 1950s and 1970s. Early pieces were made in crystal, iridescent, and pink; later pieces were made in blue-green, reddish yellow, or white. The pattern is also called Iris & Herringbone. Reproduction candy vases have been made in a variety of colors since 1977.

CRYSTAL

Bowl, 5 In.	7.00 to 10.00
Bowl, 9 1/2 In.	10.00 to 25.00
Bowl, 11 In.	45.00 to 60.00
Bowl, Beaded, 8 In.	115.00
Bowl, Ruffled, 5 In.	8.00 to 9.00
Butter, Cover	53.00
Candleholder, Pair	30.00 to 39.00
Candy Dish	115.00
Cocktail, 4 1/2 In.	21.00 to 23.00
Creamer	10.00 to 12.00
Cup	14.00 to 18.00
Cup & Saucer	22.00 to 29.00
Goblet, 5 3/4 In.	22.00 to 27.00

Nut Set	60.00
Pitcher, Footed, 9 1/2 In.	31.00 to 40.00
Plate, 5 1/2 In.	14.00 to 17.50
Plate, 8 In.	90.00
Plate, 9 In.	47.50 to 55.00
Plate, 11 3/4 In.	25.00 to 36.00
Sauce, Ruffled, 5 In.	9.00
Saucer	10.00 to 13.00
Sherbet, Footed, 2 1/2 In.	10.00 to 20.00
Sherbet, Footed, 4 In.	10.00 to 18.00
Sugar, Cover	25.00 to 28.00
Tumbler, Footed, 6 In.	25.00 to 33.00
Vase, 9 In.	23.00 to 27.50
Wine, 4 In.	13.75 to 16.00

IRIDESCENT

Bowl, 11 In.	10.00 to 13.00
Bowl, Beaded, 4 1/2 In.	5.50 to 10.00
Bowl, Ruffled, 5 In.	20.00 to 23.00
Bowl, Ruffled, 9 1/2 In.	13.00
Bowl, Ruffled, 11 In.	12.00 to 14.00
Butter, Cover	42.00 to 50.00
Candleholder, Pair	40.00
Cocktail, 4 1/2 In.	28.00 to 30.00
Creamer	10.00 to 15.00
Cup	12.00
Cup, Demitasse	475.00
Cup & Saucer	24.00 to 25.00
Pitcher, Footed, 9 1/2 In.	40.00
Plate, 5 1/2 In.	10.00 to 12.00
Plate, 9 In.	20.00 to 36.00
Plate, 11 3/4 In.	29.00 to 30.00
Saucer	8.00 to 9.00
Sherbet, Footed, 2 1/2 In.	9.00 to 14.00
Sugar, Cover	28.00
Sugar & Creamer	22.00
Tumbler, Footed, 6 In.	14.00 to 18.00
Vase, 9 In.	18.00 to 25.00
Wine, 4 In.	35.00

IRIS & HERRINGBONE, see Iris

IVEX, see Chinex Classic; Cremax

Jadite

Jadite is a color as well as a pattern. Kitchenware was made in Jadite from 1936 to 1938 by Jeannette Glass Company. A matching set of dinnerware in the same green glass was called Jane-Ray. These pieces are listed in their own section. All of the pieces of kitchenware made of Jadite were also made of a blue glass called Delphite, but it is incorrect to call any but the green dishes by the name Jadite. For more information about related patterns and colors, see Alice, Charm, Fire-King, Jane-Ray, Philbe, Square, Swirl Fire-King, Turquoise Blue, and Wheat in this book.

Ashtray, 5 3/4 In.	13.00
Bowl, 4 3/4 In.	5.00 to 6.00
Bowl, 5 7/8 In.	9.00 to 10.00
Bowl, Batter	25.00
Bowl, Leaf, Handle	8.00
Bowl, Vegetable, 8 1/4 In.	10.00
Butter, Cover, 1/4 Lb.	45.00
Canister, Coffee, 7 1/2 In.	75.00
Cup, After Dinner	10.00
Cup, Coffee, 7 Oz.	4.75
Cup, St. Dennis	7.00
Cup & Saucer	5.00
Egg Tray	15.00
Eggcup	10.00

Grill Plate	9.00
Mixing Bowl, 5 In.	6.00
Mixing Bowl, 6 1/2 In.	8.00 to 10.00
Mixing Bowl, 7 In.	12.50
Mixing Bowl, 9 In.	10.00
Mixing Bowl, Straight Sides, 9 x 4 In.	15.00
Mug, Coffee, 7 Oz.	4.00 to 10.00
Pitcher, Batter	14.00
Pitcher, Milk, 20 Oz.	18.00
Plate, 7 In.	10.00
Plate, 9 In.	8.00
Platter, Oval, 9 1/2 In.	6.50
Relish, 3 Sections	11.00
Saltshaker, 5 In.	8.00
Saucer	2.00
Shaving Mug, 8 Oz.	6.00 to 18.00
Water Dispenser, 11 x 4 1/2 In.	150.00

Jane-Ray

A plain dinnerware set with ribbed edge was made of Jadite from 1945 to 1963 by Anchor Hocking Glass Corporation, Lancaster, Ohio. The matching kitchenware sets of the same green glass are called Jadite. Other related sections in this book are Alice, Fire-King, Philbe, Square, Swirl Fire-King, Turquoise Blue, and Wheat.

JADITE

Bowl, 4 7/8 In.	3.00
Bowl, 5 In.	2.50 to 4.50
Bowl, 6 In.	6.00 to 11.00
Bowl, 7 5/8 In.	6.00

Bowl, 8 1/4 In.	10.00 to 12.50
Creamer	4.00 to 5.00
Cup	2.00 to 3.00
Cup & Saucer	6.00
Cup & Saucer, After Dinner	28.50
Plate, 7 3/4 In.	3.00 to 5.00
Plate, 9 1/8 In.	5.00 to 6.00
Platter, 9 x 12 In.	10.00 to 15.00
Saucer	.50 to 1.00
Soup, Dish	6.00 to 12.00
Sugar	4.00
Sugar, Cover	5.00 to 9.00
Sugar & Creamer, Cover	8.00 to 12.50

Jubilee

In the early 1930s the Lancaster Glass Company, Lancaster, Ohio, made this luncheon set decorated with etched flowers. It was made in a yellow shade, called topaz, and in pink. Collectors will find many similar patterns. The original Lancaster Jubilee had twelve petals and an open center on each flower.

PINK

Sugar	40.00

TOPAZ

Bowl, Handles, 9 In.	100.00
Cake Plate, Handles, 11 In.	38.00 to 45.00
Candleholder, Pair	200.00
Creamer	18.00 to 21.00
Cup	15.00
Cup & Saucer	20.00
Cup & Saucer, After Dinner, Set Of 6	75.00
Dish, Mayonnaise, 3 Piece	300.00

Goblet, 10 Oz., 6 In.	37.50 to 40.00
Plate, 7 In.	7.50 to 12.00
Plate, 8 3/4 In.	13.00 to 15.00
Plate, Sandwich, 13 In.	200.00
Saucer	6.00
Sugar	20.00
Sugar & Creamer	38.00 to 40.00
Tray, 2 Handles, 11 In.	37.50

June

June is one of very few patterns that can be dated with some accuracy from the color. Fostoria Glass Company, Fostoria, Ohio, made full dinnerware sets but changed the color. From 1928 to 1944 the glass was azure, green, or rose. Crystal was made from 1928 to 1952. If your set is topaz, it dates from 1929 to 1938. Gold-tinted glass was made from 1938 to 1944. Pieces made of color with crystal stems or bases were made only from 1931 to 1944. Reproductions have been made in azure, crystal, pink, and yellow.

AZURE

Ashtray	75.00
Candleholder, 2 In., Pair	75.00
Cordial, 4 In.	195.00
Cup	38.00
Goblet, Footed, 5 1/4 In.	39.50
Gravy Boat	325.00
Ice Bucket	175.00
Oyster Cocktail, 5 1/2 Oz.	45.00 to 60.00

Platter, 15 1/2 In. 295.00

Relish, 2 Sections,
8 1/2 In. 54.00

Salt & Pepper 250.00

Tray, Center Handle,
11 In. 85.00

CRYSTAL

Champagne, 6 In. 22.00

Cup & Saucer 22.00

Cup & Saucer,
After Dinner 35.00

Goblet, 10 Oz.,
8 1/4 In. . . . . 20.00 to 27.50

Ice Bucket 95.00

Ladle, Mayonnaise 18.00

Pitcher 395.00

Plate, 6 In. 8.00

Plate, 7 1/2 In. 14.00

Plate, 9 1/2 In. 20.00

Sherbet. 20.00

Sugar & Creamer 95.00

Tumbler, Footed,
5 1/2 In. . . . . 22.50 to 27.50

Whiskey, 2 1/2 Oz. 35.00

PINK

Champagne, 6 In. 47.50

Cup & Saucer 47.50

YELLOW

Bowl, 5 In. 25.00

Bowl, Footed, 12 In. 60.00

Candleholder, Pair 65.00

Celery Dish 65.00

Cheese Compote 60.00

Cordial, 4 In. 125.00

Creamer, Footed 30.00

Dish, Sweetmeat,
Loop Handle 35.00

Goblet, 8 1/4 In. 35.00

Oyster Cocktail,
5 1/2 Oz. 32.50

Pitcher, Footed. 495.00

Plate, 6 In. 7.00

Plate, 7 1/2 In. 8.00

Plate, 9 1/2 In. 17.50

Sherbet. 25.00

Sugar, Cover 225.00

Tumbler, Footed, 5 1/4 In. . . .32.50

Tumbler, Footed, 8 1/4 In. . . .35.00

Wine. 48.00

**KNIFE & FORK, see
Colonial**

L

Lace Edge

To add to the confusion in the marketplace, this pattern, which is most often called Lace Edge, has been called Loop, Old Colony, Open Lace, or Open Scallop. The pieces themselves are often confused with other similar patterns, such as Imperial's Laced Edge, and cups or tumblers may also be mixed up with Queen Mary or Coronation. The Hocking pattern, made by Hocking Glass Company in Lancaster, Ohio, from 1935 to 1938, can usually be identified by the familiar sunburst base common to many of that company's designs. Most of the pieces of Lace Edge were made in pink, although crystal is also found.

CRYSTAL

Bowl, 6 3/8 In. 35.00

Cup 18.00

Cup & Saucer 29.00

Plate, Torte, 16 In. 175.00

Sherbet. 17.00

Soup, Dish 73.00

PINK

Bowl, 6 3/8 In. . . . . 15.00 to 18.00

Bowl, 7 3/4 In. 19.00

Bowl, 9 1/2 In. . . . .17.00 to 25.00

Butter, Cover. . . . . .52.00 to 55.00

Candleholder, Pair 155.00

Candy Jar, Cover,
Ribbed. . . . . .41.00 to 45.00

Compote, Footed,
7 In. . . . . .18.00 to 21.50

Cup . . . . .18.00 to 23.00

Cup & Saucer . . . . .27.00 to 28.00

Flower Bowl, Crystal Frog. . 20.00

Grill Plate,
10 1/2 In. . . . . . . .18.00 to 22.00

Plate, 7 1/4 In. . . . . .17.00 to 19.00

Plate, 8 3/4 In. . . . . .14.00 to 20.00

Plate, 10 1/2 In. . . . .23.00 to 25.00

Relish, 3 Sections,
10 1/2 In. 21.00

Saucer. . . . . .11.00 to 13.00

Sherbet, Footed. 74.00

Sugar. 19.00

Sugar & Creamer. 40.00

Tumbler, 9 Oz.,
4 1/2 In. . . . . .12.00 to 16.00

Tumbler, Footed, 10 1/2 Oz.,
5 In. . . . . .56.00 to 60.00

Vase, Frosted, Without
Flowers, 7 In. 40.00

LACY DAISY, see No. 618

Lake Como

At first glance, Lake Como looks more like a piece of ceramic than a piece of glass. It is opaque white with blue decal decorations picturing a lake and part of an ancient ruin. It was made by Hocking Glass Company from 1934 to 1937.

Bowl, 6 In. 30.00

Bowl, 9 3/4 In. 52.00

Cup & Saucer 49.00

Plate, 7 1/4 In. 24.00

Plate, 9 1/4 In. 35.00
Platter, 11 In. 79.00
Salt & Pepper 49.00
Saltshaker 22.50
Sugar & Creamer 75.00

Laurel

Opaque glass was used by Mc-Kee Glass Company, Jeannette, Pennsylvania, to make Laurel dinnerware in the 1930s. The pattern, with a raised band of flowers and leaves as the only decoration, is sometimes called Raspberry Band. A few pieces have decals of a dog in the center, and that group is called Scottie Dog. The dinnerware was made in French Ivory, Jade Green, Powder Blue, or White Opal. A child's set was made with a colored rim.

GREEN
Bowl, 5 In. 6.00
Bowl, 6 In. 10.00
Bowl, 9 In. 22.00
Bowl, 11 In. 40.00
Bowl, Vegetable,
Oval, 9 3/4 In. 22.00
Candleholder, 4 In.,
Pair . . . . 30.00 to 35.00
Cheese Dish, Cover,
9 In. . . . . 40.00 to 58.00
Plate, 7 1/2 In. 9.00
Plate, 9 1/8 In. . . . . . 9.00 to 10.00
Salt & Pepper 55.00
Saucer 2.50
Sherbet . . . . 7.00 to 11.00
Sugar & Creamer, Tall 26.00
IVORY
Bowl, 5 In. 7.50
Bowl, 9 In. 19.00
Bowl, 11 In. . . . . . . 27.50 to 34.00

Bowl, Footed, 6 In. . . 8.25 to 9.00
Bowl, Vegetable,
Oval, 9 In. . . . . . . 16.00 to 18.50
Candleholder, 4 In., Pair 24.00
Cup & Saucer 8.00
Plate, 6 In. . . . . 4.25 to 5.00
Plate, 7 1/2 In. . . . . . 8.25 to 11.00
Plate, 9 1/8 In. . . . . . 9.00 to 12.00
Platter, Oval,
10 3/4 In. . . . . 20.00 to 25.00
Salt & Pepper 45.00
Saucer 3.00
Sherbet. . . . . 11.00 to 12.00
Sugar, Tall 11.00
Tumbler, 12 Oz.,
5 In. . . . . 38.00 to 40.00
WHITE
Plate, 8 1/8 In. 4.50
Saucer 1.00

LAUREL LEAF, see Peach Lustre

Lido

Lido pattern was made by the Federal Glass Company of Columbus, Ohio, in the mid-1930s. The glass was offered in crystal, Golden Glow, green, or Rose Glow.

CRYSTAL
Cup & Saucer 22.50
Dish, Mayonnaise, 2 Piece . . 50.00
Jam Jar, Cover. 40.00
Jug, 53 Oz. 75.00
Plate, 7 1/2 In. 11.00
Relish, 3 Sections, 10 In. 25.00

LILY MEDALLION, see American Sweetheart

LINCOLN DRAPE, see Princess

Lincoln Inn

Lincoln Inn was made by the Fenton Glass Company, Williamstown, West Virginia, from 1928 until c.1936. The ridged dinnerware sets were made of amber, amethyst, black, light blue, cobalt blue, crystal, green, Jadite (opaque green), pink, and red. A recent copy of the Lincoln Inn pitcher was made by Fenton Glass Company in iridized carnival glass.

AMBER
Goblet, Water 29.50
AMETHYST
Sherbet, Footed, 4 3/4 In. . . . 15.00
BLACK
Salt & Pepper 250.00
COBALT BLUE
Tumbler, Footed, 12 Oz. 40.00
GREEN
Bowl, 6 In. 11.00
Nut Dish. 65.00
Vase, 10 In. 175.00
PINK
Saucer, 5 In. 45.00
RED
Finger Bowl. 30.00
Goblet, Water 27.50
Tumbler, Footed, 9 Oz. 24.00

LINE 300, see Peacock & Wild Rose

LINE 994, see Popeye & Olive

LITTLE HOSTESS, see
Moderntone Little Host-
ess Party Set

LOOP, see Lace Edge

LORAIN, see No. 615

LOUISA, see Floragold

LOVEBIRDS, see Georgian

LYDIA RAY, see New
Century

M

Madrid

Madrid has probably had more publicity than any other Depression glass pattern. It was originally made by the Federal Glass Company, Columbus, Ohio, from 1932 to 1939, using the molds developed for Sylvan. It was made first in green, then in amber; blue and pink pieces were made for a limited time. In 1976 Federal Glass reworked the molds and made full sets of amber glass called Recollection. These can be identified by a small "76" worked into the pattern. In 1982 crystal pieces of Recollection were made. In more recent years blue, pink, and crystal pieces have been reproduced by the Indiana Glass Company. It is sometimes called Paneled Aster, Primus, and Winged Medallion.

AMBER
Bowl, 5 In. . . . . 4.50 to 9.00
Bowl, 9 3/8 In. 30.00
Bowl, Deep, 9 1/2 In. 40.00
Bowl, Vegetable, Oval,
  10 In. . . . . 15.00 to 19.00
Cake Plate,
  11 1/4 In. . . . . . . 12.50 to 18.50
Candleholder, 2 1/4 In.,
  Pair 22.00
Console, 11 In. . . . . 15.00 to 20.00
Console Set, 3 Piece 35.00
Cookie Jar, Cover 45.00
Creamer . . . . 5.00 to 8.50
Cup 9.50
Cup & Saucer 13.00
Grill Plate, 10 1/2 In. 9.50
Jell-O Mold,
  2 1/8 In. . . . . 7.00 to 12.00
Pitcher, 60 Oz.,
  8 In. . . . . 40.00 to 45.00
Plate, 6 In. . . . . 3.50 to 7.50
Plate, 7 1/2 In. . . . . . 10.00 to 15.00
Plate, 8 7/8 In. . . . . . . 5.50 to 7.00
Plate, 10 1/2 In. 45.00
Platter, Oval,
  11 1/2 In. . . . . 12.50 to 15.00
Relish, 10 1/4 In. 14.50
Sherbet . . . . 5.00 to 7.50
Soup, Dish, 7 In. . . . 12.00 to 16.00
Sugar & Creamer,
  Cover . . . . 35.00 to 45.00
Tumbler, 5 Oz., 3 7/8 In. 14.50
Tumbler, Footed, 5 Oz.,
  4 In. 18.00
Tumbler, Footed, 12 Oz.,
  5 1/2 In. 20.00
BLUE
Bowl, Vegetable, 10 In. 25.00
Cup .16.00
Cup & Saucer 30.00
Dish, Jam, 7 In. 35.00
Pitcher, 60 Oz.,
  8 In. . . . . .140.00 to 165.00
Tumbler, 12 Oz.,
  5 1/2 In. . . . . 35.00 to 40.00
CRYSTAL
Butter, Cover 60.00
Coaster,
  Hot Dish . . . . 25.00 to 50.00

Creamer 10.00
Plate, 8 7/8 In. 13.00
Plate, 10 1/2 In. 22.00
Relish, 10 1/4 In. 6.00
Sugar, Cover 40.00
GREEN
Ashtray, Square, 6 In. 225.00
Bowl, 5 In. 8.00
Bowl, 7 In. 20.00
Bowl, Vegetable,
  Oval, 10 In. 17.00
Creamer 12.00
Cup 10.00
Grill Plate,
  10 1/2 In. . . . . .8.00 to 12.50
Pitcher, 60 Oz., 8 In. 55.00
Platter, Oval, 11 1/2 In. 17.00
Salt & Pepper, 3 1/2 In. 70.00
Sugar, Cover 45.00
Tumbler, Footed, 10 Oz.,
  5 1/2 In. 37.00
PINK
Butter, Cover 65.00

MAGNOLIA, see Dogwood

Manhattan

Manhattan is another modern-looking pattern with a design made of molded circles. It was made by Anchor Hocking Glass Corporation from 1938 to 1941, primarily in crystal. A few green, pink, and red pieces are also known. The pattern has been called many names, such as Horizontal Fine Rib, Horizontal Ribbed, Horizontal Rounded Big Rib, Horizontal Sharp Big Rib, and Ribbed.

CRYSTAL

Ashtray, Round,
4 In. . . . . 8.00 to 10.00

Ashtray, Square,
4 1/2 In. 17.00

Bowl, 4 1/2 In. 7.00

Bowl, 7 1/2 In. . . . . 12.00 to 16.00

Bowl, 9 In. 15.00

Bowl, Closed Handles,
8 In. 20.00

Bowl, Handle,
5 3/8 In. . . . . 8.00 to 10.00

Bowl, Open Handle,
9 1/2 In. 32.00

Candlestick, Square,
4 1/4 In., Pair. . . . . 8.00 to 11.00

Candy Dish, Cover. 30.00

Coaster, 3 1/2 In. 11.00

Compote,
5 3/4 In. . . . . 24.00 to 30.00

Cup . . . . 12.00 to 16.00

Cup & Saucer . . . . . 17.50 to 20.00

Pitcher, 24 Oz. . . . . 20.00 to 29.00

Pitcher, Tilted,
80 Oz. . . . . 29.00 to 37.00

Plate, 6 In. . . . . 3.00 to 5.00

Plate, 8 1/2 In. . . . . 10.00 to 14.00

Plate, 10 1/4 In. . . . 12.00 to 19.00

Plate, 14 In. 20.00

Relish, 4 Sections,
14 In. . . . . 16.00 to 19.00

Sauce, Handles,
4 1/2 In. . . . . 5.00 to 7.00

Sherbet . . . . 6.00 to 8.50

Sugar . . . . 7.00 to 8.50

Tumbler, Footed,
10 Oz. . . . . 14.00 to 15.00

Vase, 8 In. . . . . 13.50 to 15.00

Wine, 3 1/2 In. . . . . . . 4.00 to 5.00

PINK

Bowl, Handle,
5 3/8 In. . . . . 9.00 to 15.00

Bowl, Open Handle,
9 1/2 In. 30.00

Compote, 5 3/4 In. 30.00

Salt & Pepper 75.00

Sherbet 12.00

Sugar & Creamer . . 18.50 to 20.00

Tumbler, Footed,
10 Oz. 15.00

RED

Relish, 4 Sections, 14 In. 25.00

**MANY WINDOWS,
see Roulette**

Martha Washington

The Cambridge Glass Company of Cambridge, Ohio, started manufacturing Martha Washington pattern in 1932. The glass was made in amber, crystal, Forest Green, Gold Krystol, Heatherbloom, Royal Blue, and ruby.

BLUE

Cocktail, 3 Oz. 12.00

CRYSTAL

Compote, 6 In. 35.00

Goblet, 9 Oz. 9.00

Plate, 10 In. 37.00

Sherbet, 6 Oz. 6.00

Sugar 10.00

Tumbler, Footed, 12 Oz. 10.00

MAYFAIR, see Rosemary

Mayfair Federal

The Mayfair patterns can easily be recognized, but if you are buying by mail, the names are sometimes confusing. Mayfair Federal is the pattern sometimes called Rosemary Arches. It was made in amber, crystal, or green by Federal Glass Company in 1934, but was discontinued because of a patent conflict with Hocking's Mayfair pattern, referred to as Mayfair Open Rose.

AMBER

Creamer. 12.00

Grill Plate 13.00

Plate, 6 3/4 In. . . . . 4.25 to 5.00

Plate, 9 1/2 In. . . . . . . 8.50 to 15.00

Saucer. 3.00

Sugar. 12.00

Tumbler, 9 Oz.,
4 1/2 In. . . . . 23.00 to 25.00

CRYSTAL

Bowl, Vegetable, Oval 16.00

Plate, 9 1/2 In. 9.00

Sugar & Creamer 22.00

GREEN

Creamer. 15.00

Plate, 6 3/4 In. 8.00

Soup, Cream, 5 In. 18.00

Sugar. 15.00

Tumbler, 9 Oz., 4 1/2 In. 26.00

Mayfair Open Rose

Mayfair Open Rose was made by Hocking Glass Company from 1931 to 1937. It was made primarily in light blue and pink, with a few green and yellow pieces. Crystal examples are rare. The cookie jar and the whiskey glass have been reproduced since 1982.

BLUE

Bowl, 5 1/2 In. 42.00

Bowl, Ruffled,
12 In. . . . . 60.00 to 80.00

Bowl, Vegetable, 7 In. 55.00

Bowl, Vegetable, Cover,
10 In. 110.00

Bowl, Vegetable, Oval,
9 1/2 In. 75.00

Cake Plate, Handles,
12 In. . . . . 65.00 to 75.00

Candy Dish, Cover. 290.00

Celery Dish, 2 Sections,
8 3/8 In. . . . . 55.00 to 65.00

Cookie Jar,
Cover . . . . 265.00 to 290.00

Creamer. . . . . 62.50 to 70.00

Cup. 50.00

Cup & Saucer . . . . . 60.00 to 68.00

Grill Plate, 9 1/2 In. 44.00

Plate, 5 3/4 In. 22.00

Plate, 8 1/2 In. 42.00

Platter, Oval, 12 1/2 In. 55.00

Relish, 4 Sections,
8 3/8 In. 60.00

Sherbet, Footed,
4 3/4 In. 65.00

Sugar 75.00

CRYSTAL

Relish, 4 Sections,
8 3/8 In. 12.00

GREEN

Grill Plate, 9 1/2 In. 50.00

Tumbler, 9 Oz., 4 1/4 In. . . . 25.00

PINK

Bowl, 5 1/2 In. 20.00

Bowl, 11 3/4 In. . . . 48.00 to 58.00

Bowl, Ruffled,
12 In. . . . . 45.00 to 46.00

Bowl, Vegetable,
10 In. . . . . 18.00 to 22.50

Bowl, Vegetable,
Cover, 10 In. . . . 80.00 to 110.00

Bowl, Vegtable,
Oval, 9 1/2 In. 22.00

Butter, Cover 65.00

Cake Plate, Footed,
10 In. . . . . 26.00 to 30.00

Candy Dish,
Cover . . . . 25.00 to 53.00

Cocktail, 2 1/2 Oz., 4 In. 70.00

Cookie Jar, Cover 40.00

Creamer. . . . . 16.00 to 30.00

Cup. . . . . 14.00 to 17.00

Decanter, Stopper,
32 Oz. . . . . 100.00 to 130.00

Decanter Set, 7 Piece 585.00

Goblet, 2 1/2 Oz., 4 In. 65.00

Pitcher, 37 Oz.,
6 In. . . . . 45.00 to 52.00

Pitcher, 60 Oz.,
8 In. . . . . 50.00 to 55.00

Pitcher, 80 Oz.,
8 1/2 In. . . . . 70.00 to 95.00

Plate, 6 In. . . . . 12.00 to 14.00

Plate, 6 1/2 In. . . . . . 9.00 to 11.00

Plate, 8 1/2 In. . . . . . 23.00 to 24.00

Plate, 9 1/2 In. . . . . . 28.00 to 50.00

Plate, Off-Center Ring,
6 1/2 In. 28.00

Platter, Handles, Oval,
12 In. . . . . 19.00 to 25.00

Salt & Pepper 50.00

Sandwich Server, Center
Handle . . . . 35.00 to 42.00

Sherbet, 2 1/4 In. . . 14.00 to 18.50

Sherbet, Footed, 3 In. 15.00

Soup, Cream,
5 In. . . . . 35.00 to 47.00

Sugar. . . . . 22.00 to 28.00

Tumbler, 13 Oz., 5 1/4 In. . . 52.00

Tumbler, Footed, 10 Oz.,
5 1/4 In. 32.00

Tumbler, Footed, 15 Oz.,
6 1/2 In. . . . . 32.00 to 36.00

Wine, 3 Oz.,
4 1/2 In. . . . . 65.00 to 75.00

YELLOW

Plate, 9 1/2 In. 130.00

Platter, Closed Handles,
Oval, 12 1/2 In. 225.00

MEADOW FLOWER,
see No. 618

MEANDERING VINE,
see Madrid

Miss America

Miss America, or Diamond Pattern, was made by Hocking Glass Company from 1933 to 1936 in many colors, including crystal, green, Ice Blue, Jadite, pink, red, and Ritz Blue. It is similar to English Hobnail but can be distinguished by the typical Hocking sunburst base and hobs that are more pointed than those of the Westmoreland pattern. In 1977 some reproduction butter dishes were made of Amberina, crystal, green, Ice Blue, pink, or red. Saltshakers, pitchers, and tumblers are also being reproduced.

CRYSTAL

Bowl, 6 1/4 In. 9.00

Bowl, Vegetable,
Oval, 10 In. 15.00

Cake Plate, Footed,
12 In. . . . . 22.00 to 23.00

Celery Dish,
10 1/2 In. . . . . 9.00 to 15.00

Coaster, 5 3/4 In. 15.00

Compote, 5 In. . . . . 13.00 to 14.00

Creamer, Footed. 9.00

Cup . . . . 8.00 to 10.00

Grill Plate,
10 1/4 In. . . . . 8.00 to 10.00

Plate, 10 1/2 In. 12.00

Relish, 4 Sections, 8 3/4 In. . . . 9.00

Salt & Pepper 28.00
Sherbet 75.00
Tumbler, 5 Oz., 4 In. 11.00
Tumbler, 10 Oz.,
 4 1/2 In. 15.00
Tumbler, 12 Oz.,
 5 3/4 In. 75.00
PINK
Bowl, 6 1/4 In. . . . . 15.00 to 20.00
Bowl, 8 In. 64.00
Bowl, Straight Sides,
 8 3/4 In. . . . . 45.00 to 65.00
Bowl, Vegetable, Oval,
 10 In. . . . . 22.00 to 32.00
Cake Plate, Footed,
 12 In. 40.00
Candy Jar, Cover,
 11 1/2 In. . . . . . 119.00 to 135.00
Celery Dish,
 10 1/2 In. . . . . 21.00 to 26.00
Coaster, 5 3/4 In. 27.00
Compote, 5 In. 21.00
Creamer, Footed . . 12.00 to 17.50
Cup & Saucer . . . . . 24.00 to 32.00
Goblet, 5 Oz., 4 3/4 In. 75.00
Goblet, 10 Oz.,
 5 1/2 In. . . . . 37.00 to 42.00
Grill Plate, 10 1/4 In. 17.00
Pitcher, Ice Lip, 65 Oz.,
 8 1/2 In. 115.00
Plate, 5 3/4 In. 6.50
Plate, 8 1/2 In. . . . . 20.00 to 22.00
Plate, 10 1/4 In. . . . 24.50 to 35.00
Platter, Oval,
 12 1/4 In. . . . . 22.00 to 25.00
Relish, 4 Sections,
 8 3/4 In. . . . . 18.00 to 21.00
Salt & Pepper . . . . . 48.00 to 50.00
Sherbet . . . . 11.50 to 14.00
Sugar 18.50
Sugar & Creamer . . 32.00 to 39.50
Tumbler, 5 Oz., 4 In. 42.50
Tumbler, 12 Oz., 5 3/4 In. . . 70.00
Tumbler, 14 Oz., 5 3/4 In. . . 66.00
Wine, 3 Oz., 3 3/4 In. 45.00

**MISS AMERICA, see also
 English Hobnail**

**MODERNE ART, see Tea
 Room**

Moderntone

Moderntone, or Wedding Band, was made by Hazel Atlas Glass Company from 1935 to 1942. The cobalt blue and the simple pattern are popular today with Art Deco enthusiasts. The pattern was made of amethyst, cobalt blue, crystal, and pink glass. It was also made of a glass called Platonite, which was covered with a variety of bright fired-on colors, including black, light or dark blue, light or dark green, red, orange, yellow, and white trimmed with a small colored rim.

AMETHYST
Bowl, 5 In. 14.00
Cup. 7.00
Plate, 5 3/4 In. 7.00
Plate, 7 3/4 In. 7.00
Plate, 10 1/2 In. 8.00
Soup, Cream, 4 3/4 In. 12.00
Soup, Cream, Ruffled,
 5 In. 15.00
COBALT BLUE
Bowl, 6 1/2 In. 70.00
Bowl, 8 3/4 In. 55.00
Butter, Metal Cover 105.00
Creamer. . . . . 6.00 to 11.00
Cup. . . . . 8.00 to 9.00
Cup & Saucer . . . . . 16.00 to 17.50
Custard Cup . . . . . 18.00 to 22.00
Plate, 5 3/4 In. 6.50
Plate, 6 3/4 In. . . . . . 6.00 to 11.00
Plate, 7 3/4 In. . . . . . 7.00 to 12.00
Plate, 8 7/8 In. . . . . 12.00 to 15.00
Plate, 10 1/2 In. . . . 17.50 to 20.00

Salt & Pepper . . . . . 25.00 to 35.00
Saltshaker. 12.00
Sherbet. 13.00
Soup, Cream,
 4 3/4 In. . . . . 20.00 to 22.00
Soup, Cream, Ruffled, 5 In. . . 48.00
Sugar. . . . . 6.00 to 11.00
Whiskey, 1 1/2 Oz. 30.00
PINK
Whiskey 15.00

Moderntone Little Hostess Party Set

The Moderntone Little Hostess Party Set was also made by Hazel Atlas in the late 1940s. This was a child's set of dishes made in Platonite with fired-on colors. We have seen blue, gray, green, maroon, orange, pink, turquoise, and yellow, but other colors were probably made.

GRAY
Cup. 8.00
Plate 6.00
Saucer. 4.00
GREEN
Tea Set, Box, 16 Piece 250.00
MAROON
Tea Set, Box, 15 Piece 225.00
ORANGE
Cup. 6.00
Plate 6.00
Saucer. 4.00
PASTELS
Tea Set, 14 Piece. 95.00
PINK
Tea Set, 15 Piece. 185.00
TURQUOISE
Cup. . . . . 7.00 to 8.00
Plate . . . . 6.00 to 7.00
Saucer. 4.00
Teapot 40.00
YELLOW
Cup. 8.00
Plate 6.00
Saucer. 4.00

Moondrops

The New Martinsville Glass Company, New Martinsville, West Virginia, made Moondrops from 1932 to the late 1940s. Collectors like the pieces with the fan-shaped knobs or stoppers. The pattern was made in amber, amethyst, black, cobalt blue, crystal, Evergreen, Ice Blue, Jadite, light green, medium blue, pink, Ritz Blue, rose, ruby, and Smoke.

CRYSTAL
Plate, 9 1/2 In. 12.00
Sherbet, 2 5/8 In. 10.00

GREEN
Cup & Saucer 13.00
Tumbler, 9 Oz.,
 4 7/8 In. . . . . 11.00 to 15.00

RED
Ashtray, Footed, 4 In. 20.00
Compote, 4 In. 20.00
Creamer,
 2 3/4 In. . . . . 17.50 to 18.00
Cup. .11.00
Cup & Saucer . . . . . 15.00 to 20.00
Goblet, 4 Oz., 4 In. 20.00
Goblet, 9 Oz.,
 6 1/4 In. . . . . 24.00 to 28.00
Plate, 6 1/8 In. 5.00
Plate, 8 1/2 In. 11.00

Plate, 9 1/2 In. 25.00
Sherbet, 2 5/8 In. 15.00
Sherbet, 4 1/2 In. 20.00
Sugar, 2 3/4 In. 14.00
Sugar & Creamer,
 2 3/4 In. 28.00
Tumbler, 8 Oz., 4 3/8 In. 15.00
Tumbler, 9 Oz.,
 4 7/8 In. . . . . 15.00 to 19.00
Tumbler, Handle,
 5 Oz., 3 5/8 In. 17.00
Whiskey,
 2 3/4 In. . . . . 10.00 to 15.00
Wine, 4 Oz., 4 In. . . 16.00 to 20.00

Moonstone

The opalescent hobnails on this pattern give it the name Moonstone. It was made by Anchor Hocking Glass Corporation, Lancaster, Ohio, from 1941 to 1946. A few pieces are seen in green.

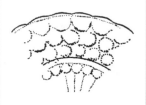

CRYSTAL
Bonbon, Heart Shape,
 Handle . . . . 10.00 to 15.00
Bowl, 5 1/2 In. 12.00
Bowl, Cigarette, Cover 17.00
Bowl, Crimped, 9 1/2 In. . . .18.00
Candleholder, Pair 16.00
Creamer. 7.00
Cup. . . . . 5.00 to 7.00
Cup & Saucer . . . . . 13.00 to 17.00
Goblet, 10 Oz.,
 5 1/2 In. . . . . 17.00 to 18.50
Plate, 6 In. 5.00
Plate, 8 1/2 In. 12.50
Plate, 10 In. 18.00
Puff Box, Cover,
 4 1/2 In. 18.00

Relish, 3 Sections,
 Cloverleaf Shape . . . 6.50 to 7.50
Sherbet, Footed. 8.50
Sugar, Footed. 7.00
Vase, Bud, 5 In. . . . . . 7.00 to 12.00

Mt. Pleasant

Mt. Pleasant, sometimes called Double Shield, was made by L. E. Smith Glass Company, Mt. Pleasant, Pennsylvania, from the mid-1920s to 1934. The pattern was made in amber, black amethyst, a very deep purple that appears black unless held in front of a strong light, cobalt blue, crystal, green, and pink. Some pieces have gold or silver trim.

BLACK AMETHYST
Bowl, Handles, 6 In. 14.00
Cake Plate, Closed Handles,
 10 1/2 In. 14.00
Candleholder, 2-Light,
 Pair . . . . 32.00 to 49.00
Creamer . . . . 14.00 to 19.00
Cup 6.50
Plate, Center Handle, 6 In. . . 11.00
Plate, Square, 8 In. 7.50
Sandwich Server, Center
 Handle, 10 In. 27.00
Sugar. . . . . .18.00 to 19.00
Tumbler, Footed. 16.50

COBALT BLUE
Candleholder, 2-Light,
 Pair 35.00
Cup. 11.00
Cup & Saucer . . . . .15.00 to 16.00

Saucer 4.50
Sherbet . . . . 15.00 to 17.00
Tumbler, Footed 18.00
Vase, 7 1/4 In. 35.00

Mt. Vernon

Mt. Vernon was made in the late 1920s through the 1940s by the Cambridge Glass Company, Cambridge, Ohio. It was made in amber, blue, crystal, Emerald Green, Heatherbloom, red, and violet.

CRYSTAL

Candleholder, Dolphin,
Pair 160.00
Compote, 4 1/2 In. 45.00
Decanter Set, 7 Piece 95.00
Goblet, 10 Oz. 10.00
Perfume Bottle, Stopper,
2 1/2 Oz. 20.00
Sherbet, 4 1/2 Oz. . . . 7.00 to 8.00
Wine, 4 1/2 In. . . . . . . 7.00 to 8.00

RED

Goblet, 10 Oz. 15.00
Relish, 3 Sections,
3 Handles, 8 In. 75.00
Sherbet, 4 1/2 Oz. 11.00

N

Navarre

Fostoria Glass Company, Fostoria, Ohio, made Navarre pattern glass from 1937 to 1980. It is an etched pattern. Some of the pieces were made on the Baroque glass blank, others on more modern shapes. It was originally made only in crystal. A few later pieces were made in color.

CRYSTAL

Bell, 6 1/2 In. . . . . . . 30.00 to 65.00
Bonbon, Footed,
7 3/8 In. . . . . 25.00 to 27.50
Bowl, Handles, 10 1/2 In. 50.00
Cake Plate, Handles,
10 In. . . . . 35.00 to 50.00
Candlestick, 3-Light,
6 3/4 In., Pair 125.00
Candlestick, 5 1/2 In. 32.50
Candy Dish,
Cover . . . . 85.00 to 100.00
Champagne, 6 Oz.,
5 5/8 In. . . . . 16.00 to 21.00
Claret, 4 1/2 Oz.,
6 1/2 In. . . . . 40.00 to 50.00
Compote,
5 1/2 In. . . . . 25.00 to 47.50
Cordial, 3/4 Oz., 3 7/8 In. 50.00
Cup & Saucer . . . . . 18.00 to 27.50
Dish, Mayonnaise, 3 Piece . . 65.00
Goblet, Footed, 10 Oz.,
7 5/8 In. . . . . 16.00 to 29.00
Nappy, 3-Cornered,
Handle, 4 5/8 In. 25.00
Oyster Cocktail,
4 Oz., 3 5/8 In. 25.00
Plate, 7 In. 14.00
Plate, 8 In. 20.00
Plate, 9 In. . . . . 45.00 to 65.00

Plate, Torte, 14 In. 55.00
Relish, 3 Sections, 10 In. 35.00
Relish, 5 Sections,
13 1/4 In. 85.00
Sherbet . . . . 12.00 to 14.00
Sugar, Footed 17.50
Sugar & Creamer,
Footed . . . . 25.00 to 40.00
Sugar & Creamer,
Individual 40.00
Tumbler, Footed, 5 Oz.,
4 5/8 In. . . . . 15.00 to 20.00
Tumbler, Footed, 13 Oz.,
5 7/8 In. . . . . 20.00 to 30.00
Vase, 10 In. 195.00
Wine, 3 1/4 Oz., 5 1/2 In. . . . 30.00

New Century

There is vast confusion about the patterns called New Century, Banded Ribbon, Lydia Ray, Ovide, and related pieces. After studying all the available books about Depression glass, the old advertisements, and checking with dealers who sell the glass, we have made these decisions. Most dealers and most people who advertise Depression glass call the pattern pictured here New Century. It has a series of ribs in the glass design. New Century was made by the Hazel Atlas Glass Company, a firm with factories in Ohio, Pennsylvania, and West Virginia, from 1930 to 1935. It is found in amethyst, cobalt blue, crystal, green, and pink. In 1970 a book listed the pattern with ribs by Hazel Atlas as Lydia Ray. In this same book, New Century was a very plain ware with no impressed or raised pattern. Sometimes it was made in black or white with fired-on colors and was called Ovide. Research shows that the ribbed pattern was advertised in the 1930s as New Century by Hazel Atlas. The plain glassware was also called New

Century. With added enamel designs, it was sometimes called Ovide, Floral Sterling, or Cloverleaf. In this book, we list no Lydia Ray or Floral Sterling. The plain glass we call Ovide.

AMETHYST
Bowl, Footed, Ruffled,
9 1/2 In. 35.00
Cup. 10.00
Tumbler, 5 Oz.,
3 1/2 In. . . . . 10.00 to 12.00
COBALT BLUE
Tumbler, 5 Oz., 3 1/2 In. . . . 12.50
Tumbler, 9 Oz.,
4 7/8 In. . . . . 13.00 to 20.00
Tumbler, 10 Oz., 5 In. 18.00
CRYSTAL
Creamer. 17.50
Vase, Footed, Ruffled,
7 3/4 In. 85.00
Wine, 2 1/2 Oz. . . . 17.00 to 35.00
GREEN
Butter, Cover 65.00
Creamer. 7.00
Decanter, Stopper 67.00
Pitcher, 60 Oz., 7 3/4 In. 38.00
Plate, 7 1/2 In. 7.00
Plate, 8 1/2 In. . . . . . . 8.00 to 9.00
Plate, 10 In. 16.00
Saltshaker 17.00
Sherbet. 8.50
Soup, Cream, Liner,
4 3/4 In. 23.00
Sugar 5.50
Tumbler, 10 Oz., 5 In. 20.00
Wine, 2 1/2 Oz. 30.00

NEW CENTURY, see also Ovide

Newport
Newport, or Hairpin, was made by Hazel Atlas Glass Company from 1936 to 1940. It is known in amethyst, cobalt blue, pink, Platonite (white), and a variety of fired-on colors.

AMETHYST
Bowl, 5 1/4 In. 26.00
Creamer. 13.50
Cup. . . . . 7.00 to 9.50
Cup & Saucer 13.50
Plate, 6 In. . . . . 4.00 to 5.00
Plate, 8 1/2 In. . . . . . . 8.00 to 10.00
Salt & Pepper 45.00
Saucer. . . . . 3.00 to 5.00
Soup, Cream,
4 3/4 In. . . . . 13.00 to 15.00
Sugar. 13.00
Sugar & Creamer 25.00
BLUE
Bowl, 4 1/4 In. 18.00
Cup & Saucer . . . . . 15.00 to 17.00
Plate, 8 1/2 In. . . . . . 12.00 to 13.00
Sandwich Server,
11 1/4 In. 38.00
Sherbet. 15.00
Soup, Cream,
4 3/4 In. . . . . 18.00 to 35.00
Sugar & Creamer 31.00
Tumbler, 9 Oz., 4 1/2 In. 35.00
PINK
Berry Set, 7 Piece 55.00
Bowl, 4 1/4 In. 7.00

Bowl, 8 1/4 In. . . . . 12.00 to 17.00
WHITE
Sugar. 5.00

NO. 601, see Avocado

No. 610
Many patterns are listed both by the original pattern number and by a name. No. 610 is often called Pyramid or Rex. It was made from 1926 to 1932 by the Indiana Glass Company. Green and pink were used more than crystal and yellow. In 1974 and 1975 reproductions were made in black and blue by Tiara.

GREEN
Bowl, Oval,
9 1/2 In. . . . . 35.00 to 45.00
Relish, 4 Sections, Center
Handle, 8 1/2 In. 50.00
YELLOW
Pickle, Oval,
9 1/2 In. . . . . 50.00 to 65.00
Sugar & Creamer, Tray. . . . 175.00
Tumbler, Footed, 8 Oz. 65.00

No. 612
Indiana Glass Company, Dunkirk, Indiana, called this pattern No. 612, but collectors call it Horseshoe. It was made from 1930 to 1933 primarily in green and yellow, with a smaller number of pink

pieces. Sugar and creamer sets were also made in crystal. Plates came in two styles, one with the center pattern, one plain.

GREEN

Bowl, 7 1/2 In.	20.00
Bowl, Vegetable, Oval, 10 1/2 In.	20.00 to 24.00
Butter, Cover	950.00
Candleholder	22.00
Creamer	15.00
Cup	10.00
Plate, 6 In.	4.00 to 7.00
Plate, 8 3/8 In.	8.00 to 9.00
Plate, 9 3/8 In.	7.00 to 14.00
Sandwich Server, 11 1/2 In.	14.00
Sherbet	14.00 to 19.00
Sugar	10.00 to 14.00

YELLOW

Bowl, 6 1/2 In.	22.00
Bowl, Vegetable, Oval, 10 1/2 In.	25.00
Candy Dish, 3 Sections	37.00
Creamer	15.00
Cup & Saucer	16.00
Pitcher, 64 Oz., 8 1/2 In.	295.00
Sherbet	12.00 to 15.00

Sugar	15.00
Tumbler, Footed, 9 Oz.	18.00

No. 615

No. 615 is often called Lorain or sometimes Basket, Bridal Bouquet, Flower Basket, or Hanging Basket. It was made by the Indiana Glass Company from 1929 to 1932 of crystal, green, and yellow. Sometimes crystal pieces have blue, green, red, or yellow borders. Reproduction pieces were made of milk glass or Olive Green.

CRYSTAL

Cup & Saucer	10.00
Plate, 7 3/4 In.	7.00
Plate, 10 1/4 In.	36.00
Sugar & Creamer	35.00

GREEN

Bowl, Oval, 9 3/4 In.	55.00
Plate, 7 3/4 In.	10.00
Plate, 10 1/4 In.	35.00

YELLOW

Bowl, 7 1/2 In.	55.00
Bowl, Oval, 9 3/4 In.	50.00 to 65.00
Cup & Saucer	15.00 to 18.00
Plate, 5 1/2 In.	10.00
Plate, 7 3/4 In.	15.00
Plate, 8 3/8 In.	25.00
Relish, 4 Sections, 8 In.	30.00 to 33.00
Saucer	4.00
Sugar, Footed	16.50 to 20.00
Sugar & Creamer	43.00
Tumbler, Footed, 9 Oz., 4 3/4 In.	25.00 to 28.00

No. 616

No. 616 is called Vernon by some collectors. It was made by Indiana Glass Company from 1930 to 1932. The pattern was made in crystal, green, and yellow. Some crystal pieces have a platinum trim.

CRYSTAL

Cup & Saucer	8.50
Plate, 8 In.	4.00

GREEN

Candy Dish, Cover	195.00
Cup & Saucer	25.00
Dish, Grapefruit	45.00
Dish, Grapefruit, 2 Piece	110.00
Finger Bowl, Liner	35.00
Grill Plate, 9 1/2 In.	29.50
Plate, 6 In.	7.50
Plate, 8 In.	14.50
Plate, Center Handle, 11 In.	47.50
Saucer	3.50
Sherbet	25.00
Tumbler, Footed, 5 In.	27.50 to 29.50

YELLOW

Saucer	5.50

No. 618

Another Indiana Glass Company pattern made from 1932 to 1937 was No. 618, or Pineapple & Floral. It is also called Meadow Flower, Lacy Daisy, or Wildflower. The pattern was made of amber, crystal, and fired-on green and red. Reproductions were made in Olive Green in the late 1960s.

AMBER

Creamer.	5.00
Cup.	8.00
Cup & Saucer	14.50
Plate, 8 3/8 In.	4.00
Plate, 9 3/8 In.	11.00
Platter, Closed Handles, 11 In.	15.00
Soup, Cream	15.00

CRYSTAL

Ashtray, 4 1/2 In.	15.00 to 16.00
Bowl, 4 3/4 In.	20.00
Bowl, 6 In.	19.00 to 22.00
Bowl, Vegetable, Oval, 10 In.	18.00 to 20.00
Cheese Compote	37.50
Compote, Diamond Shape	23.00
Creamer.	6.50
Cup.	9.00
Cup & Saucer	15.00
Pitcher, 76 Oz.	265.00
Plate, 6 In.	4.00 to 5.00
Plate, 8 3/8 In.	7.00 to 8.00
Plate, 9 1/2 In.	12.00 to 15.00
Plate, Indentation, 11 1/2 In.	12.00
Plate, Sandwich, 11 1/2 In.	13.00 to 16.00
Relish, 2 Sections, 11 1/2 In.	14.00 to 18.00
Saucer	4.00
Sherbet, Diamond Shape	6.00
Sherbet, Footed	15.00 to 20.00
Soup, Cream	18.00
Sugar, Diamond Shape	6.50 to 7.00
Tumbler, 8 Oz., 4 1/4 In.	26.00 to 32.50
Vase, Cone, Metal Holder, 12 In.	30.00

No. 620

No. 620, also known as Daisy, was made by Indiana Glass Company. In 1933 the pattern was made in crystal, and in 1940 in amber; in the 1960s and 1970s reproductions were made in dark green and milk glass. Some pieces have a fired-on red color.

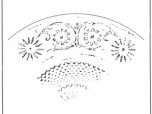

AMBER

Bowl, 4 1/2 In.	4.50 to 7.50
Bowl, Vegetable, Oval, 10 In.	14.00 to 16.00
Cake Plate, 11 1/2 In.	9.00
Creamer, Footed.	6.50
Cup.	5.00
Plate, 6 In.	2.25 to 3.00
Plate, 7 3/8 In.	6.00
Plate, 8 3/8 In.	5.50
Plate, 9 3/8 In.	8.25 to 9.00
Platter, 10 3/4 In.	11.00
Relish, 3 Sections, 8 3/8 In.	24.00
Saucer.	1.50
Sherbet, Footed	4.00 to 8.50
Soup, Cream, 4 1/2 In.	6.50 to 12.00
Sugar, Footed	6.50 to 8.00
Sugar & Creamer	14.50
Tumbler, Footed, 9 Oz.	18.00 to 20.00
Tumbler, Footed, 12 Oz.	30.00

CRYSTAL

Cup & Saucer	4.50 to 5.50
Grill Plate, 10 3/8 In.	4.00
Saucer.	.75
Soup, Cream, 4 1/2 In.	4.00

DARK GREEN

Creamer, Footed.	4.50 to 5.00

Cup.	3.00
Cup & Saucer	4.50
Plate, 7 3/8 In.	3.00
Platter, 10 3/4 In.	8.00
Tumbler, Footed, 12 Oz.	9.00 to 17.00

NO. 622, see Pretzel

NO. 624, see Christmas Candy

Normandie

A few Depression glass patterns were made in iridescent marigold color, which has been collected as carnival glass. Normandie products made in this iridescence, called Sunburst, appear in the carnival glass listings as Bouquet and Lattice; when the pattern is in the other known colors, it is called Normandie. Look for it in amber, crystal, and pink, as well as in the iridescent color. One author also lists green. It was made from 1933 to 1940.

AMBER

Bowl, 6 1/2 In.	14.00
Bowl, 8 1/2 In.	15.00
Sugar & Creamer.	15.00

IRIDESCENT

Bowl, 5 In.	3.00
Bowl, 6 1/2 In.	5.00 to 6.00
Cup & Saucer	4.00
Grill Plate, 2 Sections, 11 In.	5.00
Plate, 6 In.	2.00
Sherbet.	3.00
Sugar & Creamer.	8.00

PINK

Bowl, 8 1/2 In. 20.00
Cup & Saucer 12.00
Grill Plate, 2 Sections,
  11 In. 20.00
Plate, 6 In. 4.00
Plate, 8 In. 10.00
Platter, Oval, 11 3/4 In. 20.00
Saucer . . . . 3.75 to 4.00
Sherbet . . . . 6.00 to 8.00
Tumbler, 9 Oz.,
  4 1/4 In. . . . . 46.00 to 50.00

OATMEAL LACE, see
Princess Feather

Old Cafe

Old Cafe is one of the few patterns with only one name. It was made by the Anchor Hocking Glass Corporation, Lancaster, Ohio, from 1936 to 1938. Pieces are found in crystal, pink, and red.

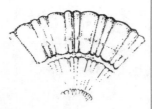

CRYSTAL

Bowl, 5 1/2 In. 6.00
Bowl, Flower Frog,
  5 1/2 In. 7.00
Candy Dish, Cover, Low,
  8 In. 10.00
Candy Dish, Red Cover,
  Low, 8 In. 18.50
Dish, Olive, Handle,
  Oval, 6 In. 5.00
Plate, 6 In. 1.75
Saucer . . . . 1.75 to 5.00
Vase, 7 1/4 In. . . . . . . 6.50 to 9.50

PINK

Bowl, 5 1/2 In. . . . . . . 6.00 to 7.00
Bowl, Handle, 5 In. . . 6.50 to 8.00
Candy Dish, Cover,
  Low, 8 In. . . . . 6.00 to 10.00
Cup. 5.00
Dish, Olive, Handle,
  Oval, 6 In. . . . . 3.00 to 7.00
Pitcher, 36 Oz., 6 In. 75.00
Pitcher, 80 Oz.,
  9 In. . . . . 69.00 to 100.00
Plate, 6 In. 12.50
Plate, 10 In. 32.00
Tumbler, 3 In. 10.00
Tumbler, 4 In. . . . . . 11.00 to 12.00
Vase, 7 1/4 In. 5.50

RED

Bowl, Handle, 5 In. 12.50
Candy Dish, Cover,
  Low, 8 In. 10.00
Cup. . . . . 5.00 to 7.50
Cup & Saucer 9.00
Tumbler, 4 In. 15.00

Old English

Old English, or Threading, was made by the Indiana Glass Company, Dunkirk, Indiana, in the late 1920s and early 1930s. It was first made in amber, crystal, and green. Pink was a later color.

AMBER
Tumbler, Footed, 4 1/2 In. . . 15.00
CRYSTAL
Eggcup. . . . . 8.00 to 8.50
Tumbler, Footed, 4 3/4 In. . . . 8.00
GREEN
Bowl, Footed, 11 In. 38.00

OLD FLORENTINE, see
Florentine No. 1

OPALESCENT HOBNAIL,
see Moonstone

OPEN LACE, see Lace Edge

OPEN ROSE, see Mayfair
Open Rose

OPEN SCALLOP, see Lace
Edge

OPTIC DESIGN, see
Raindrops

Orange Blossom

Indiana Glass Company made Orange Blossom in 1957. The pattern is the same as Indiana Custard but the milk glass items are called Orange Blossom.

WHITE
Bowl, 5 1/2 In. . . . . . . 2.50 to 6.00
Cup & Saucer 5.50
Plate, 9 3/4 In. . . . . . . 5.50 to 10.00

OREGON GRAPE, see
Woolworth

ORIENTAL POPPY,
see Florentine No. 2

Ovide

Hazel Atlas made Ovide pattern from 1929 to 1935. It was made in green at first. By 1932 it was black and by 1935 Platonite or opaque white glass was used with fired-on colors. A bright fired-on pattern of black, green, orange, yellow, and black circles and lines was one of the popular designs. Some other patterns were white with colored rims. There is great confusion between Ovide and New Century. Read the explanation under New Century.

were crystal or pink. Those with a white outside and fired-on pink or green interiors were made later, as were ruby pieces.

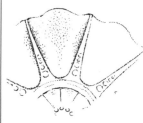

Patrician

Federal Glass Company, Columbus, Ohio, made Patrician, sometimes called Hinge or Spoke, from 1933 to 1937. Full dinner sets were made in amber and green; smaller quantities of crystal, pink, and yellow pieces were produced.

BLACK
Candy Dish, Lid 45.00
Creamer. 6.00
Creamer, Footed 6.00
Salt & Pepper 30.00
Saucer 3.00
GREEN
Cocktail, 5 Oz. 4.00
Cocktail, Footed. 3.50
Creamer. 3.00
Plate, Fired On, 6 In. 1.50
Plate, Fired On, 8 In. 4.00
Sherbet, Footed 3.00
Sugar . . . . 3.00 to 3.50
WHITE
Creamer, Red Trim 15.00
Sherbet, Platonite. 2.00
Sugar, Red Trim 15.00
Tumbler, Red Trim,
    Flowers, 9 Oz. 16.00

OVIDE, see also New Century

OXFORD, see Chinex Classic

Oyster & Pearl
Anchor Hocking Glass Corporation, Lancaster, Ohio, made only accessory pieces in the Oyster & Pearl pattern from 1938 to 1940. The first pieces

CRYSTAL
Bowl, Deep, 10 1/2 In. 20.00
Bowl, Heart Shape,
    Handle, 5 1/4 In. 7.00
Relish, 2 Sections,
    Oval, 10 1/4 In. 8.00
PINK
Bowl, 10 1/2 In. . . . 10.00 to 15.00
Bowl, Handle, 6 1/2 In. 10.00
Bowl, Heart Shape,
    Handle, 5 1/4 In. 14.00
Candleholder, 3 1/2 In.,
    Pair . . . . 9.00 to 17.50
Relish, 2 Sections,
    Oval, 10 1/4 In. 11.00
RED
Bowl, Deep,
    6 1/2 In. . . . . 14.00 to 18.00
Bowl, Handle, 5 1/4 In. 12.00
Candleholder, 3 1/2 In.,
    Pair 50.00
Plate, Sandwich, 13 1/2 In. . .35.00

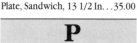

P

PANELED ASTER, see Madrid

PANELED CHERRY BLOSSOM, see Cherry Blossom

PANSY & DORIC, see Doric & Pansy

PARROT, see Sylvan

AMBER
Bowl, 5 In. . . . . .9.00 to 10.00
Bowl, 6 In. . . . . .19.00 to 22.00
Bowl, 8 1/2 In. . . . .38.00 to 45.00
Butter, Cover. 80.00
Cookie Jar, Cover 75.00
Creamer. . . . . 7.00 to 12.00
Cup . . . . 8.00 to 9.00
Cup & Saucer . . . . . 13.00 to 17.00
Grill Plate, 10 1/2 In. 12.00
Jam Jar. . . . . 17.00 to 25.00
Pitcher, 75 Oz., 8 1/4 In. . . . 90.00
Plate, 6 In. . . . . 7.00 to 8.00
Plate, 9 In. . . . . .9.00 to 11.00
Plate, 10 1/2 In. . . . . . . 5.00 to 7.00
Platter, Oval,
    11 1/2 In. . . . . . . .28.00 to 30.00
Salt & Pepper. 50.00
Saucer. . . . . .8.00 to 9.00
Sherbet. . . . . .9.00 to 14.00
Soup, Cream,
    4 3/4 In. . . . . .14.00 to 15.00
Sugar, Cover . . . . . .55.00 to 60.00
Tumbler, 5 Oz., 4 In. 28.00
Tumbler, 9 Oz.,
    4 1/4 In. . . . . .20.00 to 23.00
Tumbler, Footed,
    8 Oz., 5 1/4 In. . . .30.00 to 42.00

CRYSTAL

Bowl, 6 In.	18.00
Creamer	8.50
Jam Jar, Cover.	25.00
Plate, 7 1/2 In.	13.00
Sherbet	9.00
Soup, Cream, 4 3/4 In.	12.00
Sugar	7.50

GREEN

Bowl, 5 In.	10.00
Bowl, 6 In.	22.00
Bowl, 8 1/2 In.	32.00
Bowl, Vegetable, Oval, 10 In.	30.00
Butter, Cover	95.00
Creamer	8.00 to 10.00
Cup	7.50 to 8.50
Cup & Saucer	12.00 to 16.00
Grill Plate, 10 1/2 In.	12.00
Pitcher, 75 Oz., 8 1/4 In.	135.00
Plate, 6 In.	13.00
Plate, 7 1/2 In.	13.00
Plate, 9 In.	9.00 to 10.00
Platter, Oval, 11 1/2 In.	20.00
Salt & Pepper	55.00
Saucer	6.00
Sherbet	9.00 to 12.00
Sugar	7.00 to 10.00
Tumbler, 5 Oz., 4 In.	30.00
Tumbler, 9 Oz., 4 1/2 In.	23.00
Tumbler, 14 Oz., 5 1/2 In.	37.50

PINK

Bowl, 6 In.	24.00
Plate, 9 In.	8.00
Saucer	9.00
Sugar, Cover	60.00
Tumbler, 9 Oz., 4 1/2 In.	20.00
Tumbler, 14 Oz., 5 1/2 In.	33.00

Peach Lustre

Peach Lustre is both a pattern and a color name used for Fire-King dinnerware made by Anchor Hocking Glass Corporation from 1952 to 1963. The pattern has a laurel leaf design around the edge of the plates and bowls and the side of the cups. The pieces are a lustrous orange-yellow color. The same pattern of laurel leaves was made in 1953 in gray and was known as Gray Laurel pattern. Bubble and Boopie pattern crystal stemware was made with a similar design to go with the dinnerware.

Bowl, 4 7/8 In.	3.00 to 5.00
Bowl, 7 In.	6.00
Creamer.	3.00
Cup & Saucer	4.00
Pie Plate, 9 In.	7.00
Pitcher, Batter.	25.00
Plate, 7 3/8 In.	2.00
Plate, 9 1/8 In.	3.00 to 6.00
Plate, 11 In.	9.00
Sugar	3.00
Soup, Dish.	5.00

PEACOCK & ROSE, see Peacock & Wild Rose

Peacock & Wild Rose

Line 300 was the name used by Paden City Glass Company, Paden City, West Virginia, for the pattern now called Peacock & Wild Rose. It was made in the 1930s of black, cobalt blue, green, pink, and red. A few of the lists call this pattern Peacock & Rose.

• • • • • • • • • • • • • •

Cups are best stored by hanging them on cup hooks. Stacking cups inside one another can cause chipping.

• • • • • • • • • • • • • •

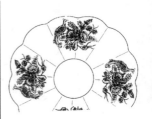

GREEN

Bowl, Footed, 9 1/2 In.	70.00

PINK

Bowl, Center Handle, 10 1/2 In.	70.00
Cake Plate, Footed, 11 In.	65.00
Compote, Footed, 6 1/2 In.	55.00

Pear Optic

Pear Optic, sometimes called Thumbprint, was made in 1929 and 1930 by the Federal Glass Company. It was made only in green and is characterized by an outside design of six-sided depressions. It is sometimes confused with Raindrops, which has an inside pattern of rounded, fingernail-shaped impressions.

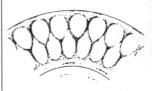

GREEN

Cup & Saucer	4.50
Plate, 8 In.	3.50

PEBBLE OPTIC, see Raindrops

Penny Line

Paden City Glass Company, Paden City, West Virginia, made Penny Line in amber,

Cheri-Glo, crystal, green, Royal Blue, and ruby. It was No. 991 in the 1932 catalog.

RUBY

Cordial	24.00
Goblet, Water	18.50
Sherbet	12.50

PETAL SWIRL, see Swirl

Petalware

Macbeth-Evans made Petalware from 1930 to 1940. It was first made in crystal and pink. In 1932 the dinnerware was made in Monax, in 1933 in Cremax. The pattern remained popular and in 1936 cobalt blue and several other variations were made. Some pieces were hand painted with pastel bands of ivory, green, and pink. Some pieces were decorated with a gold or red rim. Flower or fruit designs in bright colors were used on others. Bright bands of fired-on blue, green, red, and yellow were used to decorate some wares. All of these patterns have their own names. These include Banded Petalware, Daisy Petals, Diamond Point, Petal, Shell, and Vivid Bands.

· · · · · · · · · · · · · ·

Put a rubber collar on the faucet spout over the sink. This may save you from breaking a piece of glass or china you are washing.

· · · · · · · · · · · · · ·

COBALT BLUE

Bowl, 5 3/4 In.	12.00
Mustard, Cover	10.00
Plate, 8 In.	8.00
Saucer	3.00
Sugar	9.00

CREMAX

Bowl, 5 3/4 In.	5.00 to 5.50
Bowl, Gold Trim, 8 3/4 In.	17.00 to 30.00
Cup & Saucer	5.00
Plate, 6 In.	2.00
Plate, 8 In.	3.50 to 5.50
Plate, 9 In.	5.00
Plate, Gold Trim, 9 In.	14.00
Plate, Pastel Bands, 8 In.	7.00
Platter, Oval, 13 In.	9.00
Salver, 11 In.	7.00 to 8.00
Salver, Pastel Bands, 11 In.	11.00
Saucer	1.50
Saucer, Gold Trim	75
Saucer, Pastel Bands	1.50
Sherbet, Footed	6.00
Sherbet, Gold Trim	12.00
Soup, Cream, Handles, 4 In.	5.00 to 10.00
Sugar, Blue Trim	5.00
Sugar & Creamer, Gold Trim	11.00

CRYSTAL

Bowl, 5 3/4 In.	3.50 to 4.00
Bowl, 8 3/4 In.	9.00
Creamer	3.00
Cup	2.50
Cup & Saucer	4.00
Plate, 6 In.	1.50
Plate, 8 In.	2.00 to 3.50
Plate, 9 1/4 In.	4.00
Plate, Pastel Bands, 8 In.	8.00

Platter, Oval, 13 In.	6.00
Salver, 11 In.	5.00
Saucer	1.00
Saucer, Pastel Bands	2.00
Sugar	3.00
Tumbler, Gold Trim, 9 Oz., 4 1/2 In.	5.00

MONAX

Bowl, 5 3/4 In.	6.00 to 10.50
Bowl, 8 3/4 In.	15.00 to 17.00
Creamer	5.00 to 5.50
Cup & Saucer	6.00 to 7.50
Cup & Saucer, Floral Trim	12.00
Lamp Shade	16.00
Plate, 6 In.	2.00
Plate, 8 In.	3.50 to 6.00
Plate, 9 In.	6.00
Plate, Floral Trim, 8 In.	9.00
Plate, Gold Trim, 6 In.	2.25
Plate, Gold Trim, 8 In.	3.50
Platter, Oval, 13 In.	12.00 to 15.00
Salver, 11 In.	7.00 to 9.00
Salver, Floral Trim, 11 In.	15.00
Salver, Gold Trim, 11 In.	5.00
Saucer	1.50 to 2.50
Sherbet	6.50 to 8.50
Soup, Cream, Handles, 4 In.	9.00 to 11.00
Sugar	6.00
Sugar & Creamer	12.00
Sugar & Creamer, Floral Trim	21.50
Sugar & Creamer, Gold Trim	10.00

PINK

Bowl, 5 3/4 In.	9.00
Bowl, 8 3/4 In.	16.00
Bowl, Footed, Pheasant	35.00
Bowl, Lombardi	19.00 to 30.00
Butter, Cover	170.00
Compote, 6 In.	10.00 to 13.00
Goblet	24.00
Honey Jar, Cover	35.00 to 55.00
Plate, 6 In.	3.00
Plate, 8 In.	6.00
Platter, Oval, 13 In.	12.00
Powder Box, Cover	40.00

Punch Cup 4.00
Punch Set, 14 Piece 210.00
Saucer 2.50
Sherbet 20.00
Soup, Cream, Handles,
    4 In. 15.00
Sugar 9.00
Sugar, Pear Cover. 18.00
Sugar & Creamer 22.00

Philbe

Philbe is a Fire-King dinnerware made by the Anchor Hocking Glass Corporation from 1937 to the 1940s. It was made in blue, crystal, green, and pink. The blue sometimes has platinum trim. Philbe is the dinnerware pattern; the matching kitchenware is called Fire-King Oven Glass.

BLUE

Bowl, 5 1/2 In. 9.50
Casserole, Cover, 7 1/2 In. . . 17.00
Casserole, Cover,
    Individual. . . . . . . 7.50 to 11.00
Custard Cup, Deep, Thick . . . 4.00
Custard Cup, Rolled Edge. . . . 4.00
Measuring Cup, 1 Spout,
    8 Oz. 15.00
Mug 20.00
Pie Plate, 8 In. . . . . . 10.00 to 12.50
Refrigerator Jar, Cover,
    4 x 4 In. 18.00
Refrigerator Jar, Cover,
    4 x 8 In. 22.00
Tumbler, 10 Oz., 5 In. 85.00

PINK

Tumbler, 10 Oz., 5 In. 70.00

PHILBE, see also Fire-King

PIE CRUST, see Cremax

Pillar Flute

Pillar Flute was made by Imperial Glass Company, Bellaire, Ohio, in amber, blue, crystal, green, and a pink called Rose Marie. It was made about 1930.

BLUE

Bonbon, Crimped, 7 In. 22.50
Bowl, 6 1/2 In. 30.00
Candleholder, 2-Light, Pair . . 65.00
Celery Dish, Oval,
    8 1/2 In. 27.50
Compote, Footed, 7 In. 25.00
Cup. 18.00
Cup & Saucer 26.00
Dish, Pickle,
    Handles, 6 1/4 In. 25.00
Flower Bowl, 5 In. 25.00
Plate, 6 In. 8.00
Plate, 8 In. 18.00
Sugar & Creamer 37.50
Vase, 6 In. 65.00

**PINEAPPLE & FLORAL, see
    No. 618**

PINWHEEL, see Sierra

POINSETTIA, see Floral

Popeye & Olive

Line 994 was the original name for this Paden City Glass Company pattern. The popular name today is Popeye & Olive. It was made in cobalt blue, crystal, green, and red. The pattern was made in the 1930s, and a 1932 ad shows the red as a new color.

RED

Cup. 7.00
Plate, 8 In. 12.00
Sherbet, 3 1/4 In. . . 12.00 to 15.00
Vase, Ruffled, 7 In. 40.00

**POPPY NO. 1, see
    Florentine No. 1**

**POPPY NO. 2, see
    Florentine No. 2**

Pretzel

Pretzel, also called No. 622 or Ribbon Candy, was made by Indiana Glass Company, Dunkirk, Indiana, in the 1930s. Crystal and teal pieces were made. Some reproductions appeared in the 1970s.

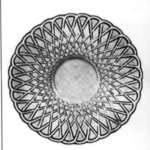

CRYSTAL

Creamer	5.00
Cup & Saucer	6.00 to 6.50
Cup Plate, Handle, 6 1/4 In.	4.00
Dish, Olive, Tab Handle, 7 In.	4.00
Dish, Pickle, Handles, 8 1/2 In.	5.00
Plate, 8 3/8 In.	5.00
Plate, Indentation, Square, 7 1/4 In.	8.00 to 8.50
Plate, Sandwich, 11 1/2 In.	9.50
Soup, Dish	9.00
Sugar	5.00
Sugar & Creamer	7.00 to 10.00

Primo

Green and Mandarin Yellow are the two colors of Primo advertised in the 1932 catalog for U.S. Glass Company.

YELLOW

Cup & Saucer	11.00 to 14.00
Tumbler, Footed, 9 Oz., 5 3/4 In.	15.00
Tumbler, Footed, 9 Oz., 5 5/8 In.	18.00

PRIMUS, see Madrid

Princess

Hocking Glass Company, Lancaster, Ohio, made the popular Princess pattern from 1931 to 1935. The first sets were made in green, then in topaz shades, which vary from yellow to apricot; or amber; so if you are assembling a set, be careful of the color variations. Pink was added last. There are blue pieces found in the West, but there is a debate about the age or origin of these pieces. Some pieces had a frosted finish, some are decorated with hand-painted flowers. Green is sometimes trimmed with gold; other colors are trimmed with platinum. This pattern is sometimes called Drape & Tassel, Lincoln Drape, or Tassel.

GREEN

Bowl, 5 In.	25.00
Bowl, Cover, Vegetable, 10 In.	22.00
Bowl, Hat Shape, Deep, 9 1/2 In.	28.50 to 45.00
Bowl, Vegetable, Oval, 10 In.	24.00
Butter, Cover	100.00
Cake Stand, 10 In.	20.00 to 22.50
Candy Jar, Cover, Footed, 8 1/2 In.	42.00 to 55.00
Cookie Jar, Cover, 7 In.	50.00
Creamer	13.00 to 15.00
Cup	11.00 to 15.00
Cup & Saucer	20.00 to 23.00
Pitcher, 37 Oz., 6 In.	42.00
Pitcher, 60 Oz., 8 In.	42.00 to 50.00
Plate, 5 1/2 In.	5.50 to 10.00
Plate, 8 1/4 In.	12.00 to 13.50
Plate, 9 1/2 In.	19.00 to 27.50
Plate, Sandwich, Handles, 11 1/2 In.	12.50
Platter, Tab Handles, 12 In.	19.00
Relish, 4 Sections, 7 1/2 In.	24.00
Salt & Pepper	48.00
Saltshaker	15.00
Saucer	9.00 to 10.00
Sherbet, Footed	16.00 to 19.00
Sugar, Cover	28.00
Tumbler, 12 Oz., 5 1/4 In.	35.00 to 37.00
Tumbler, Cone Footed, 10 Oz., 5 1/2 In.	27.00 to 29.00

PINK

Bowl, 5 In.	27.50
Bowl, Hat, Deep, 9 1/2 In.	35.00
Bowl, Vegetable, Oval, 10 In.	24.00 to 37.50
Cup	5.00 to 9.50
Cup & Saucer	19.00
Grill Plate, Tab Handles, 10 1/2 In.	8.00
Pitcher, 60 Oz., 8 In.	70.00
Plate, 5 1/2 In.	9.00
Plate, 8 In.	13.00
Plate, 9 1/2 In.	22.00
Saucer	10.00
Sherbet, Footed	20.00
Sugar & Creamer	25.00
Tumbler, 5 Oz., 3 In.	33.00
Tumbler, Cone Footed, 12 1/2 Oz., 6 1/2 In.	85.00

TOPAZ

Bowl, Tab Handles, Octagon, 9 In.	120.00
Creamer	12.00 to 14.00
Cup	7.50 to 8.50
Cup & Saucer	10.00 to 12.00
Grill Plate, 9 1/2 In.	5.00 to 15.00
Plate, 5 1/2 In.	3.50
Plate, 8 In.	9.50
Plate, 9 1/2 In.	12.00 to 14.00
Salt & Pepper	55.00
Saucer	3.50
Sherbet, Footed	30.00 to 35.00
Sugar, Cover	8.00 to 24.50
Tumbler, 5 Oz., 3 In.	26.00
Tumbler, 9 Oz., 4 In.	18.00 to 20.00
Tumbler, 12 Oz., 5 1/4 In.	17.00 to 37.00
Tumbler, Cone Footed, 10 Oz., 5 1/2 In.	20.00 to 23.00

Princess Feather

Westmoreland Glass Company made Princess Feather pattern from 1939 through 1948. It was originally made in aqua, crystal, green, and pink. In the 1960s a reproduction appeared in an amber shade called Golden Sunset. The pattern is sometimes called Early American, Flower, Oatmeal Lace, or Scroll & Star.

CRYSTAL

Candy Dish, Cover,
4 1/2 In. 35.00
Champagne 12.50
Lamp, Hand, Flint 52.00
Saltshaker 20.00
Sherbet 7.50
Sundae, Footed. 65.00
Wine 15.00

GREEN

Dish, Grapefruit, 6 1/2 In. . . 20.00

PRISMATIC LINE, see Queen Mary

PROVINCIAL, see Bubble

PYRAMID, see No. 610

Q

Queen Mary

Queen Mary, sometimes called Prismatic Line or Vertical Ribbed, was made by Anchor Hocking Glass Corporation from 1936 to 1943. It

was made first in pink, later in crystal and red.

CRYSTAL

Ashtray, Oval, 2 x 3 3/4 In. . . . 3.00
Bowl, 4 In. 3.00
Bowl, 5 In. 2.75
Bowl, 8 3/4 In. 7.00
Butter, Cover . . . . . 22.00 to 23.00
Candlestick, 2-Light,
4 1/2 In., Pair. . . . 10.00 to 13.50
Candy Jar, Cover,
7 1/4 In. . . . . 12.00 to 20.00
Celery Dish, 5 x 10 In. 10.00
Coaster-Ashtray, Square,
4 1/4 In. . . . . 3.00 to 4.50
Compote, Footed, 5 3/4 In. . . 7.00
Creamer, Oval. 5.00
Cup, Large . . . . 4.50 to 5.00
Plate, 6 In. 3.00
Plate, 6 5/8 In. 2.50
Plate, 8 1/2 In. . . . . . . 4.50 to 5.00
Plate, Sandwich,
12 In. . . . . 7.00 to 10.00
Relish, 3 Sections, 12 In. 8.50
Relish, 4 Sections, 14 In. 10.00
Saucer 4.50
Sherbet, Footed . . . . . 3.50 to 5.00
Tray, 14 In. 9.50

PINK

Bowl, 4 In. . . . . 4.00 to 5.00
Bowl, 6 In. . . . . 15.00 to 24.00
Bowl, 8 3/4 In. . . . . 16.00 to 22.00
Bowl, Handle, 4 In. . . 4.00 to 7.00
Bowl, Handles,
5 1/2 In. . . . . 5.00 to 10.00
Creamer, Oval. . . . . 3.50 to 10.00

Cup. . . . . 5.00 to 6.00
Cup & Saucer 9.00
Plate, 6 In. 4.50
Plate, Sandwich, 12 In. 12.00
Saucer. . . . . 2.50 to 3.00
Sherbet, Footed . . . . . 5.00 to 6.00
Soup, Dish 16.00
Sugar, Oval. 7.50
Tumbler, 5 Oz.,
3 1/2 In. . . . . 8.00 to 12.50
Tumbler, 9 Oz.,
4 In. . . . . 10.00 to 15.00
Tumbler, Footed,
10 Oz., 5 In. 50.00

RED

Ashtray, Oval, 2 x 3 3/4 In. . . . 3.50
Candlestick, 2-Light,
4 1/2 In., Pair. 42.00

R

Radiance

New Martinsville Glass Company in New Martinsville, West Virginia, made Radiance pattern from 1936 to 1939. It was made of amber, crystal, Emerald Green, Ice Blue, and red. A few rare pieces were made in cobalt blue.

AMBER

Candlestick, 2-Light, Pair . . . 100.00
Cordial 30.00
Sugar & Creamer 30.00

CRYSTAL

Butter, Cover. 150.00
Cheese & Cracker Set,
11 In. 45.00
Cordial 20.00
Creamer 7.00
Cup. 5.50
Punch Cup. 6.00
Sugar & Creamer, Tray 35.00

EMERALD GREEN
Compote, 6 In. 65.00
Punch Bowl 130.00

ICE BLUE
Bowl, Flared, Footed,
10 In. 50.00
Bowl, Ruffled, 12 In. 50.00
Candleholder, 2-Light,
Pair 195.00
Cheese & Cracker Set,
11 In. . . . . 45.00 to 65.00
Cup & Saucer . . . . . 24.00 to 25.00
Plate, 8 In. 20.00
Plate, Punch Bowl, 14 In. . . . 65.00
Punch Cup 13.00
Relish, 3 Sections,
8 1/2 In. . . . . 37.50 to 55.00
Sugar 20.00
Sugar & Creamer . . 40.00 to 43.00
Vase, Ruffled, 12 In. 38.00

RED
Cake Plate, Footed 125.00
Candy Dish, Cover 295.00
Cheese & Cracker Set,
11 In. 65.00
Console Set, 3 Piece 155.00
Cordial 37.50
Creamer 20.00
Cruet, Stopper,
Individual . . . . . . 65.00 to 100.00
Dish, Mayonnaise,
2 Piece 70.00
Punch Cup 12.00
Relish, 3 Sections,
8 1/2 In. 45.00
Salt & Pepper 140.00
Saucer 7.50
Sugar & Creamer 45.00
Tray, Oval 40.00
Tumbler, 9 Oz. 25.00

Raindrops
Watch out for confusion with Raindrops and another pattern called Pear Optic or Thumbprint. The rounded, fingernail-shaped impressions of the Raindrops pattern are on the inside of the pieces, the other pattern has hexagonal depressions on the outside. Federal Glass Company made crystal and green Raindrops luncheon sets from 1929 to 1933.

CRYSTAL
Tumbler, 4 Oz., 3 In. 4.00
Whiskey, 1 7/8 In. 2.00
Whiskey, 1 Oz. 6.00

GREEN
Cup & Saucer 7.00
Tumbler, 5 In. . . . . . . 8.00 to 11.00
Whiskey, 1 7/8 In. 7.00

RASPBERRY BAND, see Laurel

REX, see No. 610

RIBBED, see Manhattan

Ribbon
Black, crystal, and green pieces were made in Ribbon pattern in the 1930s. It was made by the Hazel Atlas Glass Company.

Bowl, 4 In. . . . . 10.00 to 15.00
Creamer, Footed . . . 11.00 to 13.00
Cup 4.00

Cup & Saucer . . . . . . 7.50 to 10.00
Plate, 6 1/4 In. . . . . 2.00 to 3.00
Plate, 8 In. . . . . 4.00 to 4.50
Salt & Pepper. 20.00
Saucer. . . . . 2.00 to 3.00
Sherbet, Footed. . . . . . 4.50 to 6.00
Sugar, Footed. 11.00
Sugar & Creamer, Footed . . 25.00
Tumbler, 13 Oz.,
6 1/2 In. . . . . 20.00 to 25.00

**RIBBON CANDY,
see Pretzel**

Ring
Hocking Glass Company made Ring from 1927 to 1933. The pattern, also known as Banded Ring, sometimes has colored rings added to the clear crystal, blue, green, or pink glass. The colored rings were made in various combinations of black, blue, orange, pink, platinum, red, and yellow. Some solid red pieces also were made. The design is characterized by several sets of rings, each comprised of four rings. Circle, a similar Hocking pattern, has only one group of rings.

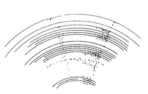

CRYSTAL
Cocktail Shaker,
11 1/2 In. . . . . 12.00 to 15.00
Decanter,
Stopper . . . . 20.00 to 32.50
Goblet, Platinum Rim,
9 Oz., 7 1/4 In. 7.00
Pitcher, 80 Oz.,
8 1/2 In. . . . . 15.00 to 18.00
Plate, 6 1/4 In. 2.50

Plate, Sandwich, Multicolored
Rings, 11 1/4 In. 9.50

Sherbet, Footed, 4 3/4 In. 4.50

Sugar & Creamer 8.00

Tumbler, 5 Oz., 3 1/2 In. 4.00

Tumbler, 9 Oz., 4 1/4 In. 4.00

Tumbler, Footed, 3 1/2 In. . . . 5.00

Whiskey, Multicolored
Rings, 1 1/2 Oz., 2 In. 8.00

GREEN

Cup & Saucer 8.00

Sandwich Server, Center
Handle 18.00

Tumbler, 5 Oz., 3 1/2 In. . . . 10.00

Tumbler, Footed, 5 1/2 In. . . . 9.00

Ring-Ding

Ring-Ding was made in 1932 by Hocking Glass Company of Lancaster, Ohio. Painted bands of green, orange, red, and yellow decorated the clear glass and gave the pattern its name.

CRYSTAL

Cocktail Shaker 25.00

Decanter, Stopper 12.00

Plate, 6 1/4 In. 3.00

Whiskey 5.00

Rock Crystal

Rock Crystal, sometimes called Early American Rock Crystal, was made in many solid colors by McKee Glass Company. Crystal was made in the 1920s; amber, blue-green, cobalt blue, crystal, green, pink, red, and yellow pieces were made in the 1930s.

AMBER

Cake Stand, Footed, 11 In. . . 25.00

Compote, Footed, 7 In. 35.00

CRYSTAL

Bowl, Footed,
12 1/2 In. . . . . 45.00 to 48.00

Bowl, Roll, 13 In. 28.00

Bowl, Scalloped, 9 In. 23.00

Candlestick, 2-Light, Pair. . . . 40.00

Candlestick, 3-Light 30.00

Candy Dish, Cover 55.00

Champagne, Footed, 6 Oz. . . 15.00

Cocktail, Footed,
3 1/2 Oz. . . . . . . 11.00 to 14.00

Compote, 7 In. 32.50

Console, Footed,
12 1/2 In. 48.00

Cordial, Footed, 1 Oz. 20.00

Cup. 16.00

Cup & Saucer 23.00

Goblet, 8 Oz. . . . . . 14.00 to 16.00

Pitcher, Tankard. 175.00

Plate, 6 In. 6.00

Plate, 8 1/2 In. . . . . . . 7.50 to 8.00

Relish, 2 Sections,
11 1/2 In. 28.00

Relish, 5 Sections,
12 1/2 In. . . . . 35.00 to 40.00

Relish, 6 Sections, 14 In. 29.00

Salt & Pepper, Bulbous 95.00

Saltshaker 32.00

Sandwich Server, Center
Handle 25.00

Saucer 6.00

Sherbet. 15.00

Sundae, Low-Footed, 6 Oz. . . 11.00

Tumbler, 5 Oz. . . . . . 6.00 to 15.00

Vase, Cornucopia. 70.00

Wine, 2 Oz. 12.00

Wine, 3 Oz. 18.00

GREEN

Bonbon, 7 1/2 In. 28.00

Bowl, Roll, 13 In. 35.00

PINK

Plate, 8 1/2 In. 12.00

Saucer. 8.00

RED

Bowl, Center Handle,
8 1/2 In. 150.00

Champagne, Footed, 6 Oz. . . 30.00

Cheese & Cracker Set 37.50

Cocktail, Footed, 3 1/2 Oz. . . 38.00

Cordial, Footed, 1 Oz. 65.00

Goblet, 8 Oz. . . . . . . 45.00 to 60.00

Plate, 7 1/2 In. 18.00

Plate, 8 1/2 In. 20.00

Plate, 10 1/2 In. 55.00

Sundae, Low-Footed, 6 Oz. . . 32.00

Tumbler, Concave, 9 Oz. 45.00

Tumbler, Straight, 12 Oz. . . . 55.00

Whiskey, 2 1/2 Oz. 48.00

Wine, 2 Oz. 45.00

Wine, 3 Oz. 50.00

ROPE, see Colonial Fluted

Rose Cameo

Rose Cameo was made by the Belmont Tumbler Company, Bellaire, Ohio, in 1933. It has been found only in green and only in six different pieces, three of which are bowls.

GREEN

Bowl, 5 In. . . . . 7.00 to 13.00

Plate, 7 In. 9.00

Sherbet. . . . . 9.00 to 10.00

Tumbler, Cone Footed,
5 In. . . . . 11.00 to 16.50

ROSE LACE, see Royal Lace

Rose Point

Rose Point was made by the Cambridge Glass Company of Cambridge, Ohio, from 1936 to 1953. The elaborate pattern was made in crystal and crystal with gold trim. A few rare pieces were made in red or amber.

CRYSTAL

Ashtray, 2 1/2 In. 50.00
Candlestick, 2-Light, 6 In.,
   Pair . . . . 110.00 to 150.00
Candlestick, 5 In. 42.50
Celery Dish, 3 Sections,
   12 In. 60.00
Cocktail, 3 Oz. . . . . . 31.00 to 35.00
Cordial, 1 Oz. 75.00
Creamer. 25.00
Cup & Saucer 50.00
Honey Dish, Cover. 150.00
Jam Jar, Cover, Liner 195.00
Oyster Cocktail,
   4 1/2 Oz. 42.50
Oyster Cocktail, Liner,
   4 1/2 Oz. 75.00
Plate, 6 1/2 In. 17.50
Relish, 3 Sections, 15 In. . . . 160.00
Relish, 5 Sections, 12 In. 85.00
Tumbler, 12 Oz., 5 1/4 In. . . 60.00
Tumbler, 15 Oz., 5 1/2 In. . . 75.00
Tumbler, Footed, 10 Oz. 32.50
Tumbler, Footed, 12 Oz. 35.00
Vase, Keyhole, 10 In. 135.00
Vase, Keyhole, 12 In. 150.00
Wine, 2 1/2 Oz. . . . 55.00 to 85.00

Rosemary

Rosemary, also called Cabbage Rose with Single Arch or Dutch Rose, was made by Federal Glass Company from 1935 to 1937. It was made in amber, green, and pink. Pieces with bases, like creamers or cups, are sometimes confused with Mayfair Federal because the molds used were those originally designed for the Mayfair pattern. The lower half of the Rosemary pieces are plain, the lower half of Mayfair Federal has a band of arches.

AMBER

Bowl, 5 In. . . . . 4.00 to 5.50
Bowl, 6 In. 25.00
Bowl, Vegetable, Oval,
   10 In. . . . . 10.00 to 15.00
Creamer, Footed. . . . 8.00 to 11.00
Cup. . . . . 5.00 to 6.00
Cup & Saucer . . . . . 8.00 to 10.00
Grill Plate . . . . 7.50 to 15.50
Plate, 6 3/4 In. . . . . . . 2.50 to 6.00
Plate, 9 1/2 In. . . . . . . 7.00 to 9.00
Platter, Oval,
   12 In. . . . . 10.50 to 16.00
Saucer. . . . . 1.50 to 4.50
Soup, Cream,
   5 In. . . . . 7.00 to 15.50
Sugar, Footed . . . . . . 8.00 to 9.00
Sugar & Creamer,
   Footed . . . . 14.00 to 20.00
Tumbler, 9 Oz.,
   4 1/4 In. 22.50

GREEN

Bowl, 5 In. 8.00
Bowl, 6 In. 29.00
Cup. 9.50
Plate, 6 3/4 In. . . . . . . 6.00 to 8.00
Plate, 9 1/2 In. 12.00
Saucer. . . . . 4.00 to 5.00
Soup, Cream, 5 In. 20.00
Sugar, Footed 12.00

PINK

Plate, 9 1/2 In. . . . . . 10.00 to 15.00
Saucer. 4.00

ROSEMARY, see also Mayfair Federal

Roulette

Anchor Hocking Glass Corporation made Roulette pattern from 1935 to 1939. Primarily green luncheon and beverage sets were manufactured, although some crystal pieces were made, as well as pink beverage sets. Collectors originally called the pattern Many Windows.

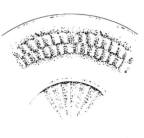

CRYSTAL

Bowl, 9 In. 20.00
Whiskey, 1 1/2 Oz.,
   2 1/2 In. 6.50

GREEN

Bowl, 9 In. 12.50
Cup. . . . . 4.00 to 6.50
Cup & Saucer . . . . . . 8.50 to 10.00
Pitcher, 64 Oz.,
   8 In. . . . . 35.00 to 45.00
Plate, 6 In. . . . . 3.00 to 3.50
Plate, 8 1/2 In. . . . . . . 5.00 to 5.50
Saucer. . . . . 3.50 to 4.00
Sherbet, Footed. 5.00
Tumbler, Cone Footed,
   10 Oz., 5 1/2 In. 22.00
Tumbler, Cone, 9 Oz.,
   4 1/8 In. 20.00
Tumbler, Footed, 10 Oz.,
   5 1/2 In. 25.00

PINK

Whiskey, 1 1/2 Oz.,
   2 1/2 In. . . . . 10.00 to 12.00

Round Robin

Sometimes a pattern was advertised by the wholesaler, but the manufacturer is unknown today. One of these is Round Robin, sometimes called Accordion Pleats. It was pictured as a luncheon set in the catalogs of the late 1920s and 1930s and offered in green, crystal, and iridescent marigold.

GREEN

Cup	5.00
Cup & Saucer	7.00
Plate, 6 In.	2.50
Plate, 8 In.	4.00
Sherbet, Footed	6.00
Sugar	6.50

Royal Lace

Royal Lace was made from 1934 to 1941. The popular pattern by Hazel Atlas Glass Company was made in cobalt blue, crystal, green, and pink, and in limited quantities in amethyst. It is sometimes called Gladiola or Rose Lace.

AMETHYST

Tumbler, Roly Poly	10.00

COBALT BLUE

Bowl, 5 In.	40.00
Bowl, Footed, 10 In.	60.00
Bowl, Vegetable, Oval, 11 In.	65.00 to 85.00
Butter, Cover	450.00 to 525.00
Candlestick, Ruffled, Pair	105.00 to 135.00
Cookie Jar, Cover	345.00
Creamer, Footed	50.00 to 55.00
Cup	35.00
Cup & Saucer	42.00 to 45.00
Grill Plate, 9 7/8 In.	42.00 to 50.00
Hot Toddy Set, 12 Piece	195.00
Pitcher, 48 Oz.	145.00 to 150.00
Pitcher, 68 Oz., 8 In.	225.00
Plate, 6 In.	12.00 to 17.00
Platter, Oval, 13 In.	65.00
Salt & Pepper	260.00 to 265.00
Sherbet, Footed	45.00
Sherbet, Metal Holder	28.00 to 35.00
Soup, Cream	38.00 to 47.00
Sugar	25.00 to 42.00
Sugar, Cover	210.00 to 215.00
Sugar & Creamer	64.00
Tumbler, 5 Oz., 3 1/2 In.	44.00 to 48.50
Tumbler, 9 Oz., 4 1/8 In.	35.00 to 47.50
Tumbler, 12 Oz., 4 7/8 In.	93.00

CRYSTAL

Bowl, 5 In.	13.00
Bowl, 10 In.	20.00 to 22.00
Butter, Cover	70.00
Candlestick, Rolled Edge, Pair	35.00
Candlestick, Ruffled, Pair	25.00
Cookie Jar, Cover	20.00 to 45.00
Creamer, Footed	8.00 to 12.00
Cup	4.00 to 9.00
Cup & Saucer	12.50 to 15.00
Grill Plate, 9 7/8 In.	12.00 to 18.00
Pitcher, 86 Oz., 8 In.	45.00

Pitcher, 96 Oz., 8 1/2 In.	48.00 to 50.00
Platter, Oval, 13 In.	18.00
Saucer	3.00 to 5.00
Sherbet, Footed	8.00 to 9.00
Soup, Cream	9.00 to 18.00
Sugar	8.00
Sugar, Cover	20.00 to 28.00
Tumbler, 5 Oz., 3 1/2 In.	15.00 to 20.00
Tumbler, 9 Oz., 4 1/8 In.	9.00 to 11.00

GREEN

Bowl, 5 In.	22.00 to 22.50
Bowl, 10 In.	28.00
Butter, Cover	45.00
Cookie Jar, Cover	75.00 to 125.00
Salt & Pepper	120.00
Sherbet, Footed	20.00 to 22.00
Soup, Cream	32.00
Sugar	15.00
Tumbler, 9 Oz., 4 1/8 In.	27.00

PINK

Bowl, 10 In.	24.00 to 40.00
Bowl, Footed, Ruffled, 10 In.	40.00 to 50.00
Bowl, Vegetable, Oval, 11 In.	35.00
Candlestick, Straight Edge, Pair	45.00
Cookie Jar, Cover	45.00 to 50.00
Cup	9.50
Cup & Saucer	19.00
Pitcher, 68 Oz., 8 In.	70.00
Platter, Oval, 13 In.	30.00 to 32.00
Salt & Pepper	58.00
Soup, Cream	24.00 to 27.50
Sugar	15.00
Sugar & Creamer	36.00
Tumbler, 9 Oz., 4 1/8 In.	16.00 to 17.50
Tumbler, 12 Oz., 4 7/8 In.	17.00

Royal Ruby

There is no reason to picture this pattern because it is the plain shape and bright red color that identifies it. Anchor Hocking Glass Corporation made it from 1939 to the 1960s and again in 1977. The same shapes were made in green and called by the pattern name Forest Green. Reproduction tumblers were made in 1977 and 1978.

Ashtray, Square,
4 1/4 In. . . . . 3.00 to 7.00
Ashtray Set, Graduated,
3 Piece 21.00
Bonbon, Leaf Shape,
6 1/2 In. 10.00
Bowl, 5 1/4 In. . . . . . . 5.00 to 6.00
Bowl, 7 1/2 In. 8.00
Bowl, 8 1/2 In. . . . . 14.00 to 25.00
Bowl, Oval, 8 In. 15.50
Bowl, Soup,
Dish . . . . 11.00 to 14.00
Bowl, Vegetable,
Oval, 11 In. 30.00
Cocktail, 3 1/2 Oz. . . 9.50 to 12.50
Creamer, Footed . . . 7.00 to 10.00
Cup. 6.00
Cup & Saucer . . . . 6.00 to 7.50
Cup & Saucer,
Square . . . . 5.50 to 7.00
Goblet, Ball Stem,
9 Oz. . . . . 8.00 to 9.00
Pitcher, Tilted,
22 Oz. . . . . 25.00 to 30.00
Pitcher, Tilted, 3 Qt. 35.00
Pitcher, Upright,
3 Qt. . . . . 40.00 to 45.00
Plate, 6 1/2 In. . . . . . . 2.00 to 3.50
Plate, 7 3/4 In. 7.50
Plate, 9 In. . . . . 9.00 to 9.50
Plate, 13 3/4 In. 19.50
Punch Bowl 34.00
Punch Cup 2.50
Punch Set, 10 Piece 70.00

Punch Set, 14 Piece 75.00
Saucer, Square. 2.00
Sherbet . . . . 5.50 to 8.00
Soup, Dish 10.00
Sugar. . . . . 6.00 to 8.00
Sugar, Footed,
Cover . . . . 13.00 to 15.50
Sugar & Creamer,
Footed . . . . 10.00 to 15.00
Tumbler, 5 Oz.,
3 1/2 In. . . . . 4.00 to 5.00
Tumbler, 9 Oz.,
4 1/8 In. . . . . 6.00 to 8.00
Tumbler, 12 Oz.,
4 7/8 In. . . . . 5.50 to 6.00
Tumbler, 13 Oz.,
5 3/8 In. 12.00
Tumbler, Footed,
2 1/2 Oz., 5 In. . . . 6.00 to 12.00
Vase, 9 In . . . . 14.00 to 15.00
Vase, Bulb, 9 In. 17.50
Vase, Hoover, 9 In. 15.00

RUSSIAN, see Holiday

S

S Pattern

Macbeth-Evans Glass Company made S Pattern, or Stippled Rose Band, from 1930 to 1935. It was made before 1932 in crystal, pink, topaz, and crystal with gold, blue, or platinum trim. The 1934 listing mentions red, green, and Monax. Other pieces were made in amber, ruby, Ritz Blue, and crystal with many colors of trim including amber, green, rose, platinum, red, silver, or white.

AMBER
Bowl, 5 1/2 In. 4.50
Cake Plate, 11 In. 36.00
Cake Plate, 13 In. 85.00
Creamer 6.00
Cup 4.00
Grill Plate, 10 1/2 In. 8.00
Plate, 6 In. 2.50
Plate, 8 In. 4.50

CRYSTAL
Bowl, Yellow Band,
5 1/2 In. . . . . 4.00 to 5.00
Creamer 6.00
Cup 3.00
Cup & Saucer 4.25
Cup & Saucer,
Yellow Band. 6.00
Plate, 8 In. 4.00
Plate, 9 1/4 In. 5.00
Plate, Yellow Band, 8 In. 3.00
Saucer, Yellow
Band . . . . 1.50 to 2.00
Sherbet, Yellow Band. 6.00
Sugar. 6.00
Sugar & Creamer. 10.00
Tumbler, 10 Oz., 4 1/4 In. 7.00

SAIL BOAT, see White Ship

SAILING SHIP, see White Ship

Sandwich Anchor Hocking

Many patterns were called Sandwich. Each company seemed to have one design with that name. The most popular were made by Anchor Hocking, Indiana Glass, and Duncan & Miller. The Anchor Hocking Glass Company Sandwich pattern was made from 1939 to 1964 and can be distinguished by the three lines around the edge of each petal. Pink and Royal Ruby were made from 1939 to 1940; crystal, Forest Green, and opaque white date from the 1950s and 1960s; amber from the 1960s.

A reproduction line was introduced in 1977 by another company in amber, blue, crystal, and Royal Ruby.

AMBER

Bowl, 8 1/2 In.	5.00
Bowl, 9 1/2 In.	25.00
Bowl, Deep, 9 1/4 In.	24.00
Bowl, Scalloped, 5 1/4 In.	6.00
Butter, Cover	35.00
Creamer	12.00
Creamer & Sugar	6.00
Plate, 7 In.	9.00
Plate, 9 In.	7.00
Salt & Pepper	38.00
Sandwich Plate, 12 In.	14.00

CRYSTAL

Bowl, 6 1/2 In.	7.50
Bowl, Oval, 8 1/4 In.	4.00 to 7.50
Bowl, Ruffled, 4 7/8 In.	5.00 to 6.00
Butter, Cover	32.00 to 45.00
Cookie Jar, Cover.	45.00
Creamer	6.00
Cup	2.50 to 3.00
Custard Cup	4.50 to 7.00
Plate, 7 In.	11.00
Plate, 8 In.	3.50
Plate, 9 In.	14.00
Punch Set, 8 Piece	40.00
Punch Set, 14 Piece	55.00 to 60.00
Sherbet, Footed	7.00 to 8.00
Sugar	6.00
Sugar, Cover	17.00 to 25.00
Sugar & Creamer	12.00
Tumbler, 3 Oz.	4.50 to 12.00

Tumbler, 5 Oz.	6.00
Tumbler, Footed, 9 Oz.	20.00 to 27.00

FOREST GREEN

Bowl, 8 In.	77.50
Bowl, Ruffled, 4 7/8 In.	3.00
Creamer.	22.50 to 25.00
Cup.	19.00
Cup & Saucer	27.00 to 32.50
Custard Cup, Liner.	4.00
Saucer	12.50
Sugar	22.00 to 27.50
Sugar & Creamer	42.00 to 44.00
Tumbler, 3 Oz.	3.50 to 5.50

ROYAL RUBY

Bowl, 6 In.	18.00

Sandwich Duncan & Miller

Sandwich Duncan & Miller is easy to recognize. The pattern was designed by Mr. Heisey's son-in-law. He added the diamond and H mark used by Heisey as part of the border design. The plates in this series have brown bottoms. The star in the center of the plate goes to the edge of the circle. Duncan & Miller had been making pattern No. 41 (Early American Lace Glass). In 1925 they started to sell Sandwich Glass. The pattern remained in production until 1955 when some of the molds were bought by other companies. The glass was made in crystal, green, amber, rose, ruby, and chartreuse (1949).

CRYSTAL

Basket, Handle, 6 1/2 In.	115.00
Bowl, 5 In.	10.00
Bowl, 7 In.	7.00
Candelabra Pair, 1-Light	145.00
Candlestick, 4 In.	27.50
Candlestick, 4 In.	25.00
Cheese Dish, Cover	95.00
Cruet.	35.00
Dish, Mayonnaise, Footed	25.00
Pitcher, Ice Lip, 64 Oz.	110.00
Plate, 7 In.	8.00
Plate, Handle, 6 In.	17.50
Relish, 2 Sections, Ring Handle	17.50
Relish, 3 Sections, 12 In.	27.50 to 37.00
Salt & Pepper, 2 1/2 In.	16.00
Sherbet.	22.00
Sugar & Creamer, Tray	10.00
Tray, Oval, 8 In.	20.00
Tumbler, Footed, 9 Oz.	21.00
Tumbler, Juice, Footed	10.00
Vase, Footed, 10 In.	65.00

GREEN

Bowl, Scalloped, 6 1/2 In.	30.00
Bowl, Scalloped, 8 In.	52.00
Cup.	15.00
Plate, 9 In.	58.00

Sandwich Indiana

Another Sandwich pattern was made by the Indiana Glass Company, Dunkirk, Indiana, from the 1920s through the 1980s. It can be distinguished by the single line around the flower petals. Only the colors changed through the years. Amber was made from the late 1920s to the 1970s, crystal in the late 1920s to the 1980s, light green in the 1930s, pink in the late 1920s through the 1930s, red from 1933 to the 1970s, and Teal Blue in the 1950s. The scroll design varies with the size of the plate. In

1969, reproduction dinner sets were made in amber, blue, crystal, green, and red. Other items have been reproduced in amber and light green since 1982.

CRYSTAL

Bowl, 7 In. 10.00
Candlestick, 8 1/2 In., Pair . . 60.00
Celery Dish, 10 1/2 In. 14.00
Cookie Jar, Cover 30.00
Cup & Saucer 5.00
Plate, 8 1/8 In. 4.00
Plate, 10 1/2 In. . . . . 8.00 to 12.00
Sherbet. 4.00

RED

Sugar, Large. 40.00

SAWTOOTH, see English Hobnail

SAXON, see Coronation

SCROLL & STAR, see Princess Feather

SHAMROCK, see Cloverleaf

Sharon

Sharon, or Cabbage Rose, was made by the Federal Glass Company from 1935 to 1939. The pattern was made in amber, crystal, green, and pink. A cheese dish was reproduced in 1976 in amber, blue, dark green, light green, and pink. Other items have been reproduced in various colors.

AMBER

Bowl, 5 In. . . . . 6.00 to 8.00
Bowl, 8 1/2 In. . . . . . 4.00 to 10.00
Bowl, 10 1/2 In. . . . 19.00 to 25.00
Bowl, Vegetable, Oval,
9 1/2 In. . . . . 14.00 to 17.00
Butter, Cover. . . . . . 40.00 to 50.00
Cake Plate, Footed,
11 1/2 In. 25.00
Candy Dish, Cover 35.00
Cheese Dish,
Cover . . . . .175.00 to 195.00
Creamer. . . . . 12.00 to 14.00
Cup. .9.00
Cup & Saucer 15.00
Jam Jar . . . . 30.00 to 35.00
Pitcher, Ice Lip, 80 Oz. 105.00
Plate, 6 In. . . . . 4.00 to 6.00
Plate, 7 1/2 In. . . . . . 14.00 to 16.00
Plate, 9 1/2 In. . . . . . . 9.00 to 11.00
Platter, Oval,
12 1/2 In. . . . . 13.00 to 18.00
Salt & Pepper . . . . . 37.00 to 40.00
Saucer. . . . . 5.00 to 5.50
Sherbet, Footed . . . 11.00 to 12.00
Soup, Cream 23.00
Soup, Dish 35.00
Sugar. 8.00
Sugar, Cover . . . . . . 26.00 to 30.00
Tumbler, Thin,
9 Oz., 4 1/8 In. 22.00
Tumbler, Thin,
12 Oz., 5 1/4 In. 40.00

CRYSTAL

Bowl, Vegetable,
Oval, 9 1/2 In. 20.00
Sherbet, Footed 15.00

GREEN

Bowl, 8 1/2 In. 18.00
Bowl, Vegetable,
Oval, 9 1/2 In. 29.00
Butter, Cover. . . . . .75.00 to 95.00
Cake Plate, Footed,
11 1/2 In. 42.00
Candy Dish, Cover 175.00
Creamer. 20.00
Plate, 6 In. 8.00
Plate, 7 1/2 In. 22.00
Plate, 9 1/2 In. 18.00
Platter, Oval, 12 1/2 In. 30.00
Salt & Pepper. 68.00
Soup, Cream . . . . . .32.00 to 45.00
Sugar. 15.00
Sugar, Cover . . . . . .37.00 to 50.00
Tumbler, Thick,
9 Oz., 4 1/8 In. 80.00

PINK

Bowl, 5 In. . . . . .8.50 to 13.00
Bowl, 6 In. . . . . .21.50 to 28.00
Bowl, 8 1/2 In. . . . .27.00 to 27.50
Bowl, 10 1/2 In. . . .32.00 to 37.50
Bowl, Vegetable, Oval,
9 1/2 In. . . . . .18.00 to 30.00
Butter, Cover. . . . . .42.00 to 50.00
Cake Plate, Footed,
11 1/2 In. . . . . . . .30.00 to 35.00
Candy Dish,
Cover. . . . . .32.00 to 50.00
Creamer . . . . .16.00 to 18.00
Cup 22.00
Cup & Saucer 28.00
Jam Jar. 150.00
Pitcher, 80 Oz. . 135.00 to 145.00
Plate, 6 In. . . . . .6.00 to 7.00
Plate, 7 1/2 In. . . . . .22.00 to 23.00
Plate, 9 1/2 In. . . . . .14.00 to 18.00
Platter, Oval,
12 1/2 In. . . . . . . .25.00 to 27.50
Salt & Pepper. . . . . .38.00 to 49.00
Saltshaker. 22.00
Saucer. . . . . .8.00 to 9.00
Sherbet, Footed. . . .11.50 to 14.00
Soup, Cream . . . . . .34.00 to 40.00
Soup, Dish . . . . .38.00 to 40.00
Sugar. 10.00
Sugar, Cover . . . . . .36.00 to 45.00

Sugar & Creamer,
Cover . . . . 30.00 to 46.00

Tumbler, Footed,
15 Oz., 6 1/2 In. 40.00

Tumbler, Thick,
9 Oz., 4 1/8 In. 38.50

Tumbler, Thin, 9 Oz.,
4 1/8 In. . . . . 30.00 to 45.00

Tumbler, Thin, 12 Oz.,
5 1/4 In. 40.00

SHEFFIELD, see Chinex Classic

SHELL, see Petalware

Shirley Temple

Shirley Temple is not really a pattern, but the dishes with the white enamel decoration picturing Shirley have become popular with collectors. The most famous were made as giveaways with cereal from 1934 to 1942. Several companies, including Hazel Atlas Glass Company and U.S. Glass, made the glassware. Sugars and creamers, bowls, plates, and mugs were made. The milk pitcher and mug have been reproduced since 1982 and the bowl has been reproduced since 1986. Other items with the Shirley Temple decal include a Fostoria Mayfair green sugar bowl and tea cup, a white mug, and an 8 7/8-inch Moderntone cobalt blue plate. In 1972 Libbey glass made six different sized tumblers.

BLUE

Bowl, Cereal 45.00
Creamer. . . . . 35.00 to 40.00
Mug . . . . 20.00 to 42.00
Plate 285.00
Sugar 48.00

Sierra

Sierra, or Pinwheel, was made by Jeannette Glass Company from 1931 to 1933. It is found in green, pink, and Ultramarine.

GREEN

Bowl, 5 1/2 In. . . . . 12.00 to 16.50
Bowl, 8 1/2 In. . . . . 25.00 to 30.00
Bowl, Vegetable,
Oval, 9 1/4 In. 90.00
Butter, Cover . . . . . 60.00 to 75.00
Creamer. 21.00
Cup. 11.00
Cup & Saucer . . . . . 19.00 to 22.00
Pitcher, 6 1/2 In. 110.00
Plate, 9 In. 18.00
Platter, Oval, 11 In. 45.00
Sugar 20.00
Sugar, Cover 40.00

PINK

Berry Set, 7 Piece 110.00
Bowl, 5 1/2 In. . . . . . 7.50 to 16.50
Bowl, 8 1/2 In. . . . . 15.00 to 20.00
Bowl, Vegetable,
Oval, 9 1/4 In. 65.00
Butter, Cover 30.00
Creamer. . . . . 10.00 to 20.00
Cup. . . . . 10.00 to 12.50
Cup & Saucer . . . . . 15.00 to 17.50
Plate, 9 In. . . . . 10.00 to 17.00

Platter, Oval,
11 In. . . . . 35.00 to 40.00
Saucer. 5.00
Sugar. . . . . 15.00 to 16.00
Tray, Serving, Handles,
10 1/4 In. . . . . . . 15.00 to 20.00

SMOCKING, see Windsor

SNOWFLAKE, see Doric

Spiral

It is easy to confuse Spiral, a Hocking Glass Company pattern, with Twisted Optic, made by Imperial. Ask to be shown examples of each, because even a picture will not be much help. Looking from the top to the base, Twisted Optic spirals right to left; Spiral twists left to right. There are a few pieces that are exceptions. Spiral pattern beverage and luncheon sets were manufactured from 1928 to 1930, mostly in green, although some pink pieces were made. It is also sometimes called Spiral Optic or Swirled Big Rib.

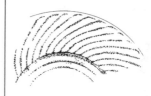

GREEN

Cup & Saucer 5.50
Ice Tub. 25.00
Plate, 6 In. . . . . 1.00 to 3.00
Plate, 8 In. . . . . 3.00 to 5.00
Platter, 12 In. 24.00
Sherbet. . . . . 2.00 to 3.00

• • • • • • • • • • • • • • • •

Never bid at an auction if you have not previewed the items.

• • • • • • • • • • • • • • • •

Spiral Flutes

Duncan & Miller Glass Company, Washington, Pennsylvania, made Spiral Flutes pattern. It was made of amber, crystal, and green glass in 1924, pink in 1926. A few pieces are reported with gold trim and in blue or Vaseline-colored glass.

AMBER
Soup, Dish.................8.00
CRYSTAL
Ashtray, Cigar Holder 27.00
Cocktail, Footed............9.00
Soup, Cream..............15.00
GREEN
Ashtray...................30.00
Compote, 4 3/8 In. 25.00
Dish, Grapefuit, Footed,
    6 3/4 In. 25.00
Nut Dish, Footed,
    Individual, 2 1/4 In. 14.00
Relish, 8 5/8 In. 15.00
Sauce, Cocktail............22.50

SPIRAL OPTIC,
    see Spiral

SPOKE, see Patrician

Sportsman Series

Hazel Atlas Glass Company made an unusual Depression glass pattern in the 1940s. It was made of cobalt blue, amethyst, or crystal with fired-on decoration. Although the name of the series was Sportsman, designs included golf, sailboats, hunting, angelfish, and a few strange choices like windmills. We list Windmill and White Ship separately, al-

though they are sometimes considered part of this pattern.

COBALT BLUE
Bowl, Fish, 6 In. 65.00
Cocktail Shaker, Fish 30.00
Cocktail Shaker, Golf......30.00
Cocktail Shaker, Polo......55.00
Ice Bowl, Polar Bear........16.00
Pitcher, Fish, Ice Lip........65.00
Pitcher, Spanish Dancers....55.00
Tumbler, Golf, 3 3/8 In 6.00
Tumbler, Polo, 4 7/8 In. 11.00
Tumbler, Polo, 8 Oz. 15.00

Spun

Spun was made by Imperial in 1935 in aqua, crystal, fired-on orange, red, and pastel colors.

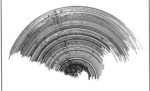

AQUA
Rose Bowl 45.00
Tumbler, Old Fashioned,
    5 In.....................7.00
Vase, 5 1/2 In. 15.00

Vase, 9 In. 65.00
Vase, Bud, 5 In...........45.00
RED
Rose Bowl 45.00
Vase, 9 In. 65.00

SQUARE, see Charm

Starlight

Starlight was made by the Hazel Atlas Company of Wheeling, West Virginia, from 1938 to 1940. Full table settings were made of cobalt blue, crystal, pink, and white. The pattern is pressed, not etched.

CRYSTAL
Plate, 8 1/2 In...............3.00
Plate, 9 In..................8.00
Saucer.....................1.50

WHITE
Cup.......................4.00
Cup & Saucer 6.00
Plate, 6 In. 3.00

STIPPLED, see Craquel

STIPPLED ROSE BAND, see
    S Pattern

• • • • • • • • • • • • • • •

When the weather is bad, the auction will probably be good. Brave storms and cold and attend the auctions in bad weather when the crowd is small and the prices low.

• • • • • • • • • • • • • • •

Strawberry

Strawberry and Cherry-Berry are similar patterns. The U.S. Glass Company made luncheon sets in this pattern in the early 1930s with strawberry decoration. Pink and green were the most commonly used colors, although crystal and iridescent marigold pieces were also made.

CRYSTAL
Dish, Pickle, Oval, 8 In...... 25.00
Sugar, Small............... 12.00
GREEN
Sugar 35.00
Sugar, Cover, Large 90.00
PINK
Pitcher,
   7 3/4 In....... 135.00 to 175.00
Plate, 6 In................ 11.00
Sherbet 9.50
Tumbler, 8 Oz., 3 5/8 In. ... 30.00

STRAWBERRY, see also Cherry-Berry

Sunburst

Crystal dinner sets were made in Sunburst pattern from 1938 to 1941 by Jeannette Glass Company of Jeannette, Pennsylvania.

CRYSTAL
Bowl, 4 3/4 In. 6.00
Bowl, 8 1/2 In. 17.00
Bowl, 10 1/4 In. 25.00
Candleholder, 2-Light,
   Pair 18.00
Creamer, Footed 12.00
Cup & Saucer 15.00
Plate, 9 In. 15.00
Sherbet, Footed 14.00

Sunflower

Sunflower was made by Jeannette Glass Company, Jeannette, Pennsylvania, in the late 1920s and early 1930s. It is most commonly found in pink and two shades of green. The darker green was used for cake plates given as a premium in sacks of flour. Small quantities of Delphite pieces also were made.

GREEN
Ashtray, 5 In.............. 14.50
Cake Plate, Footed,
   10 In. .... 8.00 to 14.00
Plate, 9 In. .... 12.00 to 16.00
Sugar & Creamer 40.00
Tumbler, Footed,
   8 Oz., 4 3/4 In. . . 25.00 to 35.00
PINK
Creamer.................. 15.00
Cup.............. 9.00 to 13.50
Plate, 9 In. 14.50

Swankyswigs

In October 1933, Kraft Cheese Company began to market cheese spreads in decorated, reusable glass tumblers. The tumbler was made in a 5-ounce size. It had a smooth beverage lip and a permanent color decoration. The designs were tested and changed as public demand indicated. Hazel Atlas Glass Company made the glasses, which were decorated by hand by about 280 girls, working in shifts around the clock. In 1937 a silk screen process was developed and the Tulip design was made by this new, faster method. The glasses were made thinner and lighter in weight. The decorated Swankyswigs were discontinued from 1941 to 1946, the war years. They were made again in 1947 and were continued through 1958. Then plain glasses were used for most of the cheese, although a few specially decorated Swankyswigs have been made since that time.

ANTIQUE
Black..................... 4.00
Blue...................... 4.00
Brown 4.00
Green 3.00
Red 10.00
BAND NO. 2
Red & Black.............. 3.00
BAND NO. 3
Blue & White.............. 3.00
BUSTLIN' BETSY
Blue..................... 4.00
Brown .... 3.50 to 4.00
Green 10.00
Orange 3.50
Red .... 3.50 to 10.00
Yellow 3.50

CARNIVAL
Red...................... 5.00

CHECKERBOARD
Blue 20.00
Green.................... 24.00
Red...................... 20.00

DAISY
Red, White & Green 10.00

FORGET-ME-NOT
Dark Blue.......... 2.75 to 10.00
Light Blue .... 2.75 to 3.00
Red...................... 3.00
Yellow.................... 3.00

KIDDIE CUP
Blue 20.00
Green............. 4.00 to 10.00
Red............... 3.50 to 4.00

POSY
Cornflower No. 2, Red 3.00

POSY CORNFLOWER
No. 1, Light Blue........... 3.00
No. 2, Dark Blue........... 3.00
No. 2, Light Blue........... 3.00
No. 2, Yellow 3.00
Red...................... 10.00

POSY CORNFLOWER NO. 1
Light Blue 3.00

POSY TULIP
Red...................... 3.00

POSY VIOLET
Violet .... 3.00 to 4.00

SAILBOAT NO. 2
Red.............. 4.00 to 18.00

STARS NO. 1
Green.................... 4.00

STARS NO. 1
Orange................... 20.00

TULIP NO. 1
Black............. 3.00 to 10.00
Dark Blue................. 4.00
Green............. 3.00 to 5.00
Red............... 4.00 to 5.00

TULIP NO. 2
Red...................... 22.00

TULIP NO. 3
Dark Blue................ 10.00

Light Blue................ 10.00
Orange.................... 3.00
Yellow.................... 3.00

SWEET PEAR, see Avocado

Swirl

Swirl, sometimes called Double Swirl or Petal Swirl, was made by Jeannette Glass Company during 1937 and 1938. Ultramarine, in a variety of shades, was the most commonly used color, but amber, Delphite, Ice Blue, and pink were also used. Some pieces have a smooth edge while others have a flower petal rim.

AMBER
Cup & Saucer 4.00
Plate, 8 In. 4.00
Plate, 9 1/4 In............. 6.00

DELPHITE
Cup...................... 4.00
Cup & Saucer 6.50
Platter, Oval, 12 In. 14.00
Sugar & Creamer, Cover 10.00

ICE BLUE
Creamer.................. 6.00
Platter, Oval, 12 In. 13.00
Soup, Dish, Handle... 7.00 to 8.00

PINK
Bowl, 5 1/4 In. 4.00
Butter, Cover............ 160.00
Candleholder, 2-Light 35.00
Candy Dish,
  Footed .... 10.00 to 12.00
Coaster................... 8.00

Cup............... 3.50 to 5.00
Cup & Saucer 6.00
Plate, 6 1/2 In. 5.00
Plate, 7 1/4 In............. 4.00
Plate, 8 In. 4.00
Plate, 9 1/4 In............. 6.00
Plate, 10 1/2 In.......... 13.00
Plate, Sandwich, 12 1/2 In. . 15.00
Saucer.................... 1.00
Soup, Dish, Lug
  Handle.......... 27.00 to 29.00
Sugar, Cover .... 4.50 to 10.00

ULTRAMARINE
Bowl, 5 1/4 In. ..... 7.00 to 13.00
Bowl, 9 In. .... 22.00 to 40.00
Candy Dish, Footed 10.00
Creamer.......... 13.00 to 15.00
Cup............. 12.00 to 14.00
Cup & Saucer 19.00
Plate, 6 1/2 In. 6.50
Plate, 7 1/4 In............. 7.00
Plate, 9 1/4 In..... 15.00 to 16.50
Plate, Sandwich, 12 1/2 In. . 25.00
Platter, Oval, 12 In........ 10.00
Salt & Pepper............ 55.00
Saucer.................... 5.00
Sherbet, Footed.... 10.00 to 17.50
Soup, Dish, Tab Handle.... 30.00
Sugar, Footed....... 8.00 to 14.00
Sugar & Creamer... 24.00 to 29.50
Tumbler, 9 Oz., 4 In. 27.00
Tumbler, 13 Oz.,
  5 1/8 In. 125.00
Tumbler, Footed, 9 Oz. 29.00
Vase, Footed, 8 1/2 In...... 17.00

Swirl Fire-King
Swirl Fire-King is named for its wide swirled border. It was made in blue, Jadite, pink, white with gold trim, and ivory with trim from 1955 to the 1960s. Other related sections in this book are Alice, Fire-King, Jane-Ray, Charm, Turquoise Blue, and Wheat.

in amber, blue, crystal, and green. The molds were later used for the Madrid pattern.

BLUE
Creamer 6.50
Plate, 7 3/8 In. 5.75
Plate, 9 1/8 In. 7.00
Saucer .... .50
Sugar 5.00
Sugar & Creamer 12.00

IVORY
Cup & Saucer .... 2.25 to 2.50
Plate, 9 1/8 In. 2.00
Saucer .... .25
Soup, Dish, 7 5/8 In. 2.00

JADITE
Creamer 5.00
Cup 3.00

PINK
Bowl, 4 7/8 In. 4.75
Bowl, Vegetable, 8 1/4 In. .. 11.00
Creamer 6.50
Cup 6.00
Cup & Saucer 7.00
Plate, 7 3/8 In. 5.75
Plate, 9 1/8 In. ...... 6.00 to 7.00
Plate, 11 In. .... 10.00 to 14.00
Saucer .... .50
Sugar, Cover 5.50

WHITE
Plate, 7 1/2 In. 3.00
Plate, 10 In. 4.00

SWIRLED BIG RIB, see Spiral

SWIRLED SHARP RIB, see Diana

Sylvan
Sylvan is often called Parrot or Three Parrot because of the center pattern on the plates. It was made by Federal Glass Company in 1931 and 1932

AMBER
Sherbet, Cone,
  Footed......... 16.00 to 20.00
Tumbler, Footed,
  5 3/4 In. 110.00

BLUE
Relish, 3 Sections, Handle... 40.00

GREEN
Bowl, 8 In................. 65.00
Butter.................... 52.50
Cup.............. 26.00 to 30.00
Cup & Saucer .... 45.00 to 50.00
Grill Plate, Square,
  10 1/2 In........ 30.00 to 33.00
Hot Plate, 5 In. 625.00
Plate, 7 1/2 In. 35.00
Plate, 9 In. .... 45.00 to 48.00
Platter, 11 In. ..... 47.50 to 50.00
Salt & Pepper 185.00
Sugar 30.00
Sugar & Creamer 80.00

T

TASSEL, see Princess

Tea Room
The very Art Deco design of Tea Room has made it popular with a group of collectors; it is even called Moderne Art by some. The Indiana Glass Company, Dunkirk, Indiana, made it from 1926 to 1931. Dinner sets were made of amber, crystal, green, and pink glass.

CRYSTAL
Sundae, Footed............70.00

GREEN
Candlestick, Pair...........75.00
Creamer...................10.00
Ice Bucket .... 60.00 to 65.00
Mustard, Cover...........235.00
Pitcher, Footed,
  64 Oz.................145.00
Salt & Pepper, Footed 75.00
Sugar.....................16.00
Sundae, Footed............75.00
Tray, Center Handle.......165.00
Tumbler, Footed,
  6 Oz., 4 3/4 In. 55.00
Tumbler, Footed,
  8 Oz., 5 1/2 In. 32.00
Tumbler, Footed,
  12 Oz., 6 1/16 In. 85.00
Vase, Ruffled, 6 1/2 In. 145.00
Vase, Ruffled, 9 1/2 In. 175.00

PINK
Creamer.......... 15.00 to 27.50
Pitcher, Footed,
  64 Oz.................165.00
Sugar............ 15.00 to 20.00
Sugar, Rectangular 25.00
Sugar & Creamer, Tray 85.00
Sundae, Footed............23.00
Tray, Rectangular 65.00
Vase, Ruffled, 6 1/2 In. 145.00

Tear Drop

Tear Drop, a pattern available in full dinnerware sets, was made by Duncan & Miller Glass Company, Washington, Pennsylvania, from 1934 to 1955. It was made only in crystal.

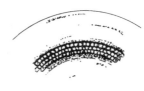

Ashtray, 3 In.	9.50
Ashtray, 5 In.	12.00
Basket, Oval, 10 In.	100.00
Butter, Metal Cover	12.00
Goblet, 7 In.	14.50
Plate, 10 1/2 In.	40.00
Plate, Handles, 6 In.	6.00
Relish, 2 Sections, Handle, 6 In.	9.50
Relish, 3 Sections, Handle, 11 In.	22.50
Relish, 5 Sections, 12 In.	29.50
Sugar, Open Handle, Large	9.00
Sugar & Creamer, Individual	20.00

Terrace

Terrace was made by Duncan & Miller in 1955 in amber, blue, crystal, and ruby.

BLUE

Plate, 2 Handles, 5 In.	30.00

CRYSTAL

Bowl, 5 In.	12.50
Cordial	45.00
Plate, 7 1/2 In.	8.50

RUBY

Ashtray, Square	35.00
Creamer	42.50

Thistle

Thistle pattern was made by Macbeth-Evans Glass Company from 1929 to 1930. The pattern pictures large thistles primarily on pink pieces, but green, crystal, and yellow dishes were also made.

CRYSTAL

Soup, Dish, Lug Handle	15.00

GREEN

Bowl, 5 1/2 In.	30.00
Cup	22.00
Plate, 8 In.	18.00

PINK

Bowl, 5 1/2 In.	20.00 to 27.00
Plate, 8 In.	7.50

THREADING, see Old English

THREE PARROT, see Sylvan

THUMBPRINT, see Pear Optic

Tradition

Imperial Glass Company of Bellaire, Ohio, made Tradition pattern glass in the 1930s. It was made in amber, amethyst, blue, crystal, green, pink, and red.

AMBER

Cocktail, 5 Oz.	12.00
Creamer	12.00
Goblet, 10 Oz.	7.00 to 9.00
Salt & Pepper	20.00 to 25.00
Sherbet	3.00 to 12.00
Sugar	12.00
Tumbler, 12 Oz.	9.00 to 10.00
Wine	3.00

AMETHYST

Creamer	20.00
Goblet, 10 Oz.	10.50
Plate, 8 In.	8.50
Sherbet	10.00
Sugar	20.00
Tumbler, 12 Oz.	15.00

BLUE

Bowl, Baked Apple, 6 In.	12.00
Goblet, 10 Oz.	18.00 to 20.00
Goblet, Juice	25.00
Plate, 8 In.	12.00
Sherbet	9.00 to 15.00
Tumbler, 12 Oz.	13.00 to 22.00
Wine	13.00 to 15.00

CRYSTAL

Pitcher, 54 Oz.	45.00
Sherbet	15.00

Tumbler, 12 Oz.... 10.00 to 13.00
Tumbler, Juice 15.00
Wine 23.00

GREEN
Goblet, 10 Oz. 20.00
Pitcher, 54 Oz. 85.00
Sherbet .... 12.50 to 15.00

PINK
Goblet, 10 Oz. 20.00
Pitcher, 54 Oz. 160.00
Sherbet 13.00
Tumbler, 12 Oz........... 20.00
Tumbler, Juice 15.00

RED
Sherbet .... 10.00 to 15.00
Tumbler, 12 Oz ... 16.00 to 20.00
Tumbler, Juice 17.00
Wine .... 20.00 to 24.00

TREE OF LIFE, see Craquel

Trojan
The Fostoria Glass Company made Trojan. The etched glass dishes were made in rose from 1929 to 1935, topaz from 1929 to 1938, and Gold Tint from 1938 to 1944. It was also made in green. Crystal bases were used on some pieces from 1931 to 1944.

ROSE
Candy Dish, Cover,
  Footed, 1/4 Lb. 215.00

• • • • • • • • • • • • • •

When moving, remember there is no insurance coverage for breakage if the items are not packed by the shipper.

• • • • • • • • • • • • • •

TOPAZ
Bowl, 5 In................45.00
Bowl, 6 In................45.00
Candleholder, 2 In., Pair 45.00
Candleholder, 3 In., Pair 45.00
Candy Dish, Cover,
  Footed, 1/2 Lb.........125.00
Compote, 6 In.............60.00
Gravy Boat, Liner 295.00
Liner, For
  Grapefruit Dish..........45.00
Sweetmeat, 2 Handles......25.00
Tumbler, Footed, 9 Oz.,
  5 1/4 In.................29.50
Tumbler, Footed, 12 Oz.,
  6 In. 24.00
Wine.....................85.00

Tulip
Tulip pattern pictures the side of a tulip in a very stylized border. It was made by the Dell Glass Company of Millville, New Jersey, during the 1930s. Amber, amethyst, blue, crystal, and green pieces were made.

AMETHYST
Bowl, 6 In.................9.00
Bowl, Oval, Oblong........25.00
Cup......................8.00
Sugar 12.50

CRYSTAL
Bowl, 7 1/2 In. 10.00
Grease Jar 15.00
Mixing Bowl, 3 Qt. 16.50

Turquoise Blue
Turquoise Blue, one of the patterns made by Anchor Hocking Glass Corporation, is a plain pattern named for its color. Mixing bowls were made in 1-pt., 1-qt., 2-qt., and 3-qt. sizes. It was made in the 1950s. Related sections in this book are Alice, Charm, Fire-King, Jadite, Jane-Ray, Peach Lustre, Philbe, Swirl Fire-King, and Wheat.

Ashtray, 3 1/2 In. 6.00
Ashtray, 4 5/8 In. 8.00
Bowl, 4 1/2 In. ...... 4.00 to 5.00
Bowl, 5 In. ...... 8.50 to 10.00
Bowl, 6 5/8 In. ..... 8.00 to 15.00
Bowl, Vegetable,
  8 In........... 12.00 to 14.00
Creamer...................5.00
Cup......................3.00
Cup & Saucer .... 4.00 to 5.00
Egg Plate,
  9 3/4 In. .... 13.00 to 14.00
Mixing Bowl, 2 Qt.........12.50
Mixing Bowl, 3 Qt.........10.00
Mixing Bowl, Tear Shape,
  1 Pt...................11.00
Mixing Bowl, Tear Shape,
  1 Qt. 8.00
Mixing Bowl, Tear Shape,
  2 Qt...................13.00
Mixing Bowl, Tear Shape,
  3 Qt. 25.00
Mug...............8.00 to 10.00
Plate, 6 1/8 In.......8.00 to 10.00
Plate, 7 In. ....9.00 to 10.00
Plate, 9 In. .... 5.00 to 9.00
Plate, 10 In. .... 15.00 to 26.00
Plate, Cup Indentation,
  9 In.............. 5.50 to 9.00
Relish, 3 Sections,
  11 1/8 In. .... 7.00 to 11.00
Roaster, 10 3/4 In. 28.00
Soup, Dish,
  6 5/8 In. .... 13.00 to 22.00
Sugar....................5.00
Sugar & Creamer 10.00

Twisted Optic

Twisted Optic is the pattern sometimes confused with Spiral. Be sure to look at the information about that pattern. Imperial Glass Company made Twisted Optic luncheon sets from 1927 to 1930 in amber, blue, canary yellow, two shades of green, and pink.

AMBER
Candleholder, 3 In.,
Pair . . . . 15.00 to 27.00
Console, 11 1/2 In. 34.00
Plate, 6 In. 7.50
Plate, 8 In. 7.50
Sherbet. 6.00

GREEN
Candy Dish,
Cover . . . . 20.00 to 25.00
Plate, 6 In. 1.00
Plate, 7 In. 3.00
Plate, 8 In. . . . . 1.50 to 4.00
Sherbet. . . . . 3.50 to 6.00

PINK
Sherbet 7.00
Sugar 6.00
Tumbler, 9 Oz., 4 1/2 In. 6.00

V

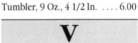

VERNON, see No. 616

Versailles

Versailles by Fostoria Glass Company was made in many colors during the years of its production, 1928 to 1944. Azure blue, green, and rose were made from 1928 to 1944, topaz from 1929 to

1938, and Gold Tint from 1938 to 1944. Crystal bases were used with colored glass from 1931 to 1944.

BLUE
Bowl, 5 In. 30.00
Bowl, Whipped Cream,
Handle 42.50
Candleholder, Pair 95.00
Champagne, 6 In. . . 32.00 to 37.50
Compote, 6 In. 110.00
Compote, 7 In. 70.00
Dish, Grapefruit 100.00
Dish, Grapefruit, 2 Piece . . .195.00
Goblet, 6 In. 39.00
Mayonnaise 95.00
Pail, Whipped Cream,
Handle 195.00
Plate, 6 In. 9.50
Plate, 8 3/4 In. 22.50
Plate, 10 1/4 In. 95.00
Salt & Pepper 225.00
Saucer, After Dinner. 25.00
Tumbler, Footed,
5 Oz., 4 1/2 In. 35.00
Tumbler, Footed,
12 Oz., 6 In. 42.00
Vase, 8 In. 275.00
Wine. 75.00

GREEN
Cake Plate, Handle,
10 1/2 In. 40.00
Dish, Mayonnaise,
Oval, 2 Piece 67.50
Ice Bucket 85.00
Jug, Footed 295.00
Plate, 7 1/2 In. 14.00
Relish, 3 Sections,
7 1/2 In. 35.00
Relish, 4 Sections 37.50
Sauce, Oval, 6 In. 67.50
Soup, Dish 75.00

Sugar & Creamer. 35.00
Tray, Service 295.00
Tumbler, Footed,
12 Oz., 6 In. . . . . .30.00 to 45.00
Vase, 9 1/4 In. 125.00

ROSE
Cup & Saucer 32.50
Dish, Grapefruit, Liner 165.00
Ice Bucket 110.00
Plate, 9 1/2 In. 40.00
Relish, 2 Sections,
8 1/2 In. 37.50
Sugar, Individual 75.00
Tumbler, Footed, 12 Oz.,
6 In. 35.00

**VERTICAL RIBBED, see
Queen Mary**

Vesper

Vesper was made by the Fostoria Glass Company of Ohio and West Virginia from 1926 to 1934. Dinner sets were made in amber, blue, crystal, and green.

AMBER
Bowl, 6 1/2 In. 24.00
Candleholder, 2 In. 25.00
Candleholder, 4 In., Pair . . . 30.00
Champagne 18.00

Cocktail 25.00
Compote, 7 In. 45.00
Cup, Footed 15.00
Cup & Saucer 22.50
Dish, Grapefruit 45.00
Goblet, Footed,
  12 Oz. . . . . 24.00 to 30.00
Ice Bucket 95.00
Pitcher, Footed. 275.00
Plate, 6 In. 5.00
Plate, 7 1/2 In. . . . . . 7.50 to 12.50
Plate, 8 1/2 In. 9.50
Plate, 10 1/2 In. 32.00
Platter, Oval, 15 In. 150.00
Tumbler, Footed, 12 Oz. . . . 22.50
Whiskey 60.00

GREEN

Bouillon, Footed. 16.00
Bouillon, Underplate 22.50
Bowl, 5 1/2 In. 12.00
Bowl, 6 1/2 In. 20.00
Bowl, Vegetable, Oval,
  9 In. 45.00
Candleholder, 4 In., Pair 40.00
Candy Dish, Cover. 125.00
Champagne 18.00
Chop Plate, 13 In. 55.00
Compote, 7 In. 30.00
Creamer 17.50
Cup & Saucer . . . . . 20.00 to 22.50
Dish, Grapefruit,
  2 Piece 110.00
Finger Bowl 18.00
Oyster Cocktail. 27.50
Pitcher, Footed. 295.00
Plate, 6 In. 4.50
Plate, 9 1/2 In. 17.50
Plate, 10 1/2 In. 30.00
Platter, 12 In. . . . . 60.00 to 100.00
Platter, Oval, 15 In. 125.00
Sauce Boat, Liner 95.00
Sauce Boat, Underplate. . . . 145.00
Saucer 5.00
Sherbet 18.00
Soup, Cream. 17.50
Sugar & Creamer, Cover. . . 175.00

Tumbler, Footed, 5 Oz. 22.50
Tumbler, Footed, 12 Oz. 29.50
Whiskey, 2 1/2 Oz. 45.00
Wine. 37.50

Victory

The Diamond Glass-Ware Company, Indiana, Pennsylvania, made Victory pattern from 1929 to 1932. It is known in amber, black, cobalt blue, green, and pink. A few pieces have gold trim.

AMBER

Bowl, 6 1/2 In. 10.50
Plate, 6 In. 6.50
Sandwich Server, Center
  Handle, 11 In. 20.00

COBALT BLUE

Bowl, 6 1/2 In. 40.00
Bowl, 8 1/2 In. 55.00
Cup & Saucer 45.00
Gravy Boat, Liner 375.00
Plate, 8 In. 30.00
Sugar & Creamer 95.00

GREEN

Bowl, 6 1/2 In. 11.00
Cup. 7.00
Cup & Saucer 11.00
Plate, 8 In. 7.00
Plate, 9 In. 16.00

PINK

Cup. . . . . 6.00 to 7.00
Cup & Saucer 12.00
Dish, Mayonnaise, Footed,
  2 Piece 50.00
Plate, 7 In. 6.00
Sandwich Server, Center
  Handle, 11 In. . . . 25.00 to 27.00

Vitrock

Vitrock is both a kitchenware and a dinnerware pattern. It has a raised flowered rim and so is often called Floral Rim or Flower Rim by collectors. It was made by Hocking Glass Company from 1934 to 1937 and resembles embossed china. It was made in white, sometimes with fired-on colors, in solid red or green, and with decal-decorated centers.

WHITE

Bowl, 5 1/8 In. 4.00
Cup & Saucer . . . . . . 5.00 to 6.00
Mixing Bowl, 7 1/2 In. 6.50
Mixing Bowl, 10 1/2 In. 14.00
Sugar & Creamer 8.00

VIVID BANDS, see Petalware

W

WAFFLE, see Waterford

Waterford

Waterford, or Waffle, pattern was made by Anchor Hocking Glass Corporation from 1938 to 1944. Crystal and pink are the most common colors; yellow and white were used less extensively. Some of the opaque white pieces also have fired-on pink and green. In the 1950s some Forest Green pieces were made.

CRYSTAL

Ashtray.....................5.00
Bowl, 4 3/4 In..............7.00
Bowl, 5 1/2 In............18.00
Bowl, 8 1/4 In......9.00 to 12.00
Butter, Cover.....18.00 to 25.00
Cake Plate, Handle,
   10 1/4 In..........4.00 to 9.00
Candy Dish, Cover, 9 In.....45.00
Coaster, 4 In.........2.00 to 3.00
Creamer............4.00 to 5.00
Cup.......................6.00
Goblet, 5 1/4 In.....8.00 to 15.00
Goblet, 5 5/8 In............16.50
Pitcher, Tilted, 42 Oz.......23.00
Plate, 6 In..................2.50
Plate, 7 1/8 In......2.00 to 5.50
Plate, 9 5/8 In.....5.00 to 10.00
Plate, Sandwich,
   13 3/4 In........6.00 to 10.00
Relish, 5 Sections,
   13 3/4 In................15.00
Salt & Pepper, Metal
   Tops............8.00 to 10.00
Salt & Pepper, Red
   Plastic Tops.......3.00 to 3.50
Saucer.............1.50 to 2.00
Sherbet, Footed.....2.00 to 6.00
Sugar..............4.00 to 5.00
Sugar, Cover...............8.00
Sugar & Creamer, Cover....15.00

GREEN

Plate, Sandwich, 13 3/4 In...24.00
Relish, White Insert,
   5 Sections, 13 3/4 In.....45.00

PINK

Bowl, 4 3/4 In.............10.00
Bowl, 5 1/2 In.............22.00
Creamer..................10.00
Cup.......................14.00
Goblet, 5 1/4 In..........125.00

Pitcher, Tilted, 80 Oz.....180.00
Plate, 9 5/8 In.............18.00
Plate, Sandwich, 13 3/4 In...24.00
Saucer.............5.00 to 6.00
Sugar, Cover..............34.00
Tumbler, Footed, 10 Oz.,
   4 7/8 In.................20.00

WEDDING BAND, see Moderntone

WESTMORELAND SAND-WICH, see Princess Feather

Wheat

Wheat glass was made by Anchor Hocking Glass Corporation from 1962 to about 1967. It is part of the Fire-King Oven Ware line. A few pieces were given added decoration. Another pattern of glass called Wheat was made by Federal Glass Company in the 1930s, but only the Anchor Hocking Glass is listed here.

WHITE

Bowl, 4 5/8 In..............3.00
Casserole, Knob Cover,
   1 1/2 Qt.................12.00
Cup.......................3.00
Plate, 10 In...............5.00
Snack Set, Box, 8 Piece.....20.00

Whirly-Twirly

Anchor Hocking made Whirly-Twirly pattern in the 1940s. It was Forest Green or red.

RED

Pitcher, 3 Qt..............50.00
Tumbler, Juice............4.50

Water Set, 9 Piece.........90.00

WHITE SAIL, see White Ship

White Ship

White Ship, also called Sailing Ship, Sail Boat, or White Sail, is really part of the Sportsman series made by Hazel Atlas in 1938. The ships are enamel decorations on cobalt blue glass.

BLUE

Cocktail Shaker...........22.50
Cup & Saucer............35.00
Pitcher, Ice Lip, 36 Oz.....45.00
Plate, 9 In...............40.00
Tumbler, 5 Oz.....10.00 to 14.00
Tumbler, 10 Oz., 4 7/8 In...22.00
Tumbler, Roly Poly,
   4 1/2 Oz.........9.00 to 11.00

WILDFLOWER, see No. 618

WILDROSE, see Dogwood

WILDROSE WITH APPLE BLOSSOM, see Flower Garden with Butterflies

---

Windmill

Windmill, or Dutch, is a part of the Sportsman series made by Hazel Atlas in 1938. Of course it pictures a landscape with a windmill.

• • • • • • • • • • • • • • •

Decorated glasses given as promotions often fade in sunlight.

• • • • • • • • • • • • • • •

Ashtray 28.00
Cocktail Shaker . . . 25.00 to 26.00
Ice Bowl . . . . 25.00 to 27.00
Pitcher, 8 1/2 In. 25.00
Tumbler, 4 5/8 In. 11.00
Tumbler, Roly Poly,
    6 Oz. . . . . 9.00 to 10.00
Tumbler, Roly Poly,
    6 Sets 45.00

Windsor

Windsor pattern, also called Diamond, Smocking, or Windsor Diamond, was made by Jeannette Glass Company, Jeannette, Pennsylvania, from 1936 to 1946. The pattern is most easily found in crystal, green, and pink, although pieces were made of Amberina, blue, Delphite, and red.

• • • • • • • • • • • • • • •
If you receive a package of glass antiques during cold weather, let it sit inside for a few hours before you unpack it. The glass must return to room temperature slowly or it may crack.
• • • • • • • • • • • • • • •

CRYSTAL
Bowl, 4 3/4 In. . . . . . . 5.00 to 6.00
Bowl, 5 In. 4.50
Bowl, Handles, 8 In. 4.00
Butter, Cover . . . . . 22.00 to 30.00
Candleholder, 3 In., Pair 14.00
Compote. . . . . 16.00 to 18.00
Creamer. 3.00
Cup. 3.25
Pitcher, 16 Oz.,
    4 1/2 In. . . . . 8.00 to 19.00
Plate, Handle, 10 1/4 In. 5.50
Platter, Oval,
    11 1/2 In. . . . . 3.00 to 6.00
Powder Jar, Cover 9.00
Relish, 2 Sections,
    11 1/2 In. 6.00
Tumbler, 5 Oz., 3 1/4 In. 4.00
Tumbler, 9 Oz., 5 In. 3.00
Tumbler, Footed,
    12 Oz., 5 In. . . . . . . 9.00 to 13.00

DELPHITE
Ashtray, 5 3/4 In. 45.00

GREEN
Ashtray, 5 3/4 In. . . 38.00 to 47.50
Bowl, 4 3/4 In. 10.00
Bowl, 8 1/2 In. 18.00
Bowl, Oval,
    9 1/2 In. . . . . 18.00 to 20.00
Butter, Cover 80.00
Chop Plate, 13 5/8 In. 40.00
Coaster, 3 1/4 In. 15.00
Cup. 9.00
Cup & Saucer . . . . . 12.00 to 16.00
Plate, 7 In. 16.00
Plate, 9 In. 18.00
Plate, Handle, 10 1/4 In. 18.50
Platter, Oval, 11 1/2 In. 20.00
Salt & Pepper 45.00
Sherbet, Footed 13.50

Sugar & Creamer 27.00
PINK
Ashtray, 5 3/4 In. 40.00
Bowl, 4 3/4 In. 6.00
Bowl, 5 3/8 In. 20.00
Bowl, 8 1/2 In. . . . . 15.00 to 20.00
Bowl, Footed,
    7 1/8 In. . . . . 25.00 to 30.00
Bowl, Handles,
    8 In. . . . . 13.00 to 17.00
Bowl, Oval, 9 1/2 In. 20.00
Butter, Cover. . . . . . 50.00 to 60.00
Cake Plate, 13 1/2 In. 18.00
Candy Jar, Cover. 30.00
Chop Plate,
    13 5/8 In. . . . . 35.00 to 45.00
Creamer. . . . . 9.00 to 10.00
Cup. . . . . 9.00 to 9.50
Pitcher, 16 Oz., 4 1/2 In. . . . 120.00
Pitcher, 52 Oz.,
    6 3/4 In. . . . . 15.00 to 30.00
Plate, 6 In. . . . . 3.50 to 5.00
Plate, 7 In. 18.00
Plate, Handle,
    10 1/4 In. . . . . 15.00 to 23.00
Platter, Oval, 11 1/2 In. 19.00
Relish, 2 Sections,
    11 1/2 In. 225.00
Salt & Pepper . . . . . 30.00 to 45.00
Saucer. 5.00
Sherbet, Footed . . . 10.00 to 11.00
Soup, Cream, 5 In. 25.00
Sugar, Cover . . . . . . 20.00 to 25.00
Sugar & Creamer, Cover 30.00
Tumbler, 5 Oz.,
    3 1/4 In. . . . . 20.00 to 22.00
Tumbler, 9 Oz., 5 In. 16.00
Tumbler, 12 Oz., 5 In. 27.00

WINDSOR DIAMOND, see Windsor

WINGED MEDALLION, see Madrid

Woolworth

Woolworth was made by Westmoreland Glass Company, Grapeville, Pennsylvania, in the early 1930s. The design, showing bunches of grapes, was also called Oregon Grape, but it is not the same as the pattern just called Grape. It was made of crystal, blue, green, and pink glass.

GREEN

Creamer..................12.00
Sugar .... 12.00 to 14.00

PINK

Plate 7.00

Tumbler..................10.00

X Design

X Design, or Criss Cross, was a Hazel Atlas pattern made from 1928 to 1932. The name indicates that the pattern has rows of X's in grids. It was made in crystal, green, pink, and white opaque glass. Only a breakfast set was made.

CRYSTAL

Bottle, Water, Small 18.00
Butter, Cover, 1 Lb. 16.00
Mixing Bowl, 5 5/8 In........8.00
Plate, 9 1/4 In............. 32.50
Reamer, Lemon.............6.00
Soup, Cream 30.00

GREEN

Butter, Cover,
    1/4 Lb............25.00 to 50.0
Butter, Cover, 1 Lb. 25.00

PINK

Butter, Cover, 1/4 Lb. 50.00
Creamer................. 18.00
Tumbler, 8 Oz. 10.00

Reproductions

PATTERN	OBJECT	COLORS	DATES
Adam	Butter dish	Green, pink	1981
American	2-piece candle night light	Crystal	1987
American	Almost all items have been reproduced	Crystal	
American	Nappy, punch bowl footed, salad bowl, torte plate	Red	1992
Avocado	Cup & saucer, pickle, handled dish, nappy, pickle, pitcher, sugar & creamer	Blue, Burnt Honey, frosted, pink, pink, red amethyst, yellow	1974
Avocado	Pitcher	Green	1979
Avocado	Berry, olive, 5 1/2-inch plate, relish, sundae, tumbler	Amber, amethyst, blue, frosted pink, green, pink, red amethyst, red-yellow	1974
Bubble	Ashtray, bowl, ivy ball, punch cup, 3 3/4-in. vase	Red	1977-1978
Cameo	Children's dishes	Green, pink, yellow	1982
Cameo	Salt & pepper shakers	Green	1982
Cameo	Salt & pepper shakers	Pink	1989
Candlewick	Bowl, candelabra, cup & saucer, cream & sugar, 2-handled jelly, plate, basket	Alexandrite, blue, pink	1987
Cape Cod	Cruet		1986
Cape Cod	Dinner set		1978
Caprice	Bashful Charlotte, butter, cream & sugar, footed juice, footed water glass, nut, relish, seashell ashtray, swan	Cobalt, light blue, Moonlight Blue	1985
Cherry Blossom	Almost all items have been reproduced in various colors since 1972		
Diana	Bowl	Pink	1986

PATTERN	OBJECT	COLORS	DATES
Early American Sandwich	Ashtray, basket, berry set, boxes, bowl, bridge set, candleholder, napkin holder, platter, pitcher, snack set, 3-part relish, tidbit, tumbler, vase	Amber, light green	1982
English Hobnail	18 pieces	Red	1980
English Hobnail	26 pieces	Pink	1983
English Hobnail	Pedestal salt dip	Crystal	1986
Floral	Shaker	Cobalt blue, dark green, pink, red	1989
Florentine No. 1	Shaker	Cobalt blue, pink, red	1989
Hazel Atlas Quilt	Kitchen shaker	Pink	1987
Heritage	5-inch bowl	Amber, crystal	1987
Heritage	5-inch bowl, 9-inch bowl, footed, cake plate, goblets, ice tea, 10-inch plate	Crystal	1992
Heritage	Goblets, ice tea, wine	Blue, pink	1992
Iris	Candy dish (bottom only), vase	Multicolored	1976
Iris	Various items	Crystal	1969
Iris	Various items	Milk glass and sprayed-on colors	1970
Iris	Vase	Crystal	1982
June	Bottom's up tumbler, custard	Black, jade	1979
June	Goblets: 6-ounce, 9-ounce, 12-ounce	Blue, crystal, yellow	1979
Madrid (called Recollection)	Various items	Amber, blue, crystal, yellow, pink, teal	1982-1990s
Madrid	Candleholder	Crystal	1977
Madrid	Dinner set	Amber	1977-1990s
Madrid	Shakers	Crystal	1978
Mayfair Open Rose	Cookie jar	Amethyst, green, pink	1982
Mayfair Open Rose	Cookie jar	Cobalt blue	1990
Mayfair Open Rose	Juice pitcher	Cobalt blue, pink	1993
Mayfair Open Rose	Salt & pepper shakers	Cobalt blue	1988
Mayfair Open Rose	Salt & pepper shakers	Green, pink	1989

PATTERN	OBJECT	COLORS	DATES
Mayfair Open Rose	Shot glass	Blue, cobalt blue, green, pink	1977
Mayfair Open Rose	Whiskey	Green, pink	1977
Miss America	Butter dish	Amberina, crystal, green, Ice Blue, pink, red	1977
Miss America	Pitcher, tumbler	Crystal, green, pink	1982
Miss America	Salt & pepper shakers	Crystal, green, pink	1977
Miss America	Various items	Cobalt blue	1987
Moonstone	Goblets, ice tea, wine	Dark & light blue	1992
Newport	Tumblers: 7-ounce, 9-ounce, 12-ounce, 16-ounce	Cobalt blue	
No. 610	Berry bowl, relish, tray, tumbler	Black, blue	1974
Princess Feather	1- and 2-piece reamers, "Gillespie" measuring cup	Various colors	1986
Royal Ruby	Tumblers: 7-ounce, 9-ounce, 12-ounce, 16-ounce	Red	1977–1978
Sandwich Anchor Hocking	Covered cookie jar	Crystal	1977
Sandwich Indiana	Basket, bridge set, candleholder, goblets, napkin holder, nappy, punch set, snack set, tidbit, vase, wine set	Amber	1982
Sandwich Indiana	Basket, candleholder, snack set, wine set	Light green	1982
Sandwich Indiana	Dinner set	Amber, crystal, dark blue, red	1969
Sandwich Indiana	Various items	Amber, blue, crystal, green, red	
Sharon	Butter dish	Amber, blue, dark green, light green, pink	1976
Sharon	Covered candy dish	Green, pink	1984
Sharon	Covered candy dish	Cobalt blue	1990
Sharon	Cheese dish	Blue, Burnt Umber, green, pink	1977
Sharon	Salt & pepper shakers	Green, pink, and other colors	1980
Sharon	Covered sugar & creamer	Pink, green	1982
Shirley Temple	Milk Pitcher, mug	Cobalt blue	1982
Shirley Temple	6 1/2-inch bowl		1986

DEPRESSION GLASS

Factories

NAME	LOCATION	DATES
Akro Agate	Clarksburg, West Virginia	1914-1951
Bartlett-Collins	Sapulpa, Oklahoma	1914-present
Belmont Tumbler Company	Bellaire, Ohio	c.1920-1952
Cambridge Glass Company	Cambridge, Ohio	1901-1958
Central Glass Works	Wheeling, West Virginia	1860s-1939
Consolidated Lamp & Glass Company	Coraopolis, Pennsylvania	1894-1933; 1936-1967
Co-Operative Flint Glass Company	Beaver Falls, Pennsylvania	1879-1934
Dell Glass Company	Millville, New Jersey	1930s
Diamond Glass-Ware Company	Indiana, Pennsylvania	1891-1931
Dunbar Flint Glass Corporation/Dunbar Glass Corporation	Dunbar, West Virginia	1913-1953
Duncan & Miller Glass Company	Washington, Pennsylvania	1893-1955
Federal Glass Company	Columbus, Ohio	1900-1971
Fenton Art Glass Company	Williamstown, West Virginia	1906-present
Fostoria Glass Company	Fostoria, Ohio; Moundsville, West Virginia	1887-1986
Hazel Atlas Glass Company	Washington, Pennsylvania; Zanesville, Ohio; Clarksburg, West Virginia; Wheeling, West Virginia	1902-1956
A. H. Heisey & Company	Newark, Ohio	1893-1956

NAME	LOCATION	DATES
Hocking Glass Company/ Anchor Hocking Glass Corporation/Anchor Hocking Corporation	Lancaster, Ohio	1905-present (Anchor Hocking Glass Corporation 1937-1969; Anchor Hocking Corporation, 1969-present)
Imperial Glass Company	Bellaire, Ohio	1904-1982
Indiana Glass Company	Dunkirk, Indiana	1907-present
Jeannette Glass Company	Jeannette, Pennsylvania	c.1900-present
Jenkins Glass Company	Kokomo, Indiana; Arcadia, Indiana	1901-1932
Lancaster Glass Company	Lancaster, Ohio	1908-1937
Libbey Glass Company	Toledo, Ohio	1892-present
Liberty Works	Egg Harbor, New Jersey	1903-1934
Louie Glass Company	Weston, West Virginia	1926-present
Macbeth-Evans Glass	Indiana (several factories); Toledo, Ohio; Charleroi, Pennsylvania; Corning, New York	1899-1936 (acquired by Corning)
McKee Glass Company	Jeannette, Pennsylvania	1853-1961
Morgantown Glass Works	Morgantown, West Virginia	Late 1800s-1972
New Martinsville Glass Manufacturing Company	New Martinsville, West Virginia	1901-1944
Paden City Glass Manufacturing Company	Paden City, West Virginia	1916-1951
Seneca Glass Company	Fostoria, Ohio; Morgantown, West Virginia	1891-present
Silex (division of Macbeth-Evans)	Corning, New York	1929-1955; sold to Corning Glass Works
L. E. Smith Glass Company	Mt. Pleasant, Pennsylvania	1907-present
Standard Glass Manufacturing Company (subsidiary of Hocking/Anchor Hocking)		1924-present

NAME	LOCATION	DATES
Tiffin Glass Company, see United States Glass Company		
United States Glass Company	Pennsylvania (several factories); Tiffin, Ohio; Gas City, Indiana; West Virginia	1891-1966
Westmoreland Glass Company	Grapeville, Pennsylvania	1890-1985

Pattern List

Note: (R) = pattern has been reproduced
* = prices and paragraph in body of book

PATTERN NAME	CROSS-REFERENCE	MANUFACTURER AND DATES	COLORS AND DESCRIPTION
ABC Stork		Belmont	Crystal, green; child's plate
*Adam (R)	Chain Daisy; Fan & Feather	Jeannette, 1932–1934	Crystal, Delphite, green, pink, yellow
Aero Optic		Cambridge, 1929	Crystal, emerald, Peach-Blo, Willow Blue
Afghan & Scottie Dog		Hazel Atlas, 1938	Blue with white decorations
*Akro Agate		Akro Agate, 1932–1951	Marbleized colored glass
*Alice	See also Charm; Fire-King Oven Ware; Jadite; Jane-Ray; Peach Lustre; Philbe; Swirl Fire-King; Turquoise Blue; Wheat	Anchor Hocking, 1940s	Jadite, opaque white; blue, pink borders
*Alpine Caprice	See also Caprice	Cambridge, 1936	Blue, crystal, pink; satin finish
*American (R)	Fostoria	Fostoria, 1915–1986	Amber, blue, crystal, green, milk glass, yellow
American Beauty	See English Hobnail		
*American Pioneer		Liberty Works, 1931–1934	Amber, crystal, green, pink
*American Sweetheart	Lily Medallion	Macbeth-Evans, 1930–1936	Blue, Cremax, Monax, pink, red; gold, green, pink, platinum, red, smokey black trim
Angel Fish	See Sportsman Series		
*Anniversary		Jeannette, 1947–1949; 1970s	Crystal, iridescent amber, pink

PATTERN NAME	CROSS-REFERENCE	MANUFACTURER AND DATES	COLORS AND DESCRIPTION
Apple Blossom		Cambridge, 1930s	Amber, blue, crystal, dark green, light green, yellow
Apple Blossom	See Dogwood		
Apple Blossom Border	See Blossoms & Band		
April		Macbeth-Evans	Pale Pink
Aramis		Dunbar, 1936	Luster colors
*Arcadia Lace		Jenkins, 1901-1932	Crystal, green, and iridescent amber glass
Arctic		Hocking, 1932	Red and white decorations
Art Moderne		Morgantown, 1929	Rose, green; black stem and foot
Artura		Indiana, c.1930	Crystal, green, pink
Athos		Dunbar, 1936	Colored stripes
*Aunt Polly		U.S. Glass, late 1920s-1935	Blue, green, iridescent
*Aurora		Hazel Atlas, late 1930s	Cobalt blue, crystal, green, pink
Autumn		McKee, 1934	French Ivory, Jade Green
*Avocado (R)	No. 601; Sweet Pear	Indiana Glass, 1923-1933	Crystal, green, pink
B Pattern	See Dogwood		
Ballerina	See Cameo		
*Bamboo Optic	See also Octagon Bamboo Optic	Liberty, 1929	Green, pink
Bananas		Indiana, c.1930	Green, pink
Banded Cherry	See Cherry Blossom		
Banded Fine Rib	See Coronation		
Banded Petalware	See Petalware		
Banded Rainbow	See Ring		
Banded Ribbon	See New Century		
Banded Rings	See Ring		
Barbra		Dunbar, 1928	Pink

PATTERN NAME	CROSS-REFERENCE	MANUFACTURER AND DATES	COLORS AND DESCRIPTION
*Baroque		Fostoria, 1936-1966	Azure, crystal, Gold Tint, ruby, topaz
Basket	See No. 615		
*Beaded Block	Frosted Block	Imperial, 1927-1930s	Amber, crystal, green, Ice Blue, pink, red, Vaseline, white; iridescent (frosted) colors
Bee Hive	See also Queen Anne	U.S. Glass, 1926	Crystal; amber, green, pink trim
Belmont Ship Plate		Belmont	Amber, crystal, green, iridescent
Berwick	See Boopie		
Beverage with Sailboats	See White Ship		
Bibi		Anchor Hocking, 1940s	Forest Green, red
Big Rib	See Manhattan		
Birch Tree	See Deerwood		
Blackberry Cluster	See Loganberry		
Blaise		Imperial, c.1930	Amber, crystal, green, Rose Marie
Blanche		Standard, c.1930	Crystal
Block	See Block Optic		
*Block Optic	Block	Hocking, 1929-1933	Amber, blue, crystal, green, pink, yellow
Block with Rose	Rose Trellis	Imperial	Crystal, green, pink
Block with Snowflake	Snowflake on Block		Green, pink; plates only
Block with Windmill	See Windmill & Checkerboard		
Blossoms & Band	Apple Blossom Border	Jenkins, 1927	Crystal, green, iridescent marigold, pink
*Boopie	Berwick	Anchor Hocking, late 1940s-1950s	Crystal, Forest Green, Royal Ruby; glasses
Bordette	See also Chinex Classic; Cremax	Macbeth-Evans, 1930-1940 (Corning Glass)	Chinex, Cremax
Bouquet & Lattice	See Normandie		

PATTERN NAME	CROSS-REFERENCE	MANUFACTURER AND DATES	COLORS AND DESCRIPTION
Bowknot		Late 1920s	Crystal, green
Bridal Bouquet	See No. 615		
Bridget		Jeannette, 1925	Green, topaz; bridge set
*Bubble (R)	Bullseye; Provincial	Hocking, 1934-1937 Anchor Hocking Glass Corporation, 1937-1965	Crystal, dark green, Milk White, pale blue, pink, Ruby Red, yellow
Bullseye	See Bubble		
*Burple		Anchor Hocking, 1940s	Crystal, Forest Green, Ruby Red; dessert sets, bowls
Butterflies & Roses	See Flower Garden with Butterflies		
Buttons & Bows	See Holiday		
*By Cracky		Smith, late 1920s	Amber, Canary, crystal, green
Cabbage Rose	See Sharon		
Cabbage Rose with Single Arch	See Rosemary		
Camellia		Jeannette, 1947-1951	Crystal
*Cameo (R)	Ballerina; Dancing Girl	Hocking, 1930-1934	Crystal, crystal with platinum rim, platinum, green, pink, yellow
*Candlewick (R)		Imperial, 1937-1982	Black, blue, brown, crystal, green, lavender, pink, red, yellow; crystal with gold; fired-on gold, red, blue, green beading
*Cape Cod (R)		Imperial, 1932-1980s	Amber, Azalea, cobalt blue, crystal, green, light blue, milk glass, ruby
*Caprice (R)	See also Alpine Caprice	Cambridge, 1936-1953	Amber, amethyst, cobalt blue, crystal, Emerald Green, light green, milk glass, Moonlight Blue, pink
Carolyn	See Yvonne		
*Caribbean	Wave	Duncan & Miller, 1936-1955	Amber, crystal, blue, red

PATTERN NAME	CROSS-REFERENCE	MANUFACTURER AND DATES	COLORS AND DESCRIPTION
Catalonian		Consolidated, 1927–1936	Amethyst, Emerald Green, Honey, jade, Spanish Rose
Centaur	Sphinx	Lancaster, 1930s	Green, yellow
*Century		Fostoria, 1926–1986	Crystal
Chain Daisy	See Adam		
Chantilly		Fostoria	Crystal
*Chantilly		Jeannette, 1960s	Crystal, pink
Charade			Amethyst, dark blue, pink
Chariot		Hocking, 1932	Red and white decorations
*Charm	See also Alice; Fire-King Oven Ware; Jadite; Jane-Ray; Peach Lustre; Philbe; Swirl Fire-King; Turquoise Blue; Wheat	Anchor Hocking, 1950–1954	Azur-ite, Forest Green, Jadite, Royal Ruby
Chateau		Fostoria, 1933–1940	Crystal
*Cherokee Rose		Tiffin, 1940s–1950s	Crystal
Cherry	See Cherry Blossom		
*Cherry-Berry	See also Strawberry	U.S. Glass, early 1930s	Crystal, green, iridescent amber, pink
*Cherry Blossom (R)	Banded Cherry; Cherry; Paneled Cherry Blossom	Jeannette, 1930–1939	Crystal, Delphite, green, Jadite, pink, red
Chesterfield		Imperial, c.1930	Amber, green, Rose Marie; iced tea set
Chico		Louie, 1936	Black, green, pink, Royal Blue, ruby, topaz; crystal handles; beverage set
*Chinex Classic	See also Cremax; Bordette; Oxford; Pie-Crust; Sheffield	Macbeth-Evans (Corning Glass), c.1938–1942	Ivory; decal decorated; colored edges
*Chintz		Fostoria, 1940–1972	Crystal
Chintz		Heisey, 1931–1938	Crystal, green, orchid, pink, yellow
*Christmas Candy	Christmas Candy Ribbon; No. 624	Indiana, 1937; 1950s	Crystal, Emerald Green, Seafoam Green, Teal Blue; luncheon sets

PATTERN NAME	CROSS-REFERENCE	MANUFACTURER AND DATES	COLORS AND DESCRIPTION
Christmas Candy Ribbon	See Christmas Candy		
*Circle	Circular Ribs	Hocking, 1930s	Crystal, green, pink
Circular Ribs	See Circle		
Classic	See Chinex Classic		
*Cleo		Cambridge, 1930	Amber, blue, crystal, green, pink, yellow
Clico		McKee, 1930	Crystal with black, green feet, Jade Green, transparent green, rose pink
*Cloverleaf	Shamrock	Hazel Atlas, 1930-1936	Black, crystal, green, pink, topaz
*Colonial	Knife & Fork	Hocking 1934-1938	Crystal, green, opaque white, pink
*Colonial Block		Hazel Atlas	1930s—black, crystal, green, pink; 1950s—white
*Colonial Fluted	Rope	Federal, 1928-1933	Crystal, green
*Colony	Elongated Honeycomb; Hexagon Triple Band	Hazel Atlas, 1930s	Crystal, green, pink
Colony		Fostoria, 1920s-1970s	Amber, blue, crystal, green, white, yellow
*Columbia		Federal, 1938-1942	Crystal, pink
Columbus		Anchor Hocking	Amber; plate only
Comet	Scroll	U.S. Glass, mid-1920s	Crystal, green, pink
Corded Optic		Federal, 1928	Crystal, green
Coronada	See Royal		
*Coronation	Banded Fine Rib; Saxon; see also Lace Edge	Anchor Hocking, 1936-1940	Crystal, dark green, pink, Ruby Red
Cosmos		Jeannette, 1950s	Crystal, golden iridescent
*Cracked Ice		Indiana, 1930s	Green, pink
Crackled	See Craquel		
*Craquel	Crackled; Stippled; Tree of Life	U.S. Glass, 1924	Crystal with green trim, blue, yellow

PATTERN NAME	CROSS-REFERENCE	MANUFACTURER AND DATES	COLORS AND DESCRIPTION
*Cremax	See also Bordette; Chinex Classic; Ivex; Oxford; Pie-Crust; Sheffield	Macbeth-Evans (Corning Glass), 1930s–1940s	Cream-colored opaque; decal decorated; colored edges
Criss Cross	See X Design		
Crossbar		Federal, mid-1930s	Crystal, Golden Glow, green, Rose Glow
Crystal Leaf		Macbeth-Evans, 1928	Crystal, green, pink
Crystolite		Heisey	Amber, crystal, Sahara, Zircon
Cube	See Cubist		
*Cubist	Cube	Jeannette, 1929–1933	Amber, blue, Canary Yellow, crystal, green, pink, Ultramarine, white
Cupid		Paden City, 1930s	Black, green, light blue, pink, yellow
Daisy	See No. 620		
Daisy J		Jeannette, 1926	Amber, green
Daisy Petals	See Petalware		
Daisy Spray & Lattice		Federal, 1928	Crystal, green
Dance of the Nudes		Consolidated, 1920s	Crystal, pink
Dancing Girl		Morgantown, 1920s–1930s	Blue, green, pink
Dancing Girl	See Cameo	Hocking	
D'Artagnan		Dunbar, 1936	Lusters
Debbra		Hocking, 1931–1933	Green, rose, topaz
*Decagon		Cambridge, 1930s	Amber, cobalt blue, green, Moonlight Blue, pink, red
Deerwood	Birch Tree	U.S. Glass, 1920s–1930s	Amber, green, pink
*Della Robbia		Westmoreland, 1920s–1930s	Amber, crystal, green, pink
*Dewdrop		Jeannette, 1954–1955	Crystal
Diamond	See Windsor		

PATTERN NAME	CROSS-REFERENCE	MANUFACTURER AND DATES	COLORS AND DESCRIPTION
Diamond Arch	Diamond Lattice	Federal, 1938–1940	Crystal, green, pink
Diamond Dart		Macbeth-Evans, 1928	Crystal, Emerald Green
Diamond Lattice	See Diamond Arch		
Diamond Panel	See Diamond Point Columns		
Diamond Pattern	See Miss America		
Diamond Point	See Petalware		
Diamond Point Columns	Diamond Panel	Hazel Altas, late 1920s–1930s	Crystal, green, iridescent, pink
*Diamond Quilted	Flat Diamond	Imperial, 1920s–1930s	Amber, black, blue, crystal, green, pink, red
Diamond Squat		Federal, 1928	Crystal; water set
*Diana (R)	Swirled Sharp Rib	Federal, 1937–1941	Amber, crystal, pink
Diane		Cambridge, 1934–1950s	Blue, crystal, Heatherbloom, pink, yellow
Diner		U.S. Glass, 1927	Amber, green, pink
Dixie		Macbeth-Evans, 1931	Green, pink; water set
*Dogwood	Apple Blossom; B Pattern; Magnolia; Wildrose	Macbeth-Evans, 1929–1934	Cremax, crystal, green, Monax, pink, yellow
Doreen		Westmoreland, 1924	Amber, blue, crystal, green, rose
*Doric	Snowflake	Jeannette, 1935–1938	Delphite, green, pink, yellow
*Doric & Pansy	Doric with Pansy; Pansy & Doric; see also Pretty Polly Party Dishes	Jeannette, 1937–1938	Crystal, pink, Ultramarine
Doric with Pansy	See Doric & Pansy		
Do-Si-Do		Smith, 1930s	Black, black with crystal
Double Shield	See Mt. Pleasant		
Double Swirl	See Swirl		
Drape & Tassel	See Princess		
Dutch	See Windmill		

PATTERN NAME	CROSS-REFERENCE	MANUFACTURER AND DATES	COLORS AND DESCRIPTION
Dutch Rose	See Rosemary		
Early American	See Princess Feather		
Early American Hobnail	See also Hobnail	Imperial, 1930s	Amber, black, blue, crystal, green, pink, red
Early American Lace		Duncan & Miller, 1932	Amber, crystal, green, rose, ruby
Early American Rock Crystal	See Rock Crystal		
Early American Sandwich (R)		Duncan & Miller, 1925-1949	Amber, chartreuse, crystal, green, pink, ruby
Early American Scroll		Heisey, 1932	Crystal
Early American Thumbprint		Heisey, 1932	Crystal, golden yellow, green, rose
Egg Harbor		Liberty, 1929	Green, rose
Elaine		Cambridge, 1934–1950s	Crystal
Elongated Honeycomb	See Colony		
Empress		Heisey, 1930-1938	Alexandrite, cobalt blue, crystal, Flamingo, Moongleam, Sahara, Tangerine
*English Hobnail (R)	American Beauty; Sawtooth; see also Miss America	Westmoreland, 1920-1970s	Amber, blue, cobalt blue, crystal, dark amber, green, pink, red, turquoise
*Everglades		Cambridge, 1933–1934	Amber, Carmen, crystal, Eleanor Blue, Forest Green
*Fairfax		Fostoria, 1927-1960	Amber, black, blue, green, orchid, pink, ruby, topaz
Fan & Feather	See Adam		
Fanfare		Macbeth-Evans	Pale pink
Feather Scroll	See Scroll Fluted		
Fieldcrest		Jenkins	Crystal, green, iridescent amber
Fine Rib	See Homespun (Jeannette)		

PATTERN NAME	CROSS-REFERENCE	MANUFACTURER AND DATES	COLORS AND DESCRIPTION
Fire-King Dinnerware	See Alice; Charm; Jane-Ray; Jadite; Peach Lustre; Philbe; Swirl Fire-King; Turquoise Blue		
*Fire-King Oven Glass	See also Philbe	Anchor Hocking, 1942-1960s	Crystal, pale blue
*Fire-King Oven Ware	See also Alice; Charm; Jadite; Jane-Ray; Peach Lustre; Philbe; Swirl Fire-King; Turquoise Blue; Wheat	Anchor Hocking, 1950s	Opaque; blue, ivory with gold or colored trim, Jadite, pink, white
*Flanders		U.S. Glass, 1914-1935	Crystal, pink, or yellow with crystal trim
Flat Diamond	See Diamond Quilted		
Flora		Imperial, c.1925	Amber, green, Rose Marie
Floradora	Floral Bouquet	Imported, 1929	Amber, amethyst, green
*Floragold	Louisa	Jeannette, 1950s	Crystal, Ice Blue, iridescent, red-yellow, Shell Pink
*Floral (R)	Poinsettia	Jeannette, 1931-1935	Amber, crystal, Delphite, green, Jadite, pink, red, yellow
*Floral & Diamond Band		U.S. Glass, 1920s	Black, crystal, green, pink
Floral Bouquet	See Floradora		
Floral Rim	See Vitrock		
Floral Sterling		Hazel Atlas, early 1930s	Black
Florentine		Fostoria, 1931-1944	Crystal; Gold Tint base; topaz base
*Florentine No. 1 (R)	Old Florentine; Poppy No. 1	Hazel Atlas, 1932-1935	Cobalt blue, crystal, green, pink, yellow; hexagonal plates
*Florentine No. 2	Oriental Poppy; Poppy No. 2	Hazel Atlas, 1932-1935	Amber, cobalt blue, crystal, green, Ice Blue, pink, yellow
Flower	See Princess Feather		
Flower & Leaf Band	See Indiana Custard		

PATTERN NAME	CROSS-REFERENCE	MANUFACTURER AND DATES	COLORS AND DESCRIPTION
Flower Band		McKee, 1934	French Ivory, Jade Green, Poudre Blue
Flower Basket	See No. 615		
Flower Garden	See Flower Garden with Butterflies		
*Flower Garden with Butterflies	Butterflies & Roses; Flower Garden; Wildrose with Apple Blossom	U.S. Glass, late 1920s	Amber, black, blue, crystal, green, pink, yellow
Flower Rim	See Vitrock		
Forest		Co-Operative Flint, 1928	Blue, green, pink
*Forest Green		Anchor Hocking, 1950-1957	Green
*Fortune		Anchor Hocking, 1937-1938	Crystal, pink
Fostoria	See American		
Fountain Swirl		Imperial, 1928-1930	Crystal, green, pink
Franklin		Fenton, 1934	Amber, crystal, ruby; beverage glasses
Frosted Block	See Beaded Block		
Frosted Ribbon		Anchor Hocking, 1940	Red
*Fruits		Hazel Atlas, 1931-1933	Crystal, green, iridescent, pink
Fuchsia		Fostoria, 1931-1944	Crystal; Wisteria base
Fuchsia		U.S. Glass, 1930s-1940s	Crystal
Full Sail		Duncan & Miller, 1925	Amber, green
Garland		Indiana	1935—Crystal; 1950s—decorated milk glass
Georgian		Hocking, 1935	Crystal, green; beverage sets
*Georgian	Lovebirds	Federal, 1931-1935	Crystal, green
Georgian		Duncan & Miller, 1928	Amber, crystal, green, rose

PATTERN NAME	CROSS-REFERENCE	MANUFACTURER AND DATES	COLORS AND DESCRIPTION
*Georgian Fenton		Fenton, c.1930	Amber, black, cobalt blue, crystal, green, pink, ruby, topaz
Gladiola	See Royal Lace		
*Gloria		Cambridge, c.1930	Amber, crystal, Emerald Green, green, Heatherbloom, pink, yellow
Gothic Arches	Romanesque	L. E. Smith, 1920s	Amber, crystal, green, yellow
Grand Slam		Federal, 1930	Crystal; bridge set
Grape	See also Woolworth	Standard, 1930s	Green, rose, topaz
Greek Key		Heisey	Crystal, Flamingo
Gray Laurel	See Peach Lustre		
Groucho		Louie, 1936	Black, green, pink, royal blue, ruby, topaz; crystal handles; beverage set
Hairpin	See Newport		
Hammered Band	Melba; Pebbled Band	L. E. Smith, early 1930s	Amethyst, black, green, pink
Hanging Basket	See No. 615		
*Harp		Jeannette, 1954–1957	Crystal, crystal with gold trim, light blue, pink
Harpo		Louie, 1936	Black, green, pink, Royal Blue, ruby, topaz; crystal handles; beverage set
Hazel Atlas Quilt (R)		Hazel Atlas, 1937–1940	Amethyst, cobalt blue, green, pink
Hazen		Imperial, c.1930	Crystal
*Heritage (R)		Federal, late 1930s–1960s	Crystal, blue, light green, pink
Hermitage		Fostoria, 1932-1945	Amber, Azure, black, crystal, Gold Tint, green, topaz, Wisteria
Hex Optic	See Hexagon Optic		
*Hexagon Optic	Hex Optic; Honeycomb	Jeannette, 1928–1932; c.1960	Blue-green, green, pink; iridized
Hexagon Triple Band	See Colony		

PATTERN NAME	CROSS-REFERENCE	MANUFACTURER AND DATES	COLORS AND DESCRIPTION
High Point		Anchor Hocking	Ruby; water set
Hinge	See Patrician		
Hob		Jenkins, 1927-1931	Crystal, green
*Hobnail	See also Early American Hobnail; Moonstone	Hocking, 1934-1936	Crystal, pink; red rims; black base
Hobstars Intaglio		Imperial, c.1930	Crystal, green, pink
*Holiday	Buttons & Bows; Russian	Jeannette, 1947-1949	Crystal, iridescent, pink, Shell Pink opaque
*Homespun	Fine Rib	Jeannette, 1939-1940	Crystal, pink
Homespun		Hazel Atlas	Cobalt blue, crystal
Homestead		Smith, 1930s	Amber, black, green, pink
Honeycomb	See Hexagon Optic		
Horizontal Fine Rib	See Manhattan		
Horizontal Ribbed	See Manhattan		
Horizontal Rounded Big Rib	See Manhattan		
Horizontal Sharp Big Rib	See Manhattan		
Horseshoe	See No. 612		
Huck Finn		Jenkins, c.1930	Crystal
Huckabee		Imperial, c.1930	Crystal
Hughes		Morgantown, 1932	Black, crystal, green, Ritz Blue, ruby; beverage sets
Ida		Imperial, c.1930	Blue, crystal, green, ruby
Imperial Hunt		Cambridge, 1932	Crystal
Imperial Optic Rib	Optic Rib	Imperial, 1927	Amberina, blue, crystal, green, iridescent
Imperial Plain Octagon	Molly	Imperial, 1927	Crystal, green, pink
Indian		Federal, c.1930	Green

PATTERN NAME	CROSS-REFERENCE	MANUFACTURER AND DATES	COLORS AND DESCRIPTION
*Indiana Custard	Flower & Leaf Band; see also Orange Blossom	Indiana, 1930s-1950s	Custard, ivory, white; bands of pastel colors
Ipswich		Heisey, 1931-1946; 1951-1953	Alexandrite, cobalt blue, crystal, Flamingo, Moongleam, Sahara
*Iris (R)	Iris & Herringbone	Jeannette, 1928-1932; 1950s	Crystal, iridescent, pink
Iris & Herringbone	See Iris		
Ivex	See also Chinex Classic; Cremax	Macbeth-Evans (Corning Glass), 1930-1940	Chinex, Cremax
Jack Frost		Federal, 1928	Crystal; crackled; water, iced tea and lemonade sets
*Jadite	See also Alice; Charm; Fire-King Oven Ware; Jane-Ray; Peach Lustre; Philbe; Swirl Fire-King; Turquoise Blue; Wheat	Jeannette, 1936-1938	Jadite
Jamestown	See Tradition		
Jane		Lancaster, c.1930	Green, pink, topaz
*Jane-Ray	See also Alice; Charm; Fire-King Oven Ware; Jadite; Peach Lustre; Philbe; Swirl Fire-King; Turquoise Blue; Wheat	Anchor Hocking, 1945-1963	Jadite
Jenkins' Basket		Jenkins	Crystal, green, iridescent amber
John		Federal, mid-1930s	Crystal, Golden Glow, green, Rose Glow
*Jubilee		Lancaster, early 1930s	Pink, yellow
*June		Fostoria, 1928-1952	Azure blue, crystal, gold-tinted, green, rose, topaz
Kashmir		Fostoria, 1930-1934	Azure, crystal, green, topaz
Katy Blue	See Laced Edge		

PATTERN NAME	CROSS-REFERENCE	MANUFACTURER AND DATES	COLORS AND DESCRIPTION
Kimberly		Duncan & Miller, 1931	Amber, crystal, green, rose
King Arthur		Indiana, c.1930	Green, pink
Knife & Fork	See Colonial		
Krinkle		Morgantown, 1924	Crystal
*Lace Edge	Loop; Old Colony; Open Lace; Open Scallop; see also Coronation; Queen Mary	Hocking, 1935–1938	Crystal, pink
Laced Edge	Katy Blue	Imperial, early 1930s	Blue, green; opalescent edge
Lacy Daisy	See No. 618		
Lafayette		Fostoria, 1931–1960	Amber, blue, burgundy, crystal, Empire Green, Gold Tint, green, rose, ruby, topaz, Wisteria
*Lake Como		Hocking, 1934–1937	Opaque white with blue decoration
Langston		Morgantown, 1932	Black, crystal, green, Ritz Blue, ruby
Lariat		Heisey	Black, crystal
Lariette		U.S. Glass, 1931	Crystal, green, pink
*Laurel	Raspberry Band; see also Scottie Dog	McKee, 1930s	Ivory, jade, Powder Blue, White Opal; child's set-colored rim
Leaf		Macbeth-Evans, early 1930s	Crystal, green, pink
Legion		Fostoria, 1931–1940	Crytal, rose, topaz
Lenox		McKee, 1930s	Crystal, green, Ritz Blue, Rose Pink
*Lido		Federal, mid-1930s	Crystal, Golden Glow, green, Rose Glow
Lily Medallion	See American Sweetheart		
Lily Pons		Indiana, c.1930	Green
Lincoln Drape	See Princess		

PATTERN NAME	CROSS-REFERENCE	MANUFACTURER AND DATES	COLORS AND DESCRIPTION
*Lincoln Inn		Fenton, 1928	Amber, amethyst, black, cobalt blue, crystal, green, Jadite, light blue, pink, red
Lindburgh	Scalloped Panels	Imperial, c.1930	Crystal, green, rose pink
Line 92	See Twitch		
Line 191	Party Line; Tiered Block; Tiered Semi-Optic	Paden City, 1928	Amber, blue, Cheri-Glo, crystal, green, Mulberry
Line 300	See Peacock & Wild Rose		
Line 412	See Peacock Reverse		
Line 550	See Sheraton		
Line 994	See Popeye & Olive		
Little Bo Peep		Anchor Hocking, 1940	Green and orange on ivory; child's line
Little Hostess	See Moderntone Little Hostess		
Little Jewel	See also New Jewel	Imperial, late 1920s–1930	Crystal, green, pink, white
Little Orphan Annie	See Orphan Annie		
Loganberry	Blackberry Cluster	Indiana, c.1930	Green, pink
Lombardi		Jeannette, 1938	Light blue; bowl only
Loop	See Lace Edge		
Lorain	See No. 615		
Lorna		Cambridge, 1930	Amber, crystal, emerald, Gold Krystol, Peach-Blo
Lotus		Westmoreland, 1920s–1930s	Amber, blue, crystal, green, rose
Louisa	See Floragold		
Lovebirds	See Georgian		
Lydia Ray	See New Century		
MacHOB		Macbeth-Evans, 1928	Crystal, Monax, pink
*Madrid (R)	Meandering Vine; Paneled Aster; Primus; Winged Medallion	Federal, 1932–1939	Amber, blue, crystal, green, pink

PATTERN NAME	CROSS-REFERENCE	MANUFACTURER AND DATES	COLORS AND DESCRIPTION
Magnolia	See Dogwood		
*Manhattan	Horizontal Fine Rib; Horizontal Ribbed; Horizontal Rounded Big Rib; Horizontal Sharp Big Rib, Ribbed	Anchor Hocking, 1938-1941	Crystal, green, pink, red
Manor		Fostoria, 1931-1944	Crystal, green, topaz
Many Windows	See Roulette		
Marguerite		Westmoreland, 1924	Amber, blue, crystal, green, rose
Marilyn		Morgantown, 1929	Green, pink
*Martha Washington		Cambridge, 1932	Amber, crystal, Forest Green, Gold Krystol, Heatherbloom, Royal Blue, ruby
Mary		Federal, mid-1930s	Crystal, Golden Glow, green, Rose Glow
Mayfair	See Mayfair Open Rose		
*Mayfair Federal		Federal, 1934	Amber, crystal, green
*Mayfair Open Rose (R)	Mayfair; Open Rose	Hocking, 1931-1937	Crystal, green, Ice Blue, pink, yellow
Meadow Flower	See No. 618		
Meandering Vine	See Madrid		
Melba	See Hammered Band		
Melon		Morgantown, 1932	Black, blue, green, ruby, opal with colors; beverage set
Memphis		Central, 1923	Amethyst, black, blue, canary, green
Midnight Rose		Fostoria, 1933-1957	Crystal
Millay		Morgantown, 1932	Black, blue, crystal, green, ruby; beverage set
Minuet		Heisey, 1939-1950s	Crystal
*Miss America (R)	Diamond Pattern; see also English Hobnail	Hocking, 1933-1936	Crystal, green, Ice Blue, Jadite, pink, red, Ritz Blue

PATTERN NAME	CROSS-REFERENCE	MANUFACTURER AND DATES	COLORS AND DESCRIPTION
Moderne Art	See Tea Room		
*Moderntone	Wedding Band	Hazel Atlas, 1935–1942	Amethyst, cobalt blue, crystal, pink, Platonite with fired-on colors
*Moderntone Little Hostess Party Set	Little Hostess	Hazel Atlas, 1940s	Fired-on colors
Molly	See Imperial Plain Octagon		
Monarch		Anchor Hocking	Ruby
Monticello		Imperial	Crystal
*Moondrops		New Martinsville, 1932–1940s	Amber, amethyst, black, cobalt blue, crystal, Evergreen, Ice Blue, jade, light green, medium blue, pink, Ritz Blue, ruby, Smoke
*Moonstone	Opalescent Hobnail; see also Hobnail	Anchor Hocking, 1941–1946	Crystal with opalescent hobnails, green
Morning Glory		Fostoria, 1931–1944	Crystal; amber base
*Mt. Pleasant	Double Shield	L. E. Smith, mid 1920s–1934	Amber, black amethyst, cobalt blue, crystal, green, pink; gold or silver trim
*Mt. Vernon		Cambridge, 1920s–1940s	Amber, blue, crystal, Emerald Green, Heatherbloom, red, violet
Mt. Vernon		Imperial, c.1930	Crystal
Mutt'N Jeff		Federal, 1928	Crystal, green; water set
Naomi		Seneca, mid-1930s	Blue, crystal
Nautilus		Cambridge, 1933–1934	Amber, crystal, Royal Blue
*Navarre		Fostoria, 1937–1980	Crystal
Nectar		Fostoria, 1934–1943	Crystal
*New Century	Banded Ribbon; Lydia Ray; see also Ovide	Hazel Atlas, 1930–1935	Amethyst, cobalt blue, crystal, green, pink
New Garland		Fostoria, 1930–1934	Amber, crystal, rose, topaz
New Jewel	See also Little Jewel	Imperial, 1931	Crystal, green, pink, white
*Newport	Hairpin	Hazel Atlas, 1936–1940	Amethyst, cobalt blue, fired-on Monax, pink, Platonite

PATTERN NAME	CROSS-REFERENCE	MANUFACTURER AND DATES	COLORS AND DESCRIPTION
No. 601	See Avocado		
*No. 610 (R)	Pyramid; Rex	Indiana, 1926-1932	Crystal, green, pink, white, yellow
*No. 612	Horseshoe	Indiana, 1930-1933	Green, pink, yellow; crystal sugar and creamer
*No. 615	Basket; Bridal Bouquet; Flower Basket; Hanging Basket; Lorain	Indiana, 1929-1932	Crystal, crystal with colored borders, green, yellow;
*No. 616	Vernon	Indiana, 1930-1932	Crystal, crystal with platinum trim, green, yellow
*No. 618	Lacy Daisy; Meadow Flower; Pineapple & Floral; Wildflower	Indiana, 1932-1937; 1960s	Amber, crystal, fired-on green, Olive Green, red
*No. 620	Daisy	Indiana	1933—crystal; 1940—amber; 1960s-1970s—dark green, milk glass
No. 622	See Pretzel		
No. 624	See Christmas Candy		
Nora Bird		Paden City, 1929-1930s	Crystal, green, pink
*Normandie	Bouquet & Lattice	Federal, 1933-1940	Amber, crystal, iridescent, pink
Oatmeal Lace	See Princess Feather		
Ocean Wave	Ripple	Jenkins, c.1930	
Octagon		Heisey, 1925-1937	Flamingo, Hawthorne, Marigold, Moongleam, Sahara, Tangerine
Octagon	Tiered Octagon; U.S. Octagon	U.S. Glass, 1927-1929	Green, pink
Octagon Bamboo Optic	See also Bamboo Optic	Liberty, 1929	Green, pink
Octagon Edge		McKee	Green, pink
*Old Cafe		Anchor Hocking, 1936-1938	Crystal, pink, red
Old Colony (Heisey)	See Victorian		
Old Colony (Hocking)	See Lace Edge		

PATTERN NAME	CROSS-REFERENCE	MANUFACTURER AND DATES	COLORS AND DESCRIPTION
*Old English	Threading	Indiana, late 1920s–early 1930s	Amber, crystal, Emerald Green, light green, pink
Old Florentine	See Florentine No. 1		
Old Sandwich		Heisey, 1931–1956	Cobalt blue, Flamingo, Moongleam, Sahara, Tangerine, Zircon
Opalescent Hobnail	See Moonstone		
Open Lace	See Lace Edge		
Open Rose	See Mayfair Open Rose		
Open Scallop	See Lace Edge		
Optic Design	See Raindrops		
Optic Rib	See Imperial Optic Rib		
*Orange Blossom	See also Indiana Custard	Indiana, 1957	Milk glass
Orchid		Heisey, 1940–1957	Crystal
Orchid		Paden City, early 1930s	Amber, black, cobalt blue, green, pink, red, yellow
Oregon Grape	See Woolworth		
Oriental Poppy	See Florentine No. 2		
Orphan Annie		Westmoreland, 1925	Amber, blue, crystal, green; breakfast set
*Ovide	See also New Century	Hazel Atlas, 1929–1935	Black, green, Platonite, white, trimmed with fired-on colors
Oxford	See also Chinex Classic; Cremax	Macbeth-Evans (Corning Glass), 1930–1940	Chinex, Cremax
*Oyster & Pearl		Anchor Hocking, 1938–1940	Crystal, pink, red, white; fired-on green, pink
Palm Optic		Morgantown, 1929	Green, pink
Panel	See Sheraton		
Paneled Aster	See Madrid		
Paneled Cherry Blossom	See Cherry Blossom		
Paneled Ring-Ding		Hocking, 1932	Black, green, orange, red, yellow, painted bands

PATTERN NAME	CROSS-REFERENCE	MANUFACTURER AND DATES	COLORS AND DESCRIPTION
Pansy & Doric	See Doric & Pansy		
Pantryline		Hocking, 1920s–1930s	
Parrot	See Sylvan		
Party Line	See Line 191		
*Patrician	Hinge; Spoke	Federal, 1933–1937	Amber, crystal, green, pink, yellow
Patrick		Lancaster, c.1930	Rose, topaz
*Peach Lustre	See also Alice; Charm; Fire-King Oven Ware; Jadite; Jane-Ray; Philbe; Swirl Fire-King; Turquoise Blue; Wheat	Anchor-Hocking 1952–1963	Orange-Yellow
Peacock & Rose	See Peacock & Wild Rose		
*Peacock & Wild Rose	Line 300; Peacock & Rose	Paden City, 1930s	Black, cobalt blue, green, pink, red
Peacock Optic		Morgantown, 1929–1930	Green, pink
Peacock Reverse	Line 412	Paden City, 1930s	Amber, black, cobalt blue, crystal, green, red, yellow
*Pear Optic	Thumbprint; see also Raindrops	Federal, 1929–1930	Green
Pebble Optic	See Raindrops		
Pebbled Band	See Hammered Band		
*Penny Line		Paden City, 1932	Amber, Cheri-Glo, crystal, green, Royal Blue, ruby
Petal	See Petalware		
Petal Swirl	See Swirl		
*Petalware	Banded Petalware; Daisy Petals; Diamond Point, Petal; Shell; Vivid Bands	Macbeth-Evans (Corning Glass), 1930–1940	Cobalt blue, Cremax, crystal, Monax, pink; gold trim; red trim; hand-painted fruit designs; fired-on blue, green, red, yellow
*Philbe	Fire-King Dinnerware; see also other Fire-King entries	Anchor Hocking, 1937–1940s	Blue, blue with platinum trim, crystal, green, pink

PATTERN NAME	CROSS-REFERENCE	MANUFACTURER AND DATES	COLORS AND DESCRIPTION
Pie-Crust	See also Chinex Classic, Cremax	Macbeth-Evans (Corning Glass), 1930-1940	Chinex, Cremax
*Pillar Flute		Imperial, c.1930	Amber, blue, crystal, green, pink
Pillar Optic		Hocking, 1935	Green
Pineapple & Floral	See No. 618		
Pineapple Optic		Morgantown, 1929	Green, rose
Pinwheel	See Sierra		
Pioneer		Federal, 1930s-1970s	Crystal, pink
Plantation		Heisey	Amber, crystal
Plymouth		Fenton, 1933	Amber, green, ruby
Poinsettia	See Floral		
Polar Bear		Hocking, 1932	Red and white decorations
Polo		Hazel Atlas, 1938	Blue with white decorations
*Popeye & Olive	Line 994	Paden City, early 1930s	Cobalt blue, crystal, green, red
Poppy No. 1	See Florentine No. 1		
Poppy No. 2	See Florentine No. 2		
Portia		Cambridge, 1932-1950s	Crystal, green, Heatherbloom, yellow
Pretty Polly Party Dishes	See also Doric & Pansy	Jeannette, 1937-1938	Children's dishes
*Pretzel	No. 622; Ribbon Candy	Indiana, 1930s-1970s	Crystal, teal
*Primo		U.S. Glass, 1932	Green, yellow
Primrose Lane		Morgantown, 1929	Green, pink
Primus	See Madrid		
*Princess	Drape & Tassel; Lincoln Drape; Tassel	Hocking, 1931-1935	Blue, green, pink, topaz; platinum trim, green with gold trim

PATTERN NAME	CROSS-REFERENCE	MANUFACTURER AND DATES	COLORS AND DESCRIPTION
*Princess Feather (R)	Early American; Flower; Oatmeal Lace; Scroll & Star; Westmoreland Sandwich	Westmoreland, 1939-1948; 1960s	Aqua, crystal, green, pink
Prismatic Line	See Queen Mary		
Provincial	See Bubble (Anchor Hocking)		
Provincial		Heisey	Crystal, Limelight
Punties		Duncan & Miller, 1931	Amber, crystal, green, rose
Puritan		Duncan & Miller, 1929	Crystal
Pyramid	See No. 610		
Pyramid Optic		Hocking	Crystal, green
Queen Anne	See also Bee Hive	Anchor Hocking, late 1930s	Crystal, pink; beverage set
*Queen Mary	Prismatic Line; Vertical Ribbed; see also Lace Edge	Anchor Hocking, 1936-1940	Crystal, pink, red
*Radiance		New Martinsville, 1936-1939	Amber, cobalt blue, crystal, green, Ice Blue, red
*Raindrops	Optic Design; Pebble Optic; see also Pear Optic	Federal, 1929-1933	Crystal, green
Rambler		Fostoria, 1935-1958	Crystal
Raspberry Band	See Laurel		
Rex	See No. 610		
Ribbed	See Manhattan		
Ribbed Octagon		Heisey, 1925-1936	Crystal, Flamingo, Hawthorne, Moongleam
*Ribbon		Hazel Atlas, 1930s	Black, crystal, green
Ribbon Candy	See Pretzel		
Ridgeleigh		Heisey, 1935-1957	Crystal, Sahara, Zircon

PATTERN NAME	CROSS-REFERENCE	MANUFACTURER AND DATES	COLORS AND DESCRIPTION
*Ring	Banded Rainbow; Banded Rings	Hocking, 1927–1932	Blue, crystal, green, pink, red; rings of black, blue, orange, pink, platinum, red, yellow
*Ring-Ding		Hocking, 1932	Painted bands of green, orange, red, yellow
Ringed Target		Macbeth-Evans, 1931	Crystal, green, pink; iced tea set
Ripple	See Ocean Wave		
*Rock Crystal	Early Americn Rock Crystal	McKee, 1920s–1930s	Amber, blue-green, cobalt blue, crystal, green, pink, red, yellow
Romanesque	See Gothic Arches		
Rope	See Colonial Fluted		
Rosalie		Cambridge, 1920s–1930s	Amber, blue, green, Heatherbloom, pink, red
Rose		Standard, c.1930	Topaz
Rose & Thorn	See Thorn		
*Rose Cameo		Belmont Tumbler, 1933	Green
Rose Lace	See Royal Lace		
*Rose Point		Cambridge	Crystal; gold trim
Rose Trellis	See Block with Rose		
*Rosemary	Cabbage Rose with Single Arch; Dutch Rose; see also Mayfair Federal	Federal, 1935–1937	Amber, green, pink
*Roulette	Many Windows	Anchor Hocking, 1935–1939	Crystal, green, pink
*Round Robin	Accordion Pleats	Late 1920s–1930s	Crystal, green, iridescent marigold
Roxana		Hazel Atlas, 1932	Crystal, white, yellow
Royal	Coronada	Fostoria, 1925–1934	Amber, black, blue, crystal, green; blue trimmed in white and yellow gold
*Royal Lace	Gladioli; Rose Lace	Hazel Atlas, 1934–1941	Amethyst, cobalt blue, crystal, green, pink

PATTERN NAME	CROSS-REFERENCE	MANUFACTURER AND DATES	COLORS AND DESCRIPTION
*Royal Ruby (R)		Anchor Hocking, 1939-1960s	Red
Russian	See Holiday		
*S Pattern	Stippled Rose Band	Macbeth-Evans, 1930-1935	Amber, crystal, green, Monax, pink, red, Ritz Blue, topaz; trimmed in amber, blue, gold, green, pink, platinum, red, rose, silver, white
Sail Boat	See White Ship		
Sailing Ship	See White Ship		
*Sandwich Anchor Hocking (R)		Anchor Hocking, 1939-1964	Amber, crystal, Forest Green, opaque white, pink, red
*Sandwich Duncan & Miller		Duncan & Miller, 1924-1955	Amber, cobalt blue, crystal, green, pink, red
*Sandwich Indiana (R)		Indiana, 1920s-1980s	Amber, crystal, light green, pink, red, Teal Blue
Saturn		Heisey, 1937-1957	Crystal, pale green
Sawtooth	See English Hobnail		
Saxon	See Coronation		
Scallop Edge		McKee	Green, pink
Scalloped Panels	See Lindburgh		
Scottie Dog	See also Laurel	McKee, 1930s	Children's set
Scrabble		Macbeth-Evans, 1931	Crystal, green, pink; iced tea set and tumblers
Scramble		Westmoreland, 1924	Amber, blue, crystal, green, rose
Scroll	See Comet		
Scroll & Star	See Princess Feather		
Scroll Fluted	Feather Scroll	Imperial, c.1930	Crystal, green, pink
Sea-Side		Jenkins	Crystal, green, iridescent amber
Semper		Louie, 1931	Green, pink, topaz; refreshment set
Shaffer		Imperial, c.1930	Amber, blue, crystal, green
Shamrock	See Cloverleaf		

PATTERN NAME	CROSS-REFERENCE	MANUFACTURER AND DATES	COLORS AND DESCRIPTION
*Sharon (R)	Cabbage Rose	Federal, 1935–1939	Amber, crystal, green, pink
Sheffield	See also Chinex Classic; Cremax	Macbeth-Evans (Corning Glass), 1930–1940	Chinex, Cremax
Shell	See Petalware		
Sheraton	Line 550; Panel	Bartlett-Collins, 1930s	Crystal
*Shirley Temple (R)		Hazel Atlas, U.S. Glass, and others, 1934–1942	Cobalt blue and white
*Sierra	Pinwheel	Jeannette, 1931–1933	Green, pink, Ultramarine
Simplicity		Morgantown	Green, pink
Smocking	See Windsor		
Snowflake	See Doric		
Snowflake on Block	See Block with Snowflake		
Soda Fountain		Indiana, c.1930	Green, pink
Soda Shop		Smith, mid-1920s	Crystal
Sommerset		Morgantown, 1932	Black, blue, crystal, green, ruby; beverage set
Spanish Fan	Spanish Lace		Crystal, green
Spanish Lace	See Spanish Fan		
Sphinx	See Centaur		
*Spiral	Spiral Optic; Swirled Big Rib; see also Twisted Optic	Hocking, 1928–1930	Green, pink
*Spiral Flutes		Duncan & Miller, 1924–early 1930s	Amber, crystal, crystal with gold trim, green, light blue, pink, Vaseline
Spiral Optic	See Spiral		
Spoke	See Patrician		
*Sportsman Series	See also White Ship; Windmill	Hazel Atlas, 1940s	Amethyst, cobalt blue, crystal with fired-on decorations
Spring Flowers		Imperial, 1920s	Crystal; plate only
Springtime		Fostoria, 1933–1944	Crystal, topaz

PATTERN NAME	CROSS-REFERENCE	MANUFACTURER AND DATES	COLORS AND DESCRIPTION
*Spun		Imperial, 1935	Aqua, crystal, fired-on orange, pastel colors, red
Square	See Charm	Anchor Hocking, 1940s–1960s	
Square		Morgantown, 1928	Crystal
Squat Optic		Federal, 1928	Crystal; water set
Squirt		Macbeth-Evans, 1931	Crystal, Emerald Green; water sets
*Starlight		Hazel Atlas, 1930s	Cobalt blue, crystal, pink, white
Stippled	See Craquel		
Stippled Rose Band	See S Pattern		
*Strawberry	See also Cherry-Berry	U.S. Glass, 1930s	Crystal, green, iridescent marigold, pink
Strawflower		Imperial, c.1930	Amber, crystal, green, Rose Marie
Stripe		Hocking, 1932	Red and white bands
*Sunburst		Jeannette, 1938–1941	Crystal
*Sunflower		Jeannette, late 1920s–early 1930s	Delphite, Emerald Green, light green, pink; opaque
Sunray		Fostoria, 1935–1944	Amber, Azure, Gold Tint, green, ruby
*Swankyswigs		Hazel Atlas, 1933–1940; 1947–1956; Bartlett-Collins, 1956–1958; 1975	5-oz. decorated tumblers
Sweet Pear	See Avocado		
*Swirl	Double Swirl; Petal Swirl	Jeannette, 1937–1938	Amber, Delphite, Ice Blue, pink, Ultramarine
*Swirl Fire-King	See also Alice; Charm; Fire-King Oven Ware; Jadite; Jane-Ray; Peach Lustre; Philbe; Turquoise Blue; Wheat	Anchor Hocking, 1955–1960s	Blue, ivory with trim, Jadite, pink, white with gold trim
Swirled Big Rib	See Spiral		
Swirled Sharp Rib	See Diana		

PATTERN NAME	CROSS-REFERENCE	MANUFACTURER AND DATES	COLORS AND DESCRIPTION
*Sylvan	Parrot; Three Parrot	Federal, 1931–1932	Amber, blue, crystal, green
Tall Boy		Federal, 1928	Green; iced tea sets
Tassel	See Princess		
*Tea Room	Moderne Art	Indiana, 1926–1931	Amber, crystal, green, pink
*Tear Drop		Duncan & Miller, 1934–1955	Crystal
*Terrace		Duncan & Miller, 1935	Amber, blue, crystal, ruby
*Thistle		Macbeth-Evans, 1929–1930	Crystal, green, pink, yellow
Thorn	Rose & Thorn	U.S. Glass, 1930s	Black, crystal, green, pink
Threading	See Old English		
Three Bands		Hocking, 1930s	Opaque white with three enameled bands
Three Parrot	See Sylvan		
Thumbprint	See Pear Optic		
Tiered Block	See Line 191		
Tiered Octagon	See Octagon		
Tiered Semi-Optic	See Line 191		
Tom & Jerry		Hazel Atlas, 1930s	Opaque white, enameled decorations
Tom & Jerry		McKee, 1940s	Black, ivory, white with black, gold, green, red decorations
*Tradition	Jamestown	Imperial, 1930s	Amber, amethyst, blue, crystal, green, pink, red
Tree of Life	See Craquel		
*Trojan		Fostoria, 1929–1944	Gold Tint, green, rose, topaz
Trudy		Standard, c.1930	Green, pink
Truman		Liberty, 1930	Green, pink
Trump Bridge		Federal, 1928	Colored enamel decorations; luncheon set
Tudor Ring		Federal, 1928	Crystal, green; water set
*Tulip		Dell, 1930s	Amber, amethyst, blue, crystal, green

PATTERN NAME	CROSS-REFERENCE	MANUFACTURER AND DATES	COLORS AND DESCRIPTION
*Turquoise Blue	See also Alice; Charm; Fire-King Oven Ware; Jadite; Jane-Ray; Peach Lustre; Philbe; Swirl Fire-King; Wheat	Anchor Hocking, 1950s	Turquoise
Twentieth Century		Hazel Atlas, 1928–1931	Crystal, green, pink
Twin Dolphin		Jenkins	Crystal, green, iridescent amber
Twist		Heisey, 1928-1937	Crystal, Flamingo, Marigold, Moongleam, Sahara
*Twisted Optic	See also Spiral	Imperial, 1927-1930	Amber, blue, Canary Yellow, green, pink
Twitch	Line 92	Bartlett-Collins, early 1930s	Green
U.S. Octagon	See Octagon		
U.S. Swirl		U.S. Glass, late 1920s	Crystal, green, pink
Vernon	See No. 616		
*Versailles		Fostoria, 1928-1944	Azure, crystal bases with colored glass, gold tinted, green, rose, topaz
Vertical Ribbed	See Queen Mary		
*Vesper		Fostoria, 1926-1934	Amber, crystal, green, blue
Victorian	Old Colony; Waffle King; Wayside Inn	Heisey, 1933-1953	Cobalt blue, crystal, Flamingo, Moongleam, Zircon
*Victory		Diamond Glass, 1929-1932	Amber, black, cobalt blue, green, pink; gold trim
Victory Model		Silex, 1938-1942	Amber, cobalt blue, green, pink; coffeepot
Viking		Imperial, 1929	Green, rose
*Vitrock	Floral Rim; Flower Rim	Hocking, 1934-1937	Green, red, white, white with fired-on colors; decal decorations

PATTERN NAME	CROSS-REFERENCE	MANUFACTURER AND DATES	COLORS AND DESCRIPTION
Vivid Bands	See Petalware		
Waffle	See Waterford		
Waffle Keg	See Victorian		
Wagner		Westmoreland, 1924	Amber, blue, green, rose
Wakefield		Westmoreland, 1933–1960s	Crystal
Washington Bicentennial		1932	Topaz; tumbler
*Waterford	Waffle	Anchor Hocking, 1938–1944; 1950s	Crystal, Forest Green, pink, white, white with fired-on pink or green, yellow
Wave	See Caribbean		
Wayside Inn	See Victorian		
Weatherford		Cambridge, 1926	Amber-Glo, emerald, Peach-Blo
Wedding Band	See Moderntone		
Westmoreland Sandwich	See Princess Feather	Anchor-Hocking, 1960s	White
*Wheat	See also Alice; Charm; fire-King Oven Ware; Jadite; Jane-Ray; Peach Lustre; Philbe; Swirl Fire-King; Turquoise Blue	Federal, early 1930s	Crystal, green, pink
*Whirly-Twirly		Anchor Hocking, 1940s	Forest Green, red
White Sail	See White Ship		
*White Ship	Beverages with Sailboats; Sail Boat; Sailing Ship; White Sail	Hazel Atlas, 1938	Blue with white decorations
Wiggle		McKee, 1925	Amethyst, amber, blue, canary, green
Wildflower	See No. 618		
Wildrose	See Dogwood		
Wildrose with Apple Blossom	See Flower Garden with Butterflies		

PATTERN NAME	CROSS-REFERENCE	MANUFACTURER AND DATES	COLORS AND DESCRIPTION
*Windmill	Dutch; see also Sportsman Series	Hazel Atlas, 1938	Blue with white decorations
Windmill & Checkerboard	Block with Windmill		Crystal, green
*Windsor	Diamond; Smocking; Windsor Diamond	Jeannette, 1936–1946	Amberina, blue, crystal, Delphite, green, pink
Windsor Diamond	See Windsor		
Winged Medallion	See Madrid		
Woodbury		Imperial, c.1930	Amber, crystal, green, Rose Marie
*Woolworth	Oregon Grape; see also Grape	Westmoreland, early 1930s	Blue, crystal, green, pink
Wotta Line		Paden City, 1933	Amber, amethyst, Cheri-Glo, crystal, ebony, green, Royal Blue, ruby, topaz
*X Design	Criss Cross	Hazel Atlas, 1928–1932	Crystal, green, pink, white; breakfast set
Yankee		Macbeth-Evans, 1931	Crystal, green, pink; water set
Yoo-Hoo		Jenkins, c.1930	
Yo-Yo		Jenkins, c.1930	
Yvonne	Carolyn	Lancaster, mid-1930s	Green, yellow
Zeppo		Louie, 1936	Black, green, pink, Royal Blue, ruby, topaz; crystal handles; beverage set

We welcome any additions or corrections to this chart. Please write to us c/o Crown Publishers, Inc., 201 E. 50th St., New York, NY 10022.

AMERICAN
DINNERWARE

Introduction

Many patterns of ceramic dinnerware were made in America from the 1930s through the 1960s. Some collectors refer to it as "Depression dinnerware," but the name used by the manufacturers was "American dinnerware," which is the name used by most collectors and dealers.

Pottery, porcelain, semiporcelain, ironstone, and other ceramic wares are included in the category of dinnerware. Most were made in potteries located in Southern Ohio and in West Virginia near the Ohio River. Each factory made many patterns for sale to gift shops and department stores. The potteries also made special patterns for use as premiums and free giveaways or to sell for low prices as store promotions.

American dinnerware patterns fall into six categories. The first patterns to be rediscovered by collectors and the first to be reproduced have been the solid-colored pottery lines such as Fiesta or Harlequin. Some of this type of dinnerware was also made in California potteries before 1960.

Many manufacturers preferred hand-painted decorations on their dinnerware. Included in this group are the pieces made by Southern Potteries under the name Blue Ridge and the pottery by Stangl of New Jersey, picturing fruit, flowers, or birds.

An unusual type of dinnerware made by Harker and others was Cameo Ware: a solid-colored plate embellished with a white decoration that appears to be cut into the colored glaze.

Realistically shaped pieces resembling corn were produced by several makers. The most important was Corn King by the Shawnee Pottery Company. Green and yellow dishes were made in full sets. Other dishes in three-dimensional shapes include the Red Riding Hood line, many figural cookie jars, a few figural teapots, and salt and pepper shakers.

Some of the dishes were made in very modern shapes with solid-colored decorations. The innovative shapes and subtle earth-tone colorings made them a favorite in the 1940s and 1950s. Examples of these are wares designed by Russel Wright for several firms and the Lu-Ray pattern by Taylor, Smith, and Taylor.

Most of the dinnerware was decorated with decal designs: colored, printed patterns applied to the dishes. The most famous of these designs,

Autumn Leaf, was made for and sold by the Jewel Tea Company. Mexican-inspired designs such as Mexicana by Homer Laughlin were popular during the late 1930s. The Hall China Company made many decal-decorated wares, including Poppy, Red Poppy, and Crocus. Black silhouette designs against light-colored dishes were popular in the 1930s, and included Silhouette by the Crooksville China Company and Taverne by the Hall China Company.

Because dishes were made by so many manufacturers, there is a problem with variations in vocabulary. Most sugar bowls made for these dinnerware sets had covers. Today many have lost the original cover and are sold as open sugars. We do not include the word *open* in the description, but we do indicate if there is a cover.

The terms "kitchenware" and "dinnerware" are used in the original sense. A dinnerware set includes all the pieces that might have been used on a dinner table, including dishes, bowls, platters, tumblers, cups, pitchers, and serving bowls. A kitchenware set has bowls and storage dishes of the type used in a kitchen and does not include dinner plates or cups. Kitchenwares include rolling pins, pie servers, and other kitchen utensils.

Colors often were given romantic names, and wherever necessary, we have used more ordinary language. So although we may describe a set as Surf Green or Persian Cream, we will list it as green or ivory. Some colors, such as Camellia (rose), Cadet (light blue), Indian Red (orange), or Dresden (deep blue), are explained in the paragraph descriptions.

It is important to remember that the descriptions of dinnerware may include many strange names. Some are the factory names, some refer to the pattern (decorations applied to the piece), and many were used by the factory to describe the shape. For example, Taverne is a pattern, Laurel is the shape of the dish used to make that pattern, and Taylor, Smith, and Taylor is the name of the company that made the dinnerware. Sometimes a name refers to both a pattern and a shape.

Pieces of American dinnerware are constantly being discovered in attics, basements, garage sales, flea markets, and antiques shops. The publications that offer them through the mail use descriptions that often include both the pattern and the shape name. Learn to recognize the shapes that were used by each maker. Authors of some of the other books about dinnerwares have arbitrarily named the pieces. Sometimes these names, although referring to the same piece, are different in different books. We have tried to cross-reference these names so you can locate them in any of the books. A list of known patterns of dinnerware, shapes, and makers is included at the end of this section.

There is a special vocabulary for every hobby.
This is an illustrated list of words that have special meaning to collectors of
Depression glass and American dinnerware.

Amethyst glass is the deep purple color of the mineral amethyst. This Newport pattern amethyst glass plate is $8\,^1/_2$ inches in diameter and sells for $10.

Autumn Leaf dinnerware was distributed by Jewel Tea Company starting in 1936. The pattern includes dark yellow and rust leaves in the border. The pattern also was used on matching table linens, metal canister sets, and other kitchen wares. This is a $2\,^1/_2$-inch-high covered sugar bowl worth $25.

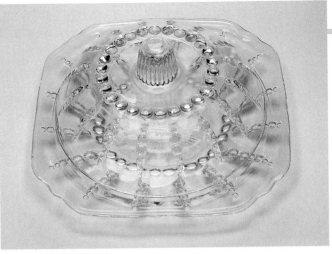

A **butter dish** is a covered dish used to hold butter on the table, or a covered storage dish used for butter in the refrigerator. Covered butter dishes for the table often have round dome covers. The butter was usually kept on the table, not in a refrigerator, so it would be soft enough to spread easily on bread. This covered butter dish is Columbia pattern. Price, $15.

If you run your finger across the surface of this Harker Pottery **cameo-ware** child's plate, you will be able to tell that the pink glaze is higher than the white design. This unusual glazing technique is found on several American dinnerware patterns. This plate is valued at $3.50.

There are two meanings for the word cameo-ware: (1) Wedgwood Pottery of England made a decorative pottery with raised white designs on a colored background and called it cameo-ware. (2) American dinnerware manufacturers made a white dinnerware with a colored glaze covering all but a silhouette design. A thick-edged stencil was used in the center of the plate. The potter then applied a thin layer of slip (liquid clay) around the stencil so the design was lower than the rest of the plate. Then a layer of colored glaze was applied around the stencil.

Candy dishes came in several different styles. The covered candy dish in Moonstone pattern at left is 6 inches wide, 2 inches high. Value, $18. The ruffled round Beaded Block candy dish with iridescent trim just below is 7 $\frac{1}{2}$ inches wide and is valued at $6. Candy dishes were usually about 5 inches in diameter, often on a pedestal foot or three small feet. Most Depression glass candy dishes were made with covers, although some were made with a ruffled edge and no cover or feet, as in the Beaded Block dish.

This Diana pattern **cereal bowl,** in the traditional size and shape, is 2 inches high, 5 inches in diameter. It is worth $8.

Cobalt blue, the dark blue color of this glass or a glaze on a piece of dinnerware, was originally made by grinding the mineral cobalt and mixing it with oxides. This Moderntone blue creamer is valued at $20.

A **cocktail glass** is a bell-shaped drinking glass with a foot and stem, usually designed to hold about three ounces. This green Colonial pattern Depression glass cocktail glass is in the typical shape. It is 4 inches high, holds 4 ounces of liquid refreshment, and is worth $24.

A **disk pitcher** is a pitcher with flattened sides. The name usually refers to Fiesta and related dinnerware patterns. The disk pitcher shape is still popular. This new Fiesta pitcher with Bugs Bunny on the side sells for $22. The color and design are new, but the shape is old.

Enamel decoration is color applied, then baked on, to the glass or ceramic. This Windmill pattern ice bowl is an example of a piece of glass with enamel decoration. It's worth $25. The white windmill is of baked-on color, the glass is blue.

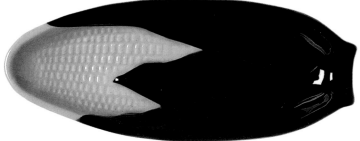

Realistic, three-dimensional shapes known as **figural shapes** were used for some patterns of dinnerware. This Corn Queen dish, 8 inches long, looks like an ear of corn. The kernels and leaves on this figural piece are raised. Value, $29.

Fire-King is the trade name used by Anchor Hocking Company of Lancaster, Ohio, for a transparent, pale blue glassware. Fire-King was popular from 1942 to the 1960s. This is a pale blue Fire-King dinner plate. Value, $6.

Fired-on colors are applied to glass, then baked under high heat at the factory. The orange Moderntone creamer is made of white glass colored with fired-on orange color. Price, $2.50.

A **goblet** has a stem. A glass without a stem is called a tumbler (see page 16). Capacity in ounces is determined by the shape. Many different names are given to stemmed glasses. The size and the shape of the bowl differs with each type.

cordial	1 ounce
wine	2–2$\frac{1}{2}$ ounce
cocktail	3–4 ounce
claret	5 ounce
champagne	5 ounce
water	8 or 9 ounce
5$\frac{3}{4}$ inch	9 ounce
7$\frac{1}{4}$ inch	15 ounce

This 4$\frac{1}{2}$-inch-high Rock Crystal goblet sells for $15.

A **gravy boat** is a bowl, often oval or round in shape. Some gravy boats have a pouring spout at one end, some at both ends. This Lu-Ray example is worth $15.

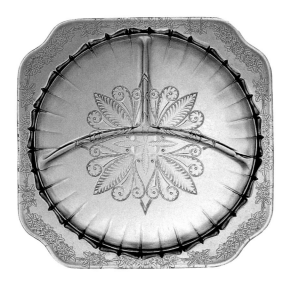

The **grill plate** first came into use in the 1920s. It is a round three-sectioned plate used to serve meat and vegetables in separate sections, similar to a modern TV-dinner tray. This Adam pattern glass piece is not a relish dish; it is a grill plate. Notice the position of the three sections, one large and two small. It is $9\frac{1}{2}$ inches in diameter and no thicker than a normal dinner plate. It sells for $16.

Hall China Company of East Liverpool, Ohio, made many different teapots, starting in the 1920s. Collectors group all of these special teapots into one category known as **Hall teapots**. There are many shapes and colors, and most were made without matching dinnerware sets. This yellow teapot with gold decoration is in the shape called Parade. It is 5 inches high. Value, $30.

A **hand-painted** design is literally painted on the piece by hand. It is not a transfer or a decal. Red Wing dinnerwares are often hand-painted, so each piece has a slightly different design. This 7-inch pitcher, worth $20, is Bob White pattern.

Incised decorations are drawn into the wet clay with a pointed tool, then the finishing colors or glazes are added. The dark lines and edges of the flowers and leaves are incised on this Stangl pottery Magnolia pattern dinnerplate worth $7.50

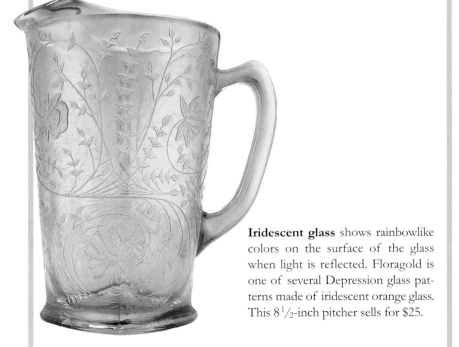

Iridescent glass shows rainbowlike colors on the surface of the glass when light is reflected. Floragold is one of several Depression glass patterns made of iridescent orange glass. This 8 1/2-inch pitcher sells for $25.

Jade-ite is a variant spelling of jadite, an opaque light-green colored glass. The hyphenated spelling is also the name of a pattern of Kitchenware made of the opaque green glass. This Jane-Ray pattern covered sugar bowl at left is made of jadite glass. Price, $10.

When two unrelated pieces are put together to make a new form such as the pink Anniversary pattern cup and sugar bowl lid, above left, it is called a **marriage**. This cup with lid was priced at $6.50 by a dealer at a Depression glass show. The lid really belongs on the Floral pattern pink sugar bowl, above right.

A set of mixing bowls of graduated sizes made to fit inside one another is called a **nest**. The smallest is number 1, and the rest are consecutively numbered. Mixing bowls often came in nested sets. This Fire-King tulip pattern set is missing the second smallest bowl. Value: $6\frac{1}{2}$-inch diameter, $8; $8\frac{1}{2}$-inch, $10; $9\frac{1}{2}$-inch, $12. Most sets have four or five bowls.

An **open salt** is a small open dish made to hold salt at the table. It was used with a tiny spoon. This $2^1/_2$-inch-tall amber English Hobnail dish looks like an eye cup, but it is an open salt, priced at $20.

Ruby glass is the deep red color of the ruby gemstone. This ruby Rock Crystal pattern saucer, $5^1/_2$ inches in diameter, is worth $15.

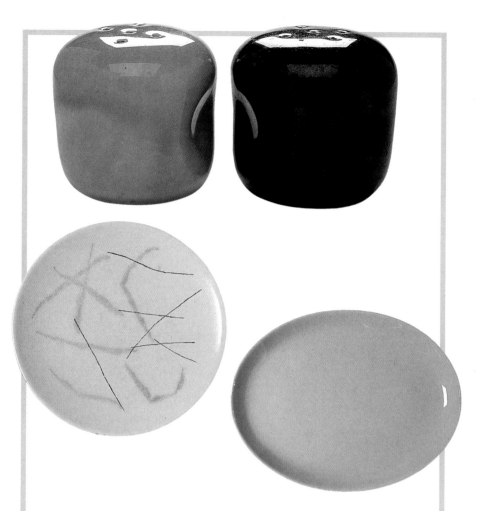

Russel Wright was a famous twentieth-century industrial designer who created many dinnerware patterns, including the most popular one ever made, American Modern. He also designed silver, glassware, furniture, woodenware, aluminum wares, and many other items. Dinnerwares designed by Russel Wright had unfamiliar shapes and a very modern look for the 1950s. The salt and pepper set (*top*) with one bean brown shaker and one chartreuse shaker, is American Modern pattern. Russel Wright dishes were sold in mix-and-match colors. The $12\frac{1}{2}$-inch Russel Wright platter (*above right*) was made by Iroquois China. It sells for $15. Although most Russel Wright patterns were made in solid colors, a few had extra decoration, such as the 8-inch Grass pattern plate (*above left*).

Salt and peppers are sets of two matching containers, one for salt, the other for pepper. The Depression glass sets were usually about 5 inches tall and sometimes had pedestal feet. The dinnerware sets were made in a variety of shapes, often low in height. This $4^1/_2$-inch-tall salt and pepper set in pink Mayfair pattern is worth $55.

A **Sandwich server** is a center-handled serving plate used for sandwiches. A **sandwich plate** is a large plate, often with handles on the sides, such as this $12^1/_2$-inch green Cherry Blossom pattern plate, which sells for $20.

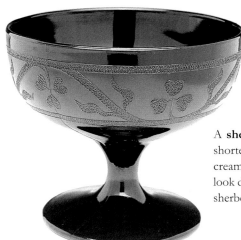

A **sherbet** is a pedestal-footed bowl, shorter than a goblet, used to serve ice cream or sherbet. Ice cream would look delicious in this black Clover Leaf sherbet worth $15.

A **stacked cream and sugar** is designed so the creamer fits on top of the sugarbowl in a small "stack." The white set on the left is a stacked cream and sugar worth $25. The gray creamer on the right, valued at $10, is part of a similar set. All of the pieces are Iroquois pattern by Russel Wright.

Starting in 1933, Kraft Cheese Company marketed cheese spreads in decorated reusable 5-ounce glass tumblers called **Swankyswigs**. When they first appeared in the grocery store, each of these glasses had a metal top and paper label and were filled with cheese. Each design had a different name. These are Posy Jonquil and Posy Tulip.

A **tumbler** does not have a stem, although it may have a foot. Capacity in ounces is determined by the shape. **Tumbler sizes** are

2½ inch	whiskey glass-3 ounce
3¾ inch	4–5 ounce
4–4½ inch	7 ounce, juice
4–6 inch	9–12 ounce iced tea, water

The 4¾-inch-high Bowknot-pattern green glass tumbler above is also called a juice glass. Value, $16.

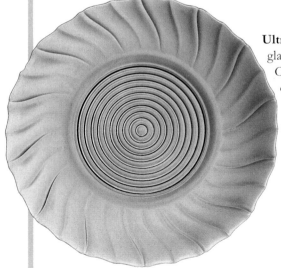

Ultramarine is a blue-green color glass made by Jeannette Glass Company. The distinctive color of Ultramarine makes it easy to spot. This Swirl pattern 9-inch plate is valued at $12.50.

Although hundreds of patterns are included in this book, many patterns were not seen at sales this year and were not included. Prices listed in this book are actual prices asked by dealers at shows, shops, and through national advertising. It is not the price you would pay at a garage sale or church bazaar. Prices are not estimates. If a high and low are given, we have recorded several sales. There is a regional variation in the prices, especially for the solid-colored wares. In general, these pieces are high-priced in the East and West, lower in the center of the country.

There have been a few reissues of dinnerwares. Harlequin was put back into production in 1979 for the Woolworth Company, the sole distributor. Complete dinner sets were made in the original colors, except that the salmon is a deeper color than the original. The sugar bowls were made with closed handles. A Fiesta look-alike has been made by Franciscan since 1978 under the name Kaleidoscope. Fiesta was reissued by Homer Laughlin China Company in 1986. The original molds and marks were used. The new Fiesta has a china body that shrinks a little more than the semivitreous clay body used before. This means that most pieces are slightly smaller than the old ones. Dinner plates and soup/cereal bowls, however, were made slightly larger to accommodate modern tastes. New molds were made for these pieces. The dinner plates are 10½ inches. The new dishes were first made in cobalt blue (darker than the original), black, white, apricot, and rose. Other colors have been added. A few of the pieces have been slightly redesigned since 1986, with variations in handles and bases. A special line was made with added cartoon decorations.

If you plan to collect dinnerware, be sure to do further research into your patterns in the books listed in the Bibliography that follows. Particular patterns can be found by using either the Depression Glass or American Dinnerware main listings, both of which are arranged alphabetically. Depression Glass begins on page 11 and American Dinnerware on page 129. There is no index of pattern names in this book because it would only duplicate the main listings. However, we have compiled lists of known Depression glass and American dinnerware patterns along with information on manufacturers, dates, alternate names, and descriptions. These can be found at the end of each section. Patterns listed in the main sections of the book are those most popular with collectors. This book is a report of prices for pieces offered for sale during the past year. Most of the patterns included in earlier books are found here because the collectors still buy these patterns. Many newly popular patterns are also included.

Bibliography

Bess, Phyllis and Tom. *Frankoma Treasures.* Privately printed, 1983 (14535 E. 13th St., Tulsa, OK 74108).

Bess, Phyllis and Tom. *Suggested Values for Frankoma Treasures.* Privately printed, 1990 (14535 E. 13th St., Tulsa, OK 74108).

Bougie, Stanley J., and David A. Newkirk. *Red Wing Dinnerware.* Privately printed, 1980 (Rte. 3, Box 141, Monticello, MN 55362).

Carlton, Carol & Jim, *Collector's Encyclopedia of Colorado Pottery.* Paducah, Kentucky: Collector Books, 1994.

Catalina Art Pottery Price List and General Sales Instructions, 1942 (catalog reprint). Privately printed, 1982 (Delleen Enge, 912 N. Signal, Ojai, CA 93023).

Chipman, Jack, and Judy Stangler. *Bauer Pottery 1982 Price Guide.* Privately printed, 1982 (16 East Holly Street, Pasadena, CA 91003).

Chipman, Jack. *Collector's Encyclopedia of California Pottery.* Paducah, Kentucky: Collector Books, 1992.

Colbert, Neva W. *Collector's Guide to Harker Pottery U.S.A.* Paducah, Kentucky: Collector Books, 1992.

Cox, Susan N. *Collectors Guide to Frankoma Pottery,* Book Two. Privately printed, 1982 (P.O. Box 2674, La Mesa, CA 92041).

Cunningham, Jo. *Autumn Leaf Story Price Guide.* Privately printed, 1979 (Box 4929, Springfield, MO 65808).

Cunningham, Jo. *Collector's Encyclopedia of American Dinnerware.* Paducah, Kentucky: Collector Books, 1982.

Cunningham, Jo. *Hall China Price Update.* Privately printed, 1982 (Box 4929, Springfield, MO 65808).

Derwich, Jenny and Mary Latos. *Dictionary Guide to United States Pottery & Porcelain (19th and 20th Century).* Privately printed, 1984 (P.O. Box 674, Franklin, MI 48025).

Dole, Pat. *Purinton Pottery.* Privately printed, 1984 (P.O. Box 4782, Birmingham, AL 35206).

Dole, Pat. *Purinton Pottery Book II.* Privately printed, 1990 (142 West Salisbury St., P.O. Box 308, Denton, NC 27239-0308).

Duke, Harvey. *Official Price Guide to Pottery and Porcelain,* 8th edition. New York: House of Collectibles, 1994.

Duke, Harvey. *Stangl Pottery.* Radnor, Pennsylvania: Wallace-Homestead, 1993.

Duke, Harvey. *Superior Quality Hall China: A Guide for Collectors.* Privately printed, 1977 (Box HB, 12135 N. State Road, Otisville, MI 48463).

Enge, Delleen. *Franciscan Ware*. Paducah, Kentucky: Collector Books, 1981.

Eva Zeisel: Designer for Industry. Chicago: University of Chicago Press, 1984.

Farmer, Linda D. *Farmer's Wife's Fiesta Inventory & Price Guide*. Privately printed, 1984 (P.O. Box 10371, Pittsburgh, PA 15234).

Fridley, A. W. *Catalina Pottery: The Early Years 1927-1937*. Privately printed, 1977 (P.O. Box 7723, Long Beach, CA 90807).

From Kiln to Kitchen: American Ceramic Design in Tableware. Springfield, Illinois: Illinois State Museum, 1980.

Gates, William C. Jr., and Dana E. Ormerod. *East Liverpool, Ohio, Pottery District Identification of Manufacturers & Marks*. Privately printed, 1982 (Society for Historical Archaeology, 1703 New Hampshire Ave., NW, Washington, DC 20009).

Hayes, Barbara, and Jean Bauer. *California Pottery Rainbow*. Privately printed, 1975 (1629 W. Washington Blvd., Venice, CA 90291).

Homer Laughlin China Company: A Fiesta of American Dinnerware. Newell, West Virginia: Homer Laughlin China Co., 1985.

Hull, Joan Gray. *Hull: The Heavenly Pottery*. 2nd edition. Privately printed, 1992 (1376 Nevada SW, Huron, SD 57350).

Hull, Joan Gray. *Hull Shirt Pocket Price List*. Privately printed, 1994 (1376 Nevada SW, Huron, SD 57350).

Huxford, Sharon and Bob. *Collectors Encyclopedia of Fiesta*, 7th edition. Paducah, Kentucky: Collector Books, 1992.

Jasper, Joanne. *The Collector's Encyclopedia of Homer Laughlin China: Reference & Value Guide*. Paducah, Kentucky: Collector Books, 1993.

Keillor, Winnie. *Dishes What Else? Blue Ridge of Course!* Privately printed, 1983 (5731 Gorivan Rd., Frankfort, MI 49635).

Kerr, Ann. *Collector's Encyclopedia of Russel Wright Designs*. Paducah, Kentucky: Collector Books, 1990.

Kerr, Ann. *Russel Wright and His Dinnerware*. Privately printed, 1981 (P.O. Box 437, Sidney, OH 45365).

Kerr, Ann. *Russel Wright Dinnerware: Designs for the American Table*. Paducah, Kentucky: Collector Books, 1985.

Kerr, Ann. *Steubenville Saga*. Privately printed, 1979 (P.O. Box 437, Sidney, OH 45365).

Klein, Benjamin. *Collector's Illustrated Price Guide to Russel Wright Dinnerware*. Smithtown, New York: Exposition Press, Inc., 1981.

Kovel, Ralph and Terry. *Kovels' Antiques & Collectibles Price List*. 27th edition. New York: Crown Publishers, 1995.

Kovel, Ralph and Terry. *Kovels' Guide to Selling, Buying, and Fixing Your Antiques and Collectibles*. New York: Crown Publishers, 1995.

Kovel, Ralph and Terry. *Kovels' Know Your Collectibles*. New York: Crown Publishers, 1981.

Kovel, Ralph and Terry. *Kovels' New Dictionary of Marks—Pottery & Porcelain 1850 to the Present*. New York: Crown Publishers, 1986.

Lehner, Lois. *Complete Book of American Kitchen and Dinner Wares.* Radnor, Pennsylvania: Wallace-Homestead Book Co., 1980.

Lehner, Lois. *Lehner's Encyclopedia of U.S. Marks on Pottery, Porcelain & Clay.* Paducah, Kentucky: Collector Books, 1988.

Mangus, Jim and Bev. *Shawnee Pottery: An Identification & Value Guide.* Paducah, Kentucky: Collector Books, 1994.

Morris, Susan. *Purinton Pottery.* Paducah, Kentucky: Collector Books, 1994.

Morris, Sue and Dave. *Watt Pottery: An Identification and Value Guide.* Paducah, KY: Collector Books, 1993.

Nelson, Maxine. *Collectible Vernon Kilns: An Identification & Value Guide.* Paducah, KY: Collector Books, 1994.

Nelson, Maxine. *Versatile Vernon Kilns.* Privately printed, 1978 (P.O. Box 1686, Huntington Beach, CA 92647).

Nelson, Maxine. *Versatile Vernon Kilns Book II.* Paducah, Kentucky: Collector Books, 1983.

Newbound, Betty. *Gunshot Guide to Values of American Made China & Pottery.* Privately printed, 1981 (4567 Chadsworth, Union Lake, MI 48085).

Newbound, Betty. *Gunshot Guide to Values of American Made China & Pottery*, Book 2. Privately printed, 1984 (4567 Chadsworth, Union Lake, MI 48085).

Newbound, Betty and Bill. *Southern Potteries Inc. Blue Ridge Dinnerware.* 3rd edition. Paducah, Kentucky: Collector Books, 1989.

Newkirk, David A. *Guide to Red Wing Prices.* Privately printed, 1982 (Rte. 3, Box 146, Monticello, MN 55362).

Nossaman, Darlene. *Homer Laughlin China: An Identification Guide,* revised edition. Privately printed, 1994 (5419 Lake Charles, Waco, TX 76710).

Piña, Leslie. *Pottery: Modern Wares 1920–1960.* Atglen, Pennsylvania: Schiffer Publishing Ltd., 1994.

Pottery 1880–1960. Encino, California: Orlando Gallery, 1973.

Rehl, Norma. *Abingdon Pottery.* Privately printed, 1981 (P.O. Box 556, Milford, NJ 08848).

Rehl, Norma. *Collectors Handbook of Stangl Pottery.* Privately printed, 1979 (P.O. Box 556, Milford, NJ 08848).

Rehl, Norma. *Stangl Pottery Part II.* Privately printed, 1982 (P.O. Box 556, Milford, NJ 08848).

Riederer, LaHoma, and Charles Bettinger. *Fiesta III, A Collector's Guide to Fiesta Dinnerware.* Privately printed, 1980 (P.O. Box 2733, Monroe, LA 71201).

Roberts, Brenda. *Collectors Encyclopedia of Hull Pottery.* Paducah, Kentucky: Collector Books, 1980.

Roberts, Brenda. *Roberts' Ultimate Encyclopedia of Hull Pottery.* Privately printed, 1992. (Rt 2, Highway 65 S., Marshall, MO 65340).

Roberts, Brenda. *Companion Guide to Roberts' Ultimate Encyclopedia of Hull Pottery.* Privately printed, 1992 (Rt. 2, Highway 65 S., Marshall, MO 65340).

Schneider, Robert. *Coors Rosebud Pottery*. Privately printed, 1984 (Box 10382S Pike Place Station, Seattle, WA 98101).

Simon, Dolores. *Red Wing Pottery with Rumrill*. Paducah, Kentucky: Collector Books, 1980.

Simon, Dolores. *Shawnee Pottery*. Paducah, Kentucky: Collector Books, 1977.

Sterling Vitrified China. Catalog, Sterling China Company, East Liverpool, Ohio, 1991.

Supnick, Mark E. *Collecting Shawnee Pottery*, Revised edition. Gas City, Indiana: L-W Book Sales, 1989. Revised 1992 prices.

Teftt, Gary and Bonnie. *Red Wing Potters & Their Wares*. 2nd edition Privately printed, 1987 (W174 N9422 Devonwood Rd., Menomonee Falls, WI 53051).

Thompson, Dennis, and W. Bryce Watt. *Watt Pottery: A Collector's Reference with Price Guide*. Atglen, Pennsylvania: Schiffer, 1994.

Vanderbilt, Duane and Janice. *The Collector's Guide to Shawnee Pottery*. Paducah, Kentucky: Collector Books, 1992.

Whitmyer, Margaret and Kenn. *Collector's Encyclopedia of Hall China*. 2nd edition. Paducah, Kentucky: Collector Books, 1994.

Clubs and Publications

CLUBS

Abingdon Pottery Collectors Club, *Abingdon Pottery Collectors Newsletter*, RR 1, Box 145, Abingdon, IL 61410.

Blue & White Pottery Club, *Blue & White Pottery Club* (newsletter), 224 12th St. NW, Center Point, IA 52405.

International Willow Collectors, *Willow Word* (newsletter), P.O. Box 13382, Arlington, TX 76094-0382.

Novelty Salt & Pepper Shakers Club, *Novelty Salt & Pepper Shakers Club Newsletter*, 581 Joy Rd., Battle Creek, MI 49017.

Red Wing Collectors Society, *Red Wing Collectors Newsletter*, 2246 95th St. NW, Maple Lake, MN 55238.

Shawnee Pottery Collector's Club, *Exclusively Shawnee* (newsletter), P.O. Box 713, New Smyrna Beach, FL 32170-0713.

PUBLICATIONS

Antique Trader Weekly (newspaper), P.O. Box 1050, Dubuque, IA 52004-1050.

Currier and Ives China (newsletter), Route 2, Box 192, Columbus, KS 66725.

Daze (newsletter), Box 57, Otisville, MI 48463.

Kovels on Antiques and Collectibles (newsletter), P.O. Box 22200, Beachwood, OH 44122.

Matching Services: China, Silver, Crystal (leaflet), Ralph and Terry Kovel (P.O. Box 22900, Beachwood, OH 44122).

National Blue Ridge Newsletter, 144 Highland Dr., Blountville, TN 37617-5404.

"Our McCoy Matters" (newsletter), P.O. Box 14255, Parkville, MO 64152.

Vernon Views (newsletter) (Vernon Kilns Pottery), P.O. Box 945, Scottsdale, AZ 85252.

A

Amber Glo

Amber Glo is a pattern made by Stangl in 1954. It was designed by Kay Hackett. The flames are orange, the background gray.

Bowl, 8 In. 20.00
Cruet, Stopper 25.00
Gravy Boat. . . . . . . 10.00 to 19.00

Amberstone

Fiesta is a popular dinnerware pattern found in solid colors. In 1967, Amberstone was made by the Homer Laughlin China Company of Newell, West Virginia, using the Fiesta shapes. The pieces were glazed a rich brown. Some pieces had black machine-stamped underglaze patterns. The pieces were used for supermarket promotions and were called Genuine Sheffield dinnerware. Full sets of dishes were made.

Bowl, 5 1/2 In. . . . . . . 2.00 to 3.50
Creamer. 5.00

Cup & Saucer 6.00
Plate, 6 In. . . . . 1.50 to 3.00
Plate, 8 In. 3.00
Plate, 10 In. 5.50
Platter, Oval, 13 In. 10.00

American Modern

Russel Wright was a designer who made dinnerware in modern shapes for many companies, including Iroquois China Company, Harker China Company, Steubenville Pottery, Paden City (Justin Tharaud and Sons), Sterling China Company, Edwin M. Knowles China Company, and Bauer Company. American Modern was made by the Steubenville Pottery Company, Steubenville, Ohio, from 1939 to 1959. The original dishes were made in Bean Brown (a shaded brown), chartreuse, coral, Granite Gray, Seafoam (blue-green), and white. The brown was replaced with Black Chutney (dark brown) during World War II. Cantaloupe, Cedar Green, and Glacier Blue were added in the 1950s. Matching linens and glassware were made.

BEAN BROWN
Bowl, Vegetable, 10 In. 55.00
Carafe, 50 Oz. 245.00
Cup & Saucer 50.00
Pitcher, Water 140.00
Plate, 8 1/4 In. 16.00
Plate, 10 In. 12.00
Refrigerator Jar 195.00
Sugar & Creamer. 45.00
Tray, Handle 275.00

BLACK CHUTNEY
Bowl, Vegetable, 10 In. 25.00
Butter, Cover. 250.00
Casserole, Cover, 12 In. . . . 60.00
Celery Dish, 13 In. 25.00
Gravy Boat 20.00
Plate, 10 In. 10.00
Plate Set, Cup Plate. 80.00

CANTALOUPE
Bowl, Vegetable, 10 In. 55.00
Casserole, Cover,
    12 In. . . . . . . 100.00 to 125.00
Cup & Saucer . . . . . 20.00 to 25.00
Plate, 10 In. . . . . . . 20.00 to 25.00

CEDAR GREEN
Bowl, Vegetable, 10 In. 35.00
Bowl, Vegetable,
    2 Sections 65.00
Celery Dish 20.00
Coffeepot, After Dinner,
    8 1/2 In. 110.00
Cup & Saucer 25.00
Pitcher 40.00
Plate, 8 In. 65.00
Teapot, 10 In. 65.00
Tumbler, Child's 150.00

CHARTREUSE

Baker, Vegetable, 10 3/4 In.	28.00
Bowl, Vegetable, Oval, 10 In.	13.00 to 20.00
Butter, Cover	110.00
Carafe, 50 Oz.	195.00
Celery Dish	22.00
Chop Plate, 13 In.	18.00
Coffeepot, After Dinner	50.00
Creamer	6.00
Cup & Saucer	4.50
Cup & Saucer, After Dinner	20.00
Gravy Boat	12.00 to 33.00
Pitcher, Water	33.00
Plate, 6 1/4 In.	3.00
Plate, 8 1/4 In.	2.00
Plate, 10 In.	4.50 to 7.50
Platter, 13 1/4 In.	20.00
Sauceboat, 8 3/4 In.	25.00
Sherbet	18.00
Soup, Dish, 2 Handles	7.00
Soup, Dish, Lug	10.00
Sugar, Cover	20.00
Tumbler, Child's	75.00

CORAL

Bowl, Vegetable, 2 Sections	55.00
Bowl, Vegetable, Cover, 12 In.	60.00
Butter, Cover	225.00
Coaster-Ashtray	14.00
Cup	9.00
Cup & Saucer	25.00
Gravy Boat	15.00 to 20.00
Pitcher, 7 1/2 In.	75.00
Plate, 6 1/4 In.	4.00
Plate, 8 1/4 In.	7.00 to 75.00
Plate, 10 In.	8.00 to 10.00
Plate, Child's	55.00
Soup, Dish, Lug	10.00
Sugar & Creamer	27.00
Teapot, 10 In.	48.00 to 65.00
Tumbler, Child's	24.00

GLACIER BLUE

Bowl, Vegetable, 2 Sections	120.00

Bowl, Vegetable, Cover, 12 In.	110.00
Casserole, Cover, 12 In.	100.00 to 125.00
Coaster-Ashtray	20.00
Coffeepot, After Dinner	125.00
Cup & Saucer	20.00 to 25.00
Plate, 10 In.	8.00

GRANITE GRAY

Bowl, Vegetable, 2 Sections	65.00 to 80.00
Bowl, Vegetable, Cover, 12 In.	50.00
Carafe, 50 Oz.	140.00 to 225.00
Casserole, Cover, 12 In.	60.00
Celery Dish	20.00
Coaster-Ashtray	14.00
Creamer	7.00 to 15.00
Cup	6.00
Cup & Saucer	8.00
Cup & Saucer, After Dinner	20.00 to 25.00
Dish, Fruit, Lug	18.00
Gravy Boat	15.00
Pitcher, Water	105.00
Plate, 6 1/4 In.	3.50 to 6.00
Plate, 8 1/4 In.	7.00 to 10.00
Plate, 10 In.	8.00 to 10.00
Platter, Oval, 13 3/4 In.	20.00
Salt & Pepper	12.00 to 20.00
Saucer	2.00
Server, Stacking	80.00
Sherbet	18.00
Soup, Dish, Lug	8.00 to 10.00
Sugar, Cover	10.00
Sugar & Creamer, Cover	25.00
Teapot, 10 In.	70.00

SEAFOAM

Bowl, Fruit, Lug, 6 1/4 In.	7.00
Casserole, Cover, 12 In.	38.00
Creamer	12.00
Pitcher, Water	65.00
Plate, 6 1/4 In.	4.00
Plate, 10 In.	8.00
Sherbet	20.00
Teapot, 10 In.	35.00
Tumbler, Child's	24.00
Wine	24.00

WHITE

Bowl, Vegetable, 2 Sections	100.00
Coffeepot, After Dinner	95.00
Plate, 10 In.	12.00
Server, Stacking	325.00

Apple Blossom

Two companies made patterns called Apple Blossom. Crooksville China of Crooksville, Ohio, made a pink flowered pattern. The pattern listed here was made by Homer Laughlin China Company of Newell, West Virginia, from 1935 to 1955. It has a flowered border and gold trim.

Casserole, Cover	32.00
Plate, 10 In.	8.00
Sugar & Creamer, Cover	28.00

Apple Franciscan

Gladding, McBean & Company made Apple pattern dishes, one of its Franciscan Ceramics "Classics" designs, beginning in 1940. The pattern is still being made, but Franciscan Ceramics is now part of Wedgwood Inc.

Ashtray, Oval...... 55.00 to 75.00
Bowl, 5 1/4 In. ...... 7.00 to 9.50
Bowl, 6 In. .... 8.00 to 16.00
Bowl, 9 In. 40.00
Bowl, Batter, 10 1/4 In. 35.00
Bowl, Salad 85.00
Bowl, Vegetable ... 25.00 to 28.00
Bowl, Vegetable, 2 Sections,
   Oval, 10 3/4 In. . 35.00 to 45.00
Butter, Cover,
   1/4 Lb. .... 25.00 to 36.00
Candleholder 35.00
Casserole, Cover, 2 1/2 Qt. . 75.00
Casserole, Cover,
   Individual...............45.00
Chop Plate,
   12 In. .... 40.00 to 60.00
Chop Plate,
   14 In. .... 65.00 to 125.00
Coffeepot,
   8 Cup .... 100.00 to 110.00
Cookie Jar ..... 140.00 to 250.00
Creamer...................8.00
Cup................ 5.00 to 8.00
Cup & Saucer ..... 10.00 to 15.00
Cup & Saucer, Jumbo 55.00
Dinner Bell 25.00
Eggcup........... 16.00 to 20.00
Gravy Boat....... 44.00 to 65.00
Jar, Marmalade, Cover.....125.00
Mixing Bowl, Large 125.00
Mixing Bowl, Medium......95.00
Mixing Bowl, Small 75.00
Mixing Bowl Set,
   Graduated, 3 Piece......350.00
Mug, 7 Oz. 15.00
Mug, 10 Oz. 80.00
Mug, 12 Oz. ..... 30.00 to 45.00
Napkin Ring, 12 Piece.....550.00
Pitcher, 1 Qt. 85.00
Pitcher, 2 Qt. 110.00
Plate, 6 In. .... 5.00 to 9.00
Plate, 8 In. 8.00
Plate, 9 1/2 In. .... 10.00 to 18.00
Plate, 10 1/2 In. .... 9.00 to 16.00
Platter, 12 In. ..... 28.00 to 40.00
Platter, 14 In. ..... 32.00 to 75.00
Platter, 17 In. ... 175.00 to 250.00

Relish,
   3 Sections......95.00 to 100.00
Salt & Pepper ..... 10.00 to 17.50
Salt & Pepper, Jumbo.......35.00
Saucer....................3.00
Saucer, Jumbo.............15.00
Sherbet...................25.00
Soup, Dish .... 15.00 to 30.00
Sugar, Cover 16.00
Sugar & Creamer 25.00
Sugar & Creamer,
   After Dinner.............45.00
Sugar & Creamer,
   Individual...............50.00
Syrup, 1 Pt. .... 85.00 to 95.00
Tea Bag Holder 12.00
Teapot, 6 Cup....80.00 to 105.00
Tidbit, 2 Tiers ..... 35.00 to 85.00
Tidbit, 3 Tiers ....45.00 to 125.00
Tumbler, 6 Oz. 10.00
Tumbler, 10 Oz. ... 22.50 to 28.00
Tureen, Large 495.00

Apple Purinton

Apple pattern was also made by Purinton Pottery of Shippenville, Pennsylvania. The hand-decorated dinnerware was made in the early 1940s. It was designed by William Blair. The apple was colored red with yellow and brown highlights, the stems and leaves were green, blue, and dark brown. The trim colors were red, cobalt blue, or blue-green.

Jug, Large.................50.00
Jug, Small 22.00
Salt 12.00
Sugar & Creamer 60.00
Sugar Shaker 10.00
Tumbler, 6 Piece 130.00

Apple Watt

The Watt Pottery Company was incorporated in Crooksville, Ohio, in 1922. They made a variety of hand-decorated potteries. The most popular is Apple pattern. It was made from the 1930s as dinnerware sets and also in kitchenwares. The company burned to the ground in 1965.

Ashtray, Oval............. 75.00
Baker, No. 96, 8 1/2 In. ... 150.00
Bean Pot, No. 75,
   Individual 300.00
Bowl, No. 73.,
   9 1/2 In. ....85.00 to 120.00
Bowl, No. 74 .... 45.00
Casserole, No. 18,
   Lug, 4 x 5 In. 275.00
Cookie Jar, No. 76, Ear Handles,
   2 Qt. .... 200.00 to 250.00
Creamer, No. 62 .... 130.00
Cup & Saucer, Large....... 55.00
Mixing Bowl, No. 4, 4 In. .. 65.00
Mixing Bowl, No. 5, 5 In. .. 56.00
Mixing Bowl, No. 6, 6 In. .. 50.00
Mixing Bowl, No. 9, 9 In. .. 45.00
Mixing Bowl, No. 63,
   6 1/2 In. ....50.00 to 80.00
Mixing Bowl, No. 64,
   7 1/2 In. 50.00
Mug, 12 Oz. 45.00
Pie Plate, No. 33, 9 In. 175.00
Pitcher, No. 6 .... 110.00
Pitcher, No. 15, 5 3/4 In. .. 125.00
Pitcher, No. 16, 6 3/4 In. . 125.00
Pitcher, No. 17,
   Ice Lip, 8 1/2 In. 220.00
Salt & Pepper,
   Hourglass 365.00

Autumn Foliage

Autumn Foliage was made by Watt Pottery from 1959 to 1965. It has brown leaves on brown stems. It is also called Brown Leaves.

Bowl, No. 73, 9 1/2 In. 70.00
Pitcher, No. 16, 2 Pt. 75.00
Sugar, No. 98 . . . . 85.00

Autumn Leaf

One of the most popular American dinnerware patterns, Autumn Leaf was made for the Jewel Tea Company, a grocery chain, beginning in 1936. Hall China Company of East Liverpool, Ohio; Crooksville China Company of Crooksville, Ohio; Harker Potteries of Chester, West Virginia; and Paden City Pottery of Paden City, West Virginia, made dishes with this design. The Autumn Leaf pattern always has the same shades of dark yellow and rust leaves. The shape of the dish varied with the manufacturer. Several special terms are used to describe these shapes, such as "bud-ray," which describes a bowl lid with a knob surrounded by raised rays. Collectors can find Autumn Leaf pattern tinware, plastic tablecloths, glassware, clocks, even painted furniture. There are several books about Autumn Leaf and a collectors club listed at the back of this book. The Jewel Tea pattern is listed here.

Baker, Fluted. 30.00
Baker, French 15.00
Bowl, 5 In. 4.00
Bowl, 5 1/2 In. 5.00
Bowl, 6 1/4 In. 9.00
Bowl, Soup, Handle 27.00
Bowl, Vegetable,
    2 Sections. 90.00
Bowl, Vegetable,
    Oval, 10 In. 12.00
Butter, 1/4 Lb. 115.00
Cake Plate, 9 1/2 In. 10.00
Casserole, Cover, 10 Oz. . . . 22.00
Casserole, Round, 2 Qt. 37.50
Coffee Server, 96 Oz.,
    8 1/4 In. 525.00
Coffeepot, Electric 275.00
Creamer. 11.00
Creamer, Ruffled 15.00
Cup, Custard. 4.00
Cup & Saucer 6.00
Cup & Saucer, Ruffled 7.00
Custard Cup 9.00
Dish, Souffle, 2 Qt. 10.00
Gravy Boat. 28.00
Gravy Boat, Underplate. 45.00
Jug, 2 1/2 Pt. 18.00
Jug, Ball, Ice Lip, No. 3 . . . . 30.00
Mixing Bowl, 9 In. 14.00
Mug, Irish Coffee,
    4 Piece 380.00
Percolator, Electric 295.00
Pickle, Oval, 9 In. 30.00
Pie Plate 9.00
Pitcher, Ball, Ice Lip 65.00
Pitcher, Ball, Jewel Tea 26.00
Pitcher, Milk, Jewel Tea 23.00

Plate, 6 In. 4.00
Plate, 7 In. 7.00
Plate, 8 In. 7.00
Plate, 9 In. . . . . 7.00 to 9.00
Plate, 10 In. . . . . . . 14.00 to 16.00
Platter, 11 1/2 In. 22.00
Platter, 13 1/2 In. 15.00
Salt & Pepper, Range 22.00
Salt & Pepper, Ruffled 16.00
Soup, Cream 28.00
Soup, Dish,
    8 1/2 In. . . . . 11.00 to 12.00
Teapot, Aladdin . . . 45.00 to 55.00
Teapot, Flare 45.00
Teapot, Newport,
    1930s . . . . 225.00 to 250.00
Tray. 120.00
Tumbler, 15 Oz.,
    5 1/2 In. 18.00
Tumbler, Frosted,
    5 1/2 In., 6 Piece 90.00

B

Ballerina

Solid-colored pottery was popular in the 1950s. Universal Potteries of Cambridge, Ohio, made Ballerina from 1947 to 1956. Ballerina was very modern in shape and had solid-colored glazes. A later line was decorated with abstract designs. The original solid-colored Ballerina dinnerware was offered in Dove Gray, Jade Green, Jonquil Yellow, and Periwinkle Blue. In 1949 chartreuse and Forest Green were added. By 1955 burgundy, charcoal, and pink were added, while some other colors had been discontinued. There was also a line called Ballerina Mist, which was a pale blue-green with decal decorations.

DOVE GRAY

Bowl, Vegetable, Cover.....12.00

Bowl, Vegetable,
Round, 9 In. 6.00

Gravy Boat................10.00

Relish, 7 In.................4.00

Sugar & Creamer, Cover....16.00

BEEHIVE, see Ring

Blue Bouquet

Standard Coffee of New Orleans, Louisiana, gave Blue Bouquet pattern dinnerware and kitchenware as a premium from the early 1950s to the early 1960s. Although it was made by the Hall China Company, East Liverpool, Ohio, it is most easily found in the South. The pattern is very plain with a thin blue border interrupted by roses. Blue Ridge also made a pattern called Blue Bouquet, but the pattern listed here is by Hall China Company.

Bowl, Fruit................5.00

Creamer, Boston 11.00

Jug, Colonial 18.00

Jug, Sunshine 20.00

Plate, 6 In.................5.00

Blue Garden

Blue Garden is a line of Hall kitchenware made in 1939. The body is cobalt blue, the design a floral decal pattern.

Teapot, Basketball,
6 Cup 495.00

Teapot, New York,
8 Cup 125.00

BLUE PARADE, see Rose Parade

Blue Willow

Willow pattern pictures a bridge, three figures, birds, trees, and a Chinese landscape. The pattern was first used in England by Thomas Turner in 1780 at the Caughley Pottery Works. It was inspired by an earlier Chinese pattern. The pattern has been copied by makers in almost every country and has been made in other colors. Many pieces of Blue Willow were made by Homer Laughlin, Sebring, and other American makers. We list dishes here from these and foreign firms.

Bowl, 8 1/2 In. 10.00

Bowl, Fruit, Royal, 5 1/2 In. ..2.00

Bowl, Homer Laughlin,
5 In. 5.50

Bowl, Royal, 10 1/4 In. 14.00

Butter Chip, Buffalo 6.00

Chop Plate, Royal,
12 1/4 In. 17.00

Creamer, Oval..............8.00

Cup, Inside Decal,
Blue Ridge 8.00

Cup, Stacking 2.50

Cup & Saucer, Stacking......4.00

Dish, Sauce 9.00

Gravy Boat, Double Spout,
Royal...................8.00

Grill Plate, 10 1/2 In. 9.50

Grill Plate, 12 1/2 In. 25.00

Plate, 5 1/2 In. 10.00

Plate, 6 In. 10.00

Plate, 13 In. 35.00

Plate, Buffalo, 5 1/2 In. 10.00

Plate, Homer Laughlin,
6 1/4 In. 2.00

Salt & Pepper............. 25.00

Saucer.............. 1.50 to 2.00

Sugar, Cover, Tapered
Base, Royal..............6.00

Sugar, Oval................8.00

Teapot 45.00

Tumbler, Blue Ridge, 5 In. . 12.00

BLACK

Cup & Saucer 36.00

Mug, 3 1/4 In. 12.00

Sugar & Creamer...........7.50

Blueberry

Stangl Pottery of Trenton, New Jersey, made Blueberry (pattern No. 3770) before 1942. The heavy red pottery dishes were glazed with a yellow border and a sgraffito decoration of blueberries in the center.

Bowl, Salad, 10 In.	40.00
Bowl, Salad, 12 In.	50.00
Cup	10.00
Cup & Saucer	13.00
Plate, 8 In.	6.00
Plate, 10 In.	8.00

Bob White

Bob White was made by Red Wing Potteries from 1956 to 1967. It was one of the most popular dinnerware patterns made by the factory. The pattern, a modern hand-painted design, shows a stylized bird and background.

• • • • • • • • • • • • • • •

China can be washed in warm water with mild soap suds. The addition of ammonia to the water will add that extra sparkle.

• • • • • • • • • • • • • • •

Cookie Jar	100.00 to 150.00
Cup & Saucer	16.00
Pitcher, 60 Oz.	35.00
Plate, 10 1/2 In.	8.00
Salt & Pepper	35.00
Salt & Pepper, Tall	20.00
Sugar	25.00
Tray, Bread, 24 In.	85.00 to 95.00

Bow Knot

Bow Knot is a variation of the Whirligig pattern. It has a piecrust rim on a Colonial shape. It was made by Blue Ridge in the 1950s. Bow Knot is colored chartreuse and brown, Whirligig is red and light blue.

Console, 13 1/2 In.	175.00
Cornucopia, 7 1/2 In.	135.00
Flowerpot	175.00
Pitcher, 5 In.	135.00
Wall Pocket, Cup & Saucer, 6 In.	150.00
Wall Pocket, Pitcher, 6 In.	150.00

C

Calico

Calico is one of the plaid designs made by Vernon Kilns of Vernon, California. The design was pink and blue with a blue border. Other related plaids are Coronation Organdy (gray and rose), Gingham (green and yellow), Homespun (cinnamon, yellow, and green), Organdie (brown and yellow), Tam O'Shanter (rust, chartreuse, and dark green), and Tweed (yellow and gray-blue).

Casserole, Individual	20.00
Custard Cup	15.00
Plate, 10 1/2 In.	20.00
Soup, Dish, 3-Lug Handle	15.00

Caliente

Every pottery company, it seemed, made a solid-colored dinnerware in the 1940s. Paden City Pottery Company, Paden City, West Virginia, made Caliente, a semiporcelain, in blue, green, Tangerine, and yellow. There is also matching ovenproof cooking ware.

BLUE

Plate, 10 In.	7.00

GREEN

Plate, 7 1/2 In.	3.00
Plate, 10 In.	7.00

TANGERINE

Bowl, 6 1/2 In.	5.00

Casserole, Yellow Cover,
  Chrome-Plated Frame 40.00
Plate, 6 1/2 In. 1.50
Plate, 8 1/2 In. 5.00
YELLOW
Plate, 7 1/2 In. 3.00

California Ivy

California Ivy was one of the most popular patterns made by the Metlox Potteries of Manhattan Beach, California. It was introduced in 1946. The pattern was named for its ivy vine border.

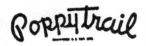

POTTERY

Coaster................. 10.00
Creamer, 2 1/2 In. 6.00
Tumbler & Coaster Set,
  13 Oz., 12 Piece 155.00

California Poppy

California Poppy is a name used by several companies. The pattern listed here was made by Blue Ridge in the 1950s. It has a hand-painted design on a Candlewick shape. The center design is two large poppies.

Bowl, Salad, 11 1/2 In. 145.00
Cup & Saucer 25.00
Plate, 5 In. 12.00
Plate, 10 In. 25.00

California Provincial

California Provincial dinnerware pictures a rooster in the center. The rooster is maroon, green, and yellow. The border is green and Coffee Brown. It was made by Metlox beginning in 1950.

Bowl, Vegetable,
  Basket, 8 In. 30.00
Jam Jar 35.00
Jug, Mustard 18.00
Plate, 6 1/2 In. 40.00
Salt & Pepper 60.00

Capistrano

Capistrano is a design picturing modern yellow-breasted swallows flying near black foliage. It was made by the Red Wing Pottery from 1953 to 1967.

Place Setting, 5 Piece 90.00
Tea Set, 3 Piece 45.00

Caprice

Caprice is a streamlined pattern made by Hall China Company from 1952 to 1957. The dishes have a leaf and floral design in pink, gray, or yellow. The designs on the smaller pieces are not the same as those on the full-sized plates. Another pattern called Caprice was made by E. M. Knowles beginning in 1954, but only Caprice made by Hall is listed here.

Plate, 11 In. 10.00
Platter, 15 In. 25.00

Casual California

Vernon Kilns made Casual California, a very popular solid-color dinnerware, from 1947 to 1956. It was made in Acacia Yellow, Dawn Pink, Dusk Gray, Lime Green, Mahogany Brown, Mocha Brown, Pine Green, Sno-white, and Turquoise Blue.

MAHOGANY BROWN
Tumbler, 14 Oz. 20.00
MOCHA BROWN
Pitcher, Water, 1 1/2 Qt. 75.00
Teapot, Redesigned 175.00
SNO-WHITE
Cup & Saucer,
  Redesigned............ 15.00

Casualstone

Casualstone is another in the family of Fiesta dinnerware. Homer Laughlin China Company, Newell, West Virginia, made the dishes for supermarket promotions under the trade name Coventry in 1970. Antique Gold Fiesta Ironstone dishes were decorated with a gold-stamped design on some pieces. Small, deep dishes were left in solid colors.

Cup & Saucer 5.00
Dish, Dessert 3.50
Saucer 1.50

Cat-Tail

Cat-Tail pattern dishes must have been found in most homes in America in the 1940s. Sears, Roebuck and Company featured the pattern from 1934 to 1956. It was made by the Universal Potteries of Cambridge, Ohio. The red and black cat-tail design was used for dinnerware and matching tinware, kitchenware, glassware, furniture, and table linens.

Bowl, Cover, Deep,
6 1/4 In. 10.00
Casserole, Cover,
8 1/4 In. 22.00
Cup & Saucer 10.00
Gravy Boat 15.00
Grill Plate, 9 3/4 In. 25.00
Pie Plate, 10 In. . . . 12.00 to 20.00
Pie Server . . . . 15.00 to 23.00
Platter, 11 1/2 In. 9.50
Tumbler, Juice,
3 1/4 In. 20.00

Century

Century pattern was made by the Homer Laughlin China Company. The ivory dinnerware had floral decals.

Berry Set, 18 Piece 100.00
Dish, Mayonnaise,
3 Piece 35.00
Plate, 6 1/4 In. 4.50
Plate, 7 3/4 In. 6.50
Plate, 9 In. 6.00

Chatelaine

Vernon Kilns of Los Angeles and Vernon, California, introduced the solid-colored Chatelaine pattern in 1953. Pieces were square with leaf handles. It was made in bronze, topaz, jade with a leaf decoration, and platinum with a leaf decoration.

JADE
Cup, Coffee 15.00

Chesterton

Chesterton was a pattern produced by Harker Pottery Company of Chester, West Virginia, from 1945 to 1965. The pieces had a gadroon border. They were made in blue, gray, green, pink, or yellow.

BLUE
Cup 3.00
Platter, Oval, 11 1/2 In. 8.00
Saucer 3.00
GRAY
Plate, 6 1/4 In. 3.00
Plate, 7 1/4 In. 4.00
Plate, 10 In. 6.00
Saucer 3.00
PINK
Cake Set, 8 Piece 25.00

Chinese Red

Chinese Red is a color used by Hall China Company, East Liverpool, Ohio. This bright red was used on many shapes of dishes. A few are listed here that are not included in the more recognizable sets.

Cookie Jar, Pretzel
Handle 95.00
Jug, Doughnut, Large 65.00
Teapot, Airflow, 6 Cup 85.00

Chintz

Chintz is a floral decorated pattern made by Vernon Kilns in about 1942 and again in 1950. The pattern in red, blue, yellow, green, and maroon resembled the English dinnerware patterns of the early nineteenth century. Another pattern named Chintz was made by Blue Ridge.

VERNON KILNS

Chocolate Pot, Footed	150.00
Chop Plate, 12 In.	25.00
Dish, Leaf Shape	28.00
Plate, 9 1/2 In.	15.00
Sugar & Creamer, Footed	75.00
Tureen, Soup	325.00

Colonial Homestead

Colonial Homestead was one of many patterns made by Royal China Company of Sebring, Ohio. The dinnerware was made in the 1940s and 1950s. The Royal China Company closed in 1986.

Bowl, 5 In.	3.00
Bowl, Vegetable, Cover, 10 In.	7.50 to 15.00
Casserole, Cover	35.00

Cup & Saucer	5.00
Gravy Boat, Liner & Ladle, 3 Piece	25.00
Plate, 6 1/2 In.	1.50 to 2.00
Plate, 9 In.	4.00
Plate, 10 In.	3.50 to 5.00
Plate, 12 In.	12.00
Plate, Tab Handle, 10 In.	12.00
Salt & Pepper	5.00 to 10.00
Salver, 12 1/4 In.	7.50
Sugar & Creamer, Cover	10.00 to 12.00
Teapot	15.00

Contempo

Contempo is a solid colored pattern made by Brusché of Los Angeles, California, in the 1950s. Herb Brusché sold his business to Bauer Pottery and the dishes were produced at a Bauer plant, although the Brusché mark was used for a few years. The Al Fresco line was glazed with glossy Hemlock Green, Coffee Brown, lime, Olive Green, Misty Grey, and Dubonnet. Later, about 1952, a second line was introduced as Contempo. It was the Al Fresco shapes glazed in a satin-finish Champagne White, Desert Beige, Indigo Brown, Pumpkin, Slate, and Spicy Green. The shapes were designed by Tracy Irwin, who also designed Monterey Moderne for Bauer. It was probably made to compete with Russel Wright's American Modern.

Bowl, 6 1/2 In.	20.00
Dish, Fruit, 5 1/2 In.	15.00

Coral Reef

Coral Reef was designed by Don Blanding for Vernon Kilns in 1938. The tropical fish in the design were colored blue, mustard, and maroon on a cream background.

MUSTARD

Cup & Saucer	55.00
Plate, 6 In.	25.00
Plate, 9 In.	50.00

Corn King

Dishes shaped like ears of corn? This novel idea became a popular reality when Corn King pattern was sold by Shawnee Pottery Company, Zanesville, Ohio, before 1954. The green and yellow pieces, three-dimensional representations of ears of corn, ranged from dinner plates to small salt and pepper shakers. Corn King has darker yellow corn kernels and lighter green leaves than a later pattern called Corn Queen.

Shawnee
U.S.A.

Butter, Cover, No. 72	60.00
Casserole, Cover, Large, No. 74	80.00
Casserole, Individual	45.00
Creamer, No. 70	28.00
Mixing Bowl, No. 5	45.00
Mug, No. 69	55.00
Pitcher, No. 71	80.00
Relish, No. 79	32.00
Teapot, Individual	82.00

Corn Queen

Corn King was redesigned slightly by Shawnee Pottery Company, Zanesville, Ohio, and continued to be marketed from 1954 to 1961. The kernels of the new line were lighter yellow and the foliage was a deeper green. It was called Corn Queen.

Butter, Cover, No. 72 ...... 65.00
Cookie Jar 120.00
Creamer, No. 70.......... 40.00
Mixing Bowl, No. 6 .... 60.00
Plate, No. 68 .... 55.00
Plate, No. 93 .... 65.00
Saucer 15.00
Sugar Cover 25.00

Coronado

Franciscan dinnerware was made by Gladding, McBean in Los Angeles, California. Coronado was a popular plain-colored art ware made from 1935 to 1942. Fifty different shapes and fifteen different colors were made. Another pattern called Coronado was made by Vernon Kilns. The Franciscan pieces are listed in this book.

CORAL
Chop Plate, Round, 14 In. . . 18.00
Creamer 8.00
Cup .... 4.00 to 5.00
Cup & Saucer 16.00
Cup & Saucer,
　After Dinner 25.00
Plate, 6 1/2 In. 4.00
Plate, 9 1/2 In. 7.00
Platter, Oval, 12 1/2 In. 24.00
Saucer 9.00
Soup, Cream.............. 7.00
Soup, Cream, Underplate... 12.00

GRAY
Cup & Saucer,
　After Dinner 18.00
Sugar & Creamer,
　After Dinner 45.00

GREEN
Bowl, 7 1/2 In. 15.50
Cup & Saucer 7.00
Cup & Saucer,
　After Dinner 18.00
Gravy Boat, Liner 18.00
Pitcher, Medium.......... 75.00
Plate, 6 1/2 In. 4.00
Plate, 9 1/2 In. 6.00
Platter, Oval, 12 1/2 In. 21.00
Saucer 1.50
Sugar, Cover 8.50

IVORY
Bowl, Salad, Underplate 65.00
Butter, Cover ..... 45.00 to 65.00
Coffeepot, After Dinner 65.00
Compote, Footed.......... 45.00
Creamer.................. 12.00
Cup & Saucer 10.00
Cup & Saucer,
　After Dinner .... 20.00 to 22.00
Plate, 6 1/2 In. ...... 3.00 to 4.00
Plate, 10 1/2 In. 12.00
Salt & Pepper 22.00
Soup, Cream.............. 8.00
Sugar & Creamer,
　After Dinner 28.00

MAROON
Cup & Saucer ...... 6.00 to 7.50
Cup & Saucer,
　After Dinner 20.00
Gravy Boat, Underplate..... 22.50
Plate, 6 1/2 In. 4.00
Plate, 9 1/2 In. 6.00
Salt & Pepper, Footed 15.00

TURQUOISE
Bowl, Vegetable,
　Oval, 13 In. 12.00
Cup & Saucer ...... 6.00 to 7.50
Cup & Saucer,
　After Dinner 18.00
Pitcher, 8 In. 5.50
Plate, 6 1/2 In. 4.00
Plate, 9 1/2 In. 6.00
Platter, Oval, 12 1/2 In. 10.00

Saucer, Soup, Cream 4.00
Soup, Cream, Underplate,
　2 Piece 12.00
Sugar & Creamer,
　After Dinner............ 28.00

WHITE
Vase, Footed, 5 1/2 In. 22.50

YELLOW
Bowl, Vegetable,
　Oval, 12 1/2 In........... 25.00
Celery Dish 15.00
Chop Plate, 12 1/2 In. 12.00
Chop Plate, Round, 14 In. . . 30.00
Creamer.................. 8.00
Cup, After Dinner.......... 15.00
Cup & Saucer .... 6.00 to 7.50
Cup & Saucer,
　After Dinner............ 18.00
Gravy Boat, Underplate..... 25.00
Pitcher, 10 1/2 In. 9.00
Plate, 6 1/2 In. ...... 3.50 to 4.00
Plate, 9 1/2 In. 6.00
Platter, Oval, 12 1/2 In. 10.00
Sugar, Cover 12.00
Sugar & Creamer, Cover 20.00

Country Garden

Three raised flowers are pictured on the Country Garden dinnerware. The pattern was made by Stangl Pottery of Trenton, New Jersey, from 1956 to 1974. Country Garden was also made by Blue Ridge and Red Wing, but only the Stangl pattern is listed here.

Don't store dishes for long periods of time in old newspaper wrappings. The ink can make indelible stains on the china.

Bowl, 8 In. 30.00
Bowl, Vegetable,
  2 Sections. . . . . . . 24.00 to 35.00
Cup. 12.00
Cup & Saucer 10.00
Plate, 6 In. 7.00
Plate, 8 In. 7.00
Salt & Pepper 14.00
Sauceboat,
  7 1/2 x 5 1/4 In. 150.00
Tidbit, 3 Tiers 40.00

Crab Apple

One of the most popular dinnerware patterns made by Southern Potteries, Inc., of Erwin, Tennessee, under the name Blue Ridge was Crab Apple. This brightly colored hand-painted dinnerware was decorated with red apples and green leaves. A thin red spatter border was used. Matching glassware was made. The pattern was in production after 1930 and was discontinued when the factory went out of business in 1957.

Plate, 8 In. 4.00
Plate, 9 1/2 In. 6.50

Platter, 15 In. 18.50
Soup, Dish, 8 In. 6.00

Crocus

Crocus was a popular name for dinnerware patterns. Prices listed are for the Crocus pattern by Hall China Company of East Liverpool, Ohio, in the 1930s. The decal-decorated dinnerware was sometimes called Holland. The design was a border of oddly shaped crocuses in black, lavender, red, green, and pink. Most pieces have platinum trim. Other firms, including Stangl Pottery and Blue Ridge, had very different-looking dinnerwares called Crocus.

Bowl, 5 1/2 In. . . . . . . 4.00 to 7.50
Bowl, Radiance, 6 In. 12.00
Bowl, Radiance, 9 In. 20.00
Coffeepot, Colonial 60.00
Mug, 4 Piece 180.00
Plate, 9 In. 8.00
Platter, 13 1/4 In. 19.00

CURIOSITY SHOP, see Old Curiosity Shop

Currier & Ives

Currier & Ives was made by the Royal China Company of Sebring, Ohio, from the 1940s. It is a blue and white pattern that was popular as a store premium. The Royal China Company closed in 1986. Currier & Ives patterns were also made by Homer Laughlin and Scio, but only the Royal China pattern is listed here.

Bowl, 5 1/2 In. . . . . . . 2.00 to 5.50
Bowl, 6 In. 9.00
Bowl, 9 In. 9.50
Bowl, Vegetable,
  10 In. . . . . 12.00 to 18.00
Calendar Plate, 1974 . . . . . . 15.00
Creamer 5.00
Cup & Saucer . . . . 2.50 to 4.00
Gravy Boat 8.00
Pie Plate, 9 In. . . . . . . 7.50 to 12.00
Pie Plate, Deep, 10 In. 12.00
Plate, 6 In. . . . . 2.50 to 6.00
Plate, 10 In. . . . . 6.00 to 7.50
Platter, 13 In. . . . . .15.00 to 18.00
Soup, Dish 9.00

Sugar 5.00
Teapot, Cover. 75.00

D

Daisy

Daisy, or Hawaiian 12-point Daisy, is a Fiesta Casual pattern made by the Homer Laughlin China Company of Newell, West Virginia. It was first made in 1962 and discontinued in 1968. Daisy pattern, on the familiar Fiesta shape, has a turquoise rim and turquoise and brown daisies in the center. Patterns named Daisy were also made by Red Wing, Stangl, and Taylor, Smith, and Taylor. Only the Homer Laughlin pattern is listed here.

Plate, 10 In. 15.00
Plate, Salad, 7 In. 12.00
Saucer 6.00

Desert Rose

Desert Rose by Franciscan is a popular pattern with today's collectors. It was introduced in 1942 by Gladding, McBean's Franciscan Ceramics. The pattern is still being made by Wedgwood, which purchased Franciscan Ceramics in 1979. The flowers on the dishes are a soft pink.

Ashtray, Individual 25.00
Ashtray, Oval,
    9 In. . . . . 50.00 to 75.00
Bowl, 5 In. 8.00
Bowl, 6 In. . . . . 8.00 to 18.00
Bowl, 9 In. 40.00
Bowl, 10 In. 95.00
Bowl, Footed, 5 1/2 In. 18.00
Bowl, Vegetable, 2 Sections,
    10 3/4 In. . . . . . . 35.00 to 45.00
Candleholder, Pair 75.00
Chop Plate, 12 In. 60.00
Cigarette Box 60.00
Coffeepot,
    8 Cup . . . . 95.00 to 125.00
Compote, Footed. 30.00
Compote, Low 60.00
Cookie Jar, Cover. 75.00
Creamer, After Dinner. 75.00
Cup & Saucer . . . . . 8.00 to 12.00
Cup & Saucer,
    After Dinner . . . . 25.00 to 45.00
Cup & Saucer,
    Jumbo. . . . . 35.00 to 55.00
Eggcup. . . . . 20.00 to 30.00
Gravy Boat. 15.00
Grill Plate. 85.00
Jam Jar . . . . 75.00 to 95.00
Mug, 12 Oz. . . . . . . 40.00 to 45.00
Napkin Rings, Box,
    4 Piece 225.00
Pitcher, 1qt. 78.00
Pitcher, 2 Qt. . . . 120.00 to 125.00
Plate, 6 1/2 In. . . . . . 6.00 to 12.00
Plate, 7 1/2 In. . . . . 10.00 to 14.00
Plate, 9 1/2 In. 18.00
Plate, 10 1/2 In. . . . 13.00 to 20.00

Platter, 19 In. . . . . . 24.00 to 40.00
Relish, 3 Sections 45.00
Salt & Pepper,
    Rosebud 20.00
Salt & Pepper, Tall 55.00
Sherbet. . . . . 25.00 to 30.00
Soup, Dish 18.00
Sugar, After Dinner. 65.00
Sugar & Creamer,
    Cover . . . . 25.00 to 35.00
Sugar & Creamer,
    Jumbo. 45.00
Syrup, 1 Qt. 85.00
Teapot . . . . 65.00 to 95.00
Tile, Square, 6 In. 95.00
Tumbler, 6 Oz. . . . . 27.00 to 35.00
Tumbler, 10 Oz. . . . 15.00 to 25.00
Tureen, Footed. 695.00
Vase, Bud. 95.00

Dogwood

Dogwood pattern was made by Homer Laughlin China Company of Newell, West Virginia. It is a decal-decorated line of dinnerware. The edges are gold, the pattern realistic pink and white sprays of dogwood. It was made in the 1960s. Another pattern named Dogwood was made by Stangl Pottery Company, Trenton, New Jersey, in 1965. It is a heavy pottery dinnerware. Other factories also used the Dogwood name for dinnerware patterns.

Bowl. 4.00
Creamer. 8.00
Cup & Saucer 5.00
Plate, 6 In. 3.00
Plate, 9 In. 5.00
Sauceboat 10.00
Saucer. 1.50
Soup, Dish 7.00
Sugar, Cover 12.00
Sugar & Creamer,
    With Sauce, 3 Piece 22.00
Teapot 45.00

E

Early California

In the late 1930s, Vernon Kilns of Vernon, California, made a solid-color line of dinnerware called Early California. The dishes, in blue, brown, green, orange, pink, turquoise, or yellow, were made to be used as mix-and-match sets. The dishes are marked with the name of the pattern.

BLUE
Eggcup 25.00
BROWN
Eggcup 16.00
MULTICOLORED
Mixing Bowl Set, Nested,
5 Piece 135.00
TURQUOISE
Eggcup 16.00

Eggshell Nautilus

Eggshell Nautilus is a shape that was made by Homer Laughlin from 1937 to the 1950s. The nautilus shell motif can been seen in the handles. The shape was decorated in many different ways.

• • • • • • • • • • • • • • •

For emergency repairs to chipped pottery, try coloring the spot with a wax crayon or oil paint. It will look a little better.

• • • • • • • • • • • • • • •

Bowl, 5 In. 7.00
Cup, Cardinal 3.00
Eggcup 15.00
Plate, 6 In. 4.00
Plate, Cardinal, 7 In. 4.00
Plate, Cardinal, 10 In. 6.00
Plate, Platinum Rim 10.00
Plate, White Rose, 9 In. 8.00
Plate, White Rose, 10 In. . . .10.00
Platter, White Rose, 11 In. . .13.00
Sauce, Cardinal 1.50
Soup, Dish, White Rose
Sugar, White Rose 15.00

El Patio

El Patio is one of many solid-color dinnerware patterns made by Franciscan from 1936 to 1956. It comes in twenty colors.

BROWN
Sugar & Creamer,
After Dinner 25.00
GREEN
Gravy Boat,
Attached Plate 22.50
REDWOOD
Butter 45.00
Coffeepot 125.00
Sugar & Creamer,
After Dinner 25.00
TURQUOISE
Sugar & Creamer,
After Dinner 25.00

• • • • • • • • • • • • • • •

Dental wax (ask your dentist about it) is a good adhesive to keep figurines on shelves, or lids on teapots.

• • • • • • • • • • • • • • •

F

FESTIVE FRUIT, see Fruit (Stangl)

Fiesta

Fiesta ware was introduced in 1936 by the Homer Laughlin China Company, Newell, West Virginia. It was originally designed by Frederick Rhead. The line was redesigned in 1969 and withdrawn in 1973. The design was characterized by a band of concentric circles, beginning at the rim. The complete Fiesta line in 1937 had 54 different pieces. Rarities include the covered onion bowl, the green disk water jug, the 10-inch cake plate, and the syrup pitcher. Cups had full-circle handles until 1969, when partial-circle handles were made. The original Fiesta colors were dark blue, Fiesta Red, light green, Old Ivory, and yellow. Later, chartreuse, Forest Green, gray, medium green, rose, and turquoise were added. From 1970 to 1972 the redesigned Fiesta Ironstone was made only in Antique Gold, Mango Red, and Turf Green. Homer Laughlin reissued Fiesta in 1986 using new colors but the original marks and molds. The new colors were apricot, black, cobalt blue, rose (pink), and white. In 1989 the company added three other colors— Periwinkle Blue, turquoise, and yellow. See American Dinnerware Introduction for more information. Most Fiesta ware was marked with the incised word Fiesta. Some pieces were hand-stamped before glazing. The word genuine was added to the mark in the 1940s. The Fiesta shape was also made with decal decorations, but these are not considered Fiesta by collectors; instead, they are collected by the pattern names. There is also a Fiesta Kitchen Kraft line, a group of kitchenware pieces made in the early 1940s in blue, green, red, or yellow. These were bake-and-serve wares. Glassware and linens were made to match the Fiesta colors.

BLUE

Bowl, 4 3/4 In. 25.00
Bowl, 5 1/2 In. . . . . 22.00 to 30.00
Carafe . . . . 180.00 to 245.00
Casserole, Cover 175.00
Chop Plate, 15 In. 45.00
Coffeepot . . . . . . 165.00 to 195.00
Compote,
  12 In. . . . . 135.00 to 145.00
Cup & Saucer . . . . . 24.00 to 45.00
Eggcup. . . . . 45.00 to 55.00
Jam Jar . . . . 205.00 to 235.00
Mixing Bowl, No. 3 . . . . 55.00
Mixing Bowl, No. 4 . . . . 75.00

Mixing Bowl, No. 5 . . . . . . 120.00
Mixing Bowl,
  No. 6. . . . . 200.00 to 295.00
Mixing Bowl, No. 7 . . . . 200.00
Mug 50.00
Mustard . . . . 195.00 to 215.00
Pitcher, 2 Pt. 60.00
Pitcher, Ice Lip 120.00
Plate, 6 In. 8.00
Plate, 9 In. 14.00
Plate, 10 1/2 In. 25.00
Relish, Multicolored Top . . 180.00
Salt & Pepper 20.00
Soup, Cream 40.00
Sugar, Cover . . . . . 35.00 to 50.00
Teapot, Medium. 150.00
Tumbler, Juice 35.00
Tumbler, Water . . . 50.00 to 55.00
Vase, Bud. . . . . 70.00 to 75.00

CHARTREUSE

Ashtray. 75.00
Bowl, 5 1/2 In. 25.00
Bowl, 6 In. 35.00
Casserole, Cover. 195.00
Chop Plate, 13 In. 65.00
Chop Plate, 15 In. 110.00
Coffeepot 240.00
Creamer. . . . . 25.00 to 30.00
Cup & Saucer . . . . . 20.00 to 30.00
Eggcup. 120.00
Gravy Boat. 40.00
Mug . . . . 30.00 to 50.00
Nappy, 8 1/2 In. . . 35.00 to 44.00
Pitcher, Disk 195.00
Pitcher, Jug, 2 Pt. . . 75.00 to 85.00
Plate, 6 In. 14.00
Plate, 7 In. . . . . 6.00 to 12.00
Plate, 9 In. . . . . . . 18.00 to 25.00
Plate, 10 In. 35.00
Salt & Pepper . . . . 30.00 to 36.00
Sauceboat . . . . 45.00 to 65.00
Saucer 10.00
Soup, Cream 40.00
Sugar, Cover . . . . . 34.00 to 40.00
Teapot, Medium. 250.00

DARK BLUE

Ashtray. 45.00

Bowl, 11 3/4 In. 195.00
Casserole, Cover. 125.00
Tumbler, Juice 30.00

FOREST GREEN

Ashtray. 55.00
Bowl, 4 3/4 In. 35.00
Bowl, 5 1/2 In. . . . 20.00 to 25.00
Chop Plate, 13 In. 40.00
Chop Plate, 15 In. 110.00
Coffeepot. . . . . . 240.00 to 275.00
Creamer. 30.00
Cup & Saucer . . . . . 25.00 to 35.00
Eggcup. 100.00
Gravy Boat. 40.00
Mug. . . . . 60.00 to 65.00
Pitcher, Disk 195.00
Plate, 6 In. 15.00
Plate, 7 In. . . . . . . 10.00 to 15.00
Plate, 9 In. . . . . . . 18.00 to 22.00
Plate, 10 In. 35.00
Salt & Pepper 40.00
Sauceboat 50.00
Soup, Cream 40.00
Sugar, Cover 120.00

GRAY

Ashtray. . . . . 75.00 to 95.00
Bowl, 4 3/4 In. . . . 20.00 to 25.00
Bowl, 5 1/2 In. 30.00
Bowl, 6 In. 40.00
Casserole,
  Cover . . . . 250.00 to 275.00
Creamer. . . . . 20.00 to 28.00
Cup & Saucer . . . . . 35.00 to 40.00
Eggcup. . . . . 95.00 to 140.00
Gravy Boat. 34.00
Mixing Bowl, No. 6 . . . . 100.00
Mug. . . . . 60.00 to 70.00
Mug, Tom & Jerry. 65.00
Nappy, 8 1/2 In. . . . 36.00 to 55.00
Pitcher, Disk . . . . 225.00 to 275.00
Plate, 6 In. . . . . 6.00 to 8.00
Plate, 9 In. . . . . . . 15.00 to 20.00
Plate, 10 In. . . . . . 38.00 to 40.00
Platter, Oval. 40.00
Salt & Pepper . . . . 35.00 to 40.00
Saltshaker. 15.00
Sauceboat . . . . 60.00 to 85.00

Saucer 3.00
Soup, Cream . . . . . . 52.00 to 70.00
Sugar, Cover 55.00
Teapot, Medium. 225.00

LIGHT GREEN

Ashtray. 40.00
Bowl, 4 3/4 In. 15.00
Bowl, 5 1/2 In. . . . . 15.00 to 22.00
Bowl, 11 3/4 In. 125.00
Candleholder, Tripod,
    Pair 270.00
Carafe. 175.00
Casserole, Cover. 165.00
Chop Plate, 13 In. 20.00
Coffeepot 140.00
Creamer. 18.00
Cup & Saucer . . . . . 22.00 to 25.00
Cup & Saucer,
    After Dinner 42.00
Eggcup. 35.00
Mixing Bowl, No. 1 . . . . 90.00
Mixing Bowl, No. 2 . . . . 65.00
Mixing Bowl, No. 3 . . . . 70.00
Mixing Bowl, No. 4 . . . . 85.00
Mixing Bowl,
    No. 5. . . . . 110.00 to 125.00
Mixing Bowl,
    No. 6. . . . . 120.00 to 135.00
Mixing Bowl, No. 7 . . . . 275.00
Mug 100.00
Nappy, 8 1/2 In. 70.00
Pitcher, Disk . . . . . . 70.00 to 80.00
Pitcher, Ice Lip . . . . 65.00 to 70.00
Plate, 6 In. . . . . 4.00 to 7.00
Plate, 9 In. . . . . 10.00 to 15.00
Plate, 10 In. . . . . 16.00 to 26.00
Saltshaker 8.00
Sugar, Cover 30.00
Tumbler, 8 Oz. . . . . 40.00 to 60.00
Vase, Bud. 48.00

MEDIUM GREEN

Ashtray. 175.00
Bowl, 5 1/2 In. . . . . 50.00 to 65.00
Chop Plate, 15 In. 24.00
Creamer. . . . . 60.00 to 75.00
Cup, After Dinner 75.00
Cup & Saucer 39.00
Mixing Bowl, No. 2 . . . . 40.00

Mixing Bowl, No .3 . . . . 95.00
Mixing Bowl, No. 6 . . . . 55.00
Mug. . . . . 40.00 to 80.00
Nappy, 8 1/2 In. 125.00
Plate, 6 In. . . . . 10.00 to 18.00
Plate, 7 In. . . . . 15.00 to 30.00
Plate, 9 In. . . . . 30.00 to 42.00
Plate, 10 In. 65.00
Platter, Oval, 12 In. 125.00
Salt & Pepper . . . . 95.00 to 145.00
Sauceboat . . . . 95.00 to 165.00
Saucer. 15.00
Teapot 130.00

OLD IVORY

Ashtray. 40.00
Bowl, 4 3/4 In. 20.00
Bowl, Tom & Jerry 370.00
Candleholder, Bulb,
    Pair 105.00
Casserole, Cover. 130.00
Chop Plate, 13 In. 25.00
Coffeepot. 145.00
Compote, 12 In. 100.00
Creamer. 18.00
Cup & Saucer,
    After Dinner. 65.00
Gravy Boat. . . . . 45.00 to 60.00
Jam Jar 225.00
Mixing Bowl, No. 1 . . . . 150.00
Mixing Bowl, No. 3 . . . . 95.00
Mixing Bowl, No. 4 . . . . 80.00
Mug. 50.00
Mug, Tom & Jerry,
    Gold Letters. 55.00
Nappy, 8 1/2 In. . . . 30.00 to 45.00
Pitcher, Disk . . . . . 95.00 to 115.00
Pitcher, Juice. 28.00
Plate, 9 In. 10.00
Plate, 10 In. . . . . 20.00 to 38.00
Plate, Calendar, 1954. . . . . . . 35.00
Salad Set, Tom & Jerry,
    Gold Letters 250.00
Saltshaker. 10.00
Soup, Cream . . . . . . 42.00 to 48.00
Teapot, Large 145.00
Tumbler, 5 Oz. . . . 18.00 to 28.00
Tumbler, 8 Oz. . . . . 35.00 to 55.00
Vase, 12 In. 695.00

Vase, Bud . . . . 50.00 to 80.00

RED

Ashtray . . . . 38.00 to 45.00
Bowl, 4 3/4 In. 22.00
Candleholder, Ball 55.00
Candleholder, Bulb,
    Pair . . . . 95.00 to 110.00
Carafe 240.00
Chop Plate, 13 In. . 35.00 to 38.00
Coffeepot . . . . . . 110.00 to 175.00
Creamer, Stick Handle. 40.00
Cup & Saucer 30.00
Cup & Saucer,
    After Dinner. 75.00
Eggcup 45.00
Gravy Boat . . . . 55.00 to 75.00
Mixing Bowl,
    No. 1 . . . . 80.00 to 160.00
Mixing Bowl, No. 3. . . . . . . 55.00
Mixing Bowl, No. 5. . . . . . . 110.00
Mug. . . . . 55.00 to 75.00
Mug, Tom & Jerry. 48.00
Mustard 125.00
Nappy, 9 1/2 In. . . . 45.00 to 65.00
Pepper Shaker. 12.00
Pitcher, Disk 145.00
Pitcher, Juice. 495.00
Plate, 6 In. 5.00
Plate, 7 In. 8.00
Plate, 10 In. . . . . . . 38.00 to 40.00
Platter, Oval, 12 In. 60.00
Relish . . . . 150.00 to 300.00
Salt & Pepper. 10.00
Sauceboat. 55.00
Saucer. . . . . 3.00 to 7.00
Soup, Cream . . . . . . 48.00 to 70.00
Sugar, Cover 45.00
Sugar & Creamer, Tray,
    3 Piece 140.00
Teapot, Large. . . 175.00 to 195.00
Teapot,
    Medium . . . . . 125.00 to 175.00
Tumbler, 5 Oz. . . . 35.00 to 40.00
Tumbler, 8 Oz. . . . 38.00 to 60.00
Vase, 10 In. 650.00
Vase, Bud . . . . 75.00 to 80.00

ROSE

Ashtray 60.00

Bowl, 4 3/4 In. . . . . 22.00 to 25.00
Bowl, 5 1/2 In. 30.00
Bowl, 6 In. 40.00
Casserole, Cover 250.00
Chop Plate, 13 In. 75.00
Chop Plate, 15 In. 80.00
Coffeepot 195.00
Creamer 30.00
Cup & Saucer . . . . . 30.00 to 40.00
Gravy Boat . . . . 45.00 to 65.00
Mug 65.00
Pitcher, Disk 165.00
Plate, 6 In. . . . . 6.00 to 12.00
Plate, 7 In. . . . . 9.50 to 15.00
Plate, 9 In. . . . . 14.00 to 20.00
Plate, 10 In. 40.00
Plate, Deep, 8 In. 42.00
Saucer 10.00
Soup, Cream . . . . . . 52.00 to 65.00
Sugar, Cover . . . . . . 40.00 to 60.00
Teapot 260.00
Tumbler, 5 Oz. . . . 30.00 to 35.00

TURQUOISE
Ashtray . . . . 30.00 to 45.00
Bowl, 4 3/4 In. . . . . 15.00 to 18.00
Bowl, 5 1/2 In. 18.00
Bowl, 6 In. 25.00
Bowl, Salad, Individual 50.00
Carafe 175.00
Chop Plate, 13 In. 24.00
Chop Plate, 15 In. 40.00
Coffeepot . . . . . . 120.00 to 165.00
Creamer 14.00
Creamer, Stick
   Handle . . . . 28.00 to 45.00
Cup & Saucer . . . . . 19.00 to 25.00
Cup & Saucer,
   After Dinner 45.00
Eggcup. 40.00
Gravy Boat 28.00
Grill Plate. 20.00
Jam Jar 185.00
Jug, 2 Pt. 55.00
Mixing Bowl, No. 1 . . . . 150.00
Mixing Bowl, No. 2 . . . . 75.00
Mixing Bowl, No. 3 . . . . 75.00
Mixing Bowl, No. 4 . . . . 85.00

Mixing Bowl, No. 7 . . . . 395.00
Mug . . . . 40.00 to 50.00
Nappy, 8 1/2 In. . . 25.00 to 38.00
Pitcher, Disk . . . . . 65.00 to 95.00
Plate, 6 In. 3.50
Plate, 7 In. 6.00
Plate, 9 In. 10.00
Plate, 10 In. . . . . . . 20.00 to 26.00
Platter, Oval, 12 In. 20.00
Relish 30.00
Salt & Pepper 12.00
Soup, Cream . . . . . 28.00 to 35.00
Soup, French, Cover 475.00
Sugar, Cover . . . . . 22.00 to 25.00
Teapot, Large 125.00
Teapot,
   Medium . . . . . . 85.00 to 135.00
Tumbler, 5 Oz. . . . 25.00 to 30.00
Tumbler, 8 Oz. . . . 38.00 to 45.00

YELLOW
Ashtray. . . . . 28.00 to 35.00
Bowl, 4 3/4 In. 16.00
Bowl, 5 1/2 In. 18.00
Bowl, 6 In. 30.00
Bowl, Salad, Individual 55.00
Casserole, Cover. 125.00
Casserole, French,
   Cover 145.00
Chop Plate, 13 In. 25.00
Chop Plate,
   15 In. . . . . 40.00 to 45.00
Coffeepot 125.00
Compote, 12 In. 75.00
Creamer. . . . . 14.00 to 22.00
Creamer, Stick Handle. 35.00
Cup & Saucer . . . . . 19.00 to 21.00
Cup & Saucer,
   After Dinner 55.00
Eggcup. 40.00
Gravy Boat. 30.00
Jug, 2 Pt. 65.00
Mixing Bowl, No. 1 . . . . 100.00
Mixing Bowl, No. 3 . . . . 75.00
Mixing Bowl, No. 3,
   Cover 720.00
Mixing Bowl, No. 4 . . . . 50.00
Mixing Bowl, No. 5 . . . . 125.00
Mixing Bowl, No. 7 . . . . 138.00

Mug. . . . . 35.00 to 48.00
Mustard 165.00
Nappy, 8 1/2 In. 25.00
Pie Plate, 9 In. 30.00
Pitcher, Disk . . . . . . 49.00 to 60.00
Pitcher, Juice. . . . . . 30.00 to 45.00
Plate, 6 In. 6.00
Plate, 7 1/2 In. 6.00
Plate, 9 In. . . . . 10.00 to 15.00
Plate, 10 In. . . . . . . 18.00 to 25.00
Plate, Deep, 8 In. 24.00
Plate, Salad, Individual 65.00
Relish, Multicolored
   Inserts. 200.00
Soup, Cream . . . . . 26.00 to 45.00
Soup, French, Cover 75.00
Sugar, Cover . . . . . 22.00 to 30.00
Teapot, Large 120.00
Teapot,
   Medium . . . . . . 95.00 to 135.00
Tumbler, 5 Oz. 25.00
Tumbler, 8 Oz. 45.00
Vase, Bud. 49.00

**FIESTA, see also Amber-
   stone; Casualstone;
   Daisy; Fiesta Kitchen
   Kraft**

FIESTA CASUAL, see Daisy

Fiesta Kitchen Kraft
Fiesta Kitchen Kraft was a
bake-and-serve line made in
the early 1940s by Homer
Laughlin China Company,
Newell, West Virginia. It was
made in red, yellow, green,
and blue.

. . . .

**It is easy to glue pieces of
broken china. Use a new
fast-setting but not instant
glue. Position the pieces
correctly, then use tape to
hold the parts together. If
the piece needs special
support, lean it in a suit-
able position in a box
filled with sand.**

. . . .

ITCHEN
RAFT

H • L • C

BLUE
Cake Server............140.00
Casserole, Cover,
  8 1/2 In................40.00
Casserole, Cover,
  Indivdual..............70.00
Spoon...................110.00

GREEN
Fork....................85.00
Platter, Oval, 12 In.........60.00

RED
Casserole, Holder,
  7 1/2 In................40.00
Salt & Pepper............85.00

YELLOW
Fork....................115.00

Forest Fruits
Forest Fruits is one of many hand-painted patterns made by Blue Ridge in the 1950s. It had yellow fruit and a dark border band.

Berry Bowl, Small..........4.00
Plate, 10 In.............6.75
Platter..................12.00

Fruit
Stangl Pottery, Trenton, New Jersey, made Fruit pattern from 1942 to 1974. The dishes had center designs that were different fruits. Some pictured apples, some pears, grapes, or other fruit. This pattern, No. 3697, was sometimes called Festive Fruit. It was marked

Terra Rose. Also listed here are Fruit pattern dishes made by Franciscan Ceramics from 1949 and by Red Wing from 1947.

Bowl, 5 1/2 In. .... 13.00 to 15.00
Bowl, 10 In. 40.00
Bowl, Vegetable, Oval,
  2 Sections..............45.00
Cruet, Stopper 35.00
Cup.....................8.00
Cup & Saucer 11.00
Gravy Boat..............15.00
Mixing Bowl Set, Nested,
  4 Piece 135.00
Pitcher, 1 Qt. 30.00
Plate, 6 In. 6.00
Plate, 8 In. .... 12.00 to 13.00
Plate, 10 In. 18.00
Saucer..................5.00
Soup, Dish, 7 1/2 In. 20.00
Sugar, Cover ...... 13.00 to 18.00
Teapot, 4 Cup............45.00
Teapot, 6 Cup............50.00
Tidbit, 3 Tiers 40.00

Fruit & Flowers
Fruit & Flowers pattern, No. 4030, was made by Stangl Pottery, Trenton, New Jersey, from 1957 to 1974. The design shows a mixed grouping of flowers, leaves, grapes, and fanciful shapes. Pieces have a colored border. Universal also made a pattern called Fruit & Flowers, but only the Stangl pattern is listed here.

Bowl, 5 1/2 In. 6.00
Creamer.................6.00
Cup & Saucer 10.00
Gravy Boat..............18.00
Plate, 6 In. 4.00
Plate, 8 In. 8.00
Plate, 10 In. 10.00

G

Gingham
Vernon Kilns, Vernon, California, made six different plaid patterns. Each plaid was given a special name. Gingham is the pattern with a dark green border and green and yellow plaid. Other related plaids are Calico (pink and blue), Coronation Organdy (gray and rose), Homespun (cinnamon, yellow, and green), Organdie (brown and yellow), Tam O'Shanter (rust, chartreuse, and dark green), and Tweed (yellow and gray-blue).

Bowl, Vegetable, 2 Sections,
  9 In. ....15.00 to 16.00
Carafe..................15.00
Casserole, Cover..........15.00
Cup & Saucer 10.00
Mixing Bowl, 8 In. 15.00
Mixing Bowl, 9 In. 20.00
Mixing Bowl Set, Nested,
  5 Piece 150.00
Pitcher, Bulb, 1/2 Pt. 25.00
Plate, 6 1/2 In. 3.00
Plate, 9 1/2 In. ......7.50 to 9.00

Greenbriar

Greenbriar was made by E. M. Knowles in 1959.

Creamer	6.50
Gravy Boat	14.00
Plate, 6 In.	2.00
Plate, 9 In.	4.50

H

Hacienda

Another Mexican-inspired pattern, Hacienda was made by Homer Laughlin China Company, Newell, West Virginia, in 1938. The dinnerware was made on the Century shape. A decal showed a bench, cactus, and a portion of the side of a Mexican home. Most pieces have red trim at the handles and at the edge of the plate. Franciscan also made a pattern called Hacienda, a green dinnerware made after 1936.

Bowl, Cereal, Franciscan	4.00
Bowl, Vegetable, Franciscan, 11 In.	12.00
Bread Plate, Franciscan	3.00
Cup, Franciscan	4.00
Plate, Dinner, Franciscan	5.00

Plate, Franciscan, 7 1/2 In.	4.00
Plate, Homer Laughlin, 6 In.	4.00
Platter, Franciscan, 14 In.	20.00
Saucer, Franciscan	2.00
Saucer, Homer Laughlin	1.00
Teapot, Homer Laughlin	29.00

Hall Teapot

Teapots of all sizes and shapes were made by the Hall China Company of East Liverpool, Ohio, starting in the 1920s. Each pot had a special design name such as Airflow or Boston. Each shape could be made in one of several colors, often with names like Cadet (light blue), Camellia (rose), Dresden (deep blue), Delphinium (purple-blue), and Indian Red (orange). Coffeepots were also made.

AIRFLOW

Cobalt, Gold	45.00
Turquoise, Gold	50.00

ALADDIN

Black, Gold, 6 Cup	28.00 to 45.00
Cobalt	45.00
Jewel Tea	95.00
Morning Glory	95.00
Yellow, Gold	40.00

AUTOMOBILE

Turquoise	750.00

BALTIMORE

Red	350.00

BASKETBALL

Red	495.00
Turquoise, Gold	550.00

BELLEVUE

Cobalt, 2 Cup	75.00

BOSTON

Addison, Gold	35.00
Cadet, Gold	30.00 to 32.00
Cobalt, 2 Cup	35.00
Crocus	225.00
Maroon, Gold	40.00
Poppy	95.00
Red	225.00
Red, 2 Cup	140.00
Yellow, Gold	30.00

CUBE

Brown	25.00

DONUT

Poppy	225.00

FOOTBALL

Maroon	750.00

FRENCH

Cadet, Gold	30.00
Cadet, Gold, 4 Cup	25.00
Cobalt, 4 Cup	45.00
Ivory, Gold	30.00
Red	125.00

GLOBE

Rose, Gold, Dripless	75.00
Turquoise, Gold, 4 Cup	125.00

HOLLYWOOD

Maroon, Gold	30.00
Red, 8 Cup	250.00 to 275.00

HOOK COVER

Cadet	125.00
Cadet, Gold	30.00
Turquoise, Gold	75.00

KANSAS

Ivory, Gold	300.00

LOS ANGELES

Canary, 4 Cup	30.00
Cobalt, Gold	75.00
Pink	45.00
Red, 4 Cup	250.00 to 275.00

MCCORMICK

Maroon	25.00

MELODY

Red	250.00

MODERNE

Marine, Gold	50.00

NAUTILUS

Emerald	145.00
Maroon	225.00

Maroon, Gold 175.00
Turquoise, Gold 125.00
Yellow, Decal, 6 Cup. 90.00

NEW YORK
Emerald, Gold. 30.00
Ivory, Gold 45.00
Maroon, 4 Cup 30.00
Poppy. 60.00
Yellow, Gold. 30.00

PARADE
Canary, Gold. 30.00
Emerald, Gold. 60.00
Turquoise, Gold 50.00
Yellow, Gold. . . . . . 65.00 to 75.00

PHILADELPHIA
Emerald, 6 Cup. 33.00
Ivory, Gold . . . . 35.00 to 38.00

PLUME
Pink .45.00

RONALD REAGAN
White . . . . 75.00 to 85.00

SAF-HANDLE
Canary, Gold. 55.00
Cobalt. 145.00

SANI-GRID
Chinese Red 35.00
Cobalt. 110.00
Maroon, Gold 95.00
Rose Parade, 3 Cup 50.00

STAR
Delphinium, Gold 95.00

STREAMLINE
Orange Poppy 135.00
Red. 185.00

TWINSPOUT
Canary 55.00
Red. 150.00

WINDSHIELD
Cobalt. 150.00
Cobalt, Gold 175.00
Delphinium, Gold 95.00
Gamebird. 275.00
Ivory, Gold Dots. 55.00
Maroon, Gold 35.00
Turquoise, Gold 95.00

Harlequin

Harlequin, a solid-color dinnerware made by Homer Laughlin China Company of Newell, West Virginia, was less expensive than Fiesta. It was made from 1938 to 1964 and sold unmarked in Woolworth stores. The rings molded into the plate were at the edge of the plate well, and the rim was plain. Dishes were made in blue, chartreuse, dark blue, Forest Green, gray, ivory, light green, maroon, mauve blue, rose, Spruce Green, Tangerine (red), turquoise, and yellow.

BLUE
Creamer, Individual 15.00
Cup. .4.00
Cup & Saucer 6.00
Cup & Saucer,
   After Dinner. 30.00
Tumbler. 30.00

CHARTREUSE
Platter, 11 In. 13.00

FOREST GREEN
Cup & Saucer 10.00
Sugar & Creamer,
   Cover 25.00

GRAY
Cup & Saucer . . . . . 10.00 to 20.00
Eggcup, Double 17.50
Pitcher, Ball 140.00
Plate, 6 In. 3.00
Sugar, Cover 17.00

LIGHT GREEN
Cup. .5.00
Jug, 22 Oz. 40.00

MAROON
Baker, Oval. 28.00
Butter, Cover, 1/2 Lb. 100.00
Cup. .4.00
Eggcup, Double 20.00
Jug, Water 60.00
Pitcher, 7 In. 7.00
Plate, 7 In. 7.00
Platter, Oval, 13 In. 40.00

MAUVE BLUE
Bowl, 5 1/2 In. 8.00
Casserole, Cover. 25.00
Eggcup 19.00
Nut Dish 15.00
Tumbler 35.00

ROSE
Bowl, 5 1/2 In. 7.00
Casserole, Cover. 85.00
Cup & Saucer 3.50
Saucer. 2.00
Tea Set, 3 Piece 100.00

SPRUCE GREEN
Bowl, 5 1/2 In. 16.00
Bowl, 9 In. 70.00
Bowl, Salad, Individual. 95.00
Creamer, High Lip 195.00
Cup & Saucer . . . . .15.00 to 25.00
Eggcup 20.00
Jug, 22 Oz. 50.00
Nut Dish 18.00
Pitcher, Water 85.00
Plate, 10 In. 20.00
Syrup. 250.00

TANGERINE
Ashtray, Basket Weave. 25.00
Creamer,
   Individual . . . . . . .15.00 to 16.50
Cup. .8.00
Cup & Saucer 9.50

Eggcup	19.00
Salt & Pepper	15.00
Saucer, After Dinner	20.00
Sugar, Cover	9.00
Syrup, Cover	160.00
Teapot	40.00

TURQUOISE

Bowl, 5 1/2 In.	4.00
Butter	80.00
Cup & Saucer	6.00 to 7.00
Gravy Boat	9.00 to 12.00
Plate, 10 In.	7.00

YELLOW

Bowl, Vegetable, Round	15.00
Butter, Cover, 1/2 Lb.	130.00
Creamer	7.00
Creamer, Individual	10.00 to 18.00
Cup & Saucer	6.00 to 8.00
Cup & Saucer, After Dinner	25.00
Nut Dish	7.00
Plate, 6 In.	2.50
Plate, 7 In.	4.50
Plate, 9 In.	7.00
Platter, 11 In.	10.00
Platter, 13 In.	11.75
Soup, Cream	15.00
Spooner	175.00
Sugar, Cover	9.75
Teapot	28.00

HAWAIIAN DAISY, see Daisy

Hawaiian Flowers

Hawaiian Flowers was a well-known Vernon Kilns, Vernon, California, tableware designed by Don Blanding. It was first made in 1939.

HAWAIIAN FLOWERS
Scripted by
Aloha
Don Blanding

VERNON KILNS
Made in U.S.A

Chop Plate, 12 In.	60.00
Eggcup	35.00
Plate, 9 1/2 In.	25.00 to 37.00

Heather Rose

Heather Rose is a decal-decorated Hall Pottery pattern. Both dinnerware and utility ware pieces were made with this decoration. It pictures a realistic-looking pale pinkish purple rose on a stem with many leaves.

SUPERIOR HALL QUALITY · DINNERWARE ·

Bowl, 9 In.	13.00
Pitcher, 3 Pt.	265.00

HOLLAND, see Crocus

Homespun

Homespun, a yellow, green, and reddish brown plaid pattern, was made by Vernon Kilns, Vernon, California. Other related plaids are Calico (pink and blue), Coronation Organdy (gray and rose), Gingham (green and yellow), Organdie (brown and yellow), Tam O'Shanter (rust, chartreuse, and dark green), and Tweed (yellow and gray-blue).

· · · · · · · · · · · · · ·

When stacking dinner plates, put a piece of felt or paper between each plate. Never put more than 24 in one stack.

· · · · · · · · · · · · · ·

UNDER GLAZE HAND PAINTED HOMESPUN VERNONWARE CALIFORNIA U.S.A

Bowl, Salad, 10 1/2 In.	85.00
Bowl, Vegetable, 2 Sections, 10 In.	25.00
Bowl, Vegetable, 9 In.	10.00
Bread Plate, 6 In.	5.00
Chop Plate, 12 In.	25.00
Chop Plate, 14 In.	25.00 to 45.00
Coaster	18.00 to 30.00
Creamer	5.00
Cup & Saucer	17.00
Eggcup	10.00 to 20.00
Gravy Boat, Streamlined, 1/2 Pt.	25.00
Gravy Boat, Streamlined, 1 Pt.	30.00
Mixing Bowl Set, 4 Piece	70.00
Mug, 9 Oz.	9.00 to 20.00
Pitcher, 1 Qt.	19.00
Plate, 6 In.	5.00 to 7.00
Plate, 7 1/2 In.	8.00 to 15.00
Plate, 9 1/2 In.	10.00 to 15.00
Plate, Oval, 10 1/2 In.	10.00
Platter, Oval, 14 In.	18.00 to 20.00

Salt & Pepper 16.00
Saucer . . . . 2.00 to 3.00
Spooner 30.00
Sugar 3.00
Sugar & Creamer, Cover 16.00
Tumbler, 4 1/4 In. 20.00

Homestead Provincial

Homestead Provincial is one of the Poppytrail patterns by Metlox.

Bowl, Lug, 5 In. 15.00
Bread Tray 45.00
Coffeepot 60.00
Salt & Pepper, Tankard,
  Small 16.00
Tankard 25.00

I

Iroquois

Russel Wright was an important industrial designer. His dinnerwares were made by at least four companies. Iroquois Casual China was a Russel Wright modern design made by Iroquois China Company, Syracuse, New York. The dinnerware was less expensive than American Modern, heavier and less breakable. It was advertised as cook-and-serve. The first pieces were marked China by Iroquois with the signature of Russel Wright. In the 1950s the ware was redesigned and the mark was changed to Iroquois Casual China by Russel Wright. The dishes were made in a number of colors, designed to be mixed and matched. Sets were often sold with pieces in several colors. The original Iroquois was glazed Avocado Yellow, Ice Blue, Lemon Yellow, Nutmeg Brown, Parsley Green, or Sugar White. In

1951 more colors were added, including aqua, Brick Red, Cantaloupe, charcoal, Lettuce Green, Oyster Gray, Pink Sherbet, and Ripe Apricot. In 1959 some Iroquois pieces were decorated with patterns and sold under other names. Glass tumblers were made in matching colors.

IROQUOIS
CASUAL CHINA
by Russel Wright

AVOCADO YELLOW
Bowl, 5 In. 6.00
Bowl, 5 3/4 In. 3.50
Bowl, 6 3/4 In. 5.00
Bowl, Vegetable,
  2 Sections, 10 In. 13.00
Bowl, Vegetable, 8 In. 12.00
Butter, Cover . . . . . 50.00 to 60.00
Carafe 120.00
Casserole, Cover,
  2 Sections, 10 In. 40.00
Casserole, Cover, 8 In. 35.00
Chop Plate, 13 1/2 In. 20.00
Coffeepot,
  After Dinner . . . . . 45.00 to 60.00
Cup & Saucer . . . . 5.00 to 6.50
Pitcher, Cover, 1 1/2 Qt. . . . 90.00
Plate, 6 In. . . . . 2.50 to 4.00
Plate, 7 1/2 In. . . . . . 5.00 to 8.00
Plate, 9 In. . . . . 4.50 to 7.00
Plate, 10 In. 6.00
Plate, Redesigned, 10 In. 7.00
Platter, Oval,
  12 3/4 In. . . . . . . 10.00 to 20.00
Platter, Oval,
  14 1/2 In. . . . . . . 14.00 to 20.00
Salt & Pepper, Stacking 12.00

CHARCOAL
Bowl, 5 1/2 In. 5.00

Butter, Cover 150.00
Cup, After Dinner 115.00
Cup & Saucer,
  After Dinner 165.00
Salt & Pepper 45.00

ICE BLUE
Bowl, 5 In. 6.00
Bowl, 5 1/2 In. 4.00
Bowl, Footed, Cover, 5 In. . . 22.00
Bowl, Vegetable,
  2 Sections, 10 In. 18.00
Bowl, Vegetable,
  8 In. . . . . 14.00 to 15.00
Bowl, Vegetable, Cover,
  2 Sections, 10 In. 40.00
Carafe . . . . 110.00 to 125.00
Casserole, Cover, 4 Qt.,
  8 In. . . . . 25.00 to 75.00
Chop Plate, 13 1/2 In. 20.00
Creamer,
  Stacking . . . . 6.00 to 12.00
Cup . . . . 4.00 to 5.00
Cup & Saucer . . . . 5.00 to 9.00
Pitcher, Cover, 1 1/2 Qt. . . . 45.00
Plate, 6 In. . . . . 3.00 to 4.00
Plate, 7 1/2 In. 5.00
Plate, 9 In. 6.00
Plate, 10 In. . . . . 6.00 to 7.00
Platter, Oval, 14 1/2 In. 16.00
Salt & Pepper, Stacking 20.00
Saucer 1.00
Sugar & Creamer,
  Stacking . . . . 14.00 to 20.00

LEMON YELLOW
Bowl, 5 In. . . . . 5.00 to 6.00
Bowl, Vegetable, 2 Sections,
  10 In. . . . . 16.00 to 22.00
Butter, Cover 38.00
Casserole, Cover, 8 In. 45.00
Cup 4.00
Cup & Saucer . . . . . . 6.00 to 10.00
Fry Pan 60.00
Gravy Boat 8.00
Plate, 7 1/2 In. 6.00
Plate, 10 In. . . . . 6.00 to 8.00
Platter, Oval, 12 3/4 In. 12.00
Platter, Oval, 14 1/2 In. 22.00
Sugar & Creamer,
  Stacking 18.00

LETTUCE GREEN

Plate, 10 In. 8.00

NUTMEG BROWN

Bowl, Vegetable, 10 In. 16.00

Butter, Cover 65.00

Chop Plate, 13 1/2 In. 24.00

Creamer, Redesigned 14.00

Creamer, Stacking 6.50

Cup & Saucer 5.00

Plate, 7 1/2 In. 6.00

Plate, 10 In. 6.00

Platter, Oval,
  12 3/4 In. . . . . . . 12.00 to 17.00

Platter, Oval, 14 1/2 In. 16.00

OYSTER GRAY

Bowl, 5 1/2 In. 6.00

Carafe 125.00

Coffeepot, After Dinner 95.00

Plate, 6 In. . . . . 4.00 to 5.00

Plate, 7 1/2 In. . . . . . . 7.00 to 8.00

Plate, 9 In. . . . . 7.00 to 8.00

Platter, Oval, 12 3/4 In. 16.00

Platter, Oval, 14 1/2 In. 20.00

PARSLEY GREEN

Bowl, Vegetable, Cover,
  2 Sections, 10 In. 50.00

Plate, 6 In. 3.50

Plate, 7 1/2 In. 4.00

Plate, 10 In. 6.00

Saucer 2.00

PINK SHERBET

Bowl, 5 1/2 In. . . . . . . 4.00 to 5.00

Butter, Cover . . . . . 65.00 to 85.00

Casserole, 8 In. . . . 18.00 to 20.00

Cup 4.00

Cup & Saucer . . . . 5.00 to 6.00

Mug, 13 Oz. 55.00

Mug, Redesigned 60.00

Pitcher, Cover,
  1 1/2 Qt., 5 1/4 In. 110.00

Pitcher, Redesigned,
  1 1/2 Qt., 5 1/4 In. 175.00

Plate, 6 In. . . . . 3.00 to 4.00

Plate, 9 In. 4.50

Plate, 10 In. 7.00

Platter, Oval,
  12 3/4 In. . . . . . . 12.00 to 15.00

Platter, Oval,
  14 1/2 In. . . . . . . 16.00 to 22.50

Saucer 2.50

Sugar & Creamer,
  Stacking . . . . 20.00 to 22.00

RIPE APRICOT

Bowl, 5 1/2 In. 4.00

Bowl, Vegetable, 8 In. 14.00

Bowl, Vegetable, Cover,
  2 Sections,
  10 In. . . . . 14.00 to 16.00

Carafe 125.00

Casserole, Cover, 2 Qt.,
  8 In. . . . . 18.00 to 20.00

Chop Plate, 13 1/2 In. 24.00

Creamer, Large 16.00

Cup & Saucer 5.00

Mug, Redesigned, 9 Oz. 65.00

Plate, 6 In. . . . . 3.00 to 4.00

Plate, 9 In. 5.50

Platter, Oval, 12 3/4 In. 20.00

Salt & Pepper, Stacking 13.00

SUGAR WHITE

Creamer, Stacking . . 8.00 to 10.00

Cup & Saucer . . . . . 10.00 to 16.00

Plate, 6 In. . . . . 4.00 to 6.00

Saltshaker, Stacking 10.00

Ivy

Ivy is a hand-painted pattern
made by Franciscan Ceramics
from 1948. Harker and Paden
City also made patterns called
Ivy, but only Franciscan Ivy is
listed here.

Ashtray,
  Individual . . . . . . 20.00 to 25.00

Bowl, 11 In. . . . . . 95.00 to 145.00

Bowl, Fruit, 5 1/4 In. 15.00

Bowl, Vegetable, 8 In. 38.00

Bowl, Vegetable,
  2 Sections, 12 In. 60.00

Bowl, Vegetable, Cover,
  2 Sections, 12 In. 150.00

Butter 65.00

Casserole, 1 1/2 Qt. 110.00

Celery Dish 45.00

Chop Plate, 11 3/4 In. 145.00

Chop Plate,
  14 In. . . . . 95.00 to 100.00

Coffeepot 225.00

Creamer 30.00

Cup & Saucer . . . . . 22.50 to 26.00

Cup & Saucer, Jumbo 65.00

Gravy Boat 55.00

Jug 145.00

Mug, 12 Oz. 12.00

Plate, 5 In. . . . . . . 10.00 to 14.00

Plate, 6 In. 8.00

Plate, 7 In. . . . . 35.00 to 45.00

Plate, 9 In. 35.00

Plate, 10 In. 30.00

Platter, 14 In. 75.00

Relish, 3 Sections 115.00

Sherbet 30.00

Soup, Dish 40.00

Sugar & Creamer, Jumbo . . . 55.00

Teapot 195.00

Tidbit, 2 Tiers 75.00

Trivet, Square, Box, 6 In. . . 125.00

Tumbler, 10 Oz. 40.00

J

Jubilee

Jubilee is a 1948 dinnerware
shape made by Homer Laughlin China of Newell, West
Virginia, and East Liverpool,
Ohio. The dinnerware called
Jubilee was a solid color line.
The colors were Celadon
Green, Shell Pink, Mist Gray,
and Cream Beige. Jubilee was
colored in different ways to
produce dinnerware patterns
with other names. Jubilee was
revived in 1977 and 1978.

CELADON GREEN

Casserole 30.00

Coffeepot	45.00
Platter, Small	12.00
Teapot	40.00

SHELL PINK

Platter, Large	15.00

K

Kitchen Kraft

Kitchen Kraft oven-to-table pieces were made by Homer Laughlin China Company, Newell, West Virginia, from the early 1930s. The pieces were made in plain solid colors or with decals. If decorated with decals, they are listed in this book under the decal's name. If solid colors, they are listed here.

BLUE

Casserole, Cover, 8 1/2 In.	60.00
Casserole, Cover, Individual	125.00 to 135.00
Casserole, Metal Stand, 7 1/2 In.	150.00
Leftover, Cover, Stacking	75.00
Spoon	95.00

GREEN

Cake Plate	40.00
Cake Server	110.00
Casserole, Cover, 8 1/2 In.	95.00
Casserole, Cover, Individual	110.00 to 115.00
Fork	70.00 to 75.00
Jar, Cover, Small	175.00
Mixing Bowl, 10 In.	54.00

Salt & Pepper	65.00
Spoon	80.00

RED

Casserole, Cover, 7 1/2 In.	45.00
Casserole, Cover, Individual	75.00 to 115.00
Jar, Refrigerator, Cover, Label	265.00
Salt & Pepper	85.00 to 90.00
Spoon	100.00

YELLOW

Cake Plate	30.00 to 45.00
Casserole, 8 1/2 In.	68.00 to 70.00
Casserole, Cover, Individual	110.00 to 115.00
Jar, Refrigerator, Cover, Large	270.00
Pie Baker, 10 In.	45.00

L

LITTLE RED RIDING HOOD, see Red Riding Hood

Lu-Ray

The characteristic slightly speckled glaze of the solid-colored Lu-Ray makes it easy to identify. Taylor, Smith, and Taylor of Chester, West Virginia, made this pattern after 1938. Pastel colors include Chatham Gray, Persian Cream, Sharon Pink, Surf Green, and Windsor Blue.

CHATHAM GRAY

Creamer	15.00
Cup & Saucer	20.00

PERSIAN CREAM

Bowl, 5 1/4 In.	4.50
Bowl, Vegetable, 9 In.	18.00
Bowl, Vegetable, Oval, 10 In.	50.00
Chop Plate	25.00
Cup & Saucer, After Dinner	22.00
Eggcup	14.00
Epergne, 8 In.	85.00
Gravy Boat, Underplate	22.00
Jug, Footed, 76 Oz.	40.00 to 65.00
Plate, 6 In.	2.00
Plate, 7 1/4 In.	4.00
Plate, 9 In.	5.00
Plate, 10 In.	10.00
Platter, 13 1/2 In.	10.00 to 13.50
Saltshaker	7.00
Saucer	2.00
Soup, Cream	48.00
Sugar & Creamer	6.00

SHARON PINK

Cup & Saucer, After Dinner	20.00 to 22.00
Grill Plate	16.00
Pitcher, Footed, 76 Oz.	60.00
Plate, 6 In.	2.00
Plate, 7 1/4 In.	12.50
Plate, 8 In.	12.00
Plate, 10 In.	10.00
Salt & Pepper	15.00
Soup, Cream	68.00
Sugar, After Dinner	40.00
Sugar & Creamer, Cover	20.00
Tumbler, 5 Oz.	40.00

SURF GREEN

Bowl, Vegetable, Oval, 10 In.	12.00
Cup & Saucer	7.00
Plate, 6 1/2 In.	2.00
Plate, 7 1/4 In.	4.00
Plate, 8 In.	12.00 to 15.00
Plate, 10 In.	10.00
Saltshaker	7.00
Soup, Cream	68.00
Sugar & Creamer	6.00
Tumbler, 9 Oz.	65.00

WINDSOR BLUE

Bowl, Vegetable, 9 In. 15.00
Casserole, Cover, 8 In. 100.00
Chop Plate 32.00
Cup & Saucer 7.50
Cup & Saucer,
   After Dinner 20.00
Gravy Boat,
   Underplate . . . . . 18.50 to 22.00
Grill Plate 18.00
Jug, Footed, 76 Oz. 50.00
Nut Dish, 4 1/2 In. 70.00
Pitcher, Footed 77.00
Plate, 7 1/4 In. 4.00
Platter, 11 3/4 In. . . 10.00 to 13.00
Platter, 13 1/2 In. 10.00
Relish, 4 Sections,
   Handle . . . . 80.00 to 95.00
Salt & Pepper 20.00
Saucer 1.00

Lute Song

Lute Song is a Red Wing pattern made in the 1960s. It was decorated with stylized pictures of musical instruments in pastel colors. The dishes were china, not pottery like many Red Wing patterns, and were one of the eight patterns made in 1960.

Butter, Cover 40.00
Coffee Server 60.00
Plate, Dinner 8.00

M

Magnolia

A wide, bright, cranberry-red band borders Magnolia pattern by Stangl Pottery, Trenton, New Jersey. The pattern, No. 3870, was made from 1952 to 1962. Another version of Magnolia by Red Wing does not have the banded edge. It was made in 1947. Both are listed here.

MAGNOLIA

Coffeepot, 8 Cup,
   Red Wing 30.00
Cup & Saucer, Stangl 8.00
Cup & Saucer, Red Wing 8.00
Plate, 6 In., Red Wing 6.00
Plate, 10 In., Red Wing 7.50
Plate, 6 In., Stangl 6.00
Plate, Dinner, Red Wing 7.50
Platter, Stangl 45.00
Saucer, Red Wing 2.50
Teapot, Stangl 65.00

Mayflower

Mayflower is a pattern by Southern Potteries (Blue Ridge) of Erwin, Tennessee. The pattern was made in the 1950s. Another Mayflower pattern was made by E. M. Knowles from 1957 to 1963. May Flower is a pattern by Vernon Kilns.

Bowl, Vegetable,
   Oval, 9 In. 20.00
Creamer 13.00
Gravy Boat 35.00
Plate, 7 In. 9.00
Plate, 8 1/2 In. 4.50
Plate, 10 1/2 In. 6.00
Sugar 25.00

Meadow Rose

Meadow Rose was a pattern made by Franciscan Ceramics of Los Angeles, California, in 1977.

Bowl, 6 In. . . . . 12.00 to 16.00
Bowl, Vegetable, Large 55.00
Butter . . . . 30.00 to 45.00
Casserole, Cover 126.00
Coaster 10.00
Creamer . . . . 25.00 to 35.00
Cup & Saucer . . . . . . 7.00 to 15.00
Mug, 7 Oz. . . . . 20.00 to 35.00
Plate, 7 In. 16.00
Plate, 9 In. . . . . 10.00 to 26.00
Platter, 14 In. 55.00
Relish, 3 Sections 65.00
Salt & Pepper 26.00
Sugar 35.00
Teapot 65.00
Tumbler, Juice 20.00

Memory Lane

Memory Lane is typical of many of the patterns made by Southern Potteries (Blue Ridge) in Erwin, Tennessee. The dishes were decorated with two hand-painted flowers with stylized leaves in pink, deep red, and yellow. There was another pattern called Memory Lane made by Royal China Company, but the pieces listed here are Blue Ridge.

Ashtray 10.00
Berry Bowl, 5 1/4 In. 4.50
Butter 18.50
Cup & Saucer . . . . 4.00 to 4.50
Plate, 6 In. 4.00

Plate, 9 1/2 In. 5.00

Salt & Pepper 12.00

Soup, Dish. . . . . 6.00 to 6.50

Mexicana

The first of the Mexican-inspired patterns that became popular as a dinnerware in the 1930s was Mexicana. This decal-decorated set, designed by Frederick Hurten Rhead, was first offered in 1938. The design shows a collection of orange and yellow pots with a few cacti. The edge of the dish well is rimmed with red or occasionally yellow, green, or blue. Almost all of the pieces are Century line, a popular Homer Laughlin dinnerware shape.

Cake Plate, Blue Trim 40.00

Casserole, Cover,
   Blue Trim, 8 1/2 In. 55.00

Casserole, Cover, Red Trim,
   7 1/2 In. . . . . 40.00 to 55.00

Casserole, Cover,
   Red Trim, 8 1/2 In. 55.00

Casserole, Red Trim,
   Individual. 80.00

Jar, Cover, Blue Trim,
   Large. 135.00

Jar, Cover, Blue Trim,
   Medium 125.00

Jar, Cover, Blue Trim,
   Small. 140.00

Jar, Cover, Red Trim,
   Large. 135.00

Jar, Cover, Red Trim,
   Medium 125.00

Jar, Cover, Red Trim,
   Small 140.00

Jug, Cover, Blue Trim. 165.00

Jug, Cover, Red Trim 125.00

Mixing Bowl Set, Red Trim,
   6, 8 & 10 In., 3 Piece 125.00

Pie Baker, Blue Trim,
   10 In. 40.00

Pie Baker, Red Trim,
   10 In. 40.00

Refrigerator, Stacking Set,
   Red Trim, 4 Piece 145.00

Salt & Pepper, Blue Trim. . . . 45.00

Salt & Pepper, Red Trim 45.00

Moby Dick

Moby Dick was a high-priced line made by Vernon Kilns in 1939. Rockwell Kent, the famous illustrator, had illustrated Herman Melville's Classic story *Moby Dick*. These illustrations were adapted for the dinnerware. Plates pictured whaling ships, other pieces showed ships and whales. The printed design was available in one of four colors: dark blue, maroon, Walnut Brown, or yellow (orange-yellow). The Ultra shape was used.

BLUE

Bowl, Vegetable, 8 In. 125.00

Chop Plate,
   12 In. . . . . 155.00 to 200.00

Plate, 5 1/2 In. 25.00

BROWN

Plate, 9 1/2 In. 35.00

MAROON

Chop Plate, 12 In. 185.00

N

Nocturne

Nocturne is a Blue Ridge pattern, hand painted with a red flower and leaves. The edge is brushed with red. It is on the Colonial shape.

Bowl, Red Trim, 5 1/4 In. 5.50

Coffeepot. 80.00

Cup & Saucer, Red Trim 7.50

Plate, 8 In. 5.50

Plate, Red Trim,
   9 1/4 In. . . . . 5.50 to 8.50

Platter, 11 In. 12.00

Platter, Red Trim, 11 In. . . . 15.00

Saucer, Red Trim 2.00

Sugar, Red Trim. 7.50

O

Old Curiosity Shop

The Old Curiosity Shop is one of many patterns made by Royal China Company of Sebring, Ohio, in the 1950s. It pictures a view of the shop and an elaborate border. The Royal China Company closed in 1986.

GREEN

Bowl, 5 1/2 In. 2.50

Bowl, Vegetable, 9 1/4 In. . . . 8.00

Cake Plate, Handles,
   10 In. 12.00

Cup & Saucer 3.00

Gravy Boat, Liner 12.50

Plate, 6 In. 2.00

Plate, 10 In. . . . . 2.50 to 6.00

Platter, 13 In. 7.50

Salt & Pepper. 7.50

Sandwich Server, Handle,
   11 1/2 In. 7.50

Soup, Dish, 8 1/2 In. 7.50

Teapot 40.00

PINK

Bowl, Vegetable, 9 1/4 In. . . 12.00
Saucer 1.00
Sugar & Creamer 3.00

ORANGE POPPY,
see Poppy

Orange Tree

Orange Tree is a line of solid-colored bowls with raised designs of orange trees or perhaps peach trees. The pattern was made by Homer Laughlin about 1920 to 1930. They were made with turquoise and perhaps other glazes.

IVORY

Bowl, 8 In. 60.00

TURQUOISE

Bowl, 7 In. 50.00
Bowl, 8 In. 60.00
Bowl, 9 In. 70.00

Organdie

Organdie is one of six different plaid patterns made by Vernon Kilns, Vernon, California, in the 1940s and 1950s. It is an overall brown pattern with a yellow and brown plaid border. Other related plaids are Calico (pink and blue), Gingham (green and yellow), Homespun (cinnamon, yellow, and green), Tam O'Shanter (rust, chartreuse, and deep green), and Tweed (yellow and gray-blue). Organdie was originally the name for a group of plaid designs made in 1937. One of these was Coronation Organdy (gray and rose).

• • • • • • • • • • • • • • •

Rubber cement solvent, available at art supply and office supply stores, has many uses. Put a few drops on a paper towel and rub off ink smudges, adhesive tape glue, and label glue from glass or porcelains.

• • • • • • • • • • • • • • •

Bowl, 5 1/2 In. 3.50
Bowl, Vegetable, 2 Sections,
    10 In. 25.00
Butter Chip 10.00
Coaster. 18.00
Creamer. 4.00
Cup. 5.00
Gravy Boat. 8.00
Pitcher 32.00
Plate, 6 1/2 In. 4.50
Plate, 7 1/2 In. 5.00
Plate, 9 1/2 In. . . . . . 6.00 to 12.00
Salt & Pepper 6.00
Saucer 2.00
Soup, Dish. 12.00
Tidbit, 7 1/2 In. 15.00

P

Pate Sur Pate

Pate Sur Pate is a solid color Harker pattern. It has a scalloped border.

TEAL

Bowl, Vegetable, 9 In.. . . . . . 15.00
Cup & Saucer 12.00

Plate, 6 In. 6.00
Plate, 8 1/2 In. 8.00
Plate, 10 1/2 In. 10.00
Platter, 12 In. 12.00
Soup, Dish, 8 3/8 In. 10.00
Sugar & Creamer 20.00

Petit Point

Petit Point was an idea that was used by many makers. The pattern had a center design that looked as if it had been stitched of colored wools. Petit Point patterns were made by Crown Pottery of Evansville, Indiana, in 1941; Leigh/Crescent of Alliance, Ohio, in 1936 for Montgomery Ward; and Taylor, Smith, and Taylor of Taylor, West Virginia, and East Liverpool, Ohio. Other similar patterns with "stitched" designs were called Petit Point Basket, Petit Point House, etc. Many are listed at the back of the book. The prices for all of the patterns are very similar, and so only one price listing is given for all Petit Point patterns.

Casserole, Cover, Harker,
    8 1/2 In. 12.00
Mixing Bowl, Deep,
    TST, 9 In. 15.00
Pie Server. 12.00
Plate, Dinner, Crooksville 8.00
Plate, Tab Handle,
    TST, 11 In. 10.00
Platter, Tab Handle,
    TST, 12 1/2 In. 12.00
Platter, Vernon Kilns,
    13 In. 12.00
Saucer, Crooksville. 2.00

Plantation Ivy

Blue Ridge made several ivy patterns. Plantation Ivy is decorated with a stylized hand-painted ivy vine in yellow and green. It was made in the 1950s.

Bowl, 5 1/2 In. 4.00
Bowl, Vegetable,
  Oval, 9 In. 13.00
Cup & Saucer 6.00
Plate, 6 In. 3.00
Plate, 9 1/2 In. 6.00

Poppy

Poppy, sometimes called Orange Poppy by collectors, was made by the Hall China Company, East Liverpool, Ohio, from 1933 through the 1950s. The decals picture realistic groups of orange poppies with a few leaves. Another Hall pattern called Red Poppy has bright red stylized flowers with black leaves and trim. Poppy is a name used by at least five companies but listed here are Poppy pattern pieces by Hall.

Bowl, 9 1/2 In. 18.00
Bowl, Soup,
  Dish, 5 1/4 In. 20.00
Bowl, Utility, 11 In. 17.00
Coffepot 35.00
Cookie Jar 85.00

Creamer 45.00
Cup & Saucer 35.00
Gravy Boat 75.00
Pie Plate . . . . 15.00 to 35.00
Pitcher, Utility 32.00
Plate, 6 In. 12.00
Plate, 7 In. 7.50
Plate, 9 In. 35.00
Spooner 100.00

Poppy & Wheat

Poppy & Wheat is a design that seems to have been made in the 1930s. It was made by Hall China Company, East Liverpool, Ohio. The design shows a realistic spray of orange flowers and wheat heads. It is sometimes called Wheat or Wild Poppy.

Coffeepot, Drip 250.00
Creamer, New York 35.00
Jug, Sunshine, No. 2 . . . . 50.00
Jug, Sunshine, No. 6 . . . . 50.00
Pitcher, Small 135.00
Teapot, 2 Cup 450.00
Teapot, New York,
  8 Cup 600.00

Poppy Trail

Metlox Potteries of California made many dinnerwares marked with the word Metlox or Poppytrail (Poppy Trail). Solid-colored wares and hand-decorated pieces were made. Listed here are solid mix-and-match pieces marked Metlox Poppy Trail. Colors include Delphinium Blue, Canary Yellow, ivory, Old Rose, Poppy Orange, rust, and Turquoise Blue.

BLUE
Coffeepot 75.00
Cup & Saucer 9.00
Dish, Fruit 10.00
Platter, Small 20.00
Soup, Dish 20.00
Tankard, Large 18.00

IVORY
Butter 20.50
Casserole, Cover 24.00
Plate, 9 1/4 In. 8.00
Platter, Oval 16.00
Platter, Round 17.00
Tom & Jerry Set 85.00

RED
Bowl, 6 In. 5.00
Bowl, Vegetable,
  2 Sections, Round, 9 In. . . . 10.00
Gravy Boat, Handle 10.00
Salt & Pepper 8.00

Provincial

Provincial is a bordered plate with a floral center made by Stangl Pottery, Trenton, New Jersey, from 1957 to 1967. Others companies used the word "Provincial" to name patterns, but only Stangl is listed here.

Bowl, 6 In. 8.00
Bowl, Vegetable, Handle,
  2 Sections, 8 In. 25.00
Butter, Cover 15.00
Casserole, Handle 15.00
Creamer 12.00
Cup & Saucer 10.00
Plate, 6 3/4 In. 4.00
Plate, Dinner 10.00
Sugar, Cover 25.00

R

Raymor

Many collectors search for pieces in the Raymor pattern. It is a stoneware made by Roseville Pottery Company of

Zanesville, Ohio, in 1952 and 1953. It was designed by Ben Siebel. One advertisement claimed the textured glaze was offered in Autumn Brown, Avocado Green, Beach Gray, Contemporary White, and Terra Cotta (rust). There were also pieces made in mottled green and black.

AVOCADO GREEN

Bowl, Vegetable, Open	22.00
Teapot	85.00

Red Poppy

Bright red flowers and black leaves were used on this popular Hall pattern called Red Poppy. The pattern, made in East Liverpool, Ohio, from 1930 through 1950, was a premium item for Grand Union Tea Company. Matching metal pieces, such as wastebaskets and bread boxes, were made, and glass tumblers are known.

Bowl, 9 In.	15.00 to 26.00
Cake Plate	16.00 to 18.00
Coffeepot	32.00

Creamer	18.00
Jug, Ball	32.00
Jug, Daniel	55.00
Jug, Radiance	20.00
Mixing Bowl, Deep, 9 In.	20.00
Pie Plate	8.00
Plate, 9 1/4 In.	7.50
Salt & Pepper	20.00

Red Riding Hood

One of the easiest patterns of American dinnerware to recognize is Red Riding Hood. Three-dimensional figures of the little girl with the red hood have been adapted into saltshakers, teapots, and other pieces. The pattern was made by the Hull Pottery Company, Crooksville, Ohio, from 1943 to 1957.

Butter	395.00
Butter, Cover	350.00 to 375.00
Cookie Jar, Closed Basket	295.00 to 395.00
Cookie Jar, Open Basket	395.00
Cookie Jar, Open Basket, Cover	250.00

Cookie Jar, Open Basket, Gold Stars On Apron	375.00 to 425.00
Creamer, Tab Handle	265.00
Creamer, Side Pour	195.00
Matchbox	495.00
Mustard	275.00
Mustard, Spoon	395.00
Pitcher	240.00
Pitcher, Milk	275.00 to 300.00
Salt & Pepper, 3 1/2 In.	85.00 to 125.00
Salt & Pepper, 4 1/2 In.	1,200.00 to 1,250.00
Salt & Pepper, 5 1/2 In.	150.00 to 200.00
Saltshaker, Large	200.00
Saltshaker, Small	45.00
Spice Jar	695.00
Sugar, Cover, Crawling	265.00
Sugar & Creamer, Head Pour	700.00
Sugar & Creamer, Side Pour	195.00 to 250.00
Teapot	275.00 to 365.00
Vase	275.00
Wall Pocket	395.00 to 500.00

Red Rooster

Red Rooster by Metlox is one of the Poppytrail line made beginning in 1955. It is easy to identify because the center design is a large red rooster.

Bowl, 6 In.	18.00
Bowl, 10 In.	15.00
Bowl, 10 1/2 x 11 1/2 In.	95.00

Bowl, Deep, 5 1/2 In. 14.00
Butter, Cover 25.00
Canister, Coffee,
  Wooden Cover 45.00
Canister, Flour,
  Wooden Cover 60.00
Canister, Sugar,
  Wooden Cover 45.00
Canister Set, 8 Piece. 275.00
Canister Set, Wooden
  Covers, 4 Piece 150.00
Coffeepot 75.00
Cookie Jar, Cover. 60.00
Creamer. 10.00
Cruet Set, Wooden
  Holder, 5 Piece 165.00
Cup. 15.00
Cup & Saucer 18.00
Pitcher, 6 In. 20.00
Pitcher, 7 1/4 In. 42.00
Plate, 7 1/2 In. 6.50
Plate, 10 In. . . . . . . .10.00 to 14.00
Plate, 12 1/2 In. 70.00
Platter, 13 In. 15.00
Salt & Pepper, Handle 15.00
Sauceboat, Handle, Spout. . .10.00
Saucer 3.50
Soup, Dish. 8.00
Stein 30.00
Sugar 12.00
Sugar, Cover 18.00
Tumbler, 10 Oz. 22.00

Refrigerator Ware

Refrigerator sets were made by the Hall China Company, East Liverpool, Ohio, from the late 1930s. For Westinghouse, the company made Phoenix (Patrician) in 1938, General (Emperor) in 1939, Hercules or Peasant Ware (Aristocrat) in 1940–1941, and Adonis (Prince) in 1952. Hall also made King and Queen oven-ware to match the Refrigerator Ware. Sears, Roebuck, Montgomery Ward, Hotpoint, and General Electric also used Hall Refrigerator Ware. In addition, the company made

some pieces sold with the Hall name: Bingo in the late 1930s, Plaza in the 1930s to the 1960s, and Norris.

Made Exclusively for WESTINGHOUSE By The Hall China Co.
MADE IN U.S.A.

G.E.
Water Server, Gray,
  Yellow 45.00
Water Server, Yellow
  Cover 25.00

HOTPOINT
Leftover, No. 4, Daffodil,
  Square, 6 3/4 In. 22.00
Leftover, Square,
  Gray, 4 3/4 In. 40.00
Water Server, Stopper
  With Cork 85.00

MONTGOMERY WARD
Leftover, Ivory,
  Rectangular 60.00

WESTINGHOUSE
Butter, General,
  Dark Green 40.00
Butter, Hercules, Yellow 40.00
Casserole, Cover, Ridged . . .15.00
Casserole, Yellow. 20.00
Leftover, General,
  Orange 30.00
Leftover, Hercules, Ivory 30.00
Leftover, Phoenix, Blue 30.00

Rhythm

Rhythm is a solid-color dinner-ware made by Homer Laughlin from about 1951 to 1958. It is a pattern with simple, mod-ern shapes. The dishes were made in many of the Harle-quin colors, including char-treuse, Forest Green, gray, maroon, and yellow. Other companies also made patterns named Rhythm, but only

Homer Laughlin Rhythm is listed here.

CHARTREUSE
Bowl, 5 1/2 In. 4.50
Cup. 6.00
Nappy, 9 In. 9.00
Plate, 7 In. 5.00
Plate, 9 In. 7.00
Platter, 13 1/2 In. 15.00
Snack Plate. 25.00
Sugar & Creamer. 15.00

FOREST GREEN
Creamer 5.00
Plate, 9 In. 7.00
Snack Plate. 25.00
Soup, Dish, 8 1/4 In. 8.00

GRAY
Cup. 6.00
Platter, 13 1/2 In. 14.00
Saucer. 1.00
Snack Plate. 25.00

TURQUOISE
Gravy Boat 25.00

YELLOW
Cup. 6.00
Nappy, 9 In. 9.00
Platter, 13 1/2 In. 14.00
Sauceboat. 12.00
Saucer. 1.00
Soup, Dish, 8 1/4 In. 8.00
Sugar 12.00

Rhythm Rose

Rhythm Rose was made by Homer Laughlin China Com-pany, Newell, West Virginia, from the mid-1940s to the mid-1950s. The pattern fea-tured a center rose decal.

Bowl, Fruit, 7 In.	5.00
Bowl, Vegetable, Oval	15.00
Cake Plate	15.00
Creamer	10.00
Cup	4.00
Gravy Boat, Underplate	22.00 to 30.00
Mixing Bowl, 6 In.	15.00
Pie Plate	20.00
Plate, 6 In.	3.00 to 5.00
Plate, 7 In.	6.00
Plate, 9 In.	8.00 to 10.00
Soup, Coupe, 8 In.	8.00
Soup, Dish	10.00
Sugar, Cover	14.00 to 15.00

Ring

Ring, sometimes called Beehive, was made by J. A. Bauer Company, Los Angeles, California, from 1932 to 1962. It was made in many colors. Bright shades include black, Burnt Orange, green, ivory, maroon, orange, and yellow. Pastel shades are chartreuse, gray, green, light yellow, olive, pale blue, pink, turquoise, and white.

BURNT ORANGE
Tumbler, 3 1/2 In.	25.00

CHARTREUSE
Casserole, 8 In.	45.00

GREEN
Butter, Cover, Round	75.00
Tumbler, 3 1/2 In.	20.00

PALE BLUE
Tumbler, 3 1/2 In.	25.00

YELLOW
Tumbler, 3 1/2 In.	20.00

Riviera

Riviera was solid-color ware made by Homer Laughlin China Company, Newell, West Virginia, from 1938 to 1950. It was unmarked and sold exclusively by the Murphy Company. Plates and cup handles were squared. Colors were ivory, light green, mauve blue, red, yellow, and, rarely, dark blue.

DARK BLUE
Butter	195.00
Mug	40.00

IVORY
Creamer	15.00
Cup & Saucer, After Dinner	25.00
Jug, 4 1/2 In.	45.00
Plate, 7 In.	12.00
Plate, 9 In.	9.00
Sugar, Cover	20.00
Syrup	145.00

LIGHT GREEN
Bowl, Oval, 9 In.	25.00
Casserole, Cover	70.00

Cup & Saucer	15.00
Jug, Cover	110.00 to 135.00
Plate, 7 In.	10.00
Saltshaker	6.00 to 10.00
Tumbler, Handle	75.00

MAUVE BLUE
Plate, 8 In.	10.00
Platter, Closed Handles, 12 In.	28.00
Platter, Square, 12 In.	50.00
Salt & Pepper	7.00
Teapot	100.00

RED
Butter, 1/2 Lb.	85.00
Creamer	9.00
Nappy, 7 In.	22.00
Plate, 5 In.	8.00
Plate, 6 In.	6.00
Plate, 9 In.	20.00
Salt & Pepper	11.00
Sugar	12.00
Syrup, Cover	115.00 to 150.00
Teapot	110.00 to 150.00
Tumbler, Juice	40.00 to 65.00

YELLOW
Bowl, Oval, 9 In.	25.00
Casserole, Cover	65.00
Creamer	8.00
Cup & Saucer	8.00 to 15.00
Jug	110.00
Mug	40.00
Nappy, 7 In.	20.00
Pitcher, Juice	110.00
Plate, 9 In.	9.00 to 18.00
Platter, Handles, 11 In.	18.00
Salt & Pepper	7.00 to 9.00

Rooster

Roosters of many sorts were used as decorations on Southern Potteries pieces. The Rooster crowing from the fence top with a sun and a barn in the distance is a pattern called Cock o' the Morn. Another pattern was known as Cock o' the Walk. Most other patterns picturing the bird are called Rooster by collectors, although Rooster was a giftware line and the dinnerware, on the Clinchfield shape, was known as Game Cock. These pieces had a rooster center and a series of red three-line designs as the border. Stangl also made a pattern called Rooster, but it is not listed here.

Ashtray, Harker. 12.00

Bowl, Cover, No. 67,
Watt 250.00

Bowl, No. 64, Watt 110.00

Coffeepot, Brown Trim,
Harker 40.00

Cookie Jar, Green Trim,
Harker 65.00

Creamer, Harker. 8.00

Creamer, No. 62,
Watt . . . . 175.00 to 235.00

Match Holder, Harker 34.00

Pitcher, No. 15, Watt 150.00

Pitcher, No. 16,
Watt . . . . 95.00 to 185.00

Stein, Harker 16.00

Sugar, Cover, Harker 10.00

Rose-A-Day

Rose-A-Day was made by Vernon Kilns of Los Angeles and Vernon, California. This pattern was made from 1956 to 1958. Dishes were decorated with a single pink stylized rose and scattered leaves. The dishes had an ivory satin finish.

Chop Plate, 13 In. 25.00

Pitcher 35.00

Plate, 6 In. 4.00

Plate, 7 1/2 In. 8.00

Plate, 10 1/2 In. 10.00

Tumbler, 8 Oz. 20.00

Rose Parade

The Hall China Company, East Liverpool, Ohio, sometimes made surprising color- and decal-decorated wares. Rose Parade has a solid Cadet Blue body with contrasting Hi-White knobs and handles. A rose decal was added to the white spaces. Sometimes the flower is pink, sometimes blue. The pattern was made from 1941 through the 1950s. Serving pieces, not dinnerware sets, were made.

Bean Pot, Tab Handle 35.00

Casserole, Cover,
Tab Handles. 28.00

Pitcher 25.00

Rose White

Rose White, first made in 1941 by Hall China Company, is similar to Rose Parade. The same shapes were used, but the pieces were all white with a slightly different rose-decal decoration. There is silver trim on many pieces.

Coffeepot, Electric 80.00

**RUSSEL WRIGHT, see
American Modern;
Iroquois; Sterling**

S

Salamina

Salamina is an important pattern made by Vernon Kilns in 1939. The pattern pictures a girl from Greenland. Each piece had a different scene. The designs were adapted from the drawings in a book by Rockwell Kent. The dinnerware was hand tinted.

Charger, 16 1/2 In. 220.00

Plate, 9 In. 120.00

Sugar & Creamer 40.00

Sculptured Daisy

Sculptured Daisy was made by Metlox Potteries of Manhattan Beach, California, as part of the Poppy Trail line in 1965.

Berry Bowl 4.00

Bowl, Cereal 6.00

Bowl, Deep, 7 In. 8.00

Creamer 6.00

Cup & Saucer . . . . . . 6.00 to 7.50

Gravy Boat 35.00

Plate, 7 1/2 In. 7.50

Plate, 10 1/2 In. . . . . 8.00 to 10.00

Plate, Luncheon 6.00

Platter, 14 In. 35.00

Sugar, Cover 8.00

Sculptured Grape

Sculptured Grape is a pattern made by Metlox Potteries of Manhattan Beach, California, as part of the Poppy Trail line from 1963 to 1975. The pattern had a sculptured grapevine colored blue, brown, and green.

Bowl, Salad 32.00

Bowl, Vegetable, Round 25.00

Cup & Saucer 8.50

Gravy Boat, Liner 35.00

Sugar & Creamer 10.00

Serenade

There were two patterns named Serenade, one by Hall, the other by Homer Laughlin. The Homer Laughlin dishes listed here were plain, made in blue, green, pink, or yellow. The Hall dishes are decorated with sprigs of orange flowers. Another pattern called Serenade was made by Edwin M. Knowles China Company.

BLUE

Cup & Saucer 16.00

Soup, Coupe 20.00

GREEN

Cup & Saucer 16.00

Gravy Boat 20.00

Nappy 20.00

Plate, 6 In. 6.00

PINK

Chop Plate 18.00

Creamer . . . . 7.00 to 15.00

Plate, 7 In. . . . . 8.00 to 12.00

Tea Set, 3 Piece 18.00

Water Set, Mug, 7 Piece . . . 350.00

YELLOW

Chop Plate 15.00

Cup 10.00

Serenade Hall

Hall China Company made a pattern called Serenade on its D-shape dishes. The dishes were decorated with sprigs of orange flowers.

• • • • • • • • • • • • • • •

Some tea and coffee stains on dishes can be removed by rubbing them with damp baking soda.

• • • • • • • • • • • • • • •

EUREKA

SERENADE PATTERN

Pitcher, 1/2 Qt., 2 Mugs, 3 Piece 175.00

Teapot 35.00

Vase, 7 In. 45.00

Silhouette

Silhouette looks just like its name. The 1930s pattern shows a black silhouette of two people eating at a table and a dog begging for food in front of the table. The plates are trimmed in platinum. The pattern, made by Crooksville China Company, Crooksville, Ohio, is similar to Taverne, but Taverne has no dog. Matching metal pieces and glasswares were made. At least five companies called their patterns Silhousette.

Bowl, Fruit, TST, 5 1/4 In. . . . 8.00

Bowl, Hall, 8 In. 24.00

Bowl, Hall, 9 In. . . . 14.00 to 30.00

Bowl, Oval, TST, 9 1/4 In. 22.00

Bowl, Vegetable,
TST, 8 3/4 In. 22.00

Casserole, Cover, Hall 45.00

Cup, Hall 9.00

Leftover, Lid,
Rectangular, Hall 30.00

Plate, TST, 6 In. 4.00

Plate, TST, 7 1/4 In. 10.00

Rolling Pin 85.00

Salt & Pepper,
Handles, Hall 125.00

Sugar & Creamer, Lid,
TST 29.00

Teapot, Tavern Band,
Hall 50.00

Star Flower

Star Flower is a pattern of dinnerware made by Stangl Pottery from 1952 to 1957.

Bowl, No. 6 . . . . 55.00

Bowl, No. 7 . . . . 65.00

Bowl, No. 9, Advertising 85.00

Bowl Set, No. 7, 8 & 9,
Nested 300.00

Casserole, Cover,
No. 54 . . . . 675.00

Dish, 5 1/2 In. 10.00

Mixing Bowl, 7 Piece 140.00

Mug, No. 501 . . . . 120.00

Pitcher, No. 15 . . . . 65.00 to 90.00

Pitcher, No. 16 . . . . 95.00

Pitcher, No. 17 . . . . 175.00

Plate, 6 In. 4.00

Plate, 10 In. 10.00

Saltshaker,
Barrel Shape . . . 75.00 to 100.00

Starburst

Franciscan Ceramics of Los Angeles, California, started in 1934 and since 1979 has been part of the English Wedgwood Group. Starburst pattern was made by the company in 1954.

• • • • • • • • • • • • • • •

Never stack cups or bowls inside one another.

• • • • • • • • • • • • • • •

Ashtray, Individual 18.00

Ashtray, Large 75.00

Ashtray, Rolled Edge 55.00

Bowl, Fruit . . . . 6.00 to 12.00

Bowl, Soup 20.00

Bowl, Vegetable, 2 Sections,
8 1/4 In. . . . . 15.00 to 16.00

Bowl, Vegetable, Oval 30.00

Coffeepot 125.00

Condiment Set, Cover,
4 Piece 105.00

Cup & Saucer . . . . . . 7.00 to 8.00

Eggcup 25.00

Gravy Boat 30.00

Gravy Boat,
Ladle . . . . 45.00 to 68.00

Mug, Large 65.00

Mustard, Cover 95.00

Pitcher, 10 In. 125.00

Plate, 6 In. 5.00

Plate, 8 In. 18.00

Plate, 10 In. . . . . . . 7.00 to 10.00

Platter, Oval,
15 In. . . . . 30.00 to 45.00

Relish, 2 Sections 45.00

Salt & Pepper, Short 14.00

Salt & Pepper, Tall 40.00

Saucer 1.50

Sugar & Creamer,
Cover 30.00

Syrup 75.00

Tray, TV 75.00

Stardust

Stardust is a pattern made by Homer Laughlin China Company of Newell, West Virginia, in the 1940s and 1950s. The dinnerware used the Skytone shapes. It had a light blue background with stylized flowers.

Cup & Saucer, Skytone 16.00

Dish, Fruit, Skytone 4.00

Plate, Skytone, 6 In. 4.00

Plate, Skytone, 10 In. 8.00

Sugar & Creamer,
Skytone 30.00

Sterling

Sterling by Russel Wright is a heavy restaurant china made by the Sterling China company in 1949. It was made in Ivy Green, Straw Yellow, Suede Gray, and Cedar Brown.

CEDAR BROWN

Platter, 13 5/8 In. 28.00

Teapot 40.00

IVY GREEN

Ashtray 65.00

Coffee Bottle 80.00

STRAW YELLOW

Ashtray 60.00

Teapot Individual,
10 Oz. 85.00

SUEDE GRAY

Ashtray 95.00

T

Tam O'Shanter

Tam O'Shanter is one of the many plaid patterns made by Vernon Kilns, Vernon, California. It is a rust, chartreuse, and dark green plaid with Forest Green border. Other related plaids are Calico (pink and blue), Coronation Organdy (gray and rose), Gingham (green and yellow), Homespun (cinnamon, yellow, and green), Organdie (brown and yellow), and Tweed (yellow and gray-blue).

Bowl, 2 Sections,
Oval, 11 1/2 In. 25.00
Creamer 3.00
Eggcup. 18.00
Flower Pot 16.00
Plate, 8 1/2 In. 15.00
Platter, Oval, 12 In. 15.00
Platter, Oval, 14 In. 19.00
Soup, Dish,
2 Lug Handles. 15.00
Tumbler, 5 1/2 In. 16.00

Tampico

Tampico, a brown, green, and watermelon-colored pattern on a Futura shape, was made by Red Wing Pottery of Red Wing, Minnesota. This modern design was introduced in 1955. Many other patterns were also made on the Futura bodies.

Bowl, Salad, 12 In. 15.00
Bowl, Vegetable,
2 Sections 20.00
Plate, 8 1/2 In. 8.00
Plate, 10 1/2 In. 12.00
Platter, Oval, 13 In. 20.00
Platter, Oval, 15 In. 35.00

Relish 25.00
Saucer 4.00

Taverne

Taverne serving pieces were made by the Hall China Company of East Liverpool, Ohio, in the 1930s. Matching dinnerware was made by Taylor, Smith, and Taylor of Chester, West Virginia. A rolling pin was made by Harker Potteries. The silhouetted figures eating at a table are very similar to those seen on the pattern Silhouette, but there is no dog in this decal. In some of the literature, Taverne is called Silhouette.

Butter, Cover 225.00
Casserole, Cover,
Footed 75.00
Jug, Ball, No. 3 . . . . 125.00
Leftover, Cover,
3 1/2 x 7 In. 59.00
Leftover, Cover,
7 x 7 In. 89.00

Thistle

Thistle, or No. 3847, is a pattern made by Stangl Pottery, Trenton, New Jersey. The hand-painted decoration is a purple thistle and green spiked thistle leaves. The dishes were made from 1951 to 1967. Thistle pattern was made by four companies, but only the Stangl pattern is listed here.

Bowl, 2 Sections,
10 1/2 In. 18.00
Bowl, 5 1/2 In. 20.00
Bowl, 8 In. . . . . . . 24.00 to 25.00
Bread Tray 12.00
Butter, Cover. 18.00
Gravy Boat, Stand 16.00
Plate, 8 In. 10.00
Salt & Pepper 10.00
Saucer. 6.00
Soup, Dish, 7 1/2 In. 10.00
Vase, 6 In 95.00

Tickled Pink

The Tickled Pink pattern listed here is a Blue Ridge design on the Colonial shape. Pink leaves and soft gray dots fill the center of the plate, which has a pink rim. Vernon Kilns also made a pattern called Tickled Pink.

Cup. 5.00
Cup & Saucer 7.00
Plate, 10 In. 6.00

Tom & Jerry
Tom & Jerry sets were made to serve the famous Christmas punch. A set was usually a punch bowl and six matching cups or mugs.

BLACK
Mug 5.00
IVORY
Mug 5.00
Mug, Gold Lettering. 39.00

Town & Country
Stangl Pottery made Town & Country pattern in a variety of colors in the 1970s. The design looks like the sponged stoneware made in the nineteenth century, but the pattern was not made just in blue. Black, green, Honey Beige, and yellow were also used. Town & Country was made by other companies. We list only Stangl here.

BLUE
Pitcher, Large 90.00
Pitcher, Water, 2 Pt. 90.00
Teapot, 5 Cup 65.00

Tulip
Tulip is a 1930s pattern made by Hall China Company, East Liverpool, Ohio. It remained popular until the 1950s. Most of the pieces were distributed by Cook Coffee of Cleveland, Ohio. Pale yellow and purple tulips were applied by decal. The ware is trimmed with silver. The same design is found on a Harker Pottery pattern called Pastel Tulip. Watt Pottery Company of Crooksville, Ohio, made a pattern called Tulip that was sold in Woolworth's stores. It was made about 1963. Other patterns called Tulip were made by Stangl Pottery; Edwin H. Knowles; Paden City Pottery;

Universal Pottery; Leigh Pottery and Crescent China Co.; and Royal Pottery. Other patterns called Tulips were made by Homer Laughlin China Company; Pottery Guild; Taylor, Smith, and Taylor; and Blue Ridge.

Bowl, Cover,
Watt, No. 600 . . . . .300.00
Bowl, Watt, No. 63. . . . . .50.00
Bowl, Watt, No. 65. . . . . .60.00
Coffee Set, Percolator,
Hall, 4 Piece 125.00
Creamer, Watt, No. 62. . . . .125.00
Cup, Hall 35.00
Cup & Saucer, Hall. 15.00
Gravy Boat, Hall 45.00
Mixing Bowl, Hall,
6 In. . . . . 20.00 to 28.00
Mixing Bowl Set,
Nesting, Watt, 4 Piece 80.00
Plate, Stangl, 6 In. 6.00
Plate, Stangl, 9 In. 10.00
Soup, Dish, Hall 15.00

Tweed
Tweed is one of the group of six plaid patterns made by Vernon Kilns from 1950 to 1955. The patterns are the same except that the colors used for the plaid pattern are different. Tweed is a yellow and gray-blue plaid. The other five related designs are Calico (pink and blue), Coronation Organdy (gray and rose), Organdie (yellow and brown), Gingham (green and yellow), Homespun

(cinnamon, yellow, and green), and Tam O'Shanter (rust, chartreuse, and dark green).

Coffee Server. 35.00
Plate, 6 1/4 In. 5.00

U

Ultra California
Ultra California is a solid color Vernon Kilns pattern made from 1937 to 1942 in Carnation, Aster, Gardenia, Buttercup, Ice Green, and Maroon.

BLUE (ASTER)
Bowl, 9 In. 27.00
PINK (CARNATION)
Plate, 7 1/2 In. 9.00
WHITE (GARDENIA)
Chop Plate, 17 In. 45.00
Tea Set, Childs, 10 Piece . . . 75.00
YELLOW (BUTTERCUP)
Teapot, After Dinner 75.00

V

Virginia Rose
Virginia Rose is the name of a shape of dishes made by Homer Laughlin China Company, Newell, West Virginia. The shapes were decorated with a variety of decal decorations. The dishes with a design of a spray of roses and green leaves is the pattern most often called Virginia Rose by collectors.

Casserole, Cover 55.00
Eggcup, Double . . . 10.00 to 13.50
Nappy, 8 In. 18.00
Plate, 6 In. 4.00
Plate, 7 In. 6.00
Plate, 10 In. 10.00
Soup, Dish 8.00
Sugar & Creamer 20.00

Vistosa

Taylor, Smith, and Taylor of Chester, West Virginia, made a solid-colored dinnerware about 1938 called Vistosa. The plates had piecrust edges, and the other pieces had some bands or ridges. The glaze colors were cobalt blue, deep yellow, light green, and Mango Red. Pieces were marked with the name Vistosa and the initials T.S. & T. Co. U.S.A.

COBALT BLUE
Plate, 9 In. 12.00
DEEP YELLOW
Bowl, Salad 145.00
Eggcup 20.00
MANGO RED
Eggcup 28.00
Jug, Ball 65.00
Plate, 9 In. 7.00

· · · · · · · · · · · · · · · ·

Stains on porcelains can be removed by soaking in a mixture of two tablespoons of Polident denture cleaner in a quart of tepid water.

· · · · · · · · · · · · · · · ·

W

WHEAT, see Poppy & Wheat

Wildfire

Great American Tea Company gave Wildfire pattern as a premium. This Hall Pottery pattern of the 1950s has a Hi-White body and flower garland decal decoration.

Bowl, 9 1/4 In. . . . . 14.00 to 18.00
Custard Cup 15.00
Plate, 9 In. 7.50
Soup, Dish 16.00

Wildflower

Wildflower was made by Edwin M. Knowles, Newell, West Virginia.

Ashtray, Individual 35.00
Ewer, 13 1/2 In. 240.00
Vase, 7 1/2 In. 55.00

WILD POPPY, see Poppy & Wheat

Woodfield

Woodfield was a dinnerware made by the Steubenville Pottery, Steubenville, Ohio. The dishes were shaped like leaves and were colored in many of the shades used for American Modern dishes, also made by the same pottery. Full dinner sets were made.

Cup 3.00
Plate, 10 1/2 In. 7.00
Salt & Pepper 10.00

Y

Yorkshire

Yorkshire was made by Metlox Potteries of Manhattan Beach, California, about 1939. Each solid-colored piece had a swirled edge. The dinnerware came in at least ten colors.

GREEN
Bowl, 9 In. 16.00
PINK
Plate, 6 1/2 In. 3.00
TURQUOISE
Plate, 6 1/2 In. 3.00
YELLOW
Plate, 9 In. 7.00

Z

Zeisel

Eva Zeisel designed the Century and Tomorrow's Classic shapes for Hall China's Hallcraft line in 1952. It remained popular until the 1960s. The solid white dinnerware, sometimes decorated with decals, is marked with her name.

HALLCRAFT

Beanpot, Casual Living 100.00
Casserole, Pinecone,
Large......... 115.00 to 125.00
Creamer................. 15.00
Cruet, Lyric 23.00
Cup & Saucer, Fern 18.00
Gravy Boat................ 35.00
Plate, Fantasy, 6 In. 6.00

Platter, 12 In. 28.00
Relish, 15 In. 15.00
Sugar.....................18.00
Sugar & Creamer, Fern 54.00

Zinnia

Zinnia is a pattern made by Red Wing Potteries of Red Wing, Minnestoa, in 1947. The dishes (Concord shape) are white with accessories of yellow, Ming Green, gray, or copper. A large zinnia is pictured on each piece. Other Zinnia patterns were made by Homer Laughlin and Blue Ridge.

Butter 22.00
Casserole, Cover..........13.00
Plate, Dinner 8.00

Good tips for care of Bauer pottery and probably for Fiesta and any other heavy, color-glazed dishes of the 1930s: Bauer is oven safe for baking up to 350 degrees. Do not use in a microwave. Do not use on a direct flame. Do not wash in an automatic dishwasher as the detergent may discolor the glaze. Do not scour. Store with felt between stacked plates to avoid scratching. Early 1930 to 1942 dishes used a lead in the glazing, so do not use scratched dishes with acidic foods. Lead poisoning is possible with prolonged use.

Factories

NAME	LOCATION	DATES
Abingdon Potteries	Abingdon, Illinois	1908-1951
American Pottery	Byesville, Ohio	1942-1965
Bauer Pottery Company	Los Angeles, California	1905-c.1958
Blair Ceramics	Ozark, Missouri	1946-1950s
Blue Ridge, see Southern Potteries		
Brusché Ceramics	Whittier, California	c.1950
Brush-McCoy	Roseville and Zanesville, Ohio	1911-1925 (combined firm of Brush Pottery and J. W. McCoy Company)
Brush Pottery	Roseville and Zanesville, Ohio	1907-present (Brush-McCoy 1911-1925)
California Ceramics	Los Angeles, California	c.1948-1954
Caribe-Sterling	Vega Baja, Puerto Rico	Early 1950s-1977
Catalina Pottery	Catalina Island, California	c.1927-1947 (name purchased by Gladding McBean Company in 1937; Catalina name remained in use until 1947)
Continental Kilns	East Liverpool, Ohio	1944-1954
H. F. Coors Company	Inglewood, California, and Golden, Colorado	1925-present
Crescent China Company	Alliance, Ohio	1920-1930 (associated with Leigh Pottery after 1926)
Crooksville China Company	Crooksville, Ohio	1902-c.1960
Crown Pottery	Evansville, Indiana	1882-1962
Flintridge China Company	Pasadena, California	1945-present
Franciscan Ceramics	Los Angeles, California	1934-present (Wedgwood Group after 1979)
Frankoma Pottery	Sapulpa, Oklahoma	1936-present

NAME	LOCATION	DATES
French Saxon China Company	East Liverpool, Ohio	1935-present
W. S. George Company	Kittanning, Pennsylvania	1880-1959
Gladding, McBean & Co.	Los Angeles, California	1875-1986 (Wedgwood Group after 1979, closed in 1986)
Gonder Ceramic Art Company	Zanesville, Ohio	1941-1957
Haeger Potteries	Dundee, Illinois	1914-present
Hall China Company	East Liverpool, Ohio	1903-present
Harker Pottery Company	Chester, West Virginia, and East Liverpool, Ohio	1890-1972
Harmony House	Mark used by Sears, Roebuck and Co.; various manufacturers	
Homer Laughlin China Company	Newell, West Virginia, and East Liverpool, Onio	1877-present
A. E. Hull Pottery Company	Crooksville, Ohio	1905-present
Iroquois China Company	Syracuse, New York	1905-1969
James River Potteries	Hopewell, Virginia	1922-1938
Edwin M. Knowles China Company	Chester and Newell, West Virginia, and East Liverpool, Ohio	1900-1963; 1975-present
Leigh Pottery	Alliance, Ohio	1926-1938 (Crescent China Company before 1926)
J. W. McCoy Company	Zanesville, Ohio	1899-1925 (Brush-McCoy Pottery Company from 1911-1925)
Metlox Potteries	Manhattan Beach, California	1935-1989
Montgomery Ward	Sold variety of patterns under own name, various manufacturers	
Paden City Pottery	Paden City, West Virginia	1914-1963
Pickard, Inc.	Chicago, Illinois	1893-present
Pope-Gosser China Company	Coshocton, Ohio	1902-1958
Pottery Guild	New York, New York	1937-1946
Purinton Pottery	Shippenville, Pennsylvania	1941-1951

NAME	LOCATION	DATES
Red Wing Potteries	Red Wing, Minnesota	1878-1967
Roseville Pottery Company	Zanesville, Ohio	1892-1954
Royal China Company	Sebring, Ohio	1933-1986
Sabin Industries	McKeesport, Pennsylvania	1946-present
Salem China Company	Salem, Ohio	1898-1967
Scio Pottery Company	Scio, Ohio	1932-1985
Sears, Roebuck and Company	Sold variety of patterns under their own name, various manufacturers	
Sebring-Limoges	Sebring, Ohio	1887-1955 (Sebring Pottery Company and Limoges China Company combined under same management c.1940)
Shawnee Pottery Company	Zanesville, Ohio	1936-1961
Southern Potteries (Blue Ridge)	Erwin, Tennessee	1917-1957
Standard Pottery Company	East Liverpool, Ohio	1886-1927
Stanford Pottery	Sebring, Ohio	1945-1961
Stangl Pottery	Flemington and Trenton, New Jersey	1930-1978
Sterling China	East Liverpool, Ohio	1917-present
Stetson China Company	Lincoln, Illinois	1919-1965
Steubenville Pottery Company	Steubenville, Ohio	1879-c.1960
Syracuse China Corporation	Syracuse, New York	1871-present
Taylor, Smith, and Taylor	Chester, West Virginia, and East Liverpool, Ohio	1901-present
Terrace Ceramics	Marietta, Ohio	1961-1975
Universal Potteries	Cambridge, Ohio	1934-1956
Vernon Kilns	Los Angeles and Vernon, California	1912-1958 (name purchased by Metlox Potteries)
Watt Pottery Company	Crooksville, Ohio	1922-1965

Pattern List

For more information on factories, see the preceding pages. Dates listed here are the approximate dates the patterns were made.

Note: * = prices and paragraph in body of book

PATTERN	SHAPE	MAKER	DATE	DESCRIPTION
ABC	Kiddieware	Stangl	Mid-1940s–1974	Solid colors
Abingdon	Square	Abingdon	1935	
Abundance	Colonial	Blue Ridge		Pear and cherries; broken green rim
Abundance	Ultra	Vernon Kilns	1939	Maroon fruit and floral border
Acacia	Kitchenware	Hall		Pastel flowers; decal
Acacia Flowers	Shellcrest	Paden City		
Acorn		Harmony House		Blue, pink; cameoware
Adam	Antique	Steubenville		Rich ivory glaze; heavily embossed
Adobestone	Ceramastone	Red Wing	1967	
Adonis	Refrigerator Ware	Hall	c.1952	Westinghouse, Turk Blue and Daffodil; General Electric; Addison and Daffodil; also called Prince
Adrian		Stangl	1972-1974	
After Glow	Montecito	Vernon Kilns	1935-1937	Yellow with ivory bottom and interior
*Airflow	Teapot	Hall	1940	Canary, Chinese Red, cobalt, turquoise, and other colors
Al Fresco		Brusché (Bauer)	1950s	
*Aladdin	Teapot	Hall	1939	Variety of colors; decals
Albany	Teapot	Hall	1930	Solid colors; gold decorations
Albert	Teapot	Hall	1940s	Celadon only; Victorian style

PATTERN	SHAPE	MAKER	DATE	DESCRIPTION
Alexandria	Candlewick	Blue Ridge		Red, yellow, and blue flowers; green leaves
Alia Jane	Round	Taylor, Smith, and Taylor	1933-1934	Decal
All Apple		Purinton		Hand painted; large apple
Alleghany	Colonial	Blue Ridge		Blue, red, yellow flowers; red rim
Allure	Classique	E. M. Knowles	1960	
Aloaha	Skyline	Blue Ridge	1950s	Gray, green, white; large leaves
Aloha		French Saxon		
Amapila	Amapila	Franciscan		Hand painted
Amarylis	Colonial	Blue Ridge		Red flowers, border, and rim
Ambassador	Regent	E. M. Knowles	1948	
*Amber Glo		Stangl	1954-1962	
*Amberstone	Fiesta	Homer Laughlin	1967	Solids; brown designs; black machine-stamped underglaze patterns
American Beauty	Minion	Paden City		Large pink rose
American Beauty		Stetson		
*American Modern	American	Steubenville (Russel Wright)	1939-1959	Bean Brown, Black Chutney, Cantaloupe, Cedar Green, chartreuse, coral, Glacier Blue, Granite Gray, blue, Seafoam, white
American Provincial		Homer Laughlin		Pennsylvania Dutch designs
Americana	A2000	Stangl	1930s	Colonial Blue, green, Tangerine, and yellow
Amhurst	Colonial	Blue Ridge		Pink flowers; center and line border
Amy		Harker		Gold trim; multicolored flowers
Anemone	Piecrust	Blue Ridge		Red flowers; two-tone green leaves
Anniversary		Salem China	1943	
Antiqua		Stangl	1972-1974	Stylized flower, gold background, brown and black border

PATTERN	SHAPE	MAKER	DATE	DESCRIPTION
Antique Leaf	Lace Edge	Blue Ridge		Red, green, black leaf border
Anytime	Anytime	Vernon Kilns	1955-1958	Bands of gray, mocha, yellow
Appalachian Spring	Candlewick	Blue Ridge		Stylized red tulip and red border
*Apple	Apple	Franciscan	1940-present	Apples and leaves border
*Apple		Purinton	1936-1959	Large center apple; scalloped rim
*Apple	Watt Ware	Watt	1930s-1965	
Apple & Pear	Woodcrest	Blue Ridge	1950s	Red apple, yellow pear, green leaves
Apple Blossom		Crooksville		Pink flowers
*Apple Blossom	Liberty	Homer Laughlin	1935-1955	Flowered border, center decoration; gold trim
Apple Crisp	Skyline	Blue Ridge	1950s	Three red apples, red rim
Apple Crunch	Piecrust	Blue Ridge	1948	Red and white apple, green leaves and border
Apple Delight		Stangl	1965-1974	Red and yellow apples, dark border
Apple Jack	Skyline	Blue Ridge	1950s	Two apples; sponged yellow background
Apples		Pottery Guild		Apple tree branch
April		Homer Laughlin		Flowered border
Aquarium	Ultra	Vernon Kilns	1938	Tropical fish
Arabesque	Arabesque	Catalina	1935	Solids
Arabian Night		Paden City		
Arcadia	Melinda	Vernon Kilns	1942; 1950-1955	Brown laurel wreath border
Ardennes	Provincial	Red Wing	1941	Laurel leaf band
Argosy		W. S. George	1930	Ivory body
Aristocrat Refrigerator Ware, see Hercules				
Aristocrat		Homer Laughlin		Flowered border
Aristocrat	Century	Salem		Delphinium Blue; black and platinum band
Arlene	Trellis	Blue Ridge		Pink tulip, blue daisy, wide blue rim
Arlington Apple	Skyline	Blue Ridge	1950s	Two red apples
Art Deco	Art Deco	Catalina	Early 1930s	Solids

PATTERN	SHAPE	MAKER	DATE	DESCRIPTION
Asbury	Pegasus	Sebring	1940s	
Ashland	Colonial	Blue Ridge		Red, light blue flowers; green rim
Astor Fruit	Astor	Blue Ridge		Aqua fruit; aqua and orange rim
Atlanta	Skyline	Blue Ridge	1950s	
Aurora	Candlewick	Blue Ridge		Two large pink flowers
Automobile	Teapot	Hall	1938	Canary, Chinese Red, maroon, common colors; sometimes with gold or silver trim
Autumn		Franciscan	1934	Leaves
Autumn Apple	Colonial	Blue Ridge	1941	Apples border; broken red rim
Autumn Ballet	Ultra	Vernon Kilns	1940	Maroon floral and leaf
Autumn Breeze	Skyline	Blue Ridge	1950s	Stylized leaves, gray, green, and rust
Autumn Fancy		Universal		Decals
*Autumn Foliage		Watt	1959-1965	Brown leaves on brown stems; also called Brown Leaves
Autumn Harvest	Versatile	Taylor, Smith, and Taylor		
Autumn Laurel	Colonial	Blue Ridge		Yellow berries, green leaves, border
Autumn Leaf		Blair		Floral decals
Autumn Leaf		Crooksville China		Floral decals
Autumn Leaf		Crown		Floral decals
*Autumn Leaf		Hall	1936-present	For Jewel Tea Co.; floral decals of dark yellow and rust leaves
Autumn Leaf		Harker Potteries		Floral decals
Autumn Leaf		Paden City		Floral decals
Avenue	Coupe, LaGrande	Crooksville		Reddish brown plant sprigs
Aztec		Stangl	1967-1968	
Aztec	Citation	Steubenville		
Aztec on Desert Sand	Citation	Steubenville		
Bachelor's Button		Stangl	1965	

PATTERN	SHAPE	MAKER	DATE	DESCRIPTION
*Ballerina	Ballerina	Universal Potteries	1947-1956	Solids; burgundy, charcoal, chartreuse, Dove Gray, Forest Green, Jade Green, Jonquil Yellow, Periwinkle Blue, pink; abstract designs; pale blue-green with decal decorations
*Baltimore	Teapot	Hall	1930s	Emerald and marine common colors
Bamboo		Blair		Stylistic bamboo design
Bamboo	Woodcrest	Blue Ridge	1950s	
Banana Tree	Montecito	Vernon Kilns	1937	Tree on ivory ground
Banded	Kitchenware	Hall	1937	Kitchenware; floral decals; solid colors: Cadet, canary, Chinese Red, cobalt, Indian Red, ivory, marine, maroon; also called Five Band
Banded Flower	Montecito	Vernon Kilns	1935-1937	Center floral designs, colored band on rim
Barbara	Colonial	Blue Ridge		Blue flowers and leaves
Bardstown	Skyline	Blue Ridge	1950s	Red flowers, outlined
Barkwood	San Marino	Vernon Kilns	1953-1958	Beige and brown; like tree bark, same as Raffia and Shantung except for color
Basket	Decal	Hall	1932-1960	Small flower basket and diamond-shaped designs
Basket	Teapot	Hall	1938	Embossed flower; canary, Chinese Red, marine common colors
Basket	Harker			Flower basket border
Basket		Leigh/Crescent		Flower basket and individual small flowers
Basket		Salem		Center flower basket; border of leaves and individual flowers
Basket of Tulips	Bonjour	Salem		Various colored tulips; platinum rim
Basket Petit Point	Victory	Salem		Decals
*Basketball	Teapot	Hall	1938	
Basketweave	Skyline	Blue Ridge	1950s	Black cross-hatch on beige background

PATTERN	SHAPE	MAKER	DATE	DESCRIPTION
Bauer, see Ring				
Beaded Apple	Colonial	Blue Ridge		Apple border, broken red rim
Beatrice	Skyline	Blue Ridge	1950s	Black-haired girl
Becky	Colonial	Blue Ridge		Large red flowers
Becky		Harker		Blue and red flowers
Beehive, see Ring				
Beige	Montecito	Vernon Kilns	1935-1937	Solid beige
Bel Air	San Marino	Vernon Kilns	1940; 1955	Three lines crossing three lines; green and brown on ivory
Bella Rosa		Stangl	1960-1962	Spray of roses and lily of the valley; pale gray background
Belle Haven	Woodcrest	Blue Ridge	1950s	Plaid tree, farm, rooster at sunrise; green rim
*Bellevue (or Bellvue)	Teapot	Hall	1920s-present	Six sizes; brown, green most common colors; some decorated with gold or decals
Bellflower	Ultra	Vernon Kilns	1939	Red print, floral
Bellemeade	Astor	Blue Ridge		Yellow flowers, blue and green leaves; brown line border
Bellflower	Ultra	Vernon Kilns	1939	Red print, floral
Bench	Deanna	E. M. Knowles		Mexican-styled jugs and cactus
Benjamin	Teapot	Hall	Early 1940s	Victorian style; see also Birch, Bowknot, Connie, Murphy, Plume
Berea Blossom	Colonial	Blue Ridge		Pastel flowers
Berkeley	Williamsburg	E. M. Knowles	1955	
Bermuda		Homer Laughlin	1977-1978	
Berry Patch	Skyline	Blue Ridge	1950s	Golden berries
Berryville	Colonial	Blue Ridge		Strawberry border; red rim
Bethany Berry	Moderne	Blue Ridge	1950s	Orange berries; gray, green, brown leaves
Betty	Candlewick	Blue Ridge		Red and yellow flowers; green leaves
Beverly	Melinda	Vernon Kilns	1942	Rose blossom border
Big Apple	Colonial	Blue Ridge		

PATTERN	SHAPE	MAKER	DATE	DESCRIPTION
Big Boy	Coffeepot	Hall		Maroon with silver trim
Bimini		Homer Laughlin	1977-1978	
Bingo, see Zephyr				
Birch	Teapot	Hall	Early 1940s	Victorian style; see also Benjamin, Bowknot, Connie, Murphy, Plume
Bird	Derwood	W. S. George		Red and brown bird on border
Bird		Blair		Sgraffito bird; also called Primitive Bird
Birdcage	Teapot	Hall	1939	Maroon most common color; embossed birds
Bird in the Heart		Universal Cambridge		
Bird Pottery		Vernon Kilns	Early 1930s	Flowers, birds, tropical fish
Birds and Flowers		Harker		Multicolored flowers, small birds
Bird's Eye	Montecito	Vernon Kilns		Floral
Bit Series	Kiddieware	Stangl	Mid-1940s-1974	
Bittersweet		Hall		Flowers
Bittersweet	Skyline	Blue Ridge	1950s	Red berries
Bittersweet		Stangl		Sgraffito decoration
Bittersweet		Universal Potteries	1942-1949	Decals; orange and yellow
Black Beauty		Hall	1935	Red flowers and leaves, black shadows
Black-Eyed Susan	Forcast	E. M. Knowles	1959	
Black Ming	Skyline	Blue Ridge	1950s	Black tree
Black Tulip		Crooksville	1950s	Hand painted; black on pink
Blackberry Lily	Colonial	Blue Ridge		Dots on pink flowers
Bleeding Heart	Candlewick	Blue Ridge		Pink flowers; blue leaves, border, and rim
Blend No. 4	Montecito	Vernon Kilns	1938	Concentric rings in browns and greens
Blend No. 10	Montecito	Vernon Kilns	1938	Concentric rings in pinks and greens
Blossom Ring		Stangl	1967/68-1970	

PATTERN	SHAPE	MAKER	DATE	DESCRIPTION
Blossom Time	Coupe	Crooksville		Off-center decoration; branch of pink flowers
Blossom Time	Concord	Red Wing	1947	Modern shapes; red flowers, green leaves, yellow and green accessory pieces
Blossom Time	Melinda	Vernon Kilns	1942	Blue blossoms
Blossom Tree	Skyline	Blue Ridge	1950s	Stylized tree; green leaves and yellow flowers
Blossoms	Shellcrest	Paden City		Large flower spray
Blossoms	Fruits	Crooksville		Red and pink flowers
Blossoms	Montecito	Vernon Kilns	1937	Blue blossom border on cream ground
Blossoms	Lido	W. S. George		Pink blossoms border
Blossomtime	Bolero	W. S. George		
Blossomtime	Accent	E. M. Knowles	1958	
Blue Bell		Stangl	c.1942	
Blue Bells	Accent	E. M. Knowles	c.1954	
Blue Bird		Crown	1941	Blue birds perched on pink apple blossoms; turquoise blue rim
Blue Blossom	Kitchenware	Hall	c.1939	Cobalt blue background, floral decals
Blue Blossoms		Crooksville		Flowers in shades of blue
Blue Bonnett	Accent	E. M. Knowles	1954	
Blue Bouquet	Candlewick	Blue Ridge		Red flowers
*Blue Bouquet	D-Line	Hall	1950-1960s	Premium for Standard coffee; thin blue border with roses
Blue Bow	Montecito	Vernon Kilns	1938	Center blue bow on ivory
Blue Carousel	Kiddieware	Stangl	Mid-1940s-1974	
Blue Daisy		Stangl	1963-1974	Blue daisies
Blue Dresden	Virginia Rose	Homer Laughlin	1949	
Blue Elf	Kiddieware	Stangl	Mid-1940s-1974	
Blue Feather	Montecito	Vernon Kilns	1938	Dark blue feather on soft blue ground
Blue Flower	Colonial	Blue Ridge		Large blue off-center flower
*Blue Garden	Kitchenware	Hall	1939	Cobalt blue background, floral decals

PATTERN	SHAPE	MAKER	DATE	DESCRIPTION
Blue Heaven	Colonial	Blue Ridge		Blue flowers, gray leaves
Blue Medallion		Homer Laughlin	1920	Decals
Blue Moon	Candlewick	Blue Ridge		Blue flowers and leaves
Blue Parade, see Rose Parade				
Blue Rhythm		Harker	1959	Cameoware
Blue Shadows	True China	Red Wing	1964	
Blue Star (Constellation)	Montecito	Vernon Kilns	1938	Dark blue stars on soft blue ground
Blue Symphony		Homer Laughlin		
Blue Tango	Colonial	Blue Ridge		Floral design
Blue Tulip		Stangl		Terra Rose mark
*Blue Willow	Trellis	Blue Ridge		Blue oriental scene, rim
*Blue Willow		Homer Laughlin	1942	Blue and pink
*Blue Willow	Cavalier	Royal China	Late 1940s–1960s	Overall oriental design; also pink, green
Blue Willow		Sebring-Limoges		
Bluebell		Paden City		Floral sprig
Bluebell		Royal China	1940s	Raised border, spray in center
Bluebell Bouquet	Candlewick	Blue Ridge		
Blueberry		Sold by Montgomery Ward	1921	Decals
*Blueberry		Stangl	c.1940	Red with yellow border; blueberries in center
Blueberry Hill	Year 'Round	Vernon Kilns	1957-1958	Blue and brown floral abstract
Bluebird		Salem		Small bluebirds on border
Bluebird	Derwood	W. S. George		Bluebird on border; thin blue rim
Bluefield	Colonial	Blue Ridge		Blue flowers; red, green leaves
Blushing Rose, see Lido Dalrymple				
Bo Peep	Kiddieware	Stangl	Mid-1940s–1974	
*Bob White		Red Wing	1956-1967	Hand painted; stylized bird; figurals
Bolero		Homer Laughlin	1977-1978	

PATTERN	SHAPE	MAKER	DATE	DESCRIPTION
Bonita		Caribe-Sterling	1950s–c.1963	Modernistic flowers
Bonita		Stangl		Della-Ware mark
Bonsai	Skyline	Blue Ridge	1950s	Gnarled tree
Bouquet	Astor	Blue Ridge		Pink and yellow flowers, pink border
Border Bouquet	LaGrande	Crooksville		Border of small flowers
Border Rim		E. M. Knowles		Border design of flowers
Border Rose		Crooksville		Continuous border design
Bosc	Colonial	Blue Ridge		Red pear, blue leaves, broken red border
*Boston	Teapot	Hall	1920	Variety of colors; gold decorated line
Botanica	Esquire	E. M. Knowles	1955–1962	Abstract decal; Russel Wright
Bountiful	Colonial	Blue Ridge		Fruit; broken green rim
Bouquet		Crown		Multicolored flowers and bow
Bouquet	Hallcraft	Hall	1950s–1960s	Random flower sprays; designed by Eva Zeisel
Bouquet		Harker		
Bouquet	Ultra	Vernon Kilns	1938	Floral; yellow rim
Bourbon Rose	Colonial	Blue Ridge		Two roses, leaves allover design
*Bow Knot	Piecrust	Blue Ridge		Chartreuse and brown variation of Whirligig
Bowknot	Teapot	Hall	Early 1940s	Victorian style; see also Benjamin, Birch, Connie, Murphy, Plume
Bowling Ball	Teapot	Hall	Late 1930s	Cobalt, turquoise
Boyce		Harker		Flowers in shades of pink
Bramwell	Colonial	Blue Ridge		Yellow, red, and blue flowers
Breakfast Nook		W. S. George		Open windows with flower trellis
Breath O'Spring	Classique	E. M. Knowles	1960	
Breckenridge	Colonial	Blue Ridge		Red flowers and leaves
Breeze	Bountiful	Salem China; French Saxon	1948	
Brentwood	Cavalier	Royal		Ironstone; bold flower center design

PATTERN	SHAPE	MAKER	DATE	DESCRIPTION
Briar Patch	Colonial	Blue Ridge		Red flowers, green leaves, all-over pattern
Briar Rose	Century	Homer Laughlin	1933	Sprays of wild roses, platinum edge
Briar Rose	San Fernando	Vernon Kilns	1944	Red and yellow roses on stem
Bridal Bouquet	Colonial	Blue Ridge		Pink flowers, yellow and green leaves
Bridal Flower		Taylor, Smith, and Taylor		
Bridge	Tricorne	Salem		Decals
Bridle Rose		W. S. George		
Brilliance	Coupe	Crooksville		Multisized pink flowers
Brim		Harker		Bold-colored flower border
Bristol Bouquet	Astor	Blue Ridge		Centered red, yellow, blue flowers; red border
Bristol Lily	Candlewick	Blue Ridge		Two yellow flowers and birds; red border
Brittany	Clinchfield	Blue Ridge		Centered woman and flowers; stylized red border
Brittany	Brittany	Homer Laughlin	1936-1950s	Colored band, flowers; plaid, stylized band
Brittany	Provincial	Red Wing	1941	Yellow rose; yellow band on rim
Brocade	True China	Red Wing	1964	
Brown Eyed Susan	Montecito; Ultra	Vernon Kilns	c.1938-1958	Yellow daisies on ivory ground
Brown Leaf	Accent	E. M. Knowles	1954	
Brown Leaves, see Autumn Foliage				
Brown Satin		Stangl		
Brownie	Candlewick	Blue Ridge		Edge design of three stylized flowers with brown center
Brunswick	Candlewick	Blue Ridge		Red, yellow, and blue flowers; green rim
Brushes	Al Fresco	Bauer		
Bryn-Mawr	Symphony	Salem		Floral sprays in brown, lavender, and gray
Bud	Concord	Red Wing	1947	
Buddah	Corinthian	Sebring		
Bunny Lunch	Kiddieware	Stangl	Mid-1940s-1974	

PATTERN	SHAPE	MAKER	DATE	DESCRIPTION
Buttercup	Colonial	Blue Ridge		
Buttercup		E. M. Knowles	1948	
Butterfly and Leaves	Trellis	Blue Ridge		Red, yellow flowers; two-tone green leaves
Cabaret	Cabaret	Franciscan		
Cactus		Blue Ridge		
Cactus	Banded; Kitchenware	Hall	1937–1940s	Decal; cactus in flowerpots
Cactus and Cowboy, see Ranger				
Cactus Banded, see Cactus (Hall)				
Cadenza	Piecrust	Blue Ridge	1948	Red and yellow flowers
Cadet Series		Salem		Fluted edge; thin bands of color
Caladium	Skyline	Blue Ridge	1950s	Yellow flower; yellow and red leaf
Calais	Astor	Blue Ridge		Center pattern of male, female, and ducks; leaf and flower border
Cal-Art		Bauer		
Calico	Colonial	Blue Ridge		Red and yellow flowers; allover pattern
*Calico	Montecito	Vernon Kilns	1949–1955	Blue border; pink and blue plaid; see also Coronation Organdy; Gingham; Homespun; Organdie; Tam O'Shanter; Tweed
Calico Chick	Coupe	Crooksville		Calico-print chickens
Calico Farm	Skyline	Blue Ridge	1950s	Red and green plaid forming scene
Calico Flower		Pottery Guild		Red band; calico-print flowers
Calico Flowers	Dartmouth	Crooksville		Calico-print tulips
Calico Fruit		Pottery Guild		Red band; calico-print fruits
Calico Fruit		Universal	1940s	White background; bright red and blue fruits
Calico Tulip		Harker		Tulip-shaped decal of calico print
*Caliente		Paden City	1940s	Solids: blue, green, Tangerine, yellow
California Casual, see Casual California				
California Heritage, see California Originals				

PATTERN	SHAPE	MAKER	DATE	DESCRIPTION
*California Ivy	Poppytrail line	Metlox	1946-1980	White, green ivy
California James Poppy	LaGrande	Crooksville		Large sprays of pastel flowers
California Originals	San Marino	Vernon Kilns	1947; 1954	Drip glaze border; Almond Yellow, Raisin Purple, Redwood Brown, Vineyard Green; also called California Heritage
*California Poppy	Candlewick	Blue Ridge		Two large center flowers
California Pottery		Bauer		Solid Colors
*California Provincial	Poppytrail line	Metlox	1950-1980	Green, maroon, and yellow rooster in center; green and brown border
California Series	Melinda, Montecito, San Fernando, San Marino, Ultra	Vernon Kilns	1930s	Red, brown, green, blue
California Shadows	San Marino	Vernon Kilns	1953; 1955	Drip glaze border; Antique Gray, Cocoa Brown
California Strawberry	Poppytrail line	Metlox	1961-1980	Red strawberries on Avocado Green vines
Call Rose	Century	Homer Laughlin		Floral decal
Callaway	Piecrust	Blue Ridge	1948	Large blue and yellow and small pink flowers
Camelot	Piecrust	Blue Ridge	1948	Light blue, purple, red, and yellow flowers
Cameo Rose	E-Shape	Hall	1970s	Gray and white leaf decorations
Cameo Rose		Harker	1940s	Solid white roses; blue, pink, gray, yellow background
Cameo Shellware	Shell	Harker	1940s	White, blue, pink, gray, yellow background; same cameo flower design as Cameo Rose; fluted plate edge
Candied Fruit	Candlewick	Blue Ridge		Different fruits; two yellow bands

PATTERN	SHAPE	MAKER	DATE	DESCRIPTION
Cantata	Piecrust	Blue Ridge	1948	Red and blue flowers
Canton	Encanto	Franciscan	1953	
*Capistrano	Anniversary	Red Wing	1953-1967	Yellow-breasted swallow, black foliage
Capri		Paden City	1933	
Capri	Rhythm Coupe	Homer Laughlin		
*Caprice	Tomorrow's Classic	Hall	1952-1957	Designed by Eva Zeisel; Pink, gray; yellow leaf and floral design
Caprice	Accent	E. M. Knowles	c.1954	
Caribe Casual		Caribe-Sterling	1950s–c.1963	
Carlise	Colonial	Blue Ridge		Blue leaves, tiny pink berries, blue rim
Carlton	Heritage	E. M. Knowles	1955	
Carmel	Melinda	Vernon Kilns	1942-1950	Embossed border; brown, yellow; same as Monterey and Philodendron, but different color
Carmen	Accent	E. M. Knowles	1958	
Carnation Beauty		Homer Laughlin	1920	Decal
Carnival	Candlewick	Blue Ridge		Red, yellow, and blue flowered border
Carnival	Fruits	Crooksville		Abstract
Carnival		Homer Laughlin	late 1930s–early 1940s	Light green, red, turquoise, yellow; later dark green and gray
Carnival		Stangl	1954-1957	Pink, green, and black abstract starlike pattern
Caroline	Skyline	Blue Ridge	1950s	Brown flowers
Carraway	Coffeepot	Hall		
Carretta Cattail	Woodcrest	Blue Ridge	1950s	Three cross-hatched cattails and leaves
Carriage		Crown		Coach and horses, manor
Casa California	Montecito	Vernon Kilns	1938	Blue; green leaves; pink flowers; yellow border
Casa del Sol	Cavalier	Royal		Indian-style design
Casablanca	Cavalier	Royal		Ironstone; large center sunflower design

PATTERN	SHAPE	MAKER	DATE	DESCRIPTION
Cascade		Sold by Montgomery Ward	1936	White with red lines; solids
Cashmere		Homer Laughlin		Border of small sprays of flowers
Cassandra	Waffle Edge	Blue Ridge		Wide blue, pink border; center flowers
*Casual California	San Marino	Vernon Kilns	1947-1956	Acacia Yellow, Dawn Pink, Dusk Gray, Lime Green, Mahogany Brown, Mocha Brown, Pine Green, Snowhite, Turquoise Blue
*Casualstone	Fiesta	Homer Laughlin	1970	Gold and yellow, plain or with design; marked Coventry
Cat and the Fiddle	Kiddieware	Stangl	Mid-1940s-1974	
*Cat-Tail	Camwood; Old Holland; Laurelle	Universal	1934-1956	For Sears, Roebuck and Co.; red and black decals
Cattail		Hall	1927	
Cattails	Trailway	Blue Ridge	1950s	Brown cattails, light blue leaves and border, brown rim
Cattails	Accent	E. M. Knowles	1955	
Cavalier	Cavalier	Homer Laughlin	1950s-1970s	Solid colors, decals, bands
Celeste	Tempo	E. M. Knowles	1961-1963	
Celestial	Criterion	E. M. Knowles	1955	
*Century	Century	Homer Laughlin	1931-	Floral decals; ivory; square shapes
Chalet	Accent	E. M. Knowles	1955	
Champagne Pinks	Colonial	Blue Ridge	1940s-1950s	Overall large floral, light pink and blue
Chanticleer	Skyline	Blue Ridge	1950s	Rooster; green stylized border
Charstone Bleu	Ceramastone	Red Wing	1967	
Chartreuse		Sold by Montgomery Ward	1936	Decals; green; green border
Chateau		Homer Laughlin		
Chateau-France		Sebring-Limoges		

PATTERN	SHAPE	MAKER	DATE	DESCRIPTION
*Chatelaine	Chatelaine	Vernon Kilns	1953	Bronze, jade, platinum, topaz
Cheerio	Skyline	Blue Ridge	1950s	Brown and green flowers; yellow dappled background
Cherokee Rose	Rope Handle	Blue Ridge	1950s	
Cherries Jubilee	Colonial	Blue Ridge		Bold cherries and leaves
Cherry		Harker		Brightly colored fruits
Cherry		Salem China	1951	
Cherry		Stangl	1940	Brown band with tan glaze and blue lines; blue band with tan glaze and yellow lines; blue band with blue glaze and green lines; cherry stems in center
Cherry		Watt	Mid-1950s	Red cherries, green stem, six-petaled flower; yellow
Cherry Blossom	Colonial	Blue Ridge		Red and yellow cherries; pink flower; border
Cherry Blossom		Harker		Sprig of cherries and flowers
Cherry Cobbler	Colonial	Blue Ridge		Pink cherries, rim
Cherry Coke	Colonial	Blue Ridge		Red cherries, border, green rim
Cherry Trim		Harker		Border of groups of cherries
*Chesterton	Royal Gadroon	Harker	1945–1965	Gray, green, blue, pink, yellow
Chevron	Gypsy Trail	Red Wing	1935	Blue, ivory, orange, turquoise, yellow
Chicken Feed	Skyline	Blue Ridge	1950s	Girl feeding chickens; green rim
Chicken Pickins	Skyline	Blue Ridge	1950s	Hen and rooster; pink and green stylized border
Chickory	Colonial	Blue Ridge		Small yellow and blue flowers
Chicory		Stangl	1961	
Children's Plates		Harker		Blue and pink cameoware; duck, teddy bear, dog
Chinese Buddha	Swig	Homer Laughlin	1950s	Buddha, vases, off-center decal

*Chinese Red (color used by Hall), see individual pattern names

| Chinling | Lotus | Vernon Kilns | 1950 | Oriental floral spray |

PATTERN	SHAPE	MAKER	DATE	DESCRIPTION
Chintz	Colonial	Blue Ridge		Allover flower pattern
*Chintz	Melinda	Vernon Kilns	1942; 1950	Floral design
Choice	Ultra	Vernon Kilns	1939	Blue print, floral
Choreography	Criterion	E. M. Knowles	1955	
Christmas Doorway	Skyline	Blue Ridge	1950s	
Christmas Tree	Colonial	Blue Ridge		
Chrysanthemum	Colonial	Blue Ridge		Blue and red flowers, yellow and black leaves
Chrysanthemum	Concord	Red Wing	1947	
Cinnabar	Colonial	Blue Ridge		Bold pink and yellow flowers, green leaves
Circus Clown	Kiddieware	Stangl	Mid-1940s–1974	
Clairborne	Colonial	Blue Ridge		Centered pink and black flowers; border
Classic	Essex	E. M. Knowles	1954-1955	
Clear Day	Cavalier	Royal		Ironstone
Cleveland	Teapot	Hall	1930s	
Clio	Corinthian	Leigh		Floral
Clive	Brittany	Homer Laughlin		Border of maroon panels and floral sprays
Clover	Clinchfield	Blue Ridge	1947-1954	Pink flowers with green clover; blue and black rim
Clover	Kitchenware	Hall	1940-1960	Bright colors; Impressionistic design
Cloverleaf, see Clover				
Coastline	Montecito	Vernon Kilns	1937	Map of Pacific Coast; blue, black on ivory ground
Cock-a-Doodle	Skyline	Blue Ridge	1950s	Rooster in center; blue rim
Cock o' the Morn	Skyline	Blue Ridge	1950s	Crowing rooster
Cock-o-the-Morn (Harker), see Engraved Rooster				
Cock O' Walk	Candlewick	Blue Ridge	1948	Center rooster; red and cream flowered border; broken green rim
Cocky-Locky	Clinchfield	Blue Ridge		Rooster; red stylized border
Cocolo	Cocolo	Franciscan		
Coffee Queen	Coffeepot	Hall		Chinese Red and Olive Green common colors; also called Duchess

PATTERN	SHAPE	MAKER	DATE	DESCRIPTION
Colleen	Ultra	Vernon Kilns	1939	Green print with red, yellow, floral
Colonial	Kitchenware	Hall	1932	Chinese Red, Daffodil, Delphinium, Golden Glo, Hi-White, ivory, Lettuce Green; decals; also called Medallion
Colonial		Salem		Red and green stencil-like decorations
Colonial		Stangl	1926	Aqua, Colonial Blue, brown, Persian Yellow, rust, silver-green, Surf White, Tangerine
Colonial Birds No. 1	Colonial	Blue Ridge		Centered bird
Colonial Birds No. 2	Colonial	Blue Ridge		Centered bird
Colonial Dogwood		Stangl		Marked Prestige
*Colonial Homestead		Royal	1950-1952	
Colonial Lady		Harker		
Colonial Rose	Colonial	Blue Ridge		Red rose, green leaves, red border, green rim
Colonial Rose		Stangl	1970-1974	
Colonial Silver		Stangl	c.1970	
Colonnes	Futura	Red Wing	1960	Pillars
Color Stitch	Colonial	Blue Ridge		Red, blue, gray border
Colorado				Brown
Columbia	Teapot	Hall		
Columbia	Williamsburg	E. M. Knowles	1948	
Columbine	Skyline	Blue Ridge	1950s	Red and white flowers; red line border
Columbine	Century	Homer Laughlin		Floral decal; off-center
Commodore		Salem		Gold medallions and trim
Conchita	Century	Homer Laughlin	1938	Mexican-inspired decal
Conchita Kitchen Kraft		Homer Laughlin	1930s	Ovenwares; Mexican-inspired decal
Concord		Continental Kilns	1944-1957	
Concord		Stangl	1957	

PATTERN	SHAPE	MAKER	DATE	DESCRIPTION
Concorde	Astor	Blue Ridge		Centered grapes; blue line border; brown edge
Confetti	Candlewick	Blue Ridge		Red, yellow, and blue flower border; gray rim
Connie	Teapot	Hall	Early 1940s	Victorian style; see also Benjamin, Birch, Bowknot, Murphy, Plume
Constance	Colonial	Blue Ridge		Centered red and yellow flowers; small flowers on border; pink rim
*Contempo	Al Fresco	Brusché (Bauer)	1952	Champagne White, Desert Beige, Indigo Brown, Pumpkin, Slate, Spicy Green
Conversation		Taylor, Smith, and Taylor	1951?	Designed by Walter Teague, gray and mustard, drawing of bird
Cookie Twins	Kiddieware	Stangl	Mid-1940s–1971	
Coors, see Rosebud				
Coral Pine	Criterion	E. M. Knowles	1954	
*Coral Reef	Ultra	Vernon Kilns	1940	Tropical fish in blue, mustard, maroon on cream ground
Coreopsis	Colonial	Blue Ridge		Yellow flowers; thin yellow border
Corn		American Pottery		
Corn		Brush-McCoy		
Corn		Paden City		
Corn		Standard Pottery		
Corn		Stanford Pottery	1946–1961	
Corn Gold		Sold by Montgomery Ward	1921	Decals
Corn Is Green		Paden City		Cornstalk center design
*Corn King	Corn King	Shawnee	1954	Yellow and green; three-dimensional
*Corn Queen	Corn Queen	Shawnee	1954–1961	Three-dimensional; lighter kernel than Corn King; dark foliage
Cornflower Blue		E. M. Knowles	1930s	Decals

PATTERN	SHAPE	MAKER	DATE	DESCRIPTION
*Coronado	50 different shapes	Franciscan	1936-1956	15 solid colors
Coronado		E. M. Knowles	1948	
Coronado	Coronado, Montecito	Vernon Kilns (grocery promotion)	1935-1939	Blue, brown, dark blue, light green, orange, pink, turquoise, yellow
Coronado Swirl		Franciscan	1936-1956	
Coronation Organdy	Montecito	Vernon Kilns	1937	Gray and rose plaid; see also Calico; Gingham; Homespun; Organdie; Tam O'Shanter; Tweed
Coronet	Coronet	Homer Laughlin	c.1935	Fluted band; ivory, green, yellow
Corsage	Astor	Blue Ridge		Pastel flowers, blue leaf border
Corsage	Lyric	E. M. Knowles	1954	
Cosmos	Skyline	Blue Ridge	1950s	Large yellow flowers
Cosmos		Stangl		Marked Prestige, cosmos flower border
Cosmos	Melinda	Vernon Kilns	1942	Red allover floral
Cottage		Harker		Flowered path leading to red-roofed cottage
Cottage (Crooksville), see Petit Point House				
Cottage Window	Montecito	Vernon Kilns	1937	Window with curtain
Country Classics		Haeger		
Country Cousin	Year 'Round	Vernon Kilns	1957-1958	People and flowers with geometric border
Country Fair	Criterion	E. M. Knowles	1955	
Country Fruit	Trailway	Blue Ridge	1950s	Plaid fruit, wide yellow border
Country Garden	Candlewick	Blue Ridge		Pink and purple flowers
Country Garden	Anniversary	Red Wing	1953	Floral
*Country Garden		Stangl	1956-1974	Three realistic flowers
Country Gentleman		W. S. George		Fruit
Country Home	Fruits	Crooksville		Cottage with mountains in background
Country Life		Stangl	1956-1967	
Country Road	Colonial	Blue Ridge		Yellow flowers; orange rim

PATTERN	SHAPE	MAKER	DATE	DESCRIPTION
Country Road		Homer Laughlin	1977–1978	
Countryside		Harker		Cottage with smoking chimney
Country Side	Montecito	Vernon Kilns	1950	Rural farm scene; marked "da Bron"
County Fair	Colonial	Blue Ridge		Fruit; green trim
Coverlet, see Cozy Cover				
Cowboys and Cactus, see Ranger				
Cowslip	Colonial	Blue Ridge		Yellow flowers
Cozy Cover	Teapot	Hall		Fleece-lined aluminum cozy to fit pot
*Crab Apple	Colonial	Blue Ridge	c.1930–1957	Hand-painted red apples with green leaves; red spatter border
Crab Orchard	Candlewick	Blue Ridge		Two apples; green rim
Cradle	Square	Blue Ridge		Blue flowers and leaves
Cranberry		Stangl		
Crazy Quilt		Homer Laughlin	1977–1978	
Crazy Rhythm	Futura	Red Wing	1960	Abstract; hand-painted
Crestone		Hull		Turquoise
Crocus	Colonial	Blue Ridge		
*Crocus	D-Line	Hall	1930s	Floral decals; black, green, lavender, pink, red; platinum trim
Crocus	True China	Red Wing	1960	Floral
Crocus		Stangl		
Cross Stitch		Blue Ridge		Black X's and dots; red and green leaves
Croydon	Sovereign	Crown	1941	Black trellis border with multicolored flowers
*Cube	Teapot	Hall		Also coffeepot, creamer, and tea tile
Cumberland	Astor	Blue Ridge	1948	Hand-painted blue and white flowers
Curiosity Shop, see Old Curiosity Shop				
Currier & Ives		Homer Laughlin	Present	Blue decal on white
*Currier & Ives	Cavalier	Royal	1940s–1986	Ironstone; scenic center design in blue and white
Currier & Ives	Coupe	Scio		
Cut-A-Way		Hall	1930	Multicolored flowers

PATTERN	SHAPE	MAKER	DATE	DESCRIPTION
Cynthia		Blue Ridge	1949	
Cynthia	Lido	W. S. George		Sprigs of small pink flowers (Peach Blossom has same decal on Bolero shape)
Daffodil	Piecrust	Blue Ridge	1948	Single flower
Dahlia	Candlewick	Blue Ridge	1948	Large red flower
Dahlia by Harker, see Deco-Dahlia				
Dahlia		Stangl	1970-1974	Blue flowered border; marked Prestige
Dainty	Montecito	Vernon Kilns	1935-1947	Dark pink leaves and flowers
Daisies	Deanna	E. M. Knowles		Field of flowers
*Daisy	Fiesta	Homer Laughlin	1962-1968	Turquoise band; turquoise and brown daisies; Casual pattern; see also Yellow Carnation; also called Hawaiian Daisy and Hawaiian 12 Point Daisy
Daisy	True China	Red Wing	1960	Floral
Daisy		Stangl	1936-1942	
Daisy	Versatile	Taylor, Smith, and Taylor		
Daisy		Watt	1949-1953	Floral
Daisy Wreath	Daisy Wreath	Franciscan		
Damask	True China	Red Wing	1964	
Damask Rose	Accent	E. M. Knowles	1954	
Dandridge Dogwood	Skyline	Blue Ridge	1950s	Single flower
Dawn Rose	Americana	E. M. Knowles	1958	
Daydream	Colonial	Blue Ridge		Gray flowers
Deanna		E. M. Knowles		
Debussy	Tempo	E. M. Knowles	1961-1963	
Debutante	Debutante	Homer Laughlin	1948-early 1960s	Solid or with decals
Deca-Flip	Coffeepot	Hall		
Deco-Dahlia		Harker		Stylized red flowers, red and black leaves
Deco-Delight		Stangl		Deco shaped; Colonial Blue, silver-green
Deep Purple		Blue Ridge		Purple flower and leaves

PATTERN	SHAPE	MAKER	DATE	DESCRIPTION
Del Mar	Del Mar	Franciscan		
Delft	Americana	E. M. Knowles	1957	Purple flower; wide yellow rim
Delft Rose	Colonial	Blue Ridge		
Delicious	Candlewick	Blue Ridge		Two painted apples with green and yellow leaves
Delight	Ultra	Vernon Kilns	1940	Blue and yellow camellias and gardenias
Della Robbia	Piecrust	Blue Ridge	1948	Border of variety of fruit
Della Robbia	Vernonware	Metlox	1965	
Delmar		Stangl	1972-1974	Gold background; brown and blue border
Delta Blue	Village Green	Red Wing	1954	Light blue with flowers
Desert Bloom	San Fernando	Vernon Kilns	1944; 1955	Rust print; small flowers on wide border
Desert Flower	Skyline	Blue Ridge	1950s	One yellow and one brown flower
Desert Mallow	Montecito	Vernon Kilns		Yellow and orange flowers
*Desert Rose	Desert Rose	Franciscan	1941-present	Border of large pink flowers and green leaves
Desert Sun	New Shape	Red Wing	1962	Geometric
Design 69		Taylor, Smith, and Taylor		Pale blue and brown
Dewberry	Colonial	Blue Ridge		Green leaves; white berry border
Dewdrop Fairies	Ultra	Vernon Kilns	1940	Blue print border on cream ground
Diana		Stangl	1972-1974	Light blue flowers and rim
Dick Tracy	Century	Homer Laughlin	1950	Decal; child's set
Dinner Rose, see Queen Rose				
Dis 'N Dot	Anytime	Vernon Kilns	1957-1958	Blue, green, and mustard off-center lines and dots
Disney	Ultra most common	Vernon Kilns	1940-1941	Various patterns based on *Fantasia*
Disraeli	Teapot	Hall	1940s	Pink only; Victorian style
Dixie Harvest (No. 3913)	Piecrust	Blue Ridge	1949	
D-Line		Hall	1936	Plain; round; floral decals
Dogwood	Skyline	Blue Ridge	1950s	Large yellow flowers
Dogwood	Dogwood	Franciscan		

PATTERN	SHAPE	MAKER	DATE	DESCRIPTION
Dogwood	Bolero	W. S. George		
*Dogwood	Century	Homer Laughlin	1960s	Pink and white floral decals
Dogwood		Stangl	1965	Della-Ware mark; raised border of pink flowers and pale green leaves
Dogwood		Taylor, Smith, and Taylor	1942	Underglaze pattern; overall flowers
Dogwood		Watt	1949-1953	Pink floral, green leaves on cream
Dolores	Melinda	Vernon Kilns	1942-1947	Floral border
Dominion	Victory	Salem		Poppies, wheat, blue flowers; decal
*Donut	Teapot	Hall	1938	Ivory with orange poppy decal common; Chinese Red, cobalt, Delphinium
Dorset		Scio		
Dragon Flower		Winfield	1940s-1950s	Stylized brown plant
Drape, see Parade				
Dream Flower	Colonial	Blue Ridge		Red, blue, and yellow flowers; dot border
Dreambirds	Colonial	Blue Ridge		Birds kissing; red rim
Dreamtime	San Marino	Vernon Kilns	1950	Swirl; green rust, yellow
Dresden		Crown	1941	Sprays of assorted flowers; gold rim
Dresden Doll	Colonial	Blue Ridge		
Driftwood	Anniversary	Red Wing	1953	Tree branch design
Dubarry	Regent	E. M. Knowles	1948	
Duchess, see Coffee Queen				
Duchess		Paden City	1942	Small flowers and scrolls
Ducky Dinners	Kiddieware	Stangl	Mid-1940s-1974	
Duet		Franciscan	1956	
Duet	Tempo	E. M. Knowles	1961-1963	
Dubonnet	Criterion	E. M. Knowles	1955	
Duff	Candlewick	Blue Ridge		Eight different fruits; gray and rust stylized background

PATTERN	SHAPE	MAKER	DATE	DESCRIPTION
Duo-Tone	Montecito	Vernon Kilns	1938	Concentric bands on rim; lavender and gray, brown and pink, green and gray, black and pink, yellow and gray, pink and green, etc.
Duraprint		Homer Laughlin	1950s	Printed decoration on simple shapes
Dutch Bouquet	Candlewick	Blue Ridge		Red tulip decoration
Dutch Iris	Candlewick	Blue Ridge		Two red and blue iris; red border
Dutch Petit Point	Tricorne; Bonjour	Salem		Decals; Dutch boy and girl in stitched pattern
Dutch Tulip	Candlewick	Blue Ridge		Centered yellow-orange tulip, green leaves
Dutch Tulip		Watt	1956	Black stylized tulip with green and red leaves on cream
Dynasty	Cavalier	Royal		Ironstone
Early American	Nautilus	Homer Laughlin	1960s	Stylized covered wagon, smoke, ships, fort
*Early California	Montecito	Vernon Kilns	1935-1947	Blue, dark blue, brown, green, ivory, maroon, orange, peach, pink, turquoise, yellow
Early Days	San Fernando	Vernon Kilns	1944; 1950-1955	1860s scene with wide floral border
Ebonite	Criterion	E. M. Knowles	c.1954	
Ecstasy	Ultra	Vernon Kilns	1940	Pink camellias on light brown print
Edgemont	Colonial	Blue Ridge		Yellow and red flowers
Edmonton		Syracuse		
Eggshell	Eggshell	Homer Laughlin	1930s-1950s	Many decal patterns
Eggshell Georgian	Eggshell Georgian	Homer Laughlin	1933-1960s	Many decal decorations; colored bands
*Eggshell Nautilus	Eggshell Nautilus	Homer Laughlin	1937-1950s	Floral; bands
Eggshell Polka Dot		Hall	1934	Matte white; ivory glaze; blue, green, red dots; floral decals
Eggshell Theme		Homer Laughlin	1940s	English look; decals; floral border
Eglantine	Clinchfield	Blue Ridge		Pink flower, red border

PATTERN	SHAPE	MAKER	DATE	DESCRIPTION
El-Chico		Bauer		
Eldorado		E. M. Knowles	1948	
*El Patio		Franciscan	1934-1954	20 different solid colors
El Rosa				Della-Ware mark; pink rose and lavender flowers; border of dark green, white, and yellow
El Vuelo		Caribe-Sterling	1950s-c.1963	Modernistic swirls
Elegant Modern		Homer Laughlin		Hotel dinnerware; decals on white
Emerald		Sold by Montgomery Ward	1921	Decals
Emma Susan	Washington Square	Taylor, Smith, and Taylor	1933-1934	Decals
Emperor, see General				
Empress	Empress	Homer Laughlin	1919-1940s	Border, many patterns
Enchantment		Harker		
Enchantment	Ultra	Vernon Kilns	1940	Blue print border
English Countryside		Hall		
English Garden	Century	Homer Laughlin	1933	Landscape design
Engraved Rooster		Harker		Cameoware; rooster standing in center; also called Cock o' the Morn
Epicure		Homer Laughlin	1955	Solid; Charcoal Gray, Dawn Pink, Snow White, Turquoise Blue; highly sculptured
Equation	Criterion Antiques	E. M. Knowles	1955	
Eureka Homewood		Hall (made for Eureka Co.)		Decal
Evening Flower	Skyline	Blue Ridge	1950s	
Evening Song	Classique	E. M. Knowles	1960	
Evening Star	Montecito	Vernon Kilns	1935-1937	Blue and ivory
Eventide	Woodcrest	Blue Ridge	1950s	Log cabin and tree in center; brown rim
Fairlawn		Stangl	1959-1962	

PATTERN	SHAPE	MAKER	DATE	DESCRIPTION
Fairmede Fruits	Clinchfield	Blue Ridge		Centered fruit, four-line border
Fairmount	Skyline	Blue Ridge	1950s	Brown and green leaves on partially brown background
Fairy Bells	Colonial	Blue Ridge		Red and purple flower bells, tan ground
Fairy Tale	Astor	Blue Ridge		Pink flowers, blue leaves, pink border
Fairyland	Ultra	Vernon Kilns	1940	Blue floral and leaf design
Falling Leaves	Colonial	Blue Ridge		Multicolored leaves; orange rim
Falmouth	Skyline	Blue Ridge	1950s	Blue and red outlined flowers; yellow swirled background
Fantasia	Skyline	Blue Ridge	1950s	Abstract leaf pattern; brown, blue, yellow
Fantasia	Ultra	Vernon Kilns	1940	Brown floral and leaf pattern
Fantasy	Kitchenware	Hall	1930s–1940s	Decal; Swedish modern bright flowers on ivory
Fantasy	Accent	E. M. Knowles	1955	
Fantasy	Concord	Red Wing	1947	Abstract
Fantasy Apple	Skyline	Blue Ridge	1950s	Stylized apples; gray rim
Far East	Shellcrest	Paden City		Oriental design
Farmer Takes a Wife	Colonial	Blue Ridge		Figures in center; yellow flowers border; green rim
Farmhouse	Woodcrest	Blue Ridge	1950s	Large scenic design
Farmyard	Skyline	Blue Ridge	1950s	Barn, farmer, tree
Fashion White		Sold by Montgomery Ward	1936	Decals
Fayette Fruit	Candlewick	Blue Ridge		Apple, pear; series of three slashes on border
Feather Fantasy	Criterion	E. M. Knowles	1955	
Feathered Friends	Skyline	Blue Ridge	1950s	Cardinal, bluejay; gray background
Federal		Sebring-Limoges	1942	
Festival	Williamsburg; Forcast	E. M. Knowles	1955; 1957	
Festival		Stangl	1961–1967	Yellow band, Della-Ware mark

PATTERN	SHAPE	MAKER	DATE	DESCRIPTION
Festive	Skyline	Blue Ridge	1950s	Black and yellow crepe paper
Festive Fruit, see Fruit (Stangl)				
Field Daisy	Colonial	Blue Ridge		Red and yellow flowers, brown leaves; broken rim
Field Daisy		Stangl	1941-1942	White daisies on blue; yellow background
*Fiesta	Fiesta	Homer Laughlin	1936-1972	Antique Gold, bright green, chartreuse, dark blue, Forest Green, gray, light green, Mango Red, Old Ivory, red, rose, Turf Green, turquoise, yellow; see also Amberstone; Casualstone; Daisy; Fiesta Ironstone; Fiesta Kitchen Kraft; Yellow Carnation
Fiesta Casual, see Daisy; Yellow Carnation				
Fiesta Ironstone	Fiesta	Homer Laughlin	1970-1972	Antique Gold, Mango Red, Turf Green
*Fiesta Kitchen Kraft		Homer Laughlin	1939-early 1940s	Bake and serve line; blue, green, red, yellow
Fiesta Wood	Fiesta	Homer Laughlin		Colored border stripes; sleeping Mexican
Fireside	Skyline	Blue Ridge	1950s	Hearth and rocker; brown rim
First Love		Stangl	1968-1973	
Fisherman	Square	Blue Ridge		Man fishing; broken black rim
Five Band, see Banded				
Five Fingers	Ultra	Vernon Kilns	1938	Autumn leaves on ivory
Five Little Pigs	Kiddieware	Stangl	Mid-1940s–1974	
Fjord	Americana	E. M. Knowles	1959	
Flaming Rose		Paden City		Brightly colored floral design
Flamingo	Gray Lure	Crooksville		Sprig of delicate flowers
Flamingo		Hall		
Flare Ware Gold Lace		Hall	1960s	Overall stars and scalloped border
Fleur de Lis	Kitchen Kraft	Homer Laughlin		
Fleur de Lis	Criterion	E. M. Knowles	1955	

PATTERN	SHAPE	MAKER	DATE	DESCRIPTION
Fleur de Lis		Vernon Kilns		Large pastel center design
Fleur de Lis Iris, see Iris (Universal)				
Fleurette	Tempo	E. M. Knowles	1959	
Flight	Skyline	Blue Ridge	1950s	Centered flying birds
Flight	Forcast	E. M. Knowles	1957	
Flight	New Shape	Red Wing	1962	Birds
Flight of the Swallows	New Art	Homer Laughlin	1930s	Foliage spray and group of flying birds
Flirt	Piecrust	Blue Ridge	1950s	Red flowers; green leaves and rim
Flora	Williamsburg	E. M. Knowles	1948-1955	
Flora		Stangl	1941	Yellow band with pink, blue, and yellow flowers; Terra Rose mark
Flora	Ultra	Vernon Kilns	1938	Floral spray
Floral	Floral	Franciscan		
Floral	Lido	W. S. George		Decal of multicolored small flowers
Floral		Paden City		
Floral		Stangl	1941-1942	
Floral		Watt		Charcoal, pinkish-blue floral
Floral Birdsong	Sabina II	Sabin	c.1946	
Floral Border		Sold by Montgomery Ward	1936	Decals
Floral Bouquet	Fairway	Taylor, Smith, and Taylor	Early 1930s	
Floral Lattice	Five Band	Hall		
Floral Plaid		Stangl	1940-1942	
Floral Series	Montecito	Vernon Kilns	1935-1937	Flowers
Florence	Squared-Off Edges	E. M. Knowles	1933-1934	Decals
Florence		Pope-Gosser	1940s	Border of small flowers
Florentine		Stangl	1958	
Floret	Ultra	Vernon Kilns	1939	Red floral
Florette		Stangl	1961-1962	
Florida	Williamsburg	E. M. Knowles	1948	
Flounce	Colonial	Blue Ridge		Red, pink, and blue cut-off flowers around edge
Flower Ballet	Ultra	Vernon Kilns	1940	Maroon border print

PATTERN	SHAPE	MAKER	DATE	DESCRIPTION
Flower Basket	Yorktown	E. M. Knowles		
Flower Bowl	Colonial	Blue Ridge		Flowers in bowl; green and yellow border
Flower Fair	Coupe	Crooksville		Muted flowers
Flower Fantasy		Blue Ridge	1954	
Flower Power		Homer Laughlin	1977-1978	
Flower Rim	Lido	W. S. George		Bands of small flowers
Flower Ring	Colonial	Blue Ridge		Red, blue, and yellow flowers; green leaves and rim
Flower Wreath	Candlewick	Blue Ridge		Purple and pink flowers and border
Floweret	Skyline	Blue Ridge	1950s	Red flowers, black rim
Flowering Berry	Candlewick	Blue Ridge		Pink and red flower border
Flowerpot	Banded	Hall		Early decal
Flowers of the Dell	New Art	Homer Laughlin	1930s	Two floral sprays
Fluffy Ruffles	Astor	Blue Ridge		Large blue flowers
Flute	Kitchenware	Hall	1935	Kitchenware; Chinese Red, Hi-White, Marine, russet; also called Ribbed
Flying Bluebird	Empress	Homer Laughlin	1920	Decal
Foliage	Tempo	E. M. Knowles	1961-1963	
Fondoso	Gypsy Trail	Red Wing	1938	Pastels; blue, turquoise, yellow
Football	Teapot	Hall	1938-1940	
Forest Flower	Shellridge	Harker		Light brown and yellow
*Forest Fruits	Skyline	Blue Ridge	1950s	Yellow fruit, dark border
Forever Yours	Shellridge	Harker		Rosebud garland
Formal		Salem		Rust and gold rim; gold border design
Forman		Hall		
Fountain	Ballerina	Universal	1950	Abstract
Four Seasons White	Four Seasons	E. M. Knowles	1959-1963	
Four Winds	Melinda	Vernon Kilns	1950	Yacht; maroon and blue border
Fox Grape	Colonial	Blue Ridge		Green leaves, dark grapes, broken rim
Foxfire	Skyline	Blue Ridge	1950s	Red leaf-shaped flowers

PATTERN	SHAPE	MAKER	DATE	DESCRIPTION
Frageria	Skyline	Blue Ridge	1950s	Red strawberries; green border
*French	Teapot	Hall	1920	Gold-decorated line
French Peasant	Colonial	Blue Ridge		Light blue rim; pink and green floral border; peasant in center
French Provincial				Silhouette decal
Frolic	Anytime	Vernon Kilns	1955	Aqua, gold, and purple abstract floral
Frontenac	Futura	Red Wing	1960	Abstract flowers
Frontier Days	Montecito	Vernon Kilns	1950; 1954	Western scene
Frosted Fruit		Stangl	1957	
Frosted Leaves	Mayfair	E. M. Knowles	1955	
*Fruit		Franciscan	1949	
Fruit		Purinton	1936-1959	Four fruits; brown X
*Fruit	Concord	Red Wing	1947	
*Fruit		Stangl	1942-1974	Center designs of fruit; also called Festive Fruit
*Fruit & Flowers		Stangl	1957-1974	Center design; colored border
Fruit & Flowers		Universal		Subdued colors; large center design
Fruit Basket		Homer Laughlin	1977-1978	
Fruit Basket		Salem		Narrow checkerboard band; border of fruit baskets
Fruit Cocktail	Astor	Blue Ridge		Different fruits; black and yellow border
Fruit Fantasy	Colonial	Blue Ridge		Painted fruits, green rim
Fruit Punch	Colonial	Blue Ridge		Various fruits; allover pattern
Fruit Ring	Clinchfield	Blue Ridge		Fruit border
Fruit Salad	Colonial	Blue Ridge	Yellow pear, red apple, blueberries; red rim	
Fruit Sherbet	Colonial	Blue Ridge		Pastel fruit; broken blue rim
Fruitdale	Melinda	Vernon Kilns	1942-1947	Flower and fruit center
Fruitful	Colonial	Blue Ridge		Painted fruit
Fruits	Utility ware	Harker		Large stem of fruit—apple and pear

PATTERN	SHAPE	MAKER	DATE	DESCRIPTION
Fruits		E. M. Knowles		Brightly colored individual fruit
Fuchsia	Colonial	Blue Ridge		
Fuchsia		Leigh/Crescent		Predominately orange and green floral spray
Fuji		Hall		Oriental-styled flower
Full Bloom	Candlewick	Blue Ridge		Two large purple and red center flowers
Futura		Red Wing	1961	Hand painted
Fuzz Ball		Hall	1930s	Pink and green
Gaity	Skyline	Blue Ridge		Red flowers
Galaxy		Stangl	1963-1970	
Game Cock, see Rooster by Blue Ridge				
Garden Design		Salem China	1940s	
Garden Flower		Stangl	1947-1957	
Garden Flowers	Colonial	Blue Ridge		Eight different flowers
Garden Lane	Colonial	Blue Ridge		Hand-painted tulips, daisies, and roses
Garden Magic	Classique	E. M. Knowles	1960	
Garden Party	Garden Party	Franciscan		
Garden Pinks	Skyline	Blue Ridge	1950s	Pink flower
Garden Plates	Montecito	Vernon Kilns	1938	Sepia and brown vegetables
Garden Trail	Shellridge	Harker		Center bouquet; floral border
Garland	Colonial	Blue Ridge		Black leaves; pastel flower border
Garland	Monarch	Crown	1941	Garland of small roses
Garland	Williamsburg	E. M. Knowles	1948	
Garland		Pickard		
Garland		Stangl	1957-1967	
Gascon		W. S. George		Bright blue flowers, gray leaves; sold by Sears, Roebuck and Co.
Gay Plaid		Blair		Yellow, green, and brown; large plaid
Gayety	San Marino	Vernon Kilns	1948; 1954	Green and rose stripes on ivory

PATTERN	SHAPE	MAKER	DATE	DESCRIPTION
General	Refrigerator Ware	Hall	1939	Westinghouse; Canary, Delphinium, Garden, Sunset, Yellow; also called Emperor
General Electric	Refrigerator Ware	Hall		G.E. logo on lid; Addison (blue) and yellow
Georgian Eggshell, see Eggshell Georgian				
Ginger Boy	Kiddieware	Stangl	Mid-1940s–1974	
Ginger Cat	Kiddieware	Stangl	Mid-1940s–1974	
Ginger Girl	Kiddieware	Stangl	Mid-1940s–1974	
Gingersnap	Gingersnap	Franciscan		
*Gingham	Montecito	Vernon Kilns	1949–1958	Green and yellow plaid; dark green border; see also Calico; Coronation Organdy; Homespun; Organdie; Tam O'Shanter; Tweed
Gingham Fruit	Trailway	Blue Ridge	1950s	Fruit with plaid leaves; gray swirled border
Gladstone	Teapot	Hall	1940	Pink/gold only; Victorian style
Glamour	Ultra	Vernon Kilns	c.1938	Blue, maroon peonies and gardenias
Glencoe	Thermal Porcelain	Coors	1920s	Brown, green, yellow, and other colors
Glenedon		Leigh		
Glenwood	Cavalier	Homer Laughlin	1961–1968	
*Globe	Teapot	Hall	Early 1940s	
Gloria		Blue Ridge	1949	
Gloriosa	Skyline	Blue Ridge	1950s	Yellow flowers
Glorious	Candlewick	Blue Ridge		One red and two blue morning glories, centered
Gloucester Fisherman	Ballerina	Universal Potteries	1950	
Godey Ladies		Salem		
Godey Prints	Victory	Salem		Decals; service plates
Gold & Cobalt	Empress	Homer Laughlin	1920	Decal

PATTERN	SHAPE	MAKER	DATE	DESCRIPTION
Gold Band		Sold by Montgomery Ward	1920-1936	Decals

Gold-decorated line of Hall teapots, see Airflow; Aladdin; Albany; Automobile; Baltimore; Basket; Basketball; Birdcage; Boston; Cleveland; Donut; Football; French; Globe; Hollywood; Hook Cover; Illinois; Los Angeles; Manhattan; Melody; Moderne; Nautilus; New York; Parade; Philadelphia; Rhythm; Saf-Handle; Sani-Grid; Star; Streamline; Surfside; Windshield; World's Fair

PATTERN	SHAPE	MAKER	DATE	DESCRIPTION
Gold Drape		Crooksville		Floral design; gold border, draped effect
Gold Floral Band		Homer Laughlin	1920	Decal
Gold Garland		Homer Laughlin	1920	Decal
Gold Initial		Sold by Montgomery Ward	1921	Decal
Gold Label	Kitchenware	Hall	1950s	Gold stamped decorations
Gold Lace over Cobalt Blue		Homer Laughlin	1920	Decal
Gold Stripe		Sold by Montgomery Ward	1936	Decals
Golden		Coors	1930s	Blue, green, ivory, orange, rose, yellow
Golden Blossom		Stangl	1964-1974	Brown blossoms, orange leaves
Golden Crown	Queen Anne	Sabin		
Golden Foliage	Four Seasons	E. M. Knowles	1960-1963	
Golden Grape		Stangl	1963-1972	
Golden Harvest	Coupe	Stangl	1953-1973	Yellow flowers, gray background
Golden Laurel		E. M. Knowles	1930	Decals
Golden Maple	Montecito	Vernon Kilns	1935-1937	Pumpkin and ivory
Golden Viking	Futura	Red Wing	1960	Geometric; gold
Golden Wheat	Rhythm Coupe	Homer Laughlin	1953-1958	
Golden Wheat	Yorktown	E. M. Knowles	1936	Decals
Golden Wreath	Accent	E. M. Knowles	1960	
Goldtrim	Briar Rose	Salem	1952	Gold rim; gold border design
Good Earth	San Fernando	Vernon Kilns		Pumpkins and corn shocks with farm buildings
Gooseberry	Candlewick	Blue Ridge		Yellow fruit and rim

PATTERN	SHAPE	MAKER	DATE	DESCRIPTION
Gourmet	Accent	E. M. Knowles	1956	
Grace	Ultra	Vernon Kilns	1939	Purple print with yellow, rose, blue; floral
Granada		French Saxon	1939-1940	Solids: blue, green, Tangerine, yellow
Granada	True China	Red Wing	1960	Floral
Grandfather's Clock	Square	Blue Ridge		Clock in hallway; broken black rim
Grandiose	Coupe	Paden City	1952	Muted large flowers
Grandmother's Garden	Colonial	Blue Ridge		
Granny Smith Apple	Skyline	Blue Ridge	1950s	Two red apples on yellow center
Grape	Teapot	Hall		Grape clusters in relief; decal decorations and/or embedded rhinestones
Grape		Stangl	1973-1974	
Grape Salad	Candlewick	Blue Ridge		Grapes with large green leaves; border and rim
Grass	Esquire	E. M. Knowles	1957-1962	Abstract decal; Russel Wright
Grass Flower	Moderne	Blue Ridge	1950s	Black and yellow flowers; green leaves and rim
*Greenbriar	Forcast	E. M. Knowles	1959	
Green Briar	Piecrust	Blue Ridge	1948	
Green Dots	Avona	Taylor, Smith, and Taylor	Early 1930s	Wide border of dots
Green Eyes	Skyline	Blue Ridge	1950s	
Green Grapes		Stangl		
Green Valley		Homer Laughlin	1977-1978	
Green Wheat	Yorktown	E. M. Knowles		Decals
Green Wheat		Leigh/Crescent		Separate wheat stalks
Greensville	Skyline	Blue Ridge	1950s	Cream and brown flower
Greenwich-stone	Ceramastone	Red Wing	1967	
Gumdrop Tree	Candlewick	Blue Ridge		Red, yellow, and red with green leaves
Gypsy	Colonial	Blue Ridge		Red, orange, and yellow flowers
Gypsy Dancer	Colonial	Blue Ridge		Red and yellow flowers; red and green border

PATTERN	SHAPE	MAKER	DATE	DESCRIPTION
Gypsy Trail		Red Wing	1930s	
Hacienda	Hacienda	Franciscan		Hacienda green
*Hacienda	Century	Homer Laughlin	1938	Decal; cactus, bench, side of Mexican house; red trim
Hall teapots, see individual names				
Hallcraft, see Bouquet; Caprice; Harlequin; Peach Blossom; Zeisel				
Ham 'n Eggs	Candlewick	Blue Ridge		Pig, hen; wide green and thin red border
Happy Days	Forcast	E. M. Knowles	1957	
Harlequin	Fantasy/ Hallcraft	Hall		Designed by Eva Zeisel
*Harlequin	Harlequin	Homer Laughlin	1938-1964; 1979	Ironstone; chartreuse, cobalt blue, dark blue, Forest Green, gray, ivory, light green, maroon, mauve blue, rose, Spruce Green, Tangerine, turquoise; 1979—deep coral, green, turquoise, yellow
Harvest	Concord	Red Wing	1947	
Harvest		Stangl		
Harvest	Ultra	Vernon Kilns	1938	Fruits in center: pears, green apples, plum, cherries, and a peach
Harvestime	Skyline	Blue Ridge	1950s	Wheat tied with bow
Hawaii	Melinda	Vernon Kilns	1942	Maroon lotus flower
Hawaiian Coral	San Marino	Vernon Kilns	1952; 1956	Spatter edge; brown, yellow, and green on cream
Hawaiian Daisy, see Daisy (Homer Laughlin)				
*Hawaiian Flowers	Ultra	Vernon Kilns	1938	Lotus in blue, maroon, mustard, pink
Hawaiian Fruit	Clinchfield; Piecrust	Blue Ridge	1948	Hand-painted pineapple and two other fruits in blue, yellow, and brown; colors repeated in border
Hawaiian 12 Point Daisy, see Daisy (Homer Laughlin)				
Hawthorne	Quena	Crown		Pastel pink and blue flowers; gold rim
Hawthorne	Hawthorne	Franciscan		
Hazel	Ranson	Scio		
Hazelnut		Universal		Decals

PATTERN	SHAPE	MAKER	DATE	DESCRIPTION
Hearthstone	Casual	Red Wing	1961	Solids; beige, orange
*Heather Rose	E-Style	Hall		Pale pinkish-purple rose on a stem with many leaves
Heavenly Days	Anytime	Vernon Kilns	1956-1958	Aqua, mocha, and pink geometric designs
Heirloom	Candlewick	Blue Ridge		Blue, yellow, and red flowers; green rim
Heirloom	Corinthian	Sebring		Wide gold floral border; garland and bouquet in center
Hen Party	Lyric	E. M. Knowles	1954	Green
Hercules	Refrigerator Ware	Hall	1940-1941	Westinghouse: Arctic Blue, canary, cobalt, Garden, Sunset, and tan; also called Aristocrat
Heritage		Stangl		
Heritance		Harker		
Heyday	San Marino	Vernon Kilns	1954-1958	Geometric circles in green and brown
Hibiscus (Crooksville), see Flamingo				
Hibiscus	San Fernando	Vernon Kilns	1944; 1954	Yellow flowers and brown print
Hidden Valley	Cavalier	Royal		Ironstone; colored band and large center stencil-like flowers
Hi-Fire		Bauer	1930s	
High Sierra	Accent	E. M. Knowles	1955	
High Stepper	Square	Blue Ridge		Rooster stepping
Highland Ivy	Piecrust	Blue Ridge	1949	Dark and light green ivy
Highlands	Criterion	E. M. Knowles	1957	
Highlight		Paden City	1948	Heavy quality oven- and craze-proof colors: Blueberry, Citron, dark green, Nutmeg, Pepper, white; Russel Wright; distributed by Justin Tharaud and Son
Hilda	Candlewick	Blue Ridge		Large red flower and smaller blue and yellow flowers
Hilo	Ultra	Vernon Kilns	1938	Light brown lotus flower
Holland, see Crocus (Hall)				

PATTERN	SHAPE	MAKER	DATE	DESCRIPTION
Holly		Stangl	1967–1972	
Hollyberry	Colonial	Blue Ridge		Traditional Christmas plant; green rim
Hollyhock	Colonial	Blue Ridge		Pink flowers; yellow line border
Hollyhock	New Art	Homer Laughlin		Decal; pink flowers on stem
Hollyhock		Universal		Multicolored flowers
*Hollywood	Teapot	Hall	Late 1920s	Variety of colors; three sizes
Homesplace	Skyline	Blue Ridge	1950s	Tree, fence, and house
*Homespun	Montecito	Vernon Kilns	1949–1958	Brown, green, and yellow plaid; see also Calico; Coronation Organdy; Gingham; Organdie; Tam O'Shanter; Tweed
Homestead	Skyline	Blue Ridge	1950s	Farm scene
Homestead	Iva-Lure	Crooksville		Winter scene
Homestead in Winter, see Homestead (Crooksville)				
*Homestead Provincial	Poppytrail line	Metlox	1952–1980	Early American folk art themes in red and green
Honolulu	Candlewick	Blue Ridge		Different fruits; green rim
Honolulu	Ultra	Vernon Kilns	1938	Yellow and blue lotus flower
*Hook Cover	Teapot	Hall	1940	Cadet, Chinese Red, Delphinium, emerald common colors
Hopscotch	Astor	Blue Ridge		Centered yellow and orange flower; cross-hatched border
Hors-d'oeuvres	Accent	E. M. Knowles	1955	
Hostess Pantry Ware		Pottery Guild	1954	Hand painted
Hotpoint	Refrigerator Ware	Hall		Addison, Chinese Red, Dresden, Green Lustre, Indian Red, maroon, Sandust, Warm Yellow Daffodil
House, see Petit Point House				
Housetops		Leigh/Crescent		Variety of buildings
Humpty Dumpty	Kiddieware	Stangl	Mid-1940s–1974	
Hunting	Iva-Lure	Crooksville		Scenic

PATTERN	SHAPE	MAKER	DATE	DESCRIPTION
Illinois	Teapot	Hall	1920s-early 1930s	Cobalt and emerald common colors
Imperial	Anytime	Vernon Kilns	1955-1956	Sgraffito; white lines on black ground
Indian Campfire	Kiddieware	Stangl	Mid-1940s-1974	
Indian Tree		Leigh/Crescent		Large floral spray; pink and blue
Indian Tree	Victory	Salem		Decals; Minton-style floral
Indiana	Teapot	Hall		Warm yellow
Ingrid	Regent	E. M. Knowles	1954	
Inspiration		Stangl	1967-1968	Marked Prestige
Intaglio		Purinton	1936-1959	Dark swirling background; white etched flower
Iris	Concord	Red Wing	1947	Brown, turquoise-green
Iris		Universal		Pastel pinks; also called Fleur de Lis Iris
Iris Bouquet		Leigh/Crescent		Brightly colored flowers
Irongate	Teapot	Hall		Made for Irongate Products Co. of New York; black
*Iroquois	Casual	Iroquois China	1959-mid-1960s	Aqua, Avocado Yellow, Brick Red, Cantaloupe, charcoal, Ice Blue, Lemon Yellow, Lettuce Green, Nutmeg, Oyster, Parsley, Pink Sherbet, Ripe Apricot, Sugar White
Iroquois Red	Ranchero	W. S. George		Red banded design
Isle of Palms	Common-wealth	James River Pottery		
Isobella		E. M. Knowles	1948	
*Ivy	Ivy	Franciscan	1948	Hand painted
Ivy	Regal	Harker		Fall colors
Ivy		Paden City		
Ivy Vine	Coupe	Crooksville		Pastel greens
Ivy Vine		Harker		Border of ivy
Jack in the Box	Kiddieware	Stangl	Mid-1940s-1974	
Jacobean	Queen Anne	Sabin	c.1946	
Jade Ware		Sebring	1940s	

PATTERN	SHAPE	MAKER	DATE	DESCRIPTION
Jamestown	Tempo	E. M. Knowles	1961–1963	
Jamoca	Jamoca	Franciscan		
Jan	Candlewick	Blue Ridge	.	Red, yellow, purple, and pink flower border
Jane Adams	Victory	Salem	1950s	Yellow and green floral sprays
Jean		Nancy	Steubenville	
Jeanette	New Yorker	Salem		Flowerpot center design
Jellico	Skyline	Blue Ridge	1950s	Two-tone red and yellow flowers
Jessamine	Piecrust	Blue Ridge	1948	Red flowers, multicolored leaves, green border
Jessica	Colonial	Blue Ridge		Red, pink, and blue flowers; pink line border
Jessica		Harker		Brightly colored flowers
Jessie		Crooksville		Pastel pink; floral sprays on border and center
Jigsaw	Skyline	Blue Ridge	1950s	Rooster
Joan of Arc	Diana	Sebring-Limoges		
Joanna	Colonial	Blue Ridge		Red and yellow flowers
Jonquil	Astor	Blue Ridge		Yellow flowers, red border
Jonquil		Paden City		Pastel flowers, border of yellow sprays
Jonquil	Tricorne	Salem		Decals
Jonquil		Stangl		
Joy	Ultra	Vernon Kilns	1940	Yellow peonies and gardenias on brown
Joyce	Colonial	Blue Ridge		Red, light blue, and dark blue flowers
J-Sunshine		Hall		Floral decals
*Jubilee	Debutante	Homer Laughlin	c.1948; 1977–1978	Pastel; Celadon Green, Cream Beige, Mist Gray, Shell Pink; solids
June Apple	Woodcrest	Blue Ridge	1950s	Broken line outlining red apples and leaves
June Bouquet	Colonial	Blue Ridge		Pink, purple, and yellow flowers
June Bride	Colonial	Blue Ridge		Pink and yellow flowers; yellow centered border
June Rose	Colonial	Blue Ridge		Pink flowers, dark leaves

PATTERN	SHAPE	MAKER	DATE	DESCRIPTION
June Rose	Coronet	Homer Laughlin	c.1935	Band of roses
Kaleidoscope	Birds	Crooksville		Floral pattern with green divider
*Kansas	Teapot	Hall		Common color dark green, with or without gold decoration
Karen	Colonial	Blue Ridge		Pink, purple, and red flowers
Karen		Sebring-Limoges	1940	
Kashmir	True China	Red Wing	1964	
Kate	Colonial	Blue Ridge		Red flower and rim
Kimberly	Moderne	Blue Ridge	1950s	
King, see Ridged				
Kingsport	Astor	Blue Ridge		Centered pink flower; inner and outer leaf border
Kitchen Bouquet	Century-Kitchen Kraft	Homer Laughlin		Floral decals
*Kitchen Kraft	Kitchen Kraft	Homer Laughlin	1930s	Red, blue; also decals under pattern name
Kitchen Shelf	Astor	Blue Ridge		Kitchenware; centered light blue and yellow borders

Kitchenware, see Acacia; Banded; Blue Blossom; Blue Garden; Cactus; Clover; Colonial; Fantasy; Flute; Gold Label; Meadow Flower; Morning Glory; No. 488; Plum Pudding; Provincial; Radiant Ware; Red Dot; Rose Parade; Rose White; Royal Rose; Saf-Handle; Sani-Grid; Shaggy Tulip; Sunshine; Thorley

PATTERN	SHAPE	MAKER	DATE	DESCRIPTION
Kitten Capers	Kiddieware	Stangl	Mid-1940s–1974	
Kitty	Harker			Blue and pink cameoware
Knowles	Esquire	E. M. Knowles	1955	Russel Wright
Kumquat		Stangl		
Kwaker	Kwaker	Homer Laughlin	1901–1940s	Floral decorations
La Gonda		Gonder	1950s	Modern shapes; aqua, pink, yellow
Lacquer Blossom	Accent	E. M. Knowles	1957	
Lady Alice	Brittany	Homer Laughlin		Maroon border; bluebells and roses
Lady Greenbriar	Nautilus	Homer Laughlin		Green border; gold trim, flowers
Lady Stratford	Nautilus	Homer Laughlin		Maroon border; gold trim, flowers

PATTERN	SHAPE	MAKER	DATE	DESCRIPTION
La Linda		Bauer	1939–1940s	Solid colors; smooth (no ridges)
Landscape		Salem	1940s	
Language of Flowers	Candlewick	Blue Ridge		Blue basket, red flowers, blue rim, writing
Lanterns	Concord	Red Wing	1947	Abstract
Largo		Universal		Border of fall leaves; small center decal
Laura	Colonial	Blue Ridge		Red flowers, red and yellow leaves
Laurel	Monarch	Crown	1941	Black and gold wreath border
Laurel		Stangl	c.1942	
Laurelton		Harker		Green, beige
Laurie	Colonial	Blue Ridge		Large pink flowers, small blue flowers
Laurita		Stangl		Della-Ware mark
Lavalette	Moderne	Blue Ridge	1950s	Pink flower; green border
Lavender Fruit	Colonial	Blue Ridge		
Lazybone		Frankoma	1953	Solids
Leaf		Taylor, Smith, and Taylor		Coral
Leaf and Flower		Harker		Cameo-type design
Leaf Ballet	Accent	E. M. Knowles	1953–1954	
Leaf Dane	Four Seasons	E. M. Knowles	1960–1963	
Leaf Spray		E. M. Knowles		Muted colors
Leaf Swirl	Shellridge	Harker		Fall colors
Leaves of Fall	Trailway	Blue Ridge	1950s	Centered leaves with outline; wide yellow border
Ledford	Candlewick	Blue Ridge		Mostly pink flowers
Lei Lani	Ultra; San Marino	Vernon Kilns	1938–1942; 1947–1955	Maroon lotus flower
Lenore	Candlewick	Blue Ridge		Pink and red tulip; red border
Lenore	Monticello; Olivia	Steubenville		
Lexington	Colonial	Blue Ridge		Gray flowers; blue leaves and rim
Lexington		Homer Laughlin		Wide solid-colored border
Lexington	Concord	Red Wing	1947	Rose

PATTERN	SHAPE	MAKER	DATE	DESCRIPTION
Lexington Rose		Red Wing		Large flowers
Liberty	Liberty	Homer Laughlin	1928-1950s	Gadroon edge; florals
Lido		Homer Laughlin	1977-1978	
Lido	Regent	E. M. Knowles	1948	
Lido Dalrymple		W. S. George		Tiny buds
Lime		Stangl	1950	
Linda	Montecito	Vernon Kilns	1940	Burgundy border; pink and blue flowers
Lipton	French; Boston	Hall		Teapots, sugars and creamers; marked Lipton Tea; maroon and warm yellow most common colors
Little Bo Peep, see Bo Peep				
Little Bouquet	LaGrande	Crooksville		Small flower grouping
Little Boy Blue	Kiddieware	Stangl	Mid-1940s–1974	
Little Mission	Montecito	Vernon Kilns	1937	Mission house
Little Quackers	Kiddieware	Stangl	Mid-1940s–1974	
Little Red Riding Hood, see Red Riding Hood				
Little Violet	Astor	Blue Ridge		Centered bunch of violets; border
Liz	Colonial	Blue Ridge		Pink and yellow flowers; red rim
Lobstar Ware		Shawnee Pottery	1954-1956	Lobster motif on white, black, or Van Dyke Brown
Lollipop Tree	Year 'Round	Vernon Kilns	1957-1958	Abstract pastel lollipops
Los Angeles		Bauer		
*Los Angeles	Teapot	Hall	1926	Variety of colors; three sizes
Lotus		Harker	1960s	Cameoware
Lotus	Concord	Red Wing	1947	
Lotus	Lotus	Vernon Kilns	1950	Red and yellow lotus flower
Louise	Virginia Rose	Homer Laughlin		
Louisiana Lace	Candlewick	Blue Ridge		
Love Song	Astor	Blue Ridge		Centered male, female, and leaves; yellow and double black border
Lucerne	Classique	E. M. Knowles	1960	
Lupine	Futura	Red Wing	1960	Floral

PATTERN	SHAPE	MAKER	DATE	DESCRIPTION
*Lu-Ray	Laurel (1932); Empire (1936)	Taylor, Smith, and Taylor	1930s-1950s	Pastels: Chatham Gray, Persian Cream, Sharon Pink, Surf Green, Windsor Blue
*Lute Song	True China	Red Wing	1960s	Musical instruments
Lyric		Stangl	1954-1957	Black and brown freeform shapes; white background
Madison		Leigh		
Madras	Square	Blue Ridge		Bold geometric
Madrid		Homer Laughlin	1977-1978	
Magic Flower	Candlewick	Blue Ridge		Red and blue flower; green border
Magnolia	Piecrust	Blue Ridge	1948	White and red flowers; green leaves; dark stems
Magnolia	Liberty	Homer Laughlin		Decal
*Magnolia	Concord	Red Wing	1947	
*Magnolia		Stangl	1952-1962	Red border
Majestic	True China	Red Wing	1960	White
Mallow		Harker		Pastel flower arrangements
Manassas	Colonial	Blue Ridge		Red leaves; green leaf border
Mandarin Red		Salem		Solid colored; bright red and white
Mandarin Tricorne	Tricorne	Salem		Red borders, white interiors
Mango	Mango	Franciscan		
Manhattan	Teapot	Hall		Stock Brown; side handle
Manhattan		Leigh/Crescent		Bordered with rings of gold
Mantilla	Tempo	E. M. Knowles	1961-1963	
Maple Leaf	Woodcrest	Blue Ridge	1950s	Stylized leaves with outlines
Maple Leaf		Salem		Fall leaf design
Maple Whirl		Stangl	1965-1967	
Mar-Crest		Western Stoneware	1950s	Dark brown, many different designs; wholesaled by Marshall Burns
Mardi Gras	Colonial	Blue Ridge	1943	Blue and pink flowers and buds; flowers cut off on plates
Mardi Gras Variant	Colonial	Blue Ridge		Red cut-off flowers

PATTERN	SHAPE	MAKER	DATE	DESCRIPTION
Margaret Rose		Homer Laughlin		Thick colored border; floral center
Marigold	Marigold	Homer Laughlin	1930s-1960s	Scalloped edge, light yellow glaze
Mariner	Candlewick	Blue Ridge		Center sailboat; blue rope border; Mariner written on plate
Marine	Montecito	Vernon Kilns	1937	Anchor and ships
Mariposa Tulip	Montecito	Vernon Kilns		Yellow flowers
Mary	Astor	Blue Ridge		Fruit and flowers, border
Mary Quite	Kiddieware	Stangl	Mid-1940s–1974	
Marylou		Hall		Floral decals; creamer and sugar
Max-i-cana	Yellowstone	Homer Laughlin	1930s	Mexican decal; man, cactus, pots; octagonal plates
May and Vieve Hamilton		Vernon Kilns		
Mayan Aztec		Frankoma		Solids
Mayfair	Esquire	E. M. Knowles	1957	
Mayfair		Leigh/Crescent		Bold flower decal
May Flower	Melinda	Vernon Kilns	1942-1955	Large floral spray
*Mayflower	Skyline	Blue Ridge	1950s	
Mayflower		E. M. Knowles	1957-1963	
Maypole	Maypole	Franciscan	1977	
Maywood		Purinton	1936-1959	Gray-blue background; white flowers
*McCormick	Teapot	Hall	1907	Golden brown oldest color; made for McCormick Tea Co.
Meadow Beauty	Colonial	Blue Ridge		Brightly colored floral border
Meadow Bloom	Montecito	Vernon Kilns	1947	Blue flowers and rose; brown border
Meadow Flowers	Kitchenware	Hall	1938	Flowers in meadow on ivory; teapot
Meadow Flowers	Coupe	Crooksville		Brightly colored floral border
Meadow Gold	Criterion	E. M. Knowles	1954	
*Meadow Rose	Meadow Rose	Franciscan	1977	

PATTERN	SHAPE	MAKER	DATE	DESCRIPTION
Meadowlea	Skyline	Blue Ridge	1950s	White flowers, brown leaves, outlined
Mealtime Special	Kiddieware	Stangl	Mid-1940s–1974	
Medallion, see also Colonial (Hall)				
Medallion		Crooksville		Small floral border
Medici	Cavalier	Royal		Ironstone; wide, elaborate scroll border
Mediterranean	True China	Red Wing	1960	Floral
Mediterranean		Stangl	1965–1974	Dark blue and black
Medley	Colonial	Blue Ridge		Blue flower and rim
Melinda	Melinda	Vernon Kilns	1942	Solid colors
Mello-Tone		Coors	Late 1930s	Pastels: Aqua Blue, Canary Yellow, Coral Pink, Spring Green
*Melody	Teapot	Hall	1939	Canary, Cobalt, Chinese Red, other colors with or without gold trim
*Memory Lane	Astor	Blue Ridge		Pink, deep red, and yellow flowers
Memory Lane		Royal		
Memphis	Colonial	Blue Ridge		Pastel flowers, brown and black leaves, hatch-mark border
Mermaid	Ballerina	Universal	1950	Abstract
Merrileaf	True China	Red Wing	1960	Floral
Mesa	Encanto	Franciscan		
Metlox Poppy Trail, see Poppy Trail				
*Mexicana	Century	Homer Laughlin	1930s	Decal; orange and yellow pots of cacti
Mexicana	Montecito, San Marino	Vernon Kilns	1950–1955	Dark brown, rust, and yellow bands on border
Mexicana		W. S. George		Colored rim
Mexicana Kitchen Kraft		Homer Laughlin	1938	Mexican decals, scenes with different colored bands
Mexi-Gren		W. S. George	1930s	Mexican-style archway, pots, blanket; green rim
Mexi-Lido		W. S. George		Mexican-style pots
Meylinda	Colonial	Blue Ridge		Red, yellow, and blue flowers; gray leaves

PATTERN	SHAPE	MAKER	DATE	DESCRIPTION
Michigan Coastline	Montecito	Vernon Kilns	1937	Lake Michigan coast; blue and black on ivory ground
Mickey	Colonial	Blue Ridge		Red and pink flowers; green and gold leaves
Middlebury	Cavalier	Royal		Ironstone; large flower-burst center design
Midnight Rose	Anniversary	Red Wing	1953	Rose
Midsummer	Victory	Salem		Decals
Midsummer		Sebring-Limoges	1940	
Milkweed Dance	Montecito; Ultra	Vernon Kilns	1940	Floral pattern in blue, maroon
Ming Blossom	Woodcrest	Blue Ridge	1950s	Oriental motif; pink flowers, brown rim
Ming Tree (No. 4387)	Woodcrest	Blue Ridge	1950s	Gnarled tree; yellow dappled background
Ming Tree	Accent	E. M. Knowles	c.1954	
Mini Flowers	Deanna	E. M. Knowles		Small red flowers
Mirador		Homer Laughlin	1977-1978	
Mirasol	Mirasol	Franciscan		
Miss Terry	Teapot	Hall		H/3 mark; gold dots; also called Ohio
*Moby Dick	Ultra	Vernon Kilns	1939	Blue, brown, maroon, and orange; whaling scene
Mod Tulip	Colonial	Blue Ridge		Two red and yellow striped tulips with green leaves
Modern		J. A. Bauer	1935	Solids
Modern California	Montecito	Vernon Kilns	1937-1947	Azure, gray, ivory, orchid, Pistachio, Sand, Straw
Modern Classic	Four Seasons	E. M. Knowles	1960-1963	
Modern Orchid	Round; Trend	Paden City		Large center orchid; gold border
Modern Tulip	Plymouth	Harker	1930s	Stencil-type tulip design; muted colors
*Moderne	Teapot	Hall	1930s	Gold foot, knob, and inside of spout
Mojave	San Marino	Vernon Kilns	1955	Brown, green, yellow bands on rim
Monk's Head	Tankard/flagon	Hall		Decal of friar's head
Monogram		Salem		Gold initialed
Montecito	Montecito	Vernon Kilns	1935	

PATTERN	SHAPE	MAKER	DATE	DESCRIPTION
Monterey		J. A. Bauer	1934-early 1940s	Burgundy, ivory, light blue, orange-red, turquoise, red-brown, yellow, white
Monterey		Stangl	1967-1968; 1970	
Monterey	Melinda	Vernon Kilns	1942; 1950-1954	Red and blue leaf border
Monterey Moderne		J. A. Bauer	1948-1962	Black, burgundy, chartreuse, dark brown, gray, Olive Green, pink, yellow
Montezuma-Aztec	Montecito	Vernon Kilns	1937	Floral and geometric Aztec design; blue, green, rose, yellow; ivory ground
Montgomery Ward	Refrigerator Ware	Hall	Early 1940s	Delphinium, Mid-white
Monticello	E-Shape	Hall	1941-1959	Border; small, individual, pale flowers (made for Sears)
Monticello		Steubenville		
Montmartre	Futura	Red Wing	1960	French street scene
Moon Flower		Salem		
Moonflower		Watt	1949-1953	Pink floral design on black; also on green
Moon Song		J. A. Bauer		
Morning	Teapot	Hall		Solid colors or decals; sets with matching sugar and creamer
Morning Blue		Stangl	1970	
Morning Glory	Kitchenware	Hall	1942-1949	Cadet Blue with Hi-White features and morning glory; decal
Morning Glory	Concord	Red Wing	1947	
Morning Glory	Shenandoah	Paden City		Floral sprays
Morning Glory	Montecito	Vernon Kilns		Turquoise and blue flowers
Morningside	Delphian	Taylor, Smith, and Taylor	Late 1920s	Flower garden scene
Moss Rose (No. 4486)	Trailway	Blue Ridge	1950s	Hand painted
Moss Rose	Criterion	E. M. Knowles	1954	
Moss Rose		Universal Potteries	1953-1955	Decals

PATTERN	SHAPE	MAKER	DATE	DESCRIPTION
Mother Hubbard	Kiddieware	Stangl	Mid-1940s–1974	
Mountain Aster	Colonial	Blue Ridge		Pink and blue flowers
Mountain Bells	Colonial	Blue Ridge		Pink flowers
Mountain Cherry		Blue Ridge	1951	
Mountain Flower		Hall	1940	Cobalt; floral design; red line treatment
Mountain Ivy	Candlewick	Blue Ridge	1951	Two-tone green leaves, border
Mountain Laurel		Stangl	1947–1957	
Mountain Nosegay	Candlewick	Blue Ridge		Blue tulip and multicolored flowers
Mountain Sweetbriar	Skyline	Blue Ridge	1950s	Pink flowers
Mt. Vernon	E-Line	Hall	1941	Wreath with center decal of pink and green flowers; for Sears, Roebuck, and Co.
Multi Flori California	Montecito	Vernon Kilns	1935–1937	Petal outlined in blue, brown, green, rose, yellow; ivory ground
Mums		Hall	1930s	Pink mums
Mums		Taylor, Smith, and Taylor		Pink flowers; black and blue leaves
Muriel	Square; Colonial	Blue Ridge		Yellow and pink floral
Murphy	Teapot	Hall	Early 1940s	Victorian style; see also Benjamin, Birch, Bowknot, Connie, Plume
Nadine	Colonial	Blue Ridge		Floral
Nassau		Homer Laughlin		Border of large roses
Nassau	Concord	Red Wing	1947	
Nasturtium	Shell-Crest; Shenandoah	Paden City	1940s	Bright orange flower
Native American	Montecito	Vernon Kilns	1935–1937	Scenes of the Southwest; soft pastel colors
Native California	Melinda	Vernon Kilns	1942–1947	Pastels: aqua, blue, green, pink, yellow
Nautical	Candlewick	Blue Ridge		
*Nautilus	Teapot	Hall	1939	Seashell design

PATTERN	SHAPE	MAKER	DATE	DESCRIPTION
Nautilus	Nautilus	Homer Laughlin	1930s-1950s	Shell handles; borders, flowers
Navajo		Crown		Navajo design; red banded rim
Navarra	Williamsburg	E. M. Knowles	1955	
Neville		W. S. George		Small rosebuds interspersed on colored border; sold by Sears, Roebuck, and Co.
New Art	New Art	Homer Laughlin	1930s	Solid colors
New Princess		Sebring-Limoges		
*New York	Teapot	Hall	1920	Gold-decorated line; many sizes
Newell	Newell	Homer Laughlin	1927-1937	Gadroon edge; florals
Newport	Teapot	Hall	Early 1930s	Solid colors, gold decoration, or black decal
Newport		Stangl	1940-1942	Blue shading from dark to pale; matte finish; sailboat
Night Flower	Skyline	Blue Ridge	1952	White flowers on dark background
Night Song	Cavalier	Royal		Ironstone; bold patterned border
No. 488	Kitchenware	Hall	1930s	Flower decal
*Nocturne	Colonial	Blue Ridge		Rose-red flower; red brushed edge
Nora	Refrigerator Ware	Hall	1950s	
Nordic		Homer Laughlin	1977-1978	
Nordic Flower	Americana	E. M. Knowles	1959	
Norma	Colonial	Blue Ridge		Pink and blue flower border, green rim
Norma		Stangl		Della-Ware mark; pear branch in center; rings of color on rim
Normandy	Skyline	Blue Ridge	1950s	Two designs—one man, one woman—on sponged willow background; brown rim
Normandy	Provincial	Red Wing	1941	Blue and maroon bands, later apple blossoms added
Normandy Plaid		Purinton	1936-1959	Red plaid

PATTERN	SHAPE	MAKER	DATE	DESCRIPTION
Norris, see Nora				Water server in blue, canary, green lustre; also called Norris
North Star Cherry	Colonial	Blue Ridge		Cherries on border; red rim
North Wind	Montecito	Vernon Kilns	1948	Dark green and lime
Northern Lights	Futura	Red Wing	1960	Geometric blue
Norway Rose		Homer Laughlin		Floral decal
Nut Tree	Nut Tree	Franciscan		
Nutcracker	Ultra	Vernon Kilns	1940	Brown print border
Oakleaf	Criterion	E. M. Knowles	1955	
Oasis		Franciscan	1955	Mondrian-type design in soft blue and gray
Obion	Candlewick	Blue Ridge		Red and yellow flowers; red border
Octagon	Octagon	Catalina	1930s	Solids
October	October	Franciscan	1977	
Ohio, see Miss Terry				
Oklahoma, see Plainsman				
*Old Curiosity Shop	Cavalier	Royal China	1940s	Scenic center design; elaborate border
Old Dutch		Sebring-Limoges		
Old English		Homer Laughlin		Decal scene with castle
Old Mexico	Alara	Limoges		
Old Orchard		Stangl	1941-1942	
Old Provincial		Red Wing	1943	Aqua, brown bottom
Olinala (Olena)-Aztec	Montecito	Vernon Kilns	1937	Floral and geometric Aztec design; blue, green, rose, yellow; ivory ground
Olivia		Stangl		Della-Ware mark
Orange Blossom	Regina	Paden City		
Orange Poppy, see Poppy (Hall)				
*Orange Tree	Orange Tree	Homer Laughlin		Raised design on outside of nested bowls
Orbit		Homer Laughlin	1960s	Streamlined design; avocado, brown, and other colors
Orchard	Ultra	Vernon Kilns	1937; 1939	Hand-painted fruit design

PATTERN	SHAPE	MAKER	DATE	DESCRIPTION
Orchard Glory	Colonial	Blue Ridge		Yellow pear and red apple; broken green rim
Orchard Song		Stangl	1962-1974	Green and orange stylized fruit
Orchard Ware		Watt	1949-1959	Two-toned drip and spattered glaze combinations
*Organdie	Montecito	Vernon Kilns	1940-1958	Overall brown pattern; yellow and brown plaid border; see also Calico; Coronation Organdy; Gingham; Homespun; Tam O'Shanter; Tweed
Organdy		Homer Laughlin		Pastel border on eggshell; green handles
Oriental Poppy	Colonial	Blue Ridge		Three red poppies; red border
Orion	Colonial	Blue Ridge		Blue flowers; blue and black leaves
Orleans	Provincial	Red Wing	1941	Red rose
Oslo	Mayfair	E. M. Knowles	1954	
Our America	Ultra	Vernon Kilns	1939	State scenes; dark blue, maroon, and Walnut Brown on cream ground
Our Barnyard Friends	Kiddieware	Stangl		
Overtrue	Cavalier	Royal		Ironstone; bold center design
Paden Rose		Paden City		Large pale rose and bud
Painted Daisy	Colonial	Blue Ridge		Red, blue, yellow, and green flowers; broken green rim
Painted Desert	Ballerina	Universal	1950	Abstract
Paisley		Stangl	1963-1967	
Palm Brocade	Melinda	Vernon Kilns	1950	Palm leaves; linen textured background, brown shades
Palm Tree	New Art	E. M. Knowles		
Palm Tree		Purinton	1936-1959	Two palm trees
Palo Alto	Encanto	Franciscan		
Pan American Lei	Lotus	Vernon Kilns	1950	Lei design on pink ground
Pandora	Colonial	Blue Ridge		Floral design
Pansy		Harker		Pastel flowers

PATTERN	SHAPE	MAKER	DATE	DESCRIPTION
Pansy, see Rio Rose				
Pantry Shelf	Yorktown	E. M. Knowles		
Paper Roses	Colonial	Blue Ridge		
*Parade	Teapot	Hall	1942	Canary common color; also called Drape
Paradise	Coupe	Homer Laughlin		
Park Lane	Heritage	E. M. Knowles	1955	
Parsley	Salem	Salem		
Partridge Berry	Skyline	Blue Ridge	1950s	Yellow pear-like flower, red berry border
Passy	Ballerina	Universal	1950	Abstract
Pastel Garden	Sabina	Sabin		
Pastel Morning Glory	D-Style	Hall	1930s	Pink flowers
Pastel Poppy	Astor	Blue Ridge		Pink flowers and border
Pastel Tulip		Harker		Floral decals
Patchwork Posy	Colonial	Blue Ridge		Red plaid; blue plaid flowers
*Pate Sur Pate		Harker		Scalloped border; solid colors
Pate-Sur-Pate	Shalimar	Steubenville		
Patio	Shell-Crest	Paden City	1907–1950s	Mexican decal decoration
Patricia	Skyline	Blue Ridge	1950s	Brown and gray flowers; also called Phoenix
Patrician, see Phoenix				
Pauda (Freesia)	Pauda	Franciscan		Hand painted
Pauline	Astor	Blue Ridge		Yellow flowers; wide yellow and thin brown border
Peach		Pottery Guild		Peaches and lavender flowers
Peach Blossom	Bolero	W. S. George		Sprigs of small pink flowers (Cynthia has same decal on Lido shape)
Peach Blossom	Hallcraft	Hall		Designed by Eva Zeisel
Peach Blossom	Accent	E. M. Knowles	1955	
Pear		Pottery Guild		Fruit grouping
Pear Turnpike		Vernon Kilns		Brown
Peasant Ware, see Hercules				
Pebble Beach	Pebble Beach	Franciscan		

PATTERN	SHAPE	MAKER	DATE	DESCRIPTION
Pedro & Conchita	Montecito	Vernon Kilns	1937	Indian man and woman
Pembrooke	Colonial	Blue Ridge		Yellow flowers; pink dot border
Pennsylvania Dutch		Purinton	1936-1959	Red and blue plaid tulips around border
Penny Serenade	Colonial	Blue Ridge		Red and blue flowers, green leaves, border
Penthouse	Yorktown	E. M. Knowles		Flowerpots
Peony	Colonial	Blue Ridge		Centered large pink flower; pink and green line border
Peony Bouquet	Candlewick	Blue Ridge		One pink and three blue flowers
Pepe	New Shape	Red Wing	1963	Geometric; Bittersweet, dark bluish-purple, and green
Peppers	Montecito	Vernon Kilns	1937	Multicolored peppers on ivory or sand ground
Periwinkle	Astor	Blue Ridge		Two-tone blue flower and leaves
Petalware		W. S. George	Late 1930s	Solid colors: black, blue, coral, ivory, pink, red, turquoise
Peter Rabbit	Kiddieware	Stangl		
*Petit Point		Crown	1941	Flower bouquet, stitch effect
*Petit Point		Leigh/Crescent		Floral border, stitch effect
*Petit Point		Sold by Montgomery Ward	1936	Decals, stitch effect
*Petit Point		Taylor, Smith, and Taylor		
Petit Point Basket		Salem		Flower basket; stitch effect
Petit Point Bouquet	Delphian	Taylor, Smith, and Taylor	Late 1920s	Stitched flowers
Petit Point House		Crooksville		Decal of stitched houses, trees; also called House
Petit Point Leaf		Crooksville		Decals, stitched
Petit Point Rose		Harker		Rose border, stitched
Petit Point Rose	Fleurette	W. S. George		Stitched floral
Petite Flowers		Stangl	1970-1974	

PATTERN	SHAPE	MAKER	DATE	DESCRIPTION
Petitpoint		Homer Laughlin	1960s	Floral decal-like stitched petit point
Petunia	Colonial	Blue Ridge		Red and blue flowers, border
Petunia		Hall	1932-1969	Pink floral decal
Phacelia	Montecito	Vernon Kilns		Pink flowers
Pheasant	LaGrande	Crooksville		Flying birds; scenic
*Philadelphia	Teapot	Hall	1923	Variety of colors, decals, or gold trim; many sizes
Philodendron	Melinda	Vernon Kilns	1942; 1950-1954	Green and yellow leaf border
Phoenix	Refrigerator Ware	Hall	1938	Westinghouse; cobalt, Delphinium, Lettuce; also called Patrician
Picardy	Clinchfield	Blue Ridge		Centered man, woman, and ducks; pink border
Picardy	Village Green	Red Wing	1960	Yellow rose
Piccadilly	Piccadilly	Homer Laughlin	1940s-1950s	Floral band
Picket Fence	Yorktown	E. M. Knowles		Brightly colored floral and fence
Picnic	Picnic	Franciscan		
Pie Crust		Stangl	1969	
Piedmont Plaid	Square	Blue Ridge		Brown plaid on yellow swirled background
Pilgrims	Skyline	Blue Ridge	1950s	Figures in center; flowered border
Pine Cone		Harker		Wispy, brown design
Pinecone	Skyline	Blue Ridge	1950s	Pinecones with gray swirled background
Pinecone Spray	Fiesta	Homer Laughlin		Decal
Pink Border	LaGrande	Crooksville		Tiny pink floral border
Pink Carousel	Kiddieware	Stangl	Mid-1940s-1974	
Pink Cosmos		Stangl	1966	Marked Prestige
Pink Dogwood	Moderne	Blue Ridge	1950s	Stylized
Pink Dogwood	Classique	E. M. Knowles	1960	
Pink Dogwood		Stangl		
Pink Fairy	Kiddieware	Stangl	Mid-1940s-1974	
Pink Lady	Vernon Ware	Metlox	1965	

PATTERN	SHAPE	MAKER	DATE	DESCRIPTION
Pink Lily		Stangl	1953-1957	
Pink Morning Glory		Hall		Early decal
Pink Moss Rose		Homer Laughlin	1920	Decal
Pink Mums		Hall	1930s	Floral decals
Pink Pastel		E. M. Knowles		Pale pink and white with pink flowers
Pink Petticoat	Colonial	Blue Ridge		Pink flowers; rim
Pink Print		Sold by Montgomery Ward	1936	Decals
Pink Rose		Homer Laughlin	1920	Decals
Pink Rose & Daisy	Plain Edge	Homer Laughlin	1920	Decals
Pink Spice	Anniversary	Red Wing	1953	Butterfly design
Pinkie	Skyline	Blue Ridge	1950s	Pink flowers; sponged center; green rim
Pintoria		Metlox	c.1939	
Pippin	Skyline	Blue Ridge	1950s	Three red apples; green rim
Plaid, see Calico; Gay Plaid; Gingham; Homespun; Organdie; Tam O'Shanter; Tweed				
Plain	Refrigerator Ware	Hall		Westinghouse ovenware: Delphinium; also called Queen
Plain	Gypsy Trail	Red Wing	1935	Blue, ivory, orange, turquoise, yellow
Plain-Jane	Lido	W. S. George	1949-present	Black, brown, gold, green, red, yellow
Plainsman		Frankoma		Also called Oklahoma
*Plantation Ivy	Skyline	Blue Ridge	1950s	Yellow and green ivy
Playful Pups	Kiddieware	Stangl	Mid-1940s-1974	
Plaza	Regrigerator Ware	Hall	1930s-1960s	Water server
Plum	Candlewick	Blue Ridge		Purple fruit
Plum		Stangl	1940	Blue, green, tan
Plum Blossom	Dynasty	Red Wing	1949	Pink or yellow flower, oriental motif; six-sided
Plum Duff	Candlewick	Blue Ridge		Two plums; gray and gold swirled background
Plum Pudding	Kitchenware	Hall		White bowls with holly decals

PATTERN	SHAPE	MAKER	DATE	DESCRIPTION
Plume	Astor	Blue Ridge		Three rose plums; rose border; light blue rim
*Plume	Teapot	Hall	Early 1940s	Victorian style; see also Benjamin, Birch, Bowknot, Connie, Murphy
Pocahontas	Common-wealth	James River Pottery		
Poinsettia	Colonial	Blue Ridge	1950	Hand-painted red flowers, gray leaves
Polka Dot	Colonial	Blue Ridge		Flowers, center, random dots
Polka Dot		Hall	1942	
Polo	Tricone	Salem		Decals
Polychrome A	Montecito	Vernon Kilns	1935-1937	Rims decorated with brightly colored blocks
Pom Pom	Candlewick	Blue Ridge		Red and blue flower; red border
Pomegranate	Montecito	Vernon Kilns	1935-1937	Pink with ivory
Pompadour	Sabina	Sabin	c.1946	
Pompeii	New Shape	Red Wing	1962	Geometric
Pony Tail	Kiddieware	Stangl	Mid-1940s–1974	
Poppy		Crown		Floral center; pastel vinelike border
Poppy	Rainbow	W. S. George		Center design of three flowers
*Poppy	C-Line	Hall	1933-1950s	Floral decals; orange poppies
Poppy	Deanna	E. M. Knowles	1948	Orange floral spray
Poppy	Shenandoah	Paden City		Floral border
*Poppy & Wheat	Radiance; Kitchenware	Hall	1933-c.1939	Orange flowers, green leaves
Poppy-Flower	Floral Edge	E. M. Knowles	1933-1934	Decals
*Poppy Trail		Metlox	1934-1942	15 solid colors, including Delphinium Blue, Canary Yellow, ivory, Old Rose, peach, Poppy Orange, rust, turquoise
Posey Shop	Triumph	Sebring-Limoges	1944-1945	
Posies	LaGrande	Crooksville		Pastel flowers
Posies	Coupe	Paden City		Abstract flowers

PATTERN	SHAPE	MAKER	DATE	DESCRIPTION
Posies		Stangl	1973	
Potpourri	Colonial	Blue Ridge		Off-centered floral; black line border
Prelude		Stangl	1949-1957	Stylized flower design
Pretty Pinks	Accent	E. M. Knowles	1957	
Primitive Bird, see Bird				
Primrose Path	Astor	Blue Ridge		Red, yellow, and blue flower border
Prince, see Adonis				
Priscilla	Clinchfield	Blue Ridge		Red and blue flowers, center and border
Priscilla	Kitchen Kraft	Homer Laughlin	1940s-1950s	Pale pink roses and sprigs of flowers
Pristine	Colonial	Blue Ridge		Blue flowers and leaves, border
Provincial	Kitchenware	Hall	1938	Clay-colored with American Indian
*Provincial		Stangl	1957-1967	Floral center; border
Provincial Blue	Poppytrail line	Metlox	1951	
Provincial Bouquet	Tempo	Knowles	1961-1963	
Provincial Fruit	Poppytrail	Metlox	c.1965-1980	Solid border with cluster of fruit in center
Provincial Tulip		Harker	1959	Cameoware
Provincial Wreath		Harker		Stoneware; Pennsylvania Dutch design
Puritan	Royal Gadroon	Harker		Plain white
Pussy Willow		W. S. George		
Quaker Maid		Harker	1960s	Dark brown, drips of lighter color
Quartette	Concord	Red Wing	1947	Four solid colors
Queen, see Plain				
Queen Anne's Lace	Skyline	Blue Ridge	1950s	Dark flowers; brown, gray, and green leaves
Queen Anne's Lace	Esquire	E. M. Knowles	1955-1962	Russel Wright; abstract decal
Queen Rose	Coupe	Crooksville		Pastel rose stem; also called Dinner Rose
Quilted Fruit		Blue Ridge	1950s	Fruit design, printed calicos

PATTERN	SHAPE	MAKER	DATE	DESCRIPTION
Quilted Ivy	Woodcrest	Blue Ridge	1950s	Red plaid, black, and yellow ivy
R.F.D.	San Fernando	Vernon Kilns	1951–1953; 1954	Brown rooster; green plaid border
Radiance, see Sunshine				
Radiant Ware	Kitchenware	Hall	1940s	Bowls; blue, green, red, yellow
Raffia	San Marino	Vernon Kilns	1953–1954	Green and brown; like tree bark; same as Barkwood and Shantung except for color
Rainbow		Hall		Hall's Radiant Ware
Rainbow	Rainbow	W. S. George	Late 1930s	Solid colors
Rainelle	Colonial	Blue Ridge		Bold pastel flowers
Raisin	Ring	Vernon Kilns		Drip glaze; solids
Rambler Rose	Aristocrat	E. M. Knowles	1930s	Decals
Rambler Rose	Eggshell Georgian	Homer Laughlin		(American Vogue backstamp), small rose sprigs
Rambler Rose		Universal		Rose medallions
Rancho	Zephyr	French Saxon		Solid dark colors
Random Harvest		Red Wing	1961	Hand-painted brown, copper, coral, green, and turquoise on flecked dish
Ranger		Stangl		Cowboys and cactus
Ranger Boy	Kiddieware	Stangl	Mid-1940s– 1974	
Ravenna	Ravenna	Homer Laughlin		Embossed rim
Rawhide		Harker	1960s	Stoneware; dark brown
Raymond	Yellowstone	Homer Laughlin	1926	Floral decal
*Raymor		Roseville (Ben Siebel)	1952–1953	Black, brown, dark green, gray, ivory, mottled green, rust; modern
Raymore	Contempora	Steubenville (Ben Siebel)		Three-dimensional rippling; charcoal, Fawn, Mist Gray, Sand White
Razzle Dazzle	Skyline	Blue Ridge	1950s	Black, gray, and red leaves; sponged background
Red & Gold		Sold by Montgomery Ward	1936	Decals
Red Apple		Blue Ridge		Center apple; green rim

PATTERN	SHAPE	MAKER	DATE	DESCRIPTION
Red Apple 1		Harker		Small, continuous apple decal
Red Apple 2		Harker		Large, individual apple decal
Red Bank		Blue Ridge		Red and blue flowers; green leaves border
Red Barn	Skyline	Blue Ridge	1950s	Red barn and fence; yellow sponged background; brown rim
Red Berry	Victory	Salem		Decals
Red Cone Flower	Clinchfield	Blue Ridge		Large red flower and bud; green, blue, and yellow leaves
Red Dot	Kitchenware	Hall		Red dot on Eggshell White
Red Ivy		Stangl	1957	
*Red Poppy	D-Line	Hall	1930-1950	Made for Grand Union Tea Company; red flowers, black leaves
*Red Riding Hood	Figural	Hull	1943-1957	Three-dimensional little girl; also called Little Red Riding Hood
Red Rooster	Skyline	Blue Ridge		Red and blue rooster center, red rim
*Red Rooster	Poppytrail line	Metlox	1955-1980	Red, yellow and green rooster; some solid red
Red Rose		Paden City		Red rose decal, rosebud decal
Red Starflower, see Starflower				
Red Tulip	Candlewick	Blue Ridge		Red tulip border
Red Tulip	Kitchen Kraft	Homer Laughlin		Decals
Red Willow	Colonial	Blue Ridge		Red oriental scene; rim
Red Wing Rose	Futura	Red Wing	1960	Rose
Reed	Gypsy Trail	Red Wing	1935	Blue, ivory, orange, turquoise, yellow
Reflection	Four Seasons	E. M. Knowles	1960-1963	

*Refrigerator Ware, see Adonis; General Electric; Hercules; Hotpoint; Montgomery Ward; Nora; Phoenix; Plaza; Ridged; Sears, Roebuck and Co.; Zephyr

Regal	Teapot	Hall		By J. Palin Thorley
Regal Rings	Queen Anne	Sabin	c.1946	
Remembrance	Citation	Steubenville		

PATTERN	SHAPE	MAKER	DATE	DESCRIPTION
Republic	Republic	Homer Laughlin	1900-1940s	Scalloped edge with embossing; florals, gold trim
Rhapsody	Colonial	Blue Ridge		Blue, pink, and yellow flowers; yellow border
Rhea	Trend	Steubenville		
Rhonda	Americana	E. M. Knowles	1958	
Rhythm	Teapot	Hall	1939	Cadet, Canary, Chinese Red common colors
*Rhythm		Homer Laughlin	1951-1958	Harlequin colors; simple, modern shapes
Rhythm		Paden City	1936	
*Rhythm Rose	Century	Homer Laughlin	Mid-1940s-1950s	Large center rose
Rialto		Stangl		Della-Ware mark; yellow flowers on blue background
Ribbed, see Flute				
Ribbon	Criterion	E. M. Knowles	1954	
Ribbon Plaid	Skyline	Blue Ridge	1950s	Green and yellow
Richmond	E-Style	Hall	1941	Granitetone; yellow daisies and other flowers
Rick-Rack		Blair		Yellow and brown
Ridge Rose	Colonial	Blue Ridge		Pink flower; broken pink border
Ridged	Refrigerator	Hall		Westinghouse ovenware; Canary; also called King
Ring-A-Round	Four Seasons	E. M. Knowles	1959-1963	
Ring-O-Roses	Piecrust	Blue Ridge	1948	Red rosebud border
*Ring		J. A. Bauer	1932-1962	Solids: black, Burnt Orange, dark blue, green, ivory, maroon, yellow; pastels: chartreuse, gray, green, light yellow, olive, pale blue, pink, turquoise, white; also called Beehive
Ringles		Stangl	1973-1974	
Rio		Salem	1943	
Rio Chico	Ultra	Vernon Kilns	1938	Pink border; center floral design
Rio Rose		Hall	1950s	Floral, some with bands and swirls; sometimes called Pansy

PATTERN	SHAPE	MAKER	DATE	DESCRIPTION
Rio Verda	Ultra	Vernon Kilns	1938	Green border; center floral design
Rio Vista	Ultra	Vernon Kilns	1938	Blue border; center floral design
Rite of Spring		Paden City		
*Riviera	Century	Homer Laughlin	1938-1950	Made for Murphy Co.; solids: blue, dark blue, ivory, light green, mauve, red, yellow
Roan Mountain Rose	Colonial	Blue Ridge		Pink flowers; bold green leaves; pink line border
Roanoke	Astor	Blue Ridge		Red, blue, and yellow flowers
Rock Garden	Skyline	Blue Ridge	1950s	Small blue and gray flowers; gray rim
Rock Castle	Skyline	Blue Ridge	1950s	Gray and brown leaves
Rock Rose	Colonial	Blue Ridge		Hand painted; pink flowers and green leaves
Rockmount		Coors	Late 1930s	Colored tableware and ovenware; blue, green, ivory, orange, rose, yellow
Rockport Rooster	Candlewick	Blue Ridge		Stylized rooster center
Rococo	Princess	Paden City	1933	
Rodelay	Tempo	E. M. Knowles	1961-1963	
Romance	Cavalier	Homer Laughlin		
Romance	Regent	E. M. Knowles	1955	
*Ronald Reagan	Teapot	Hall	1970s	Three-dimensional caricature resembling Ronald Reagan
*Rooster (or Game Cock)		Blue Ridge	1950s	Red rooster
Rooster		Harker		Blue, pink; cameoware
Rooster		Stangl	1970-1974	Gold background; rooster center
Rooster Motto	Candlewick	Blue Ridge		Rooster center; "My love will stop when this rooster crows" on border
Rope Edge	Rope Edge	Catalina	1936	Solids
Rosa	Ultra	Vernon Kilns	1938	Large single rose, border of rosebuds

PATTERN	SHAPE	MAKER	DATE	DESCRIPTION
Rosalinde	Colonial	Blue Ridge		Pink, purple, and yellow flowers
Rose	Deanna	E. M. Knowles		Pale rose and buds
Rose & Lattice	Plain edge	Homer Laughlin	1920	Decals
*Rose-A-Day	Anytime	Vernon Kilns	1956-1958	Pink rose, pastel leaves, ivory ground
Rose Bouquet	Floral edge	E. M. Knowles	1933-1934	
Rose Bud	Horizon	Steubenville		
Rose Garden	Gray Lure	Crooksville		Rose spray
Rose Garland		Crooksville	1920s	Border of tiny roses
Rose Garland Border		Homer Laughlin	1920	Decals
Rose Hill	Colonial	Blue Ridge		Pink, purple, and rose flowers
Rose Leaf		Syracuse		
Rose-Marie		Salem		Large cluster of rosebuds; platinum edge
Rose Marie		Sebring-Limoges		
*Rose Parade	Kitchenware	Hall	1941-1950s	Cadet Blue body, Hi-White knobs and handles; rose decals
Rose Point	Stafford Rose	Pope-Gosser		Embossed roses
Rose Red	Candlewick	Blue Ridge		Red flowers; green leaves border
Rose Spray		Harker		Allover pattern; tiny pink and yellow flowers
Rose Tree	Criterion	E. M. Knowles	1955	
*Rose White	Kitchenware	Hall	1941	Hi-White body; trimmed in silver with a pink floral decal
Rosebud		Coors, Golden Co.	1920-1939	Blue, green, ivory, maroon, turquoise, yellow; raised rosebud and leaf design
Rosebud	Horizon	Steubenville		
Rosedale	Melinda	Vernon Kilns	1950	Roses
Rosemont	Victoria	E. M. Knowles	1948	
Roses	Birds; Bolero	Crooksville		Multicolored flowers
Rosetta		Homer Laughlin		Bird hovering over flowers
Rosette	Colonial	Blue Ridge		Blue and yellow flowers; broken pink rim

PATTERN	SHAPE	MAKER	DATE	DESCRIPTION
Rosettes		Harker		Thin sprays of flowers on border and in center
Rosey	Moderne	Blue Ridge	1950s	
Rosita	Ranchero	W. S. George		Rose blossoms
Roundelay (No. 4499)	Trailway	Blue Ridge		
Round-up	Casual	Red Wing	1958	
Roxanna		Universal		Decals
Roxanne		Stangl	1972-1974	Blue flowers and rim
Royal	Teapot	Hall		White; some with gold
Royal Brocade	Forcast	E. M. Knowles	1957	
Royal Harvest	Coupe	Homer Laughlin		
Royal Danish		Watt	1965	Basket weave design in brown, chartreuse, cream
Royal Marina	Sebring	Sebring-Limoges	1944-1945	
Royal Rose	Kitchenware	Hall	late 1940s–early 1950s	Cadet Blue exterior; Hi-White handles and knobs; silver trim; floral decals
Royal Rose		Harker		Bright single rose decal
Royal Windsor		Salem	1950s	
Ruby	Clinchfield	Blue Ridge		Blue; large red flowers with blue centers border
Ruffled Tulip		Harker		Bright flowers
Rugosa	Colonial	Blue Ridge		Large yellow flowers with brown centers and green leaves

Russel Wright, see also American Modern; Botanica; Grass; Highlight; Iroquois; Queen Anne's Lace; Seeds; Solar; Sterling; White Clover

Russel Wright		Bauer	1945	Art pottery
Russel Wright	Vitreous restaurant ware	Sterling	1948	Cedar Brown, Ivy Green, Straw Yellow, Suede Gray
Rust Bouquet	LaGrande	Crooksville		Fall shades
Rust Floral	Lido	W. S. George		Predominantly orange flowers
Rust Tulip	Shell-Crest	Paden City		Assorted flowers
Rust Tulip	Victory	Salem		Assorted pastel flowers
Rustic		Stangl	1965-1974	
Rustic Garden		Stangl	1972-1974	Orange flowers; green border

PATTERN	SHAPE	MAKER	DATE	DESCRIPTION
Rustic Plaid	Skyline	Blue Ridge	1950s	Black plaid and rim; sponged background
Rutherford	Teapot	Hall		Smooth version of fluted kitchenware pot; white with trim, dots, or decals
Rutledge	Colonial	Blue Ridge		Blue bow, red tulips
Saf-Handle	Refrigerator Ware	Hall	1938–1960s	Chinese Red most common color; also called Sundial
*Saf-Handle	Teapot	Hall	1938	Canary most common color; also called Sundial
Sailing	Georgette	W. S. George		Variety of boats on border
Sailing	Tricorne	Salem		Decals, coral and black sailboats
*Salamina	Ultra	Vernon Kilns	1939	Scenes of Greenland with girl
Sampler	Piecrust	Blue Ridge	1948	Red flower; green border
Sampler	Victory	Salem		Decals
Sandra		Salem	1950s	
Sani-Grid	Kitchenware	Hall	1941	Decal; Chinese Red, Cadet; Hi-White handle and knobs
*Sani-Grid	Teapot	Hall	1941	Contrasting Hi-White handle and knob
Santa Anita	Melinda	Vernon Kilns	1942	Pink blossoms on border
Santa Barbara	Ultra	Vernon Kilns	1939	Brown print; blue and yellow flowers
Santa Clara	Ultra	Vernon Kilns	1939	Blue, pink print; allover flower and leaf
Santa Maria	Ultra	Vernon Kilns	1939	Purple print; blue and yellow flowers
Santa Paula	Ultra	Vernon Kilns	1939	Pink print; blue and yellow flowers
Saratoga	Skyline	Blue Ridge	1952	
Sarepta	Colonial	Blue Ridge		Multicolored flowers; yellow border
Scandia	Accent	E. M. Knowles	1954	
Scotch Plaid	Coupe	Crooksville		Plaid center design
Scroll	Accent	E. M. Knowles	1955	
*Sculptured Daisy	Poppytrail	Metlox	1965	
Sculptured Fruit		Stangl	1966–1974	Marked Prestige; fruit border

PATTERN	SHAPE	MAKER	DATE	DESCRIPTION
*Sculptured Grape	Poppytrail line	Metlox	1963-1975	Sculpted grapevine; blue, brown, green
Sculptured Zinnia	Poppytrail	Metlox	1965-1980	Sculpted zinnias; brown, green, orange, yellow-gold on cream background
Sea Fare	Forcast	E. M. Knowles	1957	
Sea Shell		Paden City		
Sears, Roebuck and Co.	Refrigerator ware	Hall		Cadet, Hi-White
Seeds	Esquire	E. M. Knowles	1956-1962	Russel Wright; abstract decal
September Song	Forcast	E. M. Knowles	1959	
Sequoia		E. M. Knowles	Late 1930s	Bright floral bouquet
*Serenade	D-Shape	Hall		Sprigs of orange flowers
*Serenade		Homer Laughlin	1940s	Solid pastels: blue, green, pink
Serenade	Classique	E. M. Knowles	1960	
Sesame		Stangl	1972-1974	Brown stylized flower and rim
Seven Seas	San Marino	Vernon Kilns	1954	Brown and blue sailboats
Sevilla				Solids, similar to Harlequin
Shadow Fruit	Skyline; Moderne	Blue Ridge	1950s	Stylized line drawing of fruit; green rim
Shadow Leaf	San Marino	Vernon Kilns	1954-1955	Red and green flowers on green swirled background; same as Trade Winds, but different colors
Shaggy Tulip	Kitchenware	Hall	Mid-1930s-mid-1940s	
Shalimar	Shalimar	Steubenville		
Shantung	San Marino	Vernon Kilns	1953	Clothlike texture; brown and green; same as Barkwood and Raffia except for color
Sheffield		Salem	1943	
Shellridge		Harker		Gold decal design
Shellware, see Cameo Shellware				
Sherry	Colonial	Blue Ridge		Red and blue flower, border
Sherwood	Anytime	Vernon Kilns	1955-1958	Brown, bronze, and gold leaves on beige background

PATTERN	SHAPE	MAKER	DATE	DESCRIPTION
Shoo Fly	Colonial	Blue Ridge		Yellow and pink flowers
Shortcake	Lido	W. S. George		Strawberry decal
Showgirl	Candlewick	Blue Ridge		Red and yellow flowers; broken green rim
Sierra		Stangl	1967/1968-1970	Marked Prestige
Sierra Madre	Ultra	Vernon Kilns	1938	Pink, green, blue border
Signal Flags	Piecrust	Blue Ridge	1948	Red and black squares
*Silhouette		Crooksville	1930s	Silhouette decal; dog included
Silhouette	Skyline	Blue Ridge	1950s	Clothlike appearance; various colors
Silhouette		Hall	1930s	Black decal
Silhouette		Harker		
Silhouette		Taylor, Smith, and Taylor		
Silver Rose		Homer Laughlin	1960s	Floral decals
Silver Spray	Accent	E. M. Knowles	1954	
Simplicity	Accent	E. M. Knowles	1955	
Skiffs	Yorktown	E. M. Knowles		
Skyblue		Homer Laughlin	1977-1978	
Skylark	Americana	E. M. Knowles	1959	
Skyline Songbirds	Skyline	Blue Ridge	1950s	Eight different birds
Skytone		Homer Laughlin		Light blue
Sleeping Mexican	Deanna	E. M. Knowles		Mexican style; man sleeping under palm tree
Slender Leaf		Harker		Gray border; graceful leaf design
Smart Set	Casual	Red Wing	1955	
Smoky Mountain Laurel	Candlewick	Blue Ridge		Solid light blue with dark blue border
Smooth		J. A. Bauer	1936-1937	Solids
Snappy	Colonial	Blue Ridge		Red and blue flower
Snowflake		Homer Laughlin	1920	Decals
Snowflake		Sold by Montgomery Ward	1936	Decals
Snowflower		E. M. Knowles	1956	Russel Wright

PATTERN	SHAPE	MAKER	DATE	DESCRIPTION
Soddy-Daisy	Skyline	Blue Ridge	1950s	Small brown and cream flowers; red and green leaves; allover pattern
Solar	Esquire	E. M. Knowles	1957-1966	Russel Wright; abstract decal
Sombrero		Pottery Guild		Brightly colored fruit in straw basket
Sonata	Skyline	Blue Ridge	1950s	Blue flowers; pink buds
Sonesta		Homer Laughlin	1977-1978	
Songbirds	Astor	Blue Ridge		Eight different bird designs
Sorrento		Homer Laughlin	1977-1978	
Southern Belle	Coupe; Iva-Lure	Crooksville		Large single rosebud
Southern Camelia	Piecrust	Blue Ridge	1948	Pink flower, blue eaves, broken blue rim
Southern Dogwood	Skyline	Blue Ridge	1950s	Hand-painted cream dogwood
Southern Rose	Melinda	Vernon Kilns	1942	Floral bouquet
Southwind	Forcast	E. M. Knowles	1959	
Sowing Seed	Square	Blue Ridge		Farmer; broken blue border
Speck Ware		J. A. Bauer	1946	Gray, pink, tan, white
Spice Islands	Montecito	Vernon Kilns	1950	Map of East and West Indies; sailing ships; marked "da Bron"
Spider, see Spring Blossom				
Spiderweb	Skyline	Blue Ridge	1950s	Various solid colors, flecked finish
Spindrift	Candlewick	Blue Ridge		Center circle of small blue, red, and yellow flowers; thin red border
Spray	Piecrust	Blue Ridge	1950s	Small black and yellow flowers; green leaves
Spray	Coupe	Crooksville		Pink ground; gray and black decal
Sprig Crocus		Hall		Several sprigs on border
Spring	Trend	Steubenville		
Spring Blossom	LaGrande	Crooksville	1940s	Delicate floral sprays; also called Spider
Spring Bouquet		Sold for Montgomery Ward	1936	Decals

PATTERN	SHAPE	MAKER	DATE	DESCRIPTION
Spring Glory	Candlewick	Blue Ridge		Hand-painted blue flower and band
Spring Hill Tulip	Colonial	Blue Ridge		Centered plaid tulips
Spring Song	Cavalier	Homer Laughlin		
Spring Song	Concord	Red Wing	1947	Birds
Springblossom	Regina	Paden City		Large multicolored pastel flowers
Springtime		W. S. George	1940s	Open window with flower trellis
Springtime		Hall		Pink flowers on Hi-White body
Springtime		Harker		Large single budding flower
Spun Gold		Stangl	1965-1967	
Square Dance	Colonial	Blue Ridge		Party set of square dancers
Squares	Skyline	Blue Ridge	1950s	Three squares and ribbon
Standard		Salem		Narrow floral sprays; blue edge
Stanhome Ivy	Skyline	Blue Ridge	1950s	Stylized green ivy sprig
*Star	Teapot	Hall	1940	Turquoise or cobalt with gold stars
Star Bright	Accent	E. M. Knowles	1957	
*Star Flower		Stangl	1952-1957	Large center flower
*Starburst		Franciscan	1954	Stylized geometric stars
Stardancer	Colonial	Blue Ridge		Two-handled vase with pink flowers
Stardust		Stangl	1967	
*Stardust	Skytone	Homer Laughlin	1940s-1950s	Light blue background; stylized flowers
Starflower		Watt	1953-1965	Red flower with yellow center and green leaves on cream; also pink on green, pink on black, white on red, white on blue, green on brown known as Silhouette
Starlight	Teapot	Hall		Band of stars; some with rhinestones
Step-Down	Coffeepot	Hall		Sugar and creamer; large and small sizes; different handles

PATTERN	SHAPE	MAKER	DATE	DESCRIPTION
Step-Round	Coffeepot	Hall		Large and small sizes; same handles
*Sterling		Sterling China Co.		Russel Wright; Ivy Green, Straw Yellow, Suede Gray, and Cedar Brown.
Still Life	Colonial	Blue Ridge		Bowl of fruit
Strathmoor	Colonial	Blue Ridge		Big dark and yellow flowers; broken rim
Stratosphere	Forcast	E. M. Knowles	1955–1957	
Strawberry	Shenandoah	Paden City		Strawberry plant border
Strawberry Patch	Colonial	Blue Ridge		Strawberries; green and blue leaves
Strawberry Sundae	Skyline	Blue Ridge	1950s	Red strawberries; broken green rim
Streamers	Skyline	Blue Ridge	1950s	Ribbons
*Streamline	Teapot	Hall	1937	Canary and Delphinium most common colors; often silver trim
Style	Ultra	Vernon Kilns	1939	Fruit and floral border
Suburbia	Forcast	E. M. Knowles	1956	
Summer Day		Salem		Blue and white flowerpot with floral sprays
Sun Drops	Astor	Blue Ridge		Yellow and orange flowers, centered; miniature flowers border
Sun Garden	San Marino	Vernon Kilns	1953	Butterflies and flowers on green ground
Sun-Glo	Olympic	Harker	c.1955	Harmony House mark
Sun Glow	Forcast	E. M. Knowles	1958	
Sun Gold	Liberty	Homer Laughlin	1953	Currier & Ives decorations
Sun Porch	Fiesta	Homer Laughlin		Decal; striped umbrella, table scene
Sunbright	Colonial	Blue Ridge		Yellow flowers, border; green line rim
Sunburst	Tempo	E. M. Knowles	1959	
Sundance	Candlewick	Blue Ridge		Large yellow flowers; border design
Sundial, see Saf-Handles				
Sunfire	Colonial	Blue Ridge		Yellow flowers, gray leaves
Sunflower		Blue Ridge	c.1947	Large flowers

PATTERN	SHAPE	MAKER	DATE	DESCRIPTION
Sundowner	Candlewick	Blue Ridge		Two blue and two yellow flowers around plate
Sungold	Candlewick	Blue Ridge		
*Sunny	Colonial	Blue Ridge		Yellow flowers
Sunny Day	Cavalier	Royal		Ironstone; large flower branch
Sunnybrook Farm	Accent	E. M. Knowles	1957	
Sunrise	Woodcrest	Blue Ridge	1950s	Sun rising behind a log cabin
Sunshine	Candlewick	Blue Ridge		Yellow flowers center; thin red border
Sunshine	Kitchenware	Hall	1933	Kitchenware; decals, lettering, solids; blue, Canary, Cadet, Chinese Red, Delphinium, Dresden Emerald, Indian Red, ivory, Lettuce, Marine, maroon, pink, rose, turquoise, yellow
Sunshine		Stangl		
Surfside	Teapot	Hall	1939	Seashell-type pot
Susan	Skyline	Blue Ridge	1950s	Rust flowers
Susan		Stangl	1972-1974	Gold daisies and rim
Susan	Trend	Steubenville		
Susannah	Colonial	Blue Ridge		Pink and red flowers; thin red border; pink rim
Swedish		Crown		Modern flowers
Sweet Clover	Candlewick	Blue Ridge		
Sweet Pea	Colonial	Blue Ridge		Pastel blue and pink flowers on border; pink rim
Sweet Pea	Empire	Taylor, Smith, and Taylor		Pink decal
Sweet Rocket	Woodcrest	Blue Ridge	1950s	Brown and pink thistles; green rim
Swing	Swing	Homer Laughlin	1938-1950s	Solid color handles, curved rims, decals
Swirl	Coupe	Crooksville		Flower sprigs on border pointing to center
Symmetry	Tempo	E. M. Knowles	1959	
Symphony	Colonial	Blue Ridge		Red flowers; blue leaves

PATTERN	SHAPE	MAKER	DATE	DESCRIPTION
T-Ball	Teapot	Hall	1948	Square or round; silver; marked Made for Bacharach, Inc. of New York
Tahiti A, B, C	Montecito	Vernon Kilns		Blue, soft rose, ivory
Tahiti	Triumph	Sebrig-Limoges	1938	
Tahitian Gold	New Shape	Red Wing	1962	Gold
*Tam O'Shanter	Montecito	Vernon Kilns	1939	Green, lime, and reddish-brown plaid; green border; see also Calico; Coronation Organdy; Gingham; Homespun; Organdie; Tweed
*Tampico	Futura	Red Wing	1955	Modernistic design
Tanglewood	Colonial	Blue Ridge		Pink flowers, green leaves, allover pattern
Tango		Homer Laughlin	1930s	Blue, green, yellow, and red solids
Taste	Ultra	Vernon Kilns	1939	Maroon fruit and floral border
*Taverne		Hall	1930s	Silhouette decal; serving pieces
*Taverne	Laurel	Taylor, Smith, and Taylor		Silhouette decal; no dog; dinnerware
Tazewell Tulips	Colonial	Blue Ridge		Striped tulips
Tea for Two/ Tea for Four	Teapot	Hall		Angled top; no decoration
Tea Rose	Accent	E. M. Knowles	c.1954	
Tea Rose		Purinton	1936-1959	Two red rosebuds and broken dark rim
Teal Rose	Aladdin	Harker	1952	Wide border, large rose
Teataster	Teapot	Hall	late 1940s	For Teamaster; oval; two compartments
Tempo	Piecrust	Blue Ridge	1948	Red and yellow flowers; green rim
Terra Rose		Stangl	1941-1942	Giftware line; dinnerware patterns called fruits or tulip
Terrace Ceramics	Corn Shape	Terrace Ceramics		
Texas Rose	Candlewick	Blue Ridge		Yellow flower
Thanksgiving Turkey	Skyline	Blue Ridge	1950s	Turkey in center

PATTERN	SHAPE	MAKER	DATE	DESCRIPTION
Theme	Theme	Homer Laughlin	1939-1990s	Embossed border of fruit; plain or decal design
Thermo-Porcelain		Coors		Canary-tone glaze with decal, white glaze with chrysanthemums
Think Pink	Candlewick	Blue Ridge		Two pink flowers, centered; dark pink border
Thistle	Trailway	Blue Ridge	1954	Thistle in center; wide gray border
Thistle		Hall		Muted floral
Thistle		French Saxon		
*Thistle		Stangl	1951-1967	Hand painted; purple and green decoration
Thistle		Universal		Decals
Thorley	Kitchenware	Hall		Small starbursts
Thorley	Teapot	Hall		
Tia Juana	Deanna	E. M. Knowles		Ivory, white background; Mexican decal
Tic Tack	Piecrust	Blue Ridge	1948	Apple, pear, cross-hatched center; broken green rim
*Tickled Pink	Colonial	Blue Ridge		Pink leaves and rim; gray dots
Tickled Pink	Anytime	Vernon Kilns	1955-1958	Pink and gray geometric designs
Tiffany	Accent	E. M. Knowles	1955	
Tiger Flower	Tiger Flower	Franciscan		Pink
Tiger Lily	Colonial	Blue Ridge		Red, yellow flowers
Tiger Lily		Stangl	1957-1962	Decal
Tiny Rose	Casual	Red Wing	1958	
Toledo Delight	Trojan	Sebring	1941-1942	
*Tom & Jerry		Hall	1930s	Tom & Jerry printed on punch bowl, mug
Tom Thumb & the Butterfly		Homer Laughlin		Child's set; decal
Touch of Black	Regina	Paden City		Pastel flower sprays with occasional black leaves
Touch of Brown		Taylor, Smith, and Taylor		Brown and white flowered decal
Tower		Leigh		

PATTERN	SHAPE	MAKER	DATE	DESCRIPTION
Town & Country		Red Wing	1946	Blue, chartreuse, Forest Green, Metallic Brown, rust, Sandy Peach
*Town & Country		Stangl	1970s	Black, blue, green, Honey, yellow; graniteware look
Trade Winds	San Marino	Vernon Kilns	1954-1956	Rust and chartreuse flowers on swirled ground; same as Shadow Leaf except color
Tradition	Regent	E. M. Knowles	1948	
Trailing Rose	Montecito	Vernon Kilns	1939	Blue and red flowers and leaves on ivory ground
Traveler		Syracuse	1937-1969	Railroad china; white, shaded pink, flying geese
Trellis	Duckbill	Crooksville	1929	Bright flowers on black trellis
Trellis	Montecito	Vernon Kilns	1935-1937	Crisscross, lattice; multiflori design
Tricorne		Salem	1934	Red-orange; stripes; modern
Trinidad		Stangl	1972-1974	White background; aqua and brown flower burst; wide borders
Triple Treat	Cavalier	Royal		Ironstone; three modernistic flowers
Tritone	Teapot	Hall	1950s	Diagonal triangular sections of colors
Trojan	Trojan	Catalina Gladding, McBean and Co.	1930-1940s	Solids
Tropical	Skyline	Blue Ridge	1920-1957	Brown bamboo with green leaves
Trotter	Coupe	Crooksville		Racing horse
True Blue	Vernonware	Metlox	1965	
Tudor Rose	Sabina	Sabin		
*Tulip	D-Line	Hall	1930s-1950s	Decals; yellow and purple tulips
Tulip		Universal		Decals
*Tulip		Stangl	1942-1973	Blue or yellow tulip; Terra Rose mark
Tulip		Salem		Tulip and bud
Tulip		E. M. Knowles		Bright orange tulip
Tulip		Paden City		Floral bouquet

PATTERN	SHAPE	MAKER	DATE	DESCRIPTION
Tulip		Leigh/Crescent		Vivid tulips
Tulip Tree		Homer Laughlin	1977-1978	
Tulip Trio	Candlewick	Blue Ridge		Three red tulips
Tulip Wreath	Coupe	Homer Laughlin		
Tulips	Kitchen Kraft	Homer Laughlin	1930s	Decals on ovenware
Tulips		Pottery Guild		
Tulips		Taylor, Smith, and Taylor		
Tuliptime	Tempo	E. M. Knowles	1961-1963	Ruffled tulips
Tuliptime	Candlewick	Blue Ridge		Red, yellow, and purple tulips; green border
Tuna Salad	Skyline	Blue Ridge	1950s	Blue and brown fish
Turkey with Acorns	Skyline	Blue Ridge	1950s	
Turtle Dove	New Shape	Red Wing	1962	Two Doves
*Tweed	Montecito	Vernon Kilns	1950-1955	Gray, blue plaid; see also Calico; Coronation Organdy; Gingham; Homespun; Organdie; Tam O'Shanter
Tweed Tex	Anniversary	Red Wing	1953	White
Twilight		Flintridge China Co.		
Twin Oaks	Accent	E. M. Knowles	c.1954	
*Twinspout	Teapot	Hall	Late 1940s	For Teamaster; round; two compartments
Twin-Tee	Teapot	Hall		Flat top; decorated in gold or decal
Two-Some	Montecito	Vernon Kilns	1938	Brown bands on cream ground
Two Step	Village Green	Red Wing	1960	Geometric design
Two-Tone	Ultra	Vernon Kilns	c.1938	Wide border in blue, green, pink
Tyrol	Olivia	Steubenville		Aster, Buttercup, Carnation, Gardenia
*Ultra California	Ultra	Vernon Kilns	1937-1942	Blue, ivory, light green, maroon, pink, yellow
Unicoi	Clinchfield	Blue Ridge		Red and blue flowered border

PATTERN	SHAPE	MAKER	DATE	DESCRIPTION
Valencia		Watt	1937-1940	Blue, green, yellow, Tangerine, burgundy; fluting on top and sides
Valley Violet	Astor	Blue Ridge		Small flowers
Vegetable Patch	Skyline	Blue Ridge	1950s	Corn and tomato on black sponged background
Veggie	Skyline	Blue Ridge	1950s	Vegetables
Veggies		Crooksville		
Vera	Ultra	Vernon Kilns	1938	Floral
Vermillion Rose	Triumph	Sebring-Limoges		
Vernon 1860	San Fernando	Vernon Kilns	1944; 1955	Scene of 1860s America in brown; floral border
Vernon Rose	San Fernando	Vernon Kilns	1944; 1950-1954	Yellow rose, blossoms; cream ground
Verona	Colonial	Blue Ridge		Large blue flowers, border
Veronica	Clinchfield	Blue Ridge		Yellow and red flowers and borders in center; wide green outer border
Vestal Rose		E. M. Knowles	1930s	Decals
Victoria	Colonial	Blue Ridge		Pink and yellow flowers; red rim
Victoria	Teapot	Hall	Early 1940s	Celadon only; Victorian style
Victoria	Americana	E. M. Knowles	1959	
Victoria	Montecito	Vernon Kilns	1939	Green flowers and leaves
Victory		Salem		Fluted border
Vienna	Victory	Salem	1940s	
Village Brown	Village Green	Red Wing	1955	Brown
Village Green	Village Green	Red Wing	1953	Green
Vine		Harker		Cameoware
Vine Yard	Vernonware	Metlox	1965	
Vine Wreath	Laurel	Taylor, Smith, and Taylor	1933-1934	Decals
Vintage	Colonial	Blue Ridge		Bold grapes, vine, and leaves
Vintage	Royal Gadroon	Harker	1947-1949	Red and green ivy
Vintage	Accent	E. M. Knowles	1953-1954	
Vintage	Lotus	Vernon Kilns	1950	Purple grapes, brown leaves
Vintage	True China	Red Wing	1960	Floral

PATTERN	SHAPE	MAKER	DATE	DESCRIPTION
Vintage Pink	Poppytrail	Metlox	1965	
Violet	Trend	Steubenville		
Violet Spray	Skyline	Blue Ridge	1950s	Off-centered large and small violet sprays
Violet Spray		Homer Laughlin	1920	Decals
*Virginia Rose	Virginia Rose	Homer Laughlin	1935–1960	Decals; spray of roses, leaves
*Vistosa		Taylor, Smith, and Taylor	1938	Solids: cobalt blue, deep yellow, light green, Mango Red
Vistosa		E. M. Knowles	1936	Solids: Cadet Blue, burgundy, red, russet, yellow
Vogue		Syracuse		
Wagon Wheels		Frankoma	1942	Solids: Clay Blue, Desert Gold, Onyx Black, Prairie Green, Red Bud
Waldorf		Sebring-Limoges	1939	
Walt Disney	Ultra/ Montecito	Vernon Kilns	1941	Fantasia; blue, brown, maroon all-over prints or borders
Waltz Time	Colonial	Blue Ridge		Pastel flowers, broken blue border
Wampum	Ranchero	W. S. George		Floral
Ward's Garland		Sold by Montgomery Ward	1936	Decals
Water Lily	Yorktown	E. M. Knowles		
Water Lily		Stangl	1949–1957	
Waterlily	Astor	Blue Ridge		Multicolored pastel flower; blue rim
Waverly		Homer Laughlin	1977–1978	
Weather Bloom	Squared-Off Edges	E. M. Knowles	1933–1934	Decals
Weathervane (No. 4277)	Skyline	Blue Ridge	1950s	House and tree; sponged yellow background; green rim
Weathervane	Forcast	E. M. Knowles	1957	
Wells	Wells	Homer Laughlin	c.1930–1935	Solid Bburnt Orange matte, green, peach, rust, yellow, some ivory with decals

PATTERN	SHAPE	MAKER	DATE	DESCRIPTION
Westinghouse, see Aristocrat; Emperor; King; Patrician; Prince; Queen				
Westwind		Frankoma	1962	Solids
Wheat	Skyline	Blue Ridge	1950s	Three golden wheat stalks
Wheat		Harker	1961	Cameoware
Wheat	Deanna; Accent	E. M. Knowles	1954	Wheat stalks
Wheat	Melinda	Vernon Kilns	1942	Sheaths of wheat and blossom sprays; Harmony House mark and "Exclusively for Sears, Roebuck and Co.," in 1950 catalog
Wheat		W. S. George		Brightly colored wheat stalks
Wheat (Hall), see Poppy & Wheat				
Wheat Sheaf	Criterion	E. M. Knowles	1955	
Wheatfield		Sebring-Limoges		
Whirligig	Piecrust; Colonial	Blue Ridge	1950s	Red and light blue flowers; green leaves and rim; same design as Bowknot but different colors
White and Embossed		Sold by Montgomery Ward	1920	Decals
White & Gold		Homer Laughlin	1920	Decals
White & Gold Carnation		Homer Laughlin	1920	Decals
White & Green Persian		Homer Laughlin	1920	Decals
White Clover		Harker		Russel Wright; engraved design; charcoal, Coral Sand, Golden Spice, Meadow Green
White Dogwood		Stangl	1965-1974	Marked Prestige; white flowered border
White Gold Ware		Sebring	1940s	
White Grape		Stangl	1967	
White Rose		Harker Potteries	1940s	Cameoware; blue or pink; outlined flowers in center
Wild Bouquet		Homer Laughlin	1977-1978	Corn-Kraft; made for Montgomery Ward

PATTERN	SHAPE	MAKER	DATE	DESCRIPTION
Wild Cherry #1	Skyline	Blue Ridge	1950s	Rust leaves; yellow cherries; broken green rim
Wild Cherry #2	Skyline	Blue Ridge	1950s	Pink and gray leaves; black rim
Wild Cherry #3	Piecrust	Blue Ridge	1950s	Cherries; yellow and brown leaves; broken green rim
Wild Irish Rose	Colonial	Blue Ridge		Red flowers border
Wild Oats		E. M. Knowles	1955	
Wild Poppy, see Poppy & Wheat				
Wild Rose		Crown	1941	Wild flowers and wheat sheaths
Wild Rose	Regent	E. M. Knowles	1948	
Wild Rose	Princess	Paden City		
Wild Rose	Colonial	Blue Ridge		Pink flowers
Wild Rose	Floral Edge	E. M. Knowles	1933-1934	Decals
Wild Rose		Homer Laughlin		Floral decals
Wild Rose		Stangl	1955-1973	
Wild Rose & Flower	Empress	Homer Laughlin	1920	Decals
Wild Strawberry	Colonial	Blue Ridge		Two strawberries; green rim
*Wildfire	D-Line	Hall	1950s	Hi-White body; floral garland decals
*Wildflower	Floral Edge	E. M. Knowles	1933-1934	Decals
Wildwood	Colonial	Blue Ridge		Red, pink, and yellow flowers, center, border
Wildwood		Stangl		
Williamsburg	Tempo	E. M. Knowles	1961-1963	
Willow	Coupe	Crooksville		Pussy willow stalks
Willow	Willow	Franciscan		
Willow Wind	Concord	Red Wing	1947	Abstract
Winchester '73	Montecito	Vernon Kilns	1950	Western scene on cream ground
Windcrest	Teapot	Hall	1940s	Canary and sponged gold; fluted; high lip
Windfall		Stangl	1955-1957	Canary
Windflower	Colonial	Blue Ridge		Fanciful red flower with green leaves
Windjammer	Clinchfield	Blue Ridge		Center sailboat; wide blue border; black rim

PATTERN	SHAPE	MAKER	DATE	DESCRIPTION
Windmill		Crown		
Windmill		Universal		
Windmill	Victory	Salem		Decals
*Windshield	Teapot	Hall	1941	Maroon and Camellia most common colors
Winesap	Skyline	Blue Ridge	1950s	Three red apples
Winged Streamliner		Homer Laughlin		Railroad china
Winnie	Skyline	Blue Ridge	1950s	Off-centered red flowers
Wishing Well	Skyline	Blue Ridge	1950s	Well, tree, and fence
Wizard of Oz	Kiddieware	Stangl	Mid-1940s–1974	
Woman in the Shoe	Kiddieware	Stangl	Mid-1940s–1974	
Wood Echo	Forcast	E. M. Knowles	1957	
Wood Rose		Stangl	1973–1974	
Wood Song		Harker		
Wood Violets	Accent	E. M. Knowles	c.1954	
*Woodfield		Steubenville		Leaf shapes; American Modern shades: Dove Gray, Golden Fawn, Salmon Pink, Tropic Rust
Woodhue	Flair	Salem		
Woodland	Round Coupe	Salem		
Woodland Gold		Metlox		Marked Poppytrail
Woodvine		Universal		Small red flowers, large leaves
World's Fair	Teapot	Hall		Cobalt and gold; trylon and perisphere embossed on side
Wren	Square	Blue Ridge		Bird; broken black rim
Wrightwood	Rainbow	E. M. Knowles	1930s	Decals
Wrinkled Rose	Colonial	Blue Ridge		Pink flower; yellow rim
Year 'Round	Year 'Round	Vernon Kilns	1957–1958	Gray, mocha, and yellow circles
Yellow Carnation	Fiesta	Homer Laughlin	1962–1968	Yellow and brown flowers on white background; yellow rim; Casual pattern; see also Daisy
Yellow Flower		Stangl	1970	

PATTERN	SHAPE	MAKER	DATE	DESCRIPTION
Yellow Matte Gold		Homer Laughlin	1920	Decals
Yellow Matte Gold Band	Plain Edge	Homer Laughlin	1920	Decals
Yellow Plaid		Blair		
Yellow Poppy	Candlewick	Blue Ridge		Off-centered pattern
Yellow Rose	D-Style	Hall		Bouquet of wild roses
Yellow Rose	Minion	Paden City	1952	
Yellow Trim Poppy	Deanna	E. M. Knowles		
Yellow Tulip, see Tulip by Stangl				
Yellowridge		Salem		Multicolored flowers
Yellowstone	Yellowstone	Homer Laughlin	c.1927	Octagonal; ivory glaze, florals
*Yorkshire	Swirled Edge	Metlox	c.1939	Solids, pastels: Delphinium Blue, Canary Yellow, Old Rose, Opal Green, Peach, Poppy Orange, Satin Ivory, Satin Turquoise, Turquoise Blue, yellow
Yorktown	Colonial	Blue Ridge		Centered bird, apple, and leaves; dark line border
Yorktown	Yorktown	E. M. Knowles	1936	Concentric Deco shape; solid colors: light yellow, maroon, Periwinkle Blue, Terra-cotta
Young in Heart	Antique	Vernon Kilns	1956-1958	Flowers in aqua, charcoal, mocha, and yellow
*Zeisel	Hallcraft/ Century and Hallcraft/ Tomorrow's Classic	Hall	1950-1960s	Solid white or decals; two modern dinnerware shapes designed by Eva Zeisel
Zephyr	Refrigerator Ware	Hall	Late 1930s	Chinese Red; also called Bingo
Zinnia	Colonial	Blue Ridge		Red, blue, and orange flowers
Zinnia		Homer Laughlin	1977-1978	
*Zinnia	Concord	Red Wing	1947	
Zodiac	Montecito	Vernon Kilns	1937	Zodiac signs

We welcome any additions or corrections to this chart. Please write to us c/o Crown Publishers, 201 E. 50th Street, New York, NY 10022.

K O V E L S

SEND ORDERS & INQUIRIES TO: **Crown Publishers, Inc.,**
c/o Random House, 400 Hahn Road,
Westminster, MD 21157

SALES & TITLE INFORMATION
1-800-733-3000

ATT: ORDER DEPT. _____

NAME _____

ADDRESS _____

CITY & STATE _____ ZIP _____

PLEASE SEND ME THE FOLLOWING BOOKS:

ITEM NO.	QTY.	TITLE		PRICE	TOTAL
884623	_____	Kovels' Antiques & Collectibles Price List 28th Edition (Available in October 1995)	PAPER	$14.95	_____
580128	_____	Kovels' American Art Pottery: The Collector's Guide to Makers, Marks, and Factory Histories	HARDCOVER	$60.00	_____
54668X	_____	American Country Furniture 1780–1875	PAPER	$14.95	_____
701375	_____	Dictionary of Marks—Pottery and Porcelain	HARDCOVER	$16.00	_____
559145	_____	Kovels' New Dictionary of Marks	HARDCOVER	$19.00	_____
568829	_____	Kovels' American Silver Marks	HARDCOVER	$40.00	_____
589443	_____	Kovels' Bottles Price List 9th Edition	PAPER	$14.00	_____
883821	_____	Kovels' Depression Glass & American Dinnerware Price List 5th Edition	PAPER	$16.00	_____
578069	_____	Kovels' Know Your Antiques Revised and Updated	PAPER	$16.00	_____
588404	_____	Kovels' Know Your Collectibles Updated	PAPER	$16.00	_____
883139	_____	Kovels' Guide to Buying, Selling, and Fixing Your Antiques and Collectibles	PAPER	$18.00	_____
883813	_____	Kovels' Quick Tips: 799 Helpful Hints on How to Care for Your Collectibles	PAPER	$12.00	_____

_____ TOTAL ITEMS

TOTAL RETAIL VALUE _____

CHECK OR MONEY ORDER ENCLOSED MADE PAYABLE
TO CROWN PUBLISHERS, INC.
or telephone 1-800-733-3000
(No cash or stamps, please)

Shipping & Handling
Charge $2.00 for one book;
50¢ for each additional book.
Please add applicable
sales tax. _____

Charge: ☐ Master Card ☐ Visa ☐ American Express
Account Number (include all digits)   Expires MO.   YR.
_____

TOTAL AMOUNT DUE _____

_____

PRICES SUBJECT TO CHANGE
WITHOUT NOTICE. If a more
recent edition of a price list has been
published at the same price, it
will be sent instead of the old edition.

Signature _____

Thank you for your order.